THE
JAMES
BEARD
COOKBOOK

Other Books By James Beard

Hors d'Oeuvre and Canapés
Cook it Outdoors
Fowl and Game Cookery (Beard on Birds)
The Fireside Cook Book
Paris Cuisine (with Alexander Watt)
Jim Beard's New Barbecue Cookbook
James Beard's New Fish Cookery
How to Eat Better for Less Money (with Sam Aaron)
The Complete Book of Outdoor Cookery (with Helen Evans Brown)
James Beard's Treasury of Outdoor Cooking
Delights and Prejudices
Menus for Entertaining
How to Eat (& Drink) Your Way Through a French (or Italian) Menu
James Beard's American Cookery
Beard on Bread
Beard on Food
Theory and Practice of Good Cooking
The New James Beard
Beard on Pasta
James Beard's Simple Foods
Love and Kisses and a Halo of Truffles: Letters to Helen Evans Brown

· THE ·
JAMES
BEARD
COOKBOOK

Third Revised Edition

In collaboration with
Isabel E. Callvert

Marlowe & Company
New York

First Marlowe & Company edition, 1996

Published by
Marlowe & Company
632 Broadway, Seventh Floor
New York, NY 10012

Text Copyright c. 1959 by James Beard
Copyright renewed 1987 by The Estate of James Beard

Manufactured in the United States of America

Library of Congress Cataloging-in-Publication Data

Beard, James, 1903–
     The James Beard cookbook / in collaboration with Isabel E.
Callvert. — 3rd, rev. ed.
        p.   cm.
     Includes index.
     ISBN 1-56924-809-5
     1. Cookery, American.   I. Title.
TX715.B3715   1996
641.5—dc20   95-49930
                                                   CIP

ISBN 1-56924-809-5

Contents

Editor's Note

James Beard made few revisions in the 1966 edition of *The James Beard Cookbook*. Just seven years after its publication it was still something of a pioneering work, and the great American food revolution was not yet in full motion. But by the time Beard's American Cookery was published in 1972, the changes in American eating habits and in national food distribution were enormous. It is hard to remember that sour cream was once an unfamiliar product (readers of the original James Beard Cookbook had to be cautioned to use commercial sour cream, not cream gone sour); that fresh chicken was available from poultry farmers and not every supermarket; and that "pasta" was still largely a matter of spaghetti, macaroni, and noodles.

Looking back on his first basic cookbook, toward the end of his career Beard noted that it was in need of a complete update. The revisions for this edition may not be as extensive as those he might have undertaken himself, but they will make the book more useful for contemporary cooks without altering its essential character. The fish chapter, for example, now incorporates the Canada Board of Fisheries rule for cooking fish, which Beard adopted in all of his later work. The food processor has been introduced. Some recipes have been deleted or rewritten, and some—obvious oversights—have been added. There are numerous other changes throughout, but this is still the book that gave us the courage to eat our lamb pink, brought classic continental dishes such as Choucroute Garnie (a Beard trademark) and Vitello Tonnato into our kitchens, and taught a whole generation of Americans how to eat better that ever before.

John Ferrone
(1987)

Note to the Third Revised Edition

This latest edition of *The James Beard Cookbook* continues the editorial aims of the previous revision—to keep the recipes workable for today's cooks while preserving the integrity of the original book, but also to take into account James Beard's rethinking on such matters as timing and temperatures. Only a handful of recipes have been deleted or replaced, a sign of the book's enduring merits. Twenty-five have been added—all qualifying as "basic" and all, I would like to think, recipes Beard might well have included the first time around.

J.F.
(1995)

Foreword

This is a basic cookbook. It is intended to help two sorts of people: first, those who are just beginning to cook and say they don't even know how to boil water, and second, those who have been trying to cook for a while and wonder why their meals don't taste like mother's cooking or the food in good restaurants.

Anybody who is conscientious enough to follow simple directions can learn to cook. For example, if you are among those who have never boiled water, this is what you do: Fill a saucepan with cold water and put it on the stove. Adjust the burner to high. Let the water heat until it bubbles and surges—and that is boiling water. I assure you in all seriousness that many of the recipes in this book are not much more complicated than these instructions on how to boil water. Most cooking, even of elaborate dishes, is merely the combining of a number of very simple operations.

A lack of knowledge about basic cookery can be somewhat inconvenient. Some years ago young friends of mine started off from New York for several months' stay in the Near East. Their luggage consisted mainly of case after case of canned goods, packaged foods and mixes, and dehydrated soups. When all the cases were stacked up on the dock, the scene looked like the receiving platform of a grocery store. The pretty young wife perched herself on a case of soup and explained that they *had* to take their food with them because she wouldn't know how to cope with the produce sold in Near Eastern markets. She had never really cooked, she admitted, except to fry hamburgers and use mixes and frozen dinners.

Now, mixes and frozen foods can be helpful when time is precious and shortcuts are necessary. But you'll never achieve confidence in your cooking ability if your culinary skill depends on using ingredients that someone else has mixed or seasoned or pre-cooked. Like almost everything else—walking, driving a car, painting a picture—you learn best by *doing*.

There are three very good reasons why you should learn basic cookery: practical, gastronomical and personal reasons. On the practical side, it's a stubborn economic fact that preparing your own food is cheaper than buying it ready-made. Gastronomically, it's a fact that home cooking is tastier and more varied. As for the personal side, it's a fact that cooking is fun, especially good cooking.

Cooking is one everyday task that can be creative. You become a creative cook by first becoming a good basic cook. Your transition from basic to creative cooking takes some doing, some actual experience in finding out what happens when you add this or change that. Once you have made this transition, you will never lack admirers. Good food has a magic appeal. You may grow old, even ugly, but if you are a good cook, people will always find the path to your door.

JAMES BEARD
(1959)

COOKING TOOLS AND TERMS

Basic Cooking Equipment

KNIVES
Large carving knife
Large chef's knife with 10- or 12-inch blade
Chef's knife with 8-inch blade
Slicing knife
Boning knife
Paring knives
Small knives for general use
Serrated bread knife
Grapefruit knife
Sharpening steel

SPOONS AND FORKS
Wooden spoons of various sizes
Slotted or perforated spoon
Long-handled spoon for basting and stirring
2 or 3 regular kitchen spoons
Ladle
Measuring spoons
Fork and spoon for tossing salad
1 large two-pronged fork

2 or 3 regular kitchen forks
Small fork for removing items from small-necked bottles

CARVING AND CHOPPING BOARDS
Large carving board, about 16 inches
Smaller carving board, about 12 inches
Small chopping boards
Chopping block
Pastry board
Bread board

DISHES AND BOWLS
Nest of mixing bowls of various sizes
Soufflé dishes
Molds of various sizes
1 or 2 kitchen platters
Ovenproof serving dishes
Shallow baking dishes
Individual ramekins and pudding molds

POTS AND PANS
Saucepans of various sizes, with lids
Double boiler
Enamel pan for boiling eggs
Large, deep braising pan with tight lid
Teakettle
Steamer with rack
Medium-sized sauté pan with lid
Large, heavy sauté pan with lid
Skillets of various sizes
Pan and basket for deep-frying
Griddle
Crêpe pan
Omelet pan
Roasting pan and rack
2 or 3 casseroles of various sizes
Loaf pans
Ring mold
Baking sheets
Tube cake pan
Cake tins

Jelly roll pan
Muffin tins
Pie tins
Flan pans with removable bottoms
Flan rings
Deep dish for quiches and pies

OTHER TOOLS

Apple corer
Ball scoop
Biscuit cutters
Bottle opener
Cake racks
Can opener
Candy thermometer
Corkscrew
Deep-fat thermometer
Eggbeater
Food mill
Funnel
Grater
Kitchen scale
Kitchen scissors
Lemon squeezer
Measuring cups, for liquid and dry measure
Meat thermometer

Mortar and pestle
Pastry brush
Pastry tube and attachments
Pepper grinder
Potato masher
Poultry shears
Rolling pin
Rubber scrapers
Salad dryer
Sieve
Sifter
Skewers
Spatulas
Strainers or colanders of various sizes
Tongs
Vegetable brush
Vegetable peeler
Wire whisks of various sizes

APPLIANCES

Electric mixer with attachments
Electric hand beater
Electric blender
Food processor

Electric skillet
Electric deep fryer
Waffle iron
Toaster

Weights and Measurements

3 teaspoons—1 tablespoon
4 tablespoons—¼ cup
1 cup—½ pint
4 cups—1 quart
4 quarts—1 gallon
1 ounce—⅛ cup or 2 tablespoons
2 ounces—¼ cup or 4 tablespoons
8 ounces—1 cup

TERMS FROM OLD RECIPES

1 wineglassful—¼ cup
1 gill—½ cup
1 saltspoon—¼ teaspoon
Butter the size of an egg—¼ cup or 2 ounces

BEANS, DRIED

White, 1 pound:
    2 cups, uncooked—6 cups, cooked
Kidney, 1 pound:
    2⅔ cups, uncooked—6¼ cups, cooked
Lima, 1 pound:
    3 cups, uncooked—7 cups, cooked

BUTTER, LARD OR VEGETABLE FAT

1 ounce—2 tablespoons
2 ounces—¼ cup or 4 tablespoons
¼ pound—½ cup
½ pound—1 cup
1 pound—2 cups

CHEESE, GRATING

1 pound—4 cups, grated

CHOCOLATE

1 ounce—1 square of baking chocolate

EGGS

4 to 6 whole eggs, shelled—1 cup
Whites of 8 to 10 eggs—1 cup

FLOUR

White: 1 pound—4 cups, sifted
Cake: 1 pound—4½ cups, sifted
Whole wheat: 1 pound—3½ cups

GELATIN

1 tablespoon—1 envelope

NUTS

Almonds: 1 pound, unshelled—1½ cups nut meats
Pecans: 1 pound, unshelled—2¼ cups nut meats
Walnuts: 1 pound, unshelled—2 cups nut meats

PASTA

Macaroni, 8 ounces:
   2 cups, uncooked—4 cups, cooked
Noodles, 8 ounces:
   2½ cups, uncooked—4 to 5 cups, cooked

Spaghetti, 8 ounces:
    2½ cups, uncooked—4 to 5 cups, cooked

RICE

1 pound, uncooked:
    2 cups, uncooked—6 cups, cooked

SUGAR

Brown: 1 pound—2¼ cups
Granulated: 1 pound—2¼ cups
Powdered: 1 pound—2¾ cups

Cooking Terms

À LA GRECQUE: Vegetables cooked in an oil and vinegar liquid with seasonings added. The term means "in the Greek style."

À LA MODE: Usually used to mean topped with ice cream. This is an American distortion of the French term meaning "in the manner of," generally followed by another word, as in *"à la mode de Caen"—"the way it is done in Caen."*

À LA RUSSE: In the Russian style. Salad à la Russe is a mixture of vegetables or vegetables and meats blended with mayonnaise.

ACIDULATED WATER: Water with vinegar or lemon juice added. Fresh vegetables and fruits are often soaked in acidulated water before cooking. Use 1 tablespoon of acid to 1 quart of water.

AL DENTE: Literally, "to the tooth." An Italian term used to describe food, especially pasta but also vegetables, cooked so it is still firm to the bite.

ASPIC: Jellied broth used to make molds of cold vegetables, meats or fish: or to mask cold foods.

AU GRATIN: Any casserole baked with a bread-crumb topping. Most people think this term means with cheese. This confusion probably stems from the fact that grated cheese is often mixed with the crumb topping.

AU JUS: In the natural juices. Meat au jus is meat served plain with pan juices, rather than with other sauce or thickened gravy.

AU POT: Means "in the pot." Generally a chicken or piece of meat cooked in a large pot with water or broth.

BAIN MARIE: The French double boiler.

BAKE: To cook in the oven.

BARBECUE: To cook over an open fire—that is, by direct heat.

BARBECUE SAUCE: A highly seasoned sauce used to baste food while it is barbecuing.

BARD: To wrap with fat or a fatty substance, such as salt pork. (Often confused with *Lard*. See page 11.) Lean pieces of meat are often barded with fat—wrapped in suet or salt pork or bacon—before cooking, to keep them from getting too dry.

BASTE: To spoon or brush liquid or melted fat over food as it cooks. Basting keeps food moist, helps flavor it and gives it a nice glaze or finish.

BEAT: To stir thoroughly with a spoon or eggbeater. The term implies a vigorous mixing.

BEURRE MANIÉ: Butter and flour kneaded together and formed into pea-sized balls. Used to thicken sauces.

BIND: To hold a mixture of foods together with mayonnaise or other sauce.

BLANCH: To pour boiling water over food and then drain almost immediately; or to parboil in water for a minute. Nuts and tomatoes are blanched in order to loosen their skins.

BLANQUETTE: A light stew; one made without browning the meat first.

BLAZE: To pour liquor over food and light it. To be sure liquor will flame, it is sometimes wise to heat it slightly before pouring it over the food. This is not necessary if the food itself is piping hot. (Also see *Flambé*, page 11.)

BLEND: To mix thoroughly, or to purée thoroughly in an electric blender or processor.

BOIL: To cook in liquid at the boiling or bubbling point.

BONE: To remove the bones from meat or fish.

BONED AND ROLLED: Certain meat cuts are boned and then rolled up and tied for roasting.

BOUILLON: A clear broth made by cooking meat, fish or vegetables in liquid and then straining the liquid. Packaged bouillon cubes, sold in grocery stores, may be used as a substitute.

BOUQUET GARNI: A selection of herbs placed in a small bag of cheesecloth and put in a broth or stock to flavor it while cooking. The bag is removed and discarded when the broth is done.

BRAISE: To brown meat or vegetables in fat, then add a small amount of liquid and finish cooking tightly covered at a low temperature. A tenderizing method good for tougher cuts of meat.

BREAD (TO BREAD): To coat meat or fish with crumbs.

BREAD CRUMBS: Soft bread crumbs used for stuffing are made with day-old bread; fine bread crumbs, with bread that is dried out and rolled or grated. For detailed instructions, see Bread chapter, page 38.

BROCHETTE: Small skewers on which pieces of meat, fish or vegetables are cooked. Food *en brochette* is generally broiled.

BROIL: To cook under or over direct heat. This can be done in the broiler section of the oven, directly under the heating unit; or over a wood, coal or charcoal fire. There are also portable electric and gas broilers.

BROTH: The liquid left after simmering vegetables, meat, fish or other foods. Also used to mean a thin soup.

BROWN (TO BROWN): To cook food in a little fat until brown.

BRUSH: To daub the surface of food lightly with some liquid or fat. You may use a pastry brush for this job or simply dribble the ingredient on with a spoon. Examples: brushing bread with melted butter; brushing top pie crusts with beaten egg.

BUTTERED CRUMBS: Fine crumbs cooked with melted butter until saturated. Used to top casseroles or to dress vegetables.

CANAPÉS: Small pieces of fried or toasted bread spread with highly seasoned toppings. Used as appetizers.

CARAMELIZE: To melt sugar until it turns liquid and brown. Example: Sugar is caramelized to coat the cups or mold for Caramel Custard.

CHARCOAL-BROILED: Broiled with the heat of a charcoal fire, directly over or in front of the coals. For instructions on how to build a charcoal fire, see page 184.

CHOP: To cut into small pieces. You may use a food chopper or a sharp, heavy knife. A large French knife with triangular blade is the best tool for chopping. Place the food to be chopped on a heavy chopping board or worktable. Rest the knife, blade down, on the food, and hold the point of the knife with your left hand. With your right hand, hold the handle and move the blade up and down, swinging the knife right and left in an arc, chopping as you go.

Do not use a meat grinder for chopping.

CLARIFY: To clear a broth of bits of food or cloudy substances by adding egg white and eggshell and beating them in over heat. The broth is then strained; the food particles cling to the egg and are separated from the liquid.

COMPOTE: A mixture of fresh or cooked fruits.

CONDIMENT: This term refers generally to seasonings and flavorings. It is used more specifically to mean prepared sauces or flavorful accompaniments for foods.

CONSOMMÉ: A clear, highly seasoned broth made from meat.

CORNED: Cured by soaking in a salt solution or brine. Example: corned beef.

CORNSTARCH: A starch, made from corn, used to thicken puddings and some sauces. Used for thickening in many oriental dishes.

COURT BOUILLON: A seasoned broth used for poaching fish.

CREAM (TO CREAM): To rub ingredients together until smooth, as in creaming butter and sugar when making a cake.

CROUTONS: Small toasted cubes of bread.

CUBE: To cut into small cubes.

CURDLING: Occasionally sauces or puddings made with eggs will separate into a watery liquid with thick, almost solid, particles in it. This is known as curdling. The sauce is still edible, but the appearance is unappetizing.

CUT IN: To cut fat into flour when making pastry.

DEVILED: Combined with sharp seasonings and cooked with a crumb topping. Or crumbed, cooked and served with a sharp (devil) sauce.

DICE: To cut into very small cubes.

DISJOINT: To cut a fowl into pieces at the joints. Example: to prepare a chicken for frying.

DOT: To cover with small bits of fat. Example: to dot a casserole with butter.

DREDGE: To cover thoroughly with a dry substance, such as flour, cornmeal or crumbs.

DRESS: To mix with sauce or flavoring just before serving. Examples: to dress cooked vegetables with melted butter; or to dress fresh greens with salad dressing.

DRIPPINGS: The juices in the pan from roasting meats.

DUST: To cover very lightly with a dry ingredient. Example: to dust the top of a sweet roll with sugar.

FILLET OR FILET: A cut of meat or fish without bones. Also used as a verb: *to fillet,* meaning to prepare such a piece of meat or fish.

FINE HERBES: Mixed herbs, chopped together and used for seasoning. Classically, includes parsley, chives, tarragon and chervil.

FLAKE: To break into small pieces. Example: to flake fish with a fork.

FLAMBÉ: To pour liquor over food and light it. This is the French term for *Blaze* (see page 8). If flambéing meat, make sure that all fat has been removed from the pan juices. The initial flaming-up can be sudden. Also make certain there is nothing above that can catch fire, and avert your face to avoid singed eyebrows.

FOLD: To combine two ingredients by turning one over into the other, using a folding motion, with a spoon. For exact instructions, see Soufflés, page 358.

FRESHLY GROUND BLACK PEPPER: Peppercorns ground in a pepper grinder as needed.

FRICASSEE: A stew of meat or fowl, which may or may not be browned and then cooked in a liquid. The liquid is thickened and served over the meat.

FRY: To cook on top of the stove in a large amount of fat.

GARNISH: To decorate. Example: to decorate cold fish platters with hard-cooked eggs, parsley, etc.

GLAZE: To give a glossy finish to food. This is done in different ways: fish or vegetables may be covered with a sauce or grated cheese, or both, and glazed under the broiler flame; onions or carrots may be steamed in butter and glazed with a little sugar added at the last minute.

The term also refers to covering cold meat or fish with aspic.

GRATE: To rub on a grater, cutting food into minute bits.

GRILL: To broil. Often used to mean cooking on a charcoal grill. The term comes from the rack (or grill) on which the food is cooked.

GRIND: To put through a grinder, cutting the food into tiny particles.

HORS D'OEUVRE: Appetizers. Generally served with cocktails.

JULIENNE: Cut into thin, long strips.

KNEAD: To press and stretch dough with the hands or with a dough hook. (See instructions, pages 39–40.)

LARD: The rendered and clarified fat of pork. Used as a cooking fat and sometimes as shortening in pie dough.

LARD (TO LARD): To insert thin strips of fat into the flesh of meat using a special larding needle. (Often confused with *Bard*. See page 7.) Fats used for this process are usually salt pork or bacon.

Legumes: Dried vegetables used in soups and casseroles. Also used as vegetables. Examples: dried lima beans, dried white pea beans.

Liaison: A thickening agent used to make a sauce. (See pages 347–348.)

Macedoine: A mixture of vegetables or fruits. Usually the ingredients are cut fairly fine.

Marinade: A seasoned sauce in which meats or other foods are soaked. Example: marinade for charcoal-grilled beef.

Marinate: To soak food in liquid, such as a marinade.

Mask: To coat or cover thoroughly, usually with a sauce or aspic.

Meringue: Stiffly beaten egg white sweetened with sugar and used as a topping on pies and certain other pastries. The pie or pastry is then put in a low oven until the egg white (meringue) browns. Meringue is sometimes shaped into cups and baked at very low heat until firm. These meringue cups are then filled with ice cream or fruit.

Mince: To chop very fine.

Pan-Broil: To cook in a skillet with little or no fat added. The pan is sometimes rubbed very lightly with fat or oil.

Parboil: To cook partially in boiling salted water or other liquid. Example: Onions are sometimes parboiled before being added to a mixture that will not require enough additional cooking to cook a raw onion. Aged hams are parboiled before baking.

Pare: To peel off the outer skin.

Pasta: The generic Italian term for spaghetti, macaroni and noodles in all their various forms.

Pâté: A paste usually made of meat or seafood. Pâtés are used as a spread for toast or crackers or they are cut in thin slices and served as a first course. They resemble very fine meat loaf.

Petits Fours: Small, rich cookies or fancy cakes.

Pilaf: Rice cooked with flavorings and sometimes broth.

Pinch: As much as you can hold between the thumb and first finger. Example: pinch of salt.

Plank: To serve on a wooden plank. Usually meat or fish arranged on a plank and surrounded with garnishes of hot vegetables.

Poach: To simmer gently in enough hot liquid to cover.

PREHEAT: To heat the pan or the oven before placing the food in it.

PURÉE: To put through a sieve or food mill until the food (usually vegetables or fruit) is a smooth paste.

RACK: A rib section of meat. A roast containing several ribs.

RAGOUT: The French term for stew.

RAMEKIN: Individual casserole; one that will hold enough food for a single portion.

REDUCE: To boil liquid until some of it has evaporated. This makes a richer mixture, since the seasonings and flavorings are more concentrated in the reduced liquid.

RENDER: To cook solid fat slowly in a skillet or in the oven until the fat melts.

ROAST: Originally this meant to cook on a spit in front of an open fire. Now means to cook in the oven, uncovered.

ROLL OUT DOUGH: To use a floured rolling pin to press dough into a flat shape. (See page 72.)

ROUX: A mixture of fat, often butter, and flour used to thicken liquid. (See page 347.)

SADDLE: A cut of meat including the entire center section of the animal; that is, both loins.

SAUTÉ: To cook on top of the stove in a very small amount of fat. (Sometimes confused with *fry,* a cooking method using a large amount of fat. See *Fry* page 11)

To sauté until colored or brown means to cook gently until golden brown on all sides.

To sauté until just soft means to cook until tender but not necessarily brown.

To sauté until transparent means to cook until the food (such as onion) has turned slightly clear.

SCALD: To heat liquid just to the boiling point, without letting it boil. Or to plunge solid food into boiling water for a minute.

SCALE: To scrape loose scales from fish.

SCORE: To make a series of slashes. Usually refers to making light gashes in the skin or outer fat of a roast. Example: to score the fat on a ham.

SEAR: To cook quickly with high heat. Usually done to seal in the juices. Example: Roasts of meat are sometimes seared quickly under high heat before being cooked more slowly to the done stage. The searing at the start seals in the juice and makes a moister roast. Searing can also mean quick browning in a pan.

SHORTENING: Fats used in cooking. Generally fats used in baking breads, cakes and pastries.

SHRED: To cut into thin slivers.

SHUCK: 1. To take the shells off certain seafood, such as clams and oysters. 2. To remove husks from corn.

SIFT: Shake through a fine sieve.

SIMMER: To cook gently below the boiling point. The liquid should be barely moving. Stews and certain sauces and all foods that need long slow cooking are generally simmered.

SKEWER: Small, thin metal rods used for spearing foods that are broiled or grilled; or very small metal pins used to fasten foods together or to close a fowl after filling it with stuffing.

SKIM: To spoon off the fat or scum forming on the surface of a liquid, or to remove the cream from milk.

SLIVER: To slice into long, thin pieces.

SOUFFLÉ: A dish made with beaten egg whites, folded in with other ingredients, so the mixture puffs up when it is baked.

SPIT: A metal rod with a sharp end used for holding meats and fish while they roast over an open fire. Charcoal units come equipped with spits for roasting.

STEAM: To cook over boiling water in a tightly covered kettle. There are special steamers—kettles with fitted racks—to do this job.

Vegetables and other foods can also be gently steamed in a little hot water or fat. The amount of water or melted fat should be much less than the amount of food to be cooked. The pan must be heavy and have a very tight cover. Cook very slowly.

STEW: To cook slowly in liquid for a long time until tender. The term usually implies a mellowing and blending of flavorings and a thorough mixing of the ingredients.

STIFF BUT NOT DRY: Egg whites are beaten "stiff but not dry" when they are used to make a mixture light and airy. Beat them just until they stand in peaks. They should still be glossy and moist-looking and not too fine-grained.

STIR: To blend ingredients by a wide, circular motion with a spoon. *Beating* implies more vigorous action.

STOCK: The liquid in which food has been cooked: meat, fish or vegetables. The basis for soup.

THICKENING AGENT: An ingredient or mixture of ingredients used to thicken liquid. It may be fat and flour, cornstarch, egg yolks, grated potato, or various other agents.

TIE: Certain cuts of meat are often boned and then rolled and tied with string so they will hold their shape while cooking.

TRUSS: To tie a fowl with the wings and legs held tightly in place so the bird holds its shape while cooking.

TRY OUT: To heat fat or fat meat, such as salt pork or bacon, until the fat melts. This is the same as *rendering.*

WHIP: To beat an ingredient quickly and thoroughly until puffy. This can be done with an eggbeater, a wire whisk, a fork or an electric mixer.

Herbs

Fresh herbs have much more zest and flavor than dried herbs, and you are fortunate if your local market carries a selection or if you can grow your own in a garden or window box.

It pays to be particular when you buy herbs in jars or tins. There is a good deal of variation in potency and flavor from brand to brand. Some packers powder herbs too finely, and this seems to cut down the flavor. Look for dried herbs that are large-leaved with a fine aroma.

Herbs can make drab dishes taste wonderful, but don't make the mistake of overdoing this magic. Too much dosing with herbs destroys the normal taste of food. Certain herbs are "made" for certain foods, and certain herbs blend well with others. The following glossary lists many popular affinities. When you experiment beyond this list, your own nose and taste buds can tell you whether you have devised an appetizing combination.

BASIL: Popular in Italian cookery. Ideal in tomato sauces, tomato juice and tomato dishes. Also good in soups and fish cocktails; with crab, shrimp and such fish as mackerel; in omelets; with veal and lamb, duck and game, and such vegetables as eggplant, zucchini, tomatoes and onions; and in green salads and sauces.

BAY LEAF: Has an assertive flavor, so use sparingly. Good in stews and pot roasts, with lentils and beans, chicken fricassees and all game, in stuffings for poultry, fish salads, gravies and sauces. Often used with other herbs.

CHERVIL: The most delicately flavored member of the parsley family. Used as a garnish and in salads, chicken and vegetable soups, and omelets (especially with other herbs); with fish, meats, poultry, and game; with asparagus and new potatoes; and in broths and sauces. Often combined with chives and parsley.

CHIVES: Not, strictly speaking, an herb but a member of the onion family. Excellent in combination with other herbs. Used as a garnish; and in salads, soups, stuffings, stews and sauces, and with all meats, poultry and vegetables.

CORIANDER (CILANTRO): Also known as Chinese parsley. Resembles Italian parsley and is sold with roots on. Has a distinctive, pungent flavor not pleasing to all and is often used in Chinese, Indian, Mexican and Latin-American dishes.

DILL WEED: Good with all fish, especially; in fish and bean soups; with lamb and veal; in creamed chicken; with beets and cabbage; in cucumber and potato salads and sour cream sauces.

FENNEL: Has a flavor resembling licorice. Use gently. Used mainly with fish, duck, goose, pork, sausage and lentils.

MARJORAM: Popular general seasoning in salads, vegetable dishes, omelets, meat dishes, poultry stuffings and sauces, and with spinach, zucchini and peas.

MINT: Use in fruit cups, mint juleps and other long drinks, with carrots and new potatoes, and, if you insist, in sauce with lamb.

OREGANO (WILD MARJORAM): More pungent than sweet marjoram; widely used in Latin and Mediterranean cookery, especially in soups, stews, meatballs, sausage and pork, stuffings, tomato sauces and barbecue sauces, and with tomatoes, zucchini and eggplant.

PARSLEY: There are two types of parsley: the common, curly parsley, and the Italian parsley with a flatter leaf. Italian parsley has a more distinctive flavor. Not just a garnish but a subtle addition to stuffings, soups, stews and sauces. Use with all fish, fish sauces, meat, poultry, game, sausage; in omelets and scrambled eggs; with peas, carrots and potatoes and in salads. Used with other herbs.

Rosemary: Used in fruit compotes and salads, especially those containing oranges; in chicken and pea soups; with salmon; in fish stuffings and stews; with steaks, lamb, poultry, game; with spinach and lima beans, and in barbecue sauces.

Sage: Very decisive flavor. Use sparingly if at all. Can be used in stuffings, chowders, stews and gravies, and with pork, duck and goose.

Savory: Used in bean, fish and pea soups; with fish; and in omelets, stews, salads and barbecue sauces. Especially good with roast lamb.

Tarragon: Widely used in salads and sauces; in mushroom, chicken and potato soups; in most egg dishes; with fish, veal, chicken and turkey, potatoes, mushrooms and spinach.

Thyme: Widely used in stuffings, stews, broths and stocks, sauces, and with all fish and meat, cheese dishes, and carrots, onions, potatoes and peas.

Spices and Seeds

Allspice: The berry of the West Indian allspice tree; sold whole or ground. Tastes like a mixture of cloves, nutmeg and cinnamon. Use in desserts. The berry is sometimes used in certain meat dishes.

Anise Seed: A pungent seed with a flavor resembling licorice. If you like the taste, use it in sauerkraut, coleslaw, creamed cabbage, cauliflower and beets, and in cookies and cakes.

Caraway Seed: Pungent. Popular in some European breads. Also used frequently with cabbage and in coleslaw, sour cream sauces, cabbage soup, cheese dishes and goulash.

Cayenne: A pungent red pepper, ground. Use sparingly. Popular in cheese dishes, highly seasoned sauces such as barbecue sauces or devil sauces, and in highly seasoned meat dishes.

Celery Seed: Seed of the celery plant; highly concentrated celery flavor. Used in some soups, stuffings, stews, barbecue sauce and boiled dressing, and in potato salad.

CHILI POWDER: The ground pulp of various chilies (Mexican peppers) sometimes combined with other spices. Used in Mexican chili dishes. Sometimes added to hot sauces, such as barbecue sauces.

CHILIES (DRIED): Small red Mexican peppers. Very hot. Use sparingly. For Mexican dishes and hot sauces.

CINNAMON: Inner bark from a tree in the East Indies; sold in pieces or ground. Very useful in desserts, fruit sauces, cakes, coffee cakes and sweet rolls; also used in some meat dishes.

CLOVE: Spicy dried buds sold whole or ground. Has wide use in cooking. Use sparingly in stocks, broths and certain meat dishes, with ham, in fruit desserts, puddings, cakes, sweet rolls and mince and pumpkin pies.

CORIANDER: Sold in seed form or ground. Totally different in flavor from fresh coriander and commonly used as one of the ingredients in curries.

CUMIN: A ground seasoning important in Mexican dishes. Used in chili dishes, stews, meat loaf, soups, cheese appetizers, cheese sauces and some barbecue sauces.

CURRY: A mixture of several spices with a touch of herbs. There are many blends of curry powder: some are mild, some hot, some pungent. Used in oriental dishes and marinades, in East Indian curries and in some sauces and salads.

GINGER: A pungent root. Comes dried in pieces, ground, candied or in syrup. Can be bought fresh in most markets. Used in certain fish dishes and soups, in some meat dishes, in cakes, cookies and puddings, with poached fruits and fruit compotes, and in oriental dishes and marinades.

MACE: The outer coating of the nutmeg. Comes ground. Flavor similar to nutmeg. Used in some stews, seafood dishes and meat dishes, and in cakes, cookies and desserts.

MUSTARD (DRIED): The ground seeds of the mustard plant. Very hot. Used in meat dishes, fish dishes, sauces, appetizers and salad dressings. Mixed with a little water or white wine as a condiment for meats.

NUTMEG: The kernel of an apricot from Indonesia. Sold whole or ground. Buy it whole and grate it; the flavor is better. Used in some meat dishes, soups, puddings and desserts, and to top sweet milk drinks.

PAPRIKA: A sweet and pungent red pepper, ground. Used in Hungarian dishes. Hungarian paprika has the most flavor. Use in soups, stews, sauces and sour cream sauces, and with veal or chicken.

Pepper: Sold whole (peppercorns), white, black or pink, coarsely cracked or ground. Buy whole and grind it yourself in a pepper grinder for general use. Coarsely cracked pepper is excellent for special recipes, such as Steak au Poivre. Whole peppercorns are used in making stocks and broths and for flavoring some meat dishes.

Green peppercorns are unripe pepper berries, usually packed in brine, and very pungent in flavor. Used in sauces with fish, meat and poultry dishes.

Poppy Seed: Dried seeds of the poppy, most commonly used on breads and rolls, also in fish and meat dishes, with noodles and in cookies, cakes and pastries.

Saffron: The dried stigma of the saffron flower, a species of crocus. Very expensive. Very pungent. Use carefully or it will have a medicinal taste; only a pinch is needed. Colors food yellow. Used in Spanish dishes, rice, some fish and fish sauces, with veal and chicken and in some buns, cakes and frostings.

Sesame Seed: Crisp seeds with a nut-like flavor. Used on breads and rolls and on barbecued fish, for coating chicken before broiling and as a topping for various soups and vegetable dishes. Also used in candy.

Condiments, Flavorings, Garnishes

Almonds (Chopped, Toasted): Sold in cans or packages already chopped and toasted. Used as a garnish or in certain sauces.

To make your own chopped, toasted almonds: Soak shelled almonds in hot water until you can slip off the skins. Heat butter or oil and toss the almonds in the hot fat, cooking them until they are golden brown. Chop coarsely. Or chop first and then cook in fat.

Anchovy: A tiny, herring-like fish, smoked, packed in oil and canned. Very salty and pungent. Used in some sauces, in salads, as an hors d'oeuvre, as a garnish on cold dishes and with fish dishes.

Anchovy Paste: A paste made of anchovies. Used in some hors d'oeuvre spreads. Added to sauces.

Bouillon Cubes: Concentrated broth of meat or chicken, sold in cubes or granulated. Combined with hot water, makes broth. Used to enrich stews, soups and sauces.

Capers: Tiny pickled buds of the caper shrub, sold in bottles. Used with fish as a garnish, with fish salads and in sauces for fish or mutton.

Catsup: Tomato pickle sauce. Used to spice certain sauces, such as barbecue sauces. Use sparingly. Its sour-sweet taste can dominate.

Caviar: The roe of the sturgeon. A very expensive delicacy often served as a first course or as an appetizer. Used as a garnish on some fish dishes. Golden caviar (whitefish roe) is also available. Red caviar (salmon roe) is less expensive. Sold in jars in most grocery stores.

Chutney: A sweet fruit pickle usually served with curries but excellent with some cold foods. Sold bottled. Chutneys vary considerably. Each packing firm has its own recipe. Try some of the fine imports.

Cider: The juice of apples. Fermented, it becomes hard cider. Used in some chicken and ham dishes. Also used to prepare extra-rich apple sauce and other apple dishes. Sold in jugs.

Cognac: Brandy from the Cognac region in France. Used extensively in elegant cookery.

Corn Syrup: Sweet syrup made from cornstarch. Useful in preparing candies and cake frostings. Sold bottled.

Foie Gras: Preserved goose liver imported from Europe. Elegant as an appetizer or first course. Used as garnish on special dishes. Very expensive.

Garlic: Strong-flavored member of the onion family. Comes in tight bulbs. Each section of the bulb is called a "clove." Also available in powdered form. Use with discretion. Valuable in flavoring many soups, sauces, meat dishes, fish dishes and stuffings. Used in Italian, Spanish, Mexican and many oriental dishes.

Gelatin: Used to thicken broths for aspics. Unflavored gelatin comes in boxes containing several envelopes of the powdered mixture. The powder in each envelope will jelly about $1\frac{3}{4}$ to 2 cups of liquid. Follow directions on the package.

Grand Marnier: A delicious French liqueur with an orange flavor. Good for fruit desserts and for flavoring dessert sauces.

Horseradish: A very hot-flavored root. Can be bought whole and grated at home or bought ready-grated and bottled with vinegar. Used in hot and pungent sauces, with certain fish dishes, pork, other rich meats, beef and in some appetizers.

Juniper Berries: Berries of the juniper tree. Used in cooking game and in marinades for game.

Kirsch: A brandy made from the pits of black cherries. Very dry. Use it on fruits and in fruit desserts.

Mustard: Although many of our best prepared mustards still come from France, there are now a number of good domestic brands. Look for Dijon-style mustards or herbed mustards.

Olive Oil: The best oil for cooking or salad dressings. It is imported from France, Italy, Spain and Greece, and comes in several grades, including "extra virgin" (the best), "virgin" and "pure."

Olives: Many kinds of olives are to be found, both green and ripe (nearly black in color); packed in brine, oil, or wine vinegar and oil; stuffed, usually with pimiento, or unstuffed; tiny Niçoise olives or colossal Spanish olives. France, Spain, Italy and Greece are the main suppliers, and olives are also produced in California.

Pâté De Foie Gras: A pâté made with rich goose livers. The genuine pâté comes from France in cans and is very expensive. American versions of it are made with chicken livers. Used as an hors d'oeuvre or garnish.

Pimiento: A sweet red pepper put up in cans and jars. Used in some sauces and as a garnish for cold dishes.

Salt: Aside from the regular salt, there is a coarse salt that can be ground at home in a salt grinder or used as is in brining or with certain dishes, such as Pot au Feu. For coarse salt, buy either Malden's or regular kosher salt. Another form of salt, rock salt, in large hunks, is used when freezing ice cream in an old-fashioned freezer, and to hold the heat in baking shellfish.

Sauerkraut: Cabbage in brine; packaged in cans or in plastic and sold in meat markets or delicatessens. Used in many French, German and central European dishes.

Sour Cream: A commercial dairy product, sold in cartons. It is not spoiled cream but cream to which bacteria have been added. It has the consistency of whipped cream. Often served with baked potatoes; excellent with some soups (such as borscht) and meat dishes, with fruit, and combined with mayonnaise for salads.

SOY SAUCE: A sauce made from soybeans and used extensively in oriental cookery in place of salt. It adds color and flavor to marinades. Sold bottled.

SUET: The firm fat from the loin and kidney section of beef. When rendered, it makes good fat for frying or deep-fat frying certain foods, such as potatoes. Solid suet is chopped and used in puddings, such as plum pudding, and in old-fashioned mince pie.

TABASCO SAUCE: A very hot sauce. Use it sparingly in hot, spicy sauces. It comes bottled.

TOMATO PASTE: A thick tomato concentrate. Sold in small cans or tubes. Used to enrich the flavor of and to thicken tomato or other sauces.

TOMATO PURÉE: Thick, sieved tomato sold in cans. Not as concentrated as tomato paste but used in much the same way.

TRUFFLES: A richly perfumed fungus that grows underground in parts of Europe. The black truffle is most often found in France; the white, in the Piedmont region of Italy. They are used with certain meat and poultry dishes, and in pâtés or stuffings. Very expensive.

VANILLA BEAN: The long, thin bean of the vanilla plant. Vanilla flavoring is popular for desserts, cakes, cookies and puddings. The bean gives a fresher, more pungent flavor than the prepared flavoring. Scrape it, or place a vanilla bean in a large jar and fill with sugar. Use the sugar for making desserts. Use a piece of vanilla bean in the syrup when poaching fruit.

VERMOUTH (DRY): A white wine flavored with herbs and seasonings. Used in certain sauces and for basting certain fish and meats. Can be used in recipes calling for white wine.

VINEGAR: The best vinegar for general purposes is a good wine vinegar—white or red. Also try sherry wine vinegar. Cider vinegar is another all-purpose vinegar. For salads there are many herb-flavored vinegars and fruit vinegars to choose among.

WINES AND LIQUEURS: In addition to the vermouth, Grand Marnier, kirsch and Cognac mentioned above, many wines and liqueurs are valuable in cooking. Dry red wine in sauces for red meats; dry white for fish and chicken; and dry sherry, dry Madeira and Marsala for certain dishes. Liqueurs offer a wide variety of flavorings for fruits and desserts. The best are Grand Marnier and kirsch. Other good liqueurs are Benedictine, Chartreuse (both sweet and flavored with herbs and peels); Cointreau and

Triple Sec (orange flavored); crème de cacao (chocolate); and crème de menthe (mint). If you can find it, eau-de-vie de framboise—the essence of raspberries—is a delightful addition to many fruit dishes. It is very expensive.

Note: Avoid such items as "cooking sherry," and never use a poor wine in your sauces. If the wine is not good enough to drink, it is not fit to use in the kitchen. The poor flavor will be noticeable and will ruin any food in which it is used.

APPETIZERS

The French phrase *hors d'oeuvre* is an idiomatic expression that means something unusual—out of the general pattern. As a culinary term it means a side dish, generally served as an appetizer. To be genuinely appetizing, hors d'oeuvre should be unusual and tempting. A bowl of peanuts, pretzels or potato chips will not do.

In this chapter you will find suggestions that call for no more work than opening a bag of salted nuts but that give much more satisfying results. You will find enough variety to arrange a large and hearty spread for a big cocktail party.

If you are serving hors d'oeuvre to be followed by dinner, keep your dinner menu in mind. If you are having a rich, heavy dinner, don't serve a rich, filling appetizer. Select, instead, something crisp and fresh, such as raw vegetables with a sour cream sauce. If you are having a light meal, say a sautéed chicken, start with hearty hors d'oeuvre, such as tiny hot biscuits stuffed with foie gras. If you are having a fish dinner, don't serve fish appetizers. Serve something made with vegetables, meat or cheese.

Whatever you select, keep hot hors d'oeuvre hot and cold hors d'oeuvre nicely chilled. Put the hot dip sauce over an alcohol flame or electric plate. Serve hot stuffed biscuits folded in a napkin. Arrange shrimp or crisp greens on a bed of crushed ice. There is nothing appetizing about lukewarm celery or cold chili dip with fat congealing on top.

Appetizers with Sauces

One of the most popular and easiest of appetizers is a flavorful sauce and food to dip into it. For suggestions on sauces, see the following pages. There you will find a variety, both hot and cold. Surprisingly enough, cold, crisp foods, such as raw vegetables, are not only good with cold sauces but also tasty dunked into a hot oil dip, a hot curry dip or a hot chili dip. And hot meats and sausages combine amazingly well with a cold sauce, such as a highly seasoned sour cream. Here is a list of suggested foods to use with the sauces:

RAW, CRISP VEGETABLES (CRUDITÉS)

Radishes
Green onions
Carrot strips
Green pepper strips
Tiny raw artichokes
Cauliflowerets
Quartered Belgian endive
Celery strips
Cucumber strips
Tiny clusters of watercress
Cherry tomatoes

MEATS, HOT AND COLD

Small fingers of cold baked ham
Thin slices of cooked Virginia ham, rolled and fastened with toothpicks
Thin slices of highly seasoned salami, rolled and fastened with toothpicks
Thin slices of tongue, rolled and fastened with toothpicks
Peeled slices of hot knockwurst on toothpicks (simmer knockwurst in hot water for 15 minutes; then peel and slice)
Tiny hot sausages on toothpicks

SEAFOOD

Cooked shrimp (see pages 136–141)
Chunks of cooked lobster meat on toothpicks
Cold poached scallops on toothpicks (page 134)

OTHER FOODS

Crisp breadsticks
Crisp tortillas
Potato chips heated and crisped
Corn chips

Cold Sauces

SOUR CREAM DIPS

1. To 1 cup of sour cream add 1 tablespoon of chili sauce, 1 teaspoon of dry mustard, 1 medium grated onion, 1 teaspoon of Worcestershire sauce, 1 tablespoon of chopped chives and $\frac{1}{2}$ teaspoon each of salt and freshly ground black pepper. Mix well and chill for 1 hour to mellow.

2. To 1 cup of sour cream add 1 tablespoon of chili sauce, 1 medium grated onion, 1 teaspoon of curry powder, a dash of Worcestershire sauce and salt to taste.

3. To 1 cup of sour cream add 1 tablespoon of chili sauce, 1 minced clove of garlic, $\frac{1}{2}$ tablespoon of bottled horseradish well drained (or $\frac{1}{2}$ tablespoon of fresh horseradish), a pinch of dry mustard and 1 tablespoon of chopped parsley, and salt and pepper to taste.

4. To $\frac{1}{2}$ cup of sour cream add $\frac{1}{2}$ cup of fine cottage cheese, 2 tablespoons of mayonnaise, 1 tablespoon of chili sauce, 1 tablespoon of chopped chives, 1 tablespoon of chopped parsley, 1 tablespoon of finely minced green pepper, and salt and pepper to taste.

5. To 1 cup of sour cream add 2 tablespoons of mayonnaise, 3 boneless and skinless sardines, mashed, 1 tablespoon of chopped chives, 1 tablespoon of chopped parsley and lemon juice to taste.

VARIATION

Substitute anchovies for the sardines.

LIVERWURST DIP

Mash 1 pound of good liverwurst and thin it down with sour cream. Add 1 medium grated onion, 2 tablespoons of finely chopped dill pickle and a good tablespoon of sharp prepared mustard. Taste for seasoning and add salt and pepper if necessary.

BLUE CHEESE DIP

Mash ¼ pound of sharp blue cheese and thin it with 1 cup of sour cream. Add a medium-sized grated onion and 1 teaspoon of freshly ground black pepper.

ELENA'S SALSA FRIA

In a bowl blend together 2 cups chopped ripe tomatoes, a 4-ounce can of chopped green chilies, 1 chopped medium onion, 1 tablespoon of chopped fresh coriander, 1 teaspoon of oregano, 1 tablespoon of olive oil, 2 tablespoons of wine vinegar, a 16-ounce can of tomatillas, chopped, and salt and pepper to taste. Chill until ready to use, and serve as a dip or as a condiment with hot or cold meats or fish.

Hot Sauces

CURRY SAUCE DIP

Use the Curry Sauce recipe (page 354), making it with tomato juice and thickening with tomato paste. Keep hot in a chafing dish or electric skillet.

CHILI DIP

Substitute chili powder for the curry powder in the Curry Sauce (page 354) and use as a hot dip.

CHILI CON QUESO

Combine 2 finely chopped cloves of garlic with a 28-ounce can of Italian plum tomatoes and cook down over medium heat for 20 minutes, stirring occasionally. Add 2 4-ounce cans of chopped green chilies, and continue to cook until thickened. Stir in 1½ cups of rich cream sauce (see page 349) and 1 pound of shredded jack cheese. Taste for seasoning. Do not allow to boil after the cheese has been added. Serve warm as a dip for breadsticks, corn chips, or raw vegetables.

HOT OIL DIP

Mince 2 cloves of garlic and 1 large onion and sauté them in ½ cup of butter until just limp. Add 1 cup of olive oil, 1 teaspoon of basil, 1 cup of red wine and a small can of tomato paste. Simmer for ½ hour and season to taste with salt and pepper.

HOT PICKLE DIP

Mince 1 large onion and ½ green pepper and sauté gently in 3 tablespoons of melted butter until just soft. Sprinkle with 1 teaspoon of oregano or 1 teaspoon of basil and add 1 bottle of tomato chili sauce. Season to taste with salt, freshly ground black pepper and a dash of dry mustard. Simmer gently for 5 to 8 minutes, or until all the flavorings are blended. Thin down with sour cream or heavy cream, but do not boil after the cream is added or it will curdle.

This dip is exceptionally good with little sausages, slices of hot frankfurter or knockwurst, or any other cubes of meat suitable for dipping.

Hot Biscuit Hors d'Oeuvre

BISCUITS WITH FOIE GRAS

Make a rich biscuit dough (see page 45) and cut into tiny biscuits. Bake until brown and puffed. Split the biscuits and stuff with foie gras.

BISCUITS WITH HAM

Prepare miniature biscuits as above and fill them with thin slices of hot baked ham.

VARIATION

Make miniature Cheese Biscuits (see page 46) and stuff with thin slices of baked ham.

BISCUITS WITH SAUSAGE

Cook little pork sausages in dry white wine to cover, simmering them gently for 10 to 15 minutes. Pour off the wine and let the sausages brown slowly, turning to color them on all sides. Make miniature biscuits and fill them with the hot sausages.

VARIATION

Cook the sausages in the wine, but do not brown. Roll them in biscuit dough and bake according to directions for Frankfurter Surprise, page 47.

Meat Hors d'Oeuvre

STEAK TARTARE

Mix 1 pound of finely ground lean beef (have the butcher grind it twice) with $1\frac{1}{2}$ teaspoons of salt, 2 to 3 teaspoons of dry mustard, 1 clove of garlic grated, 1 onion grated, a dash or two of Worcestershire sauce and $\frac{1}{2}$ cup of finely chopped parsley. Heap in a bowl and pat smooth. Surround with thin slices of rye or pumpernickel bread cut into fingers, or thin pieces of toasted rye or pumpernickel. Let guests spread their own. Have a pepper grinder nearby for those who like to top this raw steak spread with freshly ground black pepper.

HOT MEATBALLS

Mix ground round steak as for Steak Tartare (see above) and roll into small balls the size of walnuts. Brown quickly in hot olive oil, but do not cook through. They should be rare in the center. Spear each one with a toothpick and serve piping hot with a good mustard.

NEAR EASTERN MEATBALLS

See Lamb, page 261. These are good with hot Curry Sauce Dip (page 27).

ROAST BEEF

Buy a rib roast of beef and roast it just to the rare stage (see page 191). Serve it in paper-thin slices on well-buttered rye bread, and have a selection of mustards. This is a good way to feed a large group at a big cocktail party. You can let the guests make their own sandwiches.

BAKED HAM ON BREAD

Bake a ham—preferably a fine country-cured and aged ham—in any of the ways suggested on pages 282–284. Serve the ham in thin slices on well-buttered pieces of bread. Use this for a large cocktail party.

CHARCOAL-GRILLED MEATS

Prepare these hors d'oeuvre on your outdoor charcoal grill. If you have several of the small, portable grills, you can place them in various spots around your patio or garden and let the guests grill their own food. For instructions on how to build a charcoal fire, see page 184.

Grilled Sirloin Cubes: Cut sirloin of beef into small cubes about 1 to 1½ inches square and soak in the following marinade: equal parts of olive oil and red wine, seasoned with freshly ground black pepper, Worcestershire sauce, rosemary and grated garlic. Turn the meat often to be sure it is evenly bathed and let it soak for 2 or 3 hours. Arrange the cubes on small metal skewers and grill quickly just until crusty brown on all sides. The meat should be rare in the center.

Shish Kebab: Prepare miniature shish kebab on small skewers (see Lamb, pages 260–261).

Grilled Chicken Hearts: Allow 4 to 6 hearts per serving. Marinate them in a sauce made of equal parts of olive oil, sherry and soy sauce seasoned with grated garlic and dry mustard. Let them soak in this marinade for 3 or 4 hours, and turn them now and then to be sure they are evenly bathed. Arrange the hearts on small skewers and broil over charcoal until crisp brown on all sides. This will take about 7 to 8 minutes.

VARIATION

Add a touch of curry powder to the marinade.

Grilled Chicken Livers: Prepare as you do Chicken Hearts (see above), but grill a much shorter time. Allow about 4 minutes for the livers to cook—2 minutes to a side. They are better if they are pinkish rare in the center.

VARIATION

For each chicken liver, allow ½ bacon slice. Put the bacon slices in the oven on a flat tray and cook at 325° until they are just transparent. After the livers have soaked in the marinade, wrap each one in half a bacon slice and fasten with a toothpick. Spear on small skewers and grill until the bacon is crisp.

Grilled Sausages: Cook little pork sausages in dry white wine to cover, simmering them gently for 10 minutes. Drain and put on small skewers, running the skewer through the sausages the long way. Grill over charcoal until crisp and brown.

Grilled Frankfurters: Spear tiny frankfurters and grill until crisp. Serve with a mustard-seasoned sour cream dip.

COLD MEATS

Good cold hams, sausages, and ready-prepared meats, sliced very thin and served with thinly sliced rye and pumpernickel bread, make tasty appetizers. Pass the pepper grinder and a variety of sharp mustards. Here are some meat suggestions:

Prosciutto, sliced paper thin

Westphalian Ham, sliced very thin

Ready-cooked Virginia Ham or Smithfield Ham, sliced thin

Salami, sliced thin

Liverwurst: The best is found in the German markets. Look for smoked liverwurst.

Tongue, cured or smoked ready-to-eat, sliced very thin. Horseradish is a good condiment for this meat.

PÂTÉS

Of course good imported pâté de foie gras is an elegant choice, but if that seems too expensive to you, shop around for good domestic pâtés. Many food shops carry their own make. Look for a hearty country pâté or one made with chicken livers, duck or rabbit. Or to make your own country pâté, see the recipe on page 281. Serve pâtés chilled and turned out on a platter. Surround with thin slices of toast or very firm bread.

Fish Hors d'Oeuvre

ANCHOVIES

Serve as suggested for sardines, page 34, but garnish with chopped hard-cooked egg and black garlic olives instead of lemon wedges.

SMOKED FISH

Fine delicatessens and food shops carry a variety of smoked fish that can be used for hors d'oeuvre. If you buy canned smoked fish, try to find fish that has been put up in olive oil. Serve smoked fish on a platter with toast fingers, or arrange on toast fingers beforehand. Garnish with lemon wedges. Here are some suggestions:

Smoked Salmon: Nova Scotia and Scotch smoked salmon are found in slab in many good shops and should be sliced thin. Smoked salmon is also available vacuum packed and ready sliced.

Smoked Sturgeon: This is sometimes found in tins, but whole smoked sturgeon is carried by fine food shops. Have it sliced very thin.

Smoked Whitefish: Have the dealer skin and bone the fish for you, if you do not know how to do it.

Smoked Eel: Cut thin fillets from this meaty fish and arrange on a platter or on toast fingers. Serve with lemon slices or wedges.

Shop around in your area. Many regions of the country have their own specialties in smoked fish.

CAVIAR

Fine imported caviar is very expensive. If you splurge, be sure to get the best, with the least amount of salt. Keep it cold. When ready to serve, heap it in a glass bowl resting on a bed of ice. Serve simply with toast fingers or thin slices of dark bread lightly buttered and cut into fingers. Provide lemon wedges for those who like the added tang. Allow 2 ounces of caviar per serving.

Red Caviar: This is salmon roe. It is available in most food shops. Chill it well and turn it out on a plate. Accompany with toast fingers, a bowl of chopped raw onion, a bowl of sour cream and lemon wedges.

CELERY STUFFED WITH RED CAVIAR

Thin down cream cheese with a little heavy cream and beat in red caviar to taste. Add a dash of lemon juice and stuff into celery stalks. Garnish with chopped chives.

SHRIMP WITH DIP SAUCE

Serve shrimp cooked and peeled but with tails left on (see Shrimp, page 136) with a sharp dip. Choose any of those suggested on pages 26–28.

TEMPURA—See Shrimp, page 141.

BROILED SHRIMP

Follow directions for Broiled Shrimp, page 140, and grill them over charcoal.

BROILED MARINATED SCALLOPS

Follow directions for Broiled Marinated Scallops, pages 131–132, and grill on tiny skewers over charcoal.

SEVICHE—See page 135.

PAN-FRIED OYSTERS AND CLAMS

Pan-fry small oysters and clams according to directions for Pan-Fried Clams, page 117. Spear with toothpicks and serve with a sharp Tartar Sauce (page 345).

SARDINES

Buy tins of tiny sardines put up in olive oil. The best come from Portugal and France. Arrange on a serving plate and garnish with lemon wedges. Serve with toast strips. Or arrange a sardine on each toast strip and garnish with a bit of chopped parsley.

Cheese Hors d'Oeuvre

BLUE CHEESE SANDWICHES

Use a very creamy blue cheese; or cream Roquefort with a little heavy cream or sour cream. Spread on thin, finger-size slices of firm bread or toast and top with very thin slices of tiny white onion. Serve open-faced or top with another slice of the bread lightly buttered.

CELERY STUFFED WITH BLUE CHEESE

Make the Blue Cheese Dip (page 27), using $\frac{1}{2}$ cup of sour cream instead of 1 cup. Stuff celery stalks with this and top with chopped chives.

TOMATOES STUFFED WITH BLUE CHEESE

Stuff tiny tomatoes with the Blue Cheese Dip (page 27), using ½ cup of sour cream, instead of 1 cup. Top with chopped chives.

CHEESE STRAWS—See page 58.

Stuffed Egg Hors d'Oeuvre

Hard-cook eggs according to directions on pages 88–89. Cool, shell and cut into halves the long way. Scoop out the yolk and flavor in any of the following ways:

With mayonnaise: Use about 2 tablespoons of mayonnaise for 6 mashed egg yolks. Add ½ teaspoon of mustard, 1 teaspoon of chopped chives and 1 tablespoon of finely chopped parsley. Taste for seasoning and add salt if necessary. Heap into the whites and garnish with a dash of paprika. Chill.

With anchovy paste: (This comes in tubes.) Allow about 1 teaspoon of the paste to 6 mashed egg yolks. Add ½ tablespoon of very finely chopped raw onion and a dash of lemon juice. Heap into the whites and garnish with one or two parsley leaves. Chill.

With smoked ham pâté: (This comes in tins.) Allow about 1½ table-spoons of the pâté for 6 mashed egg yolks. Add mayonnaise to moisten and heap in the whites. Top with a little chopped chive. Chill.

With cold dip sauce: Mash the yolks and moisten with any of the cold dip sauces (see pages 26–27). Taste for seasoning and heap into the whites. Garnish with chopped chives, chopped parsley or tiny strips of pimiento. Chill.

Vegetable
Hors d'Oeuvre

STUFFED ARTICHOKE HEARTS

Buy the tiny, canned artichoke hearts. Drain thoroughly and stuff with Salad à la Russe (see page 327) or any of the basic seafood salads (pages 342–343), chopped very fine. Or stuff with Mixed Tuna Salad (see page 342). Chill.

ARTICHOKE AS AN HORS D'OEUVRE—See page 381.

STUFFED MUSHROOMS—Serve hot Stuffed Mushrooms, page 419.

STUFFED TOMATOES

Serve tiny tomatoes, hollowed out and stuffed with Salad à la Russe (page 327), finely chopped Seafood Salad (pages 342–343) or Mixed Tuna Salad (page 342).

STUFFED CELERY

See suggestions under Cheese Hors d'Oeuvre, page 34, and Caviar, page 33.

VEGETABLES À LA GRECQUE

Serve any of the Vegetables à la Grecque suggested in the Salad chapter, page 326. Serve on thin slices of bread with mayonnaise, or serve on individual plates.

VEGETABLES WITH DIPS—See under Appetizers with Sauces, page 25.

BEETS IN SOUR CREAM—See page 329.

CUCUMBERS IN SOUR CREAM—See page 330.

Other Foods for Hors d'Oeuvre

OLIVES

Choose any variety that you like: garlic olives, green-ripe olives, ripe olives, green olives, stuffed olives. If you cannot find garlic olives in your area, buy ripe olives, drain thoroughly and cover with olive oil. Add 1 or 2 minced garlic cloves. Rebottle, cover and stand in a cool place for a week. Drain, chill and serve.

AVOCADO

Dice avocado and spear each piece with a toothpick. Arrange in a shallow dish and cover with Vinaigrette Sauce (page 343).

SANDWICH SPREADS

Prepare any of the meat, fish or seafood salads, but chop all ingredients very fine or put through a grinder. Use as a spread for tiny, open-faced sandwiches and garnish with chopped chives or chopped parsley.

MELON

Cut melons with a melon-ball scoop and wrap each melon ball with a thin piece of prosciutto (see Ham, page 282). Fasten with toothpicks.

PINEAPPLE

Prepare cubes of fresh pineapple as you do melon balls.

BREAD

Within the memory of old timers (including me), bread-making was routine in every household, and no proper wife thought of serving bakery-made products. Baking day came once or twice a week, depending on the size of the family, and on this occasion you were irresistibly tempted to haunt the kitchen. What wonderful yeasty smells of warm bread! What delicious aromas of cinnamon and other spices from sweet rolls and coffee cakes! How beautiful the brown, crusty loaves looked as they came out of the oven! I can think of no taste sensation to equal the joy of that first crunchy bite through the crust of the miniature loaf my mother always made just for my benefit.

The local baker and the grocery store bread counter can never re-create the atmosphere of the kitchen on baking day. And though you can sometimes find fine bakery products, they never compare to the best of the homemade.

Undoubtedly housewives gave up bread-making and turned to baker's bread because the job seemed so endless and tiring. But modern methods have cut the time; modern equipment has taken over the muscle work. Now with little or no trouble we can once again have the joy of baking day with its rich smells and its wonderful results. If you have a mixer to which you can attach a bread hook, baking bread is as easy as mashing potatoes or whipping cream.

Aside from the old-fashioned yeast breads, there are many quick bread foods, such as biscuits, muffins and waffles, that can be made on very short notice. These, with recipes for heating regular breads with seasonings, give added variety to the "staff of life" so important in our diets.

Yeast Breads

Here are some general rules for making bread:

Kneading dough: If you do not have a mixer with a dough hook attachment, knead the dough by hand. First, turn the dough out of the mixing bowl onto a lightly floured board or worktable. Dust your hands with a little flour to keep them from sticking to the dough. Be careful to use the least amount of flour necessary on the board and on your hands. If you work too much extra flour into the dough as you knead it, the bread will be tough.

Next, push your fingers into the dough and then press down with the heels of your hands, rolling the dough back and forth as you press. Turn it often—a quarter circle turn at a time—and fold it over now and then to be sure the dough is kneaded in all directions and on all sides. Keep pressing in with your fingers and rolling with the heels of your hands until the dough is elastic and satiny in texture.

Letting dough rise: In order to rise properly, dough must be kept at a warm temperature and out of all drafts. Place the dough in a large bowl and cover it lightly with a clean towel. Put the bowl in a spot where the temperature remains at a constant 80° to 90°: near a warm stove or on a table in front of a sunny window. Be sure to let the dough rise the correct amount. If it rises too little, the bread will be heavy and soggy; if it rises too much, the bread will be coarse in texture.

Baking bread: The right oven temperature for baking bread is 375°. When done, the loaves should have medium brown crusts and give a rather hollow sound when tapped lightly on top.

Note: Some flours have greater powers of absorption than others and the quantity required for a good dough may vary as much as one cup in a recipe calling for 4 to 6 cups. As a consequence, all measurements for flour given here are approximate.

BASIC WHITE BREAD (2 Loaves)

This is the simplest bread recipe I know, and it is foolproof if you measure ingredients carefully.

1 package of active dry yeast	2 tablespoons of sugar
	4 tablespoons of butter
2 cups of lukewarm milk, approx. 110° (or 2 cups of warm water; or 1 cup of milk, 1 cup of water)	1 tablespoon of salt
	5 to 6 cups of all-purpose flour

Mix the yeast in a large bowl with ½ cup of the warm milk and the sugar, and let stand for a few minutes to "proof"—that is, begin to bubble and ferment, which shows the yeast is active. Melt the butter in the remaining milk and add the salt. Combine with the yeast mixture.

Add the flour a cup at a time, and stir it in with a wooden spoon. Continue mixing until the dough is thoroughly blended. If you are using an electric mixer equipped with a dough hook, knead at a moderately slow speed for about 3 or 4 minutes, adding more flour if necessary, until the dough is smooth and pulls away from the side of the bowl. If you are kneading by hand, turn the dough out on a floured board or tabletop, then knead according to instructions on page 39.

When the dough is smooth and satiny, transfer to a well-buttered bowl, and cover with a towel. Place in a warm spot to rise until double in bulk. This should take about 1 to 2 hours. Deflate the dough by punching it firmly two or three times, turn out on a lightly floured board, and knead for another minute or so. Divide it into 2 equal parts. Shape into loaves and place into well-buttered bread pans. Cover and set in a warm spot to rise a second time until doubled in bulk. Bake in a 375° oven until nicely brown and hollow-sounding when rapped. This will take 40 to 45 minutes.

VARIATION

Cinnamon Bread: Divide the dough into 2 equal parts, roll out rather thin, and spread with soft butter. Sprinkle with cinnamon and sugar and roll it up like a jelly roll. Arrange in buttered bread tins. Cover with a towel, place in a warm spot and allow to rise until double in bulk. Bake in a 375° oven until nicely browned on top and done. This will take 40 to 45 minutes.

This cinnamon bread is especially good when toasted or heated.

YEAST ROLLS

Make the dough for Basic White Bread (see page 39) and follow directions for bread up to the point of shaping the dough into loaves. Divide the dough into 6 equal parts and roll each portion between your hands until it is a long sausage shape. Cut these long rolls into 3-inch pieces. Tie each piece in a loose knot and shape into a roll. Arrange on a greased baking sheet and cover lightly with a towel. Place in a warm spot to rise again for 25 minutes. Brush the tops of the rolls with melted butter and bake in a 425° oven until nicely browned and done. This will take about 15 minutes.

VARIATIONS

With sesame seed: After you brush the rolls with butter, sprinkle them with sesame seed. Bake as above.

With poppy seed: After brushing the rolls with butter, sprinkle them with poppy seed. Bake as above.

Onion rolls: Sauté finely chopped onion in butter and sprinkle liberally over the tops of the rolls just before baking.

PARKER HOUSE ROLLS

Follow the directions for the Basic White Bread (page 39) up to the point of shaping into loaves. Instead, roll the dough out with a lightly floured rolling pin until it is about ½ inch thick. Using a 3-inch cookie cutter, cut the dough into rounds, spread each round with melted butter and fold over into a half circle. Arrange on baking sheets, cover and let rise for 25 minutes. Brush with butter and bake in a 425° oven for 15 minutes, or until browned and done.

CINNAMON ROLLS

Follow the directions for Basic White Bread (page 39) up to the point of shaping the dough into loaves. Instead, roll the dough out with a lightly floured rolling pin until it is about ½ inch thick. Spread the surface with soft butter, and sprinkle it with brown sugar, cinnamon and sultana raisins. Roll up as for a jelly roll and cut the roll into 1-inch slices. Arrange these on a well-buttered baking sheet, cover and let rise for 25 minutes. Brush with melted butter, sprinkle with a little cinnamon and bake at 425° for 15 minutes or until brown and done.

VARIATION

Grease muffin tins with butter, add a layer of brown sugar and more butter and top with the cut roll. Let rise, brush with butter and bake. You may add nuts to the brown sugar and butter in the muffin tins if you wish.

CUBAN OR FRENCH-STYLE BREAD (2 Loaves)

This is a quick French bread and especially good if eaten hot out of the oven.

1¹/₂ packages of active dry yeast
2 cups of lukewarm water
1 tablespoon of salt

1 tablespoon of sugar
5 to 6 cups of all-purpose flour
Cornmeal

Dissolve the yeast in the warm water and add the salt and sugar, stirring thoroughly. Add the flour a cup at a time, beating it in with a wooden spoon (or use the dough hook on the electric mixer at low speed). Add enough flour to make a smooth dough. When the dough is thoroughly mixed, cover it with a towel, put it in a warm spot (see instructions, page 40) and let it rise until double its bulk. Turn the dough out onto a lightly floured board or worktable and shape it into long, French-style loaves or round, Italian-style loaves. Or shape into small, individual loaves. Arrange these on a baking sheet heavily sprinkled with cornmeal. Allow to rise for 5 minutes.

Slash the tops of the loaves in two or three places with a knife, brush them with water and place them in a cold oven. Set the oven for 400°. Place a pan of boiling water in the oven, and bake the loaves until they are crusty and done. This should take about 35 minutes.

VARIATIONS

With sesame or poppy seed: Sprinkle the tops of the loaves with sesame seed or poppy seed before putting them in the oven.

Garlic bread: After the bread is baked, split the loaves the long way. Spread the inside with softened butter seasoned with chopped garlic and chopped parsley. Put the loaves together again and return to the oven to heat through.

MABELLE JEFFCOTT'S GRAHAM BREAD (2 to 3 Loaves)

This recipe makes a moist, firm bread with plenty of body. As people used to say: "It sticks to your ribs."

1 13-ounce can of
   evaporated milk
2 cups of hot water
¼ cup of melted butter
3 tablespoons of sugar
2 tablespoons of salt
2 packages of active dry
   yeast

½ cup of warm water
3 cups of coarse graham
   flour
5 to 6 cups of all-purpose
   flour

Mix the evaporated milk with the hot water, the melted butter and sugar and salt. Let cool to lukewarm 100° to 115°. Dissolve the yeast in ½ cup of warm water, and add this to the lukewarm milk mixture. Add the graham flour, then the white flour—enough to make a smooth, satiny dough. Use the electric mixer, with the dough hook attachment, at slow speed to add the flour, or beat it in gradually with a wooden spoon (see instructions under Basic White Bread, page 39). Continue mixing with the dough hook until the dough is elastic and satiny; or turn the dough out onto a lightly floured board and knead by hand (see instructions for kneading, page 39).

Put the dough in a buttered bowl, cover lightly with a cloth or towel and place in a warm spot to rise (page 40). When the dough is about double in bulk, turn it out onto a lightly floured board and divide into 2 or 3 portions. Mold these into loaf shapes and put in buttered bread tins. Cover and allow to rise again, but only until about 1½ its original bulk. This bread should not be too light; it should have a firm texture and plenty of body.

Bake at 375° about 1 hour or until browned and done. The finished bread will make a hollow sound when lightly tapped on top.

BRIOCHE

This rich French dough can be made into the traditional buns with little topknots, or it can be shaped any way you choose. It makes an excellent bread or bun to serve guests at breakfast, luncheon or, toasted, at teas.

1½ packages of active dry
   yeast
½ cup of lukewarm water
4 cups of all-purpose flour
1½ teaspoons of salt

2 tablespoons of sugar
6 eggs
1 cup of melted butter
1 egg yolk, mixed with 2
   tablespoons of cream

Dissolve the yeast in the warm water and mix it with 1 cup of the flour. This makes a spongy mixture. Cover it with a towel and set aside in a warm spot to rise until double in bulk (see instructions, page 40). Blend the rest of the flour and the salt and sugar, and stir in 3 unbeaten eggs. Continue stirring until smooth, adding the melted butter gradually. Add the other 3 eggs, one at a time, beating the mixture well after each addition. Finally add the yeast-flour "sponge," when it has doubled in bulk, and mix it in thoroughly. Cover the bowl and place it in a warm spot to let the dough rise. When it is double in bulk, deflate the dough by punching it down two or three times. Put it in the refrigerator until ready to use.

Divide it into two unequal portions: about ⅔ of the dough in one portion and ⅓ in the other. Form the larger portion of dough into individual small balls that will fit into a muffin tin. Shape the rest of the dough into an equal number of smaller balls of dough. Butter muffin tins (or use brioche molds). Place a large ball of dough in each muffin tin and top with a smaller ball of dough. Or you may shape the dough into rolls or buns; or, if you like large loaves, put it in buttered bread tins.

Cover the shaped dough and allow it to rise until almost double in bulk. Brush the tops well with beaten egg and cream, and bake in a 375° oven until nicely browned and done. Individual brioche will take about 25 minutes; large loaves, about ¾ hour.

BRIOCHE RING

Make the brioche dough according to instructions above. Remove the dough from the refrigerator and turn it out onto a floured board. Using a lightly floured rolling pin, roll out the dough and spread the surface with soft butter. Mix together ½ cup each of finely chopped raisins, nuts, cherries and brown sugar, and flavor with 2 tablespoons of Cognac. Spread this over the dough and roll it up as for a jelly roll. Arrange the roll in a circle on a buttered baking sheet and slash the roll around the outside edge with scissors or a sharp knife. Cover the roll and allow it to rise. Just before baking, brush the top with melted butter and sprinkle with granulated sugar. Bake at 375° until lightly browned and done. This will take about 45 minutes.

Quick Breads

The biscuit and muffin mixes on the market have all but eliminated the old do-it-yourself method. Actually, there is nothing in the bread line that is simpler to make than biscuit or muffin dough. At the most it takes only a minute or two longer than starting with a mix. The results are well worth the small amount of extra time.

BASIC BISCUIT DOUGH

2 cups of all-purpose flour	**4 tablespoons of shortening**
1 tablespoon of double-acting baking powder	**$^3/_4$ cup of milk (approx.)**
$^1/_2$ teaspoon of salt	

Sift the dry ingredients together into a bowl. Cut in the shortening with two knives or work it in well with your fingertips. For shortening use butter, margarine, vegetable shortening or lard. Butter, of course, is best.

Stir in just enough milk to make a smooth, soft dough, not too sticky to be handled. Turn the dough out onto a lightly floured board or worktable and knead it gently for about 1 minute (see kneading instructions, page 39). Use this dough in any of the following ways:

Square biscuits: Pat the dough down with your hands or roll it lightly with a floured rolling pin. If you like fluffy biscuits, roll it out $^1/_2$ inch thick; if you like crunchy biscuits, roll it thinner—$^1/_4$ inch thick. Cut the dough into $1^1/_2$-inch strips and then cut each strip into $1^1/_2$-inch pieces. Arrange these squares on a buttered baking sheet and bake at 450° for 12 to 15 minutes, or until lightly browned and done.

Round biscuits: Roll the dough and cut into rounds with a cutter. Arrange on a buttered baking sheet and bake as above.

Rich biscuits: Roll the dough and cut into squares or rounds. Dip each biscuit in melted butter before arranging on a baking sheet. Bake as above.

Fluffy biscuits: Substitute evaporated milk or light cream for the milk in the basic biscuit recipe. Roll the dough $^3/_4$ inch thick and cut into squares or rounds. Dip each biscuit in melted butter and arrange very close together on a greased baking sheet. Bake as above.

Parsley biscuits: Add 3 tablespoons of parsley, finely chopped, to the biscuit dough as you mix it.

Cheese biscuits: Add $\frac{1}{3}$ cup of grated sharp cheese to the biscuit dough as you mix it.

Pungent biscuits: Sauté $\frac{3}{4}$ cup of finely chopped onion in 6 tablespoons of butter until just soft. Season to taste with salt and pepper. Prepare the biscuit dough and add 3 tablespoons of finely chopped parsley as you mix it. Roll the dough out very thin, cut in any desired shape and top each biscuit with a bit of the sautéed onion. Bake as above.

Marmalade biscuits: Roll the basic biscuit dough $\frac{1}{2}$ inch thick and cut it in squares. Arrange on a buttered baking sheet and top each with a dab of orange marmalade. Bake as above.

SHORTCAKE

Follow the directions for Basic Biscuit Dough (page 45), but substitute heavy cream for the milk and add 3 tablespoons of sugar. After you have turned the dough out onto a floured board and kneaded it for 1 minute, divide it into 2 portions, one a little larger than the other. With a lightly floured rolling pin, roll the larger portion of dough into a circle approximately 9 inches across and $\frac{1}{2}$ inch thick. Roll the smaller portion of dough into a circle about 7 inches across and a little less than $\frac{1}{2}$ inch thick. Grease a round baking pan and place the larger circle of dough on the bottom. Spread it with soft butter and top with the second circle of dough. Bake at 450° until nicely browned and cooked through. This will take about 20 minutes.

Remove the cooked shortcake to a serving plate and using a pancake turner or spatula, take off the top circle. Cover the lower half with sliced or crushed, sugared strawberries. Replace the top circle and garnish with sugared whole berries. Serve with heavy cream, whipped cream or sour cream.

Note: For a very special flavor, add a little Grand Marnier to the strawberries when you crush them.

DUMPLINGS

Make the Basic Biscuit Dough (page 45) but add enough extra milk to make the dough moist and fairly soft. About an additional $\frac{1}{4}$ cup of milk should be right. You do not want a runny batter; the dumplings must hold their shape when dropped into the liquid from the end of a spoon.

To cook dumplings: These morsels are usually added to the top of a stew or fricassee. Drop small spoonfuls over the surface and space them well apart, for the dumplings swell with cooking. Cover the pan tightly and do not remove the cover for 20 minutes.

VARIATIONS

Parsley dumplings: Add ½ cup of finely chopped parsley to the dumpling dough.

Herbed dumplings: Add ¼ cup of finely chopped parsley and ¼ cup of finely chopped chives to the dough. Or add 1 teaspoon of your favorite herb (basil, oregano, thyme, etc.) and ½ cup of chopped parsley.

FRANKFURTER SURPRISE

This is a "special" for children's parties.

Make the Basic Biscuit Dough (page 45) and roll it out ¼ inch thick. Cut it into oblong pieces, the length of a frankfurter and 3 to 4 inches wide. Spread each piece with mustard, and add a dab of fried onion and a bit of catsup. Place a frankfurter on each piece of dough and roll it up. Pinch the dough together around the frankfurter. Arrange these rolls on a buttered baking sheet, brush them well with melted butter and bake at 400° until the dough is crisp and brown and the frankfurters cooked through. This will take about 20 minutes.

CORNMEAL MUFFINS

2 cups of sifted all-purpose flour

3 teaspoons of double-acting baking powder

2 tablespoons of sugar

½ teaspoon of salt

⅔ cup of yellow cornmeal

1 egg, beaten

¾ cup of milk

½ cup of melted butter

Sift the flour and measure 2 cups. (Flour increases in bulk with sifting. About 1¾ cups of flour will measure 2 cups after sifting.) Combine the flour with the baking powder, sugar and salt, and sift again. Add the cornmeal, the beaten egg, the milk, and mix well. Blend in the melted butter.

Butter muffin tins and fill ⅔ full with batter. Bake in a 400° oven until light and fluffy and delicately browned. These muffins will cook in about 25 minutes.

VARIATION

Cornbread: Pour muffin batter into a greased 8- by 8-inch baking pan and bake as above.

CORNMEAL SOUFFLÉ OR SPOONBREAD

2 cups of milk	4 tablespoons of butter
1 teaspoon of salt	4 well-beaten egg yolks
1 cup of cornmeal	4 stiffly beaten egg whites

Bring the milk and salt to a boil, then reduce the heat. Slowly add the cornmeal, stirring constantly until the mixture is smooth and thick. Add the butter and set aside to cool slightly. Beat the egg yolks well and stir into the cooled mixture. Beat the egg whites until stiff but not dry and slowly fold into the cornmeal mixture (to fold, see instructions, page 358). Pour the batter into a well-buttered casserole and bake at 375° for 35 to 40 minutes, or until light, puffy and browned on top. Serve from the casserole with a spoon, and pass plenty of butter, salt and pepper.

CORN MUFFINS

2 cups of all-purpose flour	1 egg, well beaten
3 teaspoons of double-acting baking powder	3 tablespoons of melted butter
1 teaspoon of salt	1 cup of fresh corn kernels or 1 cup of canned, whole corn kernels
1 tablespoon of sugar	
1 cup of milk	

Sift the dry ingredients together. Combine the milk, melted butter and beaten egg. Add the corn kernels to the milk and then mix in the dry ingredients thoroughly. Pour into buttered muffin tins or into a buttered shallow baking dish. Bake at 425° for 18 to 20 minutes or until puffed and brown on top.

POPOVERS

These delicious, puffy morsels have a reputation for being most difficult to make. Actually, they are simple to prepare if you follow these rules:

1. Be sure the milk and eggs are at room temperature when you mix
the batter.

2. Beat the eggs thoroughly.

3. Be sure the muffin tins are piping hot, and be sure the oven is hot
enough when you start to cook the popovers.

4. Do not open the oven door while the popovers are cooking. If they
have failed to "pop," there's nothing you can do to help anyway, and if
you let cold air into the oven it may prevent them from rising.

2 eggs	¹/₄ teaspoon of salt
1 cup of all-purpose flour	2 tablespoons of melted
1 cup of milk	butter

Beat the eggs until they are light and thoroughly aerated. Add the flour,
milk and salt, and beat until well blended. Finally, add the melted butter
and stir it in thoroughly. Set the oven at 450°, and when it is almost hot
enough, butter iron (or other metal) muffin tins and put them to heat in
the oven. When the tins are piping hot and the oven has reached 450°,
remove the muffin tins and fill each about ¹/₃ full of batter. Bake at 450°
for 20 minutes, then reduce the heat to 350° and finish baking for another 20 minutes. Good popovers are well browned, crisp and crunchy,
without any sticky dough in the center.

BLUEBERRY MUFFINS

2 cups of sifted all-purpose flour	³/₄ teaspoon of cinnamon
3 teaspoons of double-acting baking powder	³/₄ cup of milk
3 tablespoons of sugar	1 egg, well beaten
¹/₄ teaspoon of salt	¹/₂ cup of melted butter
	1 cup of blueberries

Sift the flour and measure 2 cups (see instructions for Cornmeal
Muffins, page 47). Combine the sifted flour with the baking powder,
sugar, salt and cinnamon and sift again. Combine the milk and beaten
egg, and mix with the dry ingredients. Add the melted butter and blend
thoroughly. Fold in the blueberries. Butter muffin tins and fill each one

$^2/_3$ full with the batter. Bake at 400° for about 25 minutes or until brown and puffy and done through.

QUICK COFFEE CAKE

This cake is not only a fine treat for breakfast, but also a good quick dessert for luncheon or supper.

1$^1/_2$ cups of sifted all-
purpose flour

2 teaspoons of double-acting
baking powder

$^1/_2$ teaspoon of salt

1 teaspoon of cinnamon

$^1/_2$ cup of sugar

1 egg, well beaten

$^1/_2$ cup of milk

3 tablespoons of melted
butter

Butter, cinnamon and sugar
for topping

Sift flour and measure 1$^1/_2$ cups (see instructions for Cornmeal Muffins, page 47). Add the flour to the baking powder, salt, cinnamon and sugar, and sift again. Combine the beaten egg, milk and melted butter, and stir into the dry ingredients. Beat until smooth and thoroughly mixed. Pour the batter into a buttered, 8-inch-square pan, dot the top liberally with butter and sprinkle with sugar and cinnamon. Bake at 400° for 25 minutes or until brown, puffy and done through.

SWEET MILK WAFFLES

This is the old, traditional waffle recipe, and in my opinion it makes the tastiest waffles.

2 cups of sifted all-purpose
flour

2$^1/_2$ teaspoons of double-
acting baking powder

$^3/_4$ teaspoon of salt

2 eggs

1$^1/_2$ cups of milk

$^1/_4$ cup of melted butter

Sift flour and measure 2 cups (see instructions for Cornmeal Muffins, page 47). Add the baking powder and salt, and sift again. Beat the eggs until light and lemon-colored, then beat in the milk. Gradually add the dry ingredients and blend until smooth. Finally, add the melted butter and mix it in thoroughly. Bake in a hot waffle iron until the steaming ceases.

VARIATIONS

Sweet Waffles: Add ⅓ cup of sugar and a dash of vanilla to the batter.

Bacon Waffles: Add ⅔ cup of crumbled crisp bacon to the batter.

SOUR CREAM WAFFLES

This batter will seem rather stiff, but don't be alarmed. It makes waffles that are light, crisp and very delicious.

2 eggs	**¹/₂ teaspoon of baking soda**
1 cup of sour cream	**³/₄ teaspoon of salt**
1¹/₂ cups of all-purpose flour	**6 tablespoons of melted butter**
2 teaspoons of baking powder	

Beat the eggs until light and lemon-colored. Gradually beat in the sour cream. Sift the dry ingredients together and stir them into the egg-cream mixture. Finally, add the melted butter and blend thoroughly. Bake in a hot waffle iron until the steaming ceases.
Note: This batter also makes fine pancakes.

Heated and Seasoned Breads

Hot seasoned breads are especially popular with charcoal-grilled meats, but they are also a flavorful addition to buffet suppers and informal luncheons and dinners.

GARLIC BREAD

1. Rub the crust of a loaf of French bread with a cut clove or two of garlic. Heat the bread in a 350° oven for about 12 minutes. Cut it into thick slices and serve with Garlic Butter (see page 355).

2. Split loaves of French bread the long way. For each long loaf, melt ¼ pound of butter with 3 finely chopped or crushed cloves of garlic. Brush this garlic butter on the cut surfaces of the two halves of the bread and toast or broil until nicely browned and crisp. Cut into pieces.

3. Use regular bread of good, firm texture and slice it rather thin. Spread the slices well with Garlic Butter (see page 355) and then stand them upright in a deep baking dish, pushing the slices together into a loaf shape. Brush the top with melted garlic butter and heat in a 350° oven for 15 minutes.

HERB BREAD

1. Chop rather coarsely 1 small bunch of Italian parsley (or, if the Italian variety is not available, use the regular curly parsley) and 1 bunch of green onions or scallions. Mix with ¼ pound of softened butter and spread between the halves of a loaf of French bread cut the long way. Season to taste with salt and pepper and put the halves together again. Heat in a 350° oven for 15 to 18 minutes. Cut into thick slices.

2. Cut loaves of French bread the long way and spread the halves with Rosemary Butter (see Herb Butter, page 354). Sprinkle with finely chopped parsley and coarsely cut green onions or scallions. Toast the halves under the broiler for 5 to 6 minutes or until crisp at the edges.

SESAME BREAD

Use French or Italian bread and cut through the center of the loaf. Spread the halves with Parsley Butter (page 354) and sprinkle liberally with sesame seed. Toast under the broiler until the bread is crisp and the seeds lightly browned.

CHEESE TOAST

Cut French bread the long way and spread the halves with Parsley Butter (see page 354). Sprinkle well with grated Parmesan cheese or Romano cheese. Heat in a 350° oven, or toast under the broiler flame until the bread is crisp and the cheese melted and blended with the butter.

CINNAMON TOAST

Toast regular bread slices on one side. Butter the untoasted sides lavishly and sprinkle with brown sugar and cinnamon. Run under the broiler flame for a few minutes to melt the sugar. Serve while very hot.

CROUTONS

Cut stale bread into small cubes and bake slowly in a 275° oven until crisp and well browned. Serve these with soup.

If you wish to serve the croutons with vegetables or noodles, after browning them in the oven sauté them in hot butter until they are sizzling hot and buttery.

BREAD CRUMBS

You can buy ready-made bread crumbs in packages, but if you make your own you can use up stale bread that would otherwise be wasted. There are two types of bread crumbs: soft crumbs and fine, dry crumbs. Soft crumbs are used in many stuffings, particularly those in which the crumbs are soaked in milk and then squeezed dry. Fine crumbs are also used in stuffings, particularly those which combine several solid foods, such as mushrooms, ground or chopped meats and crumbs. Fine crumbs are used on the top of casseroles and to bread meats or fish.

Soft Bread Crumbs: Break or cut stale bread slices into small cubes ½ to 1 inch across, or grind in a food processor or electric blender.

Fine Bread Crumbs: Dry out slices of stale bread in a slow oven (250°), or toast very slowly under a low broiler flame until thoroughly dry all the way through and delicately browned. Roll into crumbs with a rolling pin, grate on a grater, or grind in a food processor or electric blender. These dry crumbs will keep if stored in a tightly covered jar.

Buttered Bread Crumbs: Sauté fine, dry bread crumbs in plenty of melted butter until they are thoroughly saturated, buttery and brown. These buttered crumbs are often used as a dressing for cooked vegetables.

CHEESE

Like wine, cheese is a fermented food. Centuries ago man found that while fresh milk might spoil almost overnight, fermented milk was tasty and would keep—a most important discovery, considering the many thousands of years that mankind got along without refrigeration.

In European farm homes, cheese-making has long been routine. Different regions have developed their own versions and variations, with the gratifying result that today we have an immense choice of cheeses of different flavors and textures.

Natural cheese contains high food value and can be used in many ways. It can be eaten plain, in sauces, as flavoring and as the main ingredient in such dishes as rarebit. It is versatile, being useful in every dinner course from appetizer to dessert, and in every meal from breakfast to supper.

The best cheese is *natural* cheese, well aged. It can be creamy or dry and crumbly. It is never rubbery. The many processed cheeses on the market are poor substitutes for natural cheese. They lack the flavor and texture of the old-fashioned product.

From the standpoint of cooking and eating, cheeses fall into several categories: those good as appetizers; those good for cooking when a definite cheese flavor is needed; those that melt well; those that grate well; those good for eating plain or with fruit; those that are rich and creamy and good choices for dessert.

Cheeses good for general cooking

The following are the best choices for a cheese soufflé, melted cheese sandwiches, or any dish in which the cheese flavor predominates:

Switzerland Swiss (Emmenthal)
Gruyère
Aged cheddar

The best Swiss and Gruyère come from Switzerland. Most American Swiss cheese is too young and rubbery.

Fine aged American cheddar is made in New York State and Vermont, and milder versions come from Wisconsin and Oregon. Elsewhere around the country cheddar is made for local consumption. Look for good *natural* cheddar, well aged and sharp.

These three cheeses are also excellent grated for use on top of casseroles and vegetable dishes, and they are delicious eaten plain or with fruit. In fact, they are all-purpose cheeses.

Cheeses good for grating

Grated cheese for topping casseroles is best if it is dry and hard. Parmesan from Italy is probably the best known, but others are good choices too. Try any of the following:

Parmesan (from Italy)   Dry, aged Swiss or Gruyère
Romano (from Italy)   Dry, aged cheddar

Buy cheese by the piece and grate it yourself. It's cheaper.

Cheeses good for melting

The following cheeses melt well for sandwiches or for cheese toppings:

Swiss, Gruyère, cheddar (See "Cheeses good for general cooking")
Jack cheese (a light, creamy cheese from California)
Mozzarella (soft and bland; made in Italy and America)
Muenster (a mild cheese that can be substituted for Mozzarella)

Cheeses good for appetizers

Although any sharp cheese is good as an appetizer, the blue cheeses are perhaps most suitable. These are the cheeses with the bluish-green mold streaked through them. At their best, they are ripe, aged and have a sharp tang. They can be served plain or spread on toast fingers, or made into sandwiches with raw onion slices. They give added zip to dip sauces and can be used creamed to stuff celery. Don't put them in salad dressings; they overpower the delicate greens. Serve blue cheese separately with the salad course, if you like. The following are the best:

Roquefort
Gorgonzola
Stilton

The true Roquefort comes from France and is the aristocrat of the blue cheeses. It is also the most expensive.

Gorgonzola is the Italian version of blue cheese. It is imported, but there are also fine Gorgonzolas made in this country. A good Gorgonzola is rich and creamy.

Stilton is the English blue cheese. It is made in tall, round molds and the British like to scoop out the top and add fine port wine to keep the cheese moist.

There are Danish blue and several American blue cheeses. Some of these can be excellent if ripe and sharp.

Cheeses especially good for dessert

These are rich, creamy cheeses best served with fresh fruit at the end of the meal. They must be taken from the refrigerator some time before serving, or they will be hard and tasteless.

Brie   Bel Paese
Camembert   Tallegio
Pont-l' Evêque

The best Brie and Camembert come from France though some made in America (notably in California and Illinois) are almost as good. These are runny cheeses with a hard outer crust. Serve with melba toast or French bread.

Pont-l'Evêque is always imported from France. Like Brie and Camembert, it is runny and rich.

Bel Paese is a cream-like Italian cheese, delicious with fruit. Tallegio, a rich but mild cheese, also comes from Italy.

Cheeses for general purposes

Any good well-aged cheese can be served with fruit for dessert or a mid-day snack or be eaten plain with a cold buffet. Great favorites are:

Gruyère	Oka
Switzerland Swiss (Emmenthal)	Port-Salut
Aged cheddar	Dutch Edam

Dutch Edam is the round red cheese from Holland. To serve: Cut a slice from the top and dig the cheese out with a cheese knife.

All cheese eaten plain should be served at room temperature. Ice-cold cheese never has as fine a texture nor as definite a flavor. To enjoy cheese at its best, serve a tray of various types and eat them with a good firm bread or crusty French rolls. The salted cracker so often passed with the cheese tray detracts from the flavor of good natural cheese.

WELSH RAREBIT (Serves 4)

1 pound of sharp cheddar, grated

1 tablespoon of butter

1 cup of ale or beer

1 egg

1 teaspoon of dry mustard

2 teaspoons of Worcestershire sauce

Use a chafing dish or a double boiler. Heat water in the lower section and melt the butter in the upper section. Add the grated cheese and stir until it melts. Very slowly add the ale or beer, blending it in. Beat the egg slightly with the mustard and Worcestershire sauce, and add a few spoonfuls of the cheese mixture. Then slowly stir the egg mixture into the cheese, being sure that they blend thoroughly. Do not let the water boil, and do not let the cheese mixture get too hot or the egg will curdle. As soon as it is hot through, serve it over well-buttered toast.

CHEESE PUDDING (Serves 4)

**¹/₂ pound of cubed sharp
  cheddar**

4 slices of bread

Butter

3 eggs

1 cup of milk

Salt

Paprika

Butter the bread well and cut into cubes. Beat the eggs, add the milk, about ¹/₂ teaspoon of salt and 1 teaspoon of paprika. Stir in the cheese cubes and the bread cubes and pour into a buttered casserole. Bake in a 325° oven for about 40 minutes, or until brown and bubbly and cooked through.

CHEESE STRAWS

Make a rich pastry dough (page 76), substituting grated sharp cheddar cheese for half of the flour. Chill the dough and roll out to ¹/₄-inch thickness on a floured board. Transfer to a floured baking sheet and cut in strips about ¹/₂-inch wide, and then cut these in 5- to 6-inch lengths. Bake in a 400° oven for 6 to 8 minutes or until cooked through and crisp. Serve with cocktails.

SWISS CHEESE FONDUE (Serves 4)

Make this fondue in a heavy pan that can be placed over an alcohol flame to keep hot; or make it in an electric skillet.

**1¹/₂ pounds of grated
  Gruyère or Switzerland
  Swiss cheese**

1 clove of garlic

1 cup of dry white wine

4 teaspoons of cornstarch

3 tablespoons of kirsch

Salt to taste

Rub the pan with the garlic clove. Add the cheese, and as it starts to melt, thin it down with the white wine. Stir until the wine and cheese are thoroughly blended. Dissolve the cornstarch in the kirsch and stir this into the cheese mixture. Continue cooking and stirring until the mixture is thickened and creamy. Season to taste with salt. Keep hot over an alcohol flame or in an electric skillet. Pass cubes of French bread which are speared with forks and then dunked in the hot fondue. If the cheese mixture gets too thick, add a little more kirsch.

The following quiche recipes may be served as main dishes for luncheon or late breakfast; they are also suitable as a first course for dinner.

QUICHE LORRAINE (Serves 4 to 8)

Not the classic but one of many versions.

Cream cheese pastry (see page 77)	Pinch nutmeg
1 egg white	5 eggs
6 rashers of bacon	1½ cups of light cream
¾ cup of shredded Gruyère cheese	Salt to taste
	Chopped parsley

Prepare an 8- or 9-inch pie shell. Place a sheet of foil in shell and fill with rice or beans (these may be used again for the same purpose) to keep crust from puffing. Bake at 425° for 8 to 10 minutes. Remove foil and rice or beans. Brush the crust with lightly beaten egg white or whole egg, and bake for another 2 minutes to seal the crust.

Cook bacon through but not to the crumbly, crisp stage. Drain, cut in pieces and arrange in cooked pie shell. Add cheese and nutmeg. Beat eggs and cream together lightly, season to taste and add chopped parsley. Bake at 350° for 30 minutes or till set and a knife comes out clean when inserted 1½ inches from center. Serve warm, in wedges.

SWISS ONION TART (Serves 4 to 8)

Cream cheese pastry (see page 77)	Nutmeg
5 tablespoons of butter	¾ cup of shredded Gruyère cheese
1 large onion, thinly sliced	5 eggs
Salt	1¼ cups of light cream

Melt butter in a heavy saucepan. Add onion. Cover tightly and steam over medium heat. Onions should wilt and give off excess liquid. Drain. Season with salt and nutmeg.

Arrange onions and cheese in semi-cooked pastry shell. Beat eggs and cream together, and add 1 teaspoon salt and $^1/_4$ teaspoon nutmeg. Pour over onions, and place tart in a 375° oven for about 35 minutes or until a knife comes out clean when inserted $1^1/_2$ inches from center.

Allow to rest 15 minutes before serving.

CHEESE SOUFFLÉS—See pages 359–360.

CHEESE OMELET—See page 95.

CHEESE SAUCES—See page 350.

Desserts

Many people are "sweet conscious" and overemphasize the importance of desserts. In restaurants, they look first at the dessert list; at home, they plan the dessert and build the rest of the meal around it.

Sweets do have their place, but they should be kept in balance with other foods. After a heavy, rich dinner a heavy, rich dessert only makes one miserable. Heavy meals should conclude with a simple, refreshing fruit course or a light soufflé. Bulkier desserts, such as cakes and pies, are ideal to round out a light meal of leftovers or a one-dish meal of soup or salad.

You will find suggestions for fruit and soufflé desserts in the Fruit chapter, page 142, and under Soufflés, page 358.

Here are good basic cakes, pies and puddings—most of them old favorites, but some with new twists.

Cakes

Cake mixes are deservedly popular. They save time and trouble, and if you have a cake-eating family that demands a constant supply, mixes are your standbys. But I must say that no mix can produce cake equal to genuine homemade cake prepared with the freshest of eggs, the best butter and real—not imitation—flavoring. Even if you find making a cake from scratch too difficult for everyday baking, you should undertake the job for special occasions, such as birthdays. You may even find it much more fun than you expected. If you have an electric mixer, the tiring part of the work is eliminated.

Successful cake-baking is not difficult if you pay careful attention to a few simple rules.

1. Be sure your oven thermostat is accurate. If you have doubts, place an oven thermometer inside the stove and check its temperature with that registered on the oven control. If they are not the same, call the maintenance division of your local gas or power company and have the oven thermostat repaired.

2. Read the recipe thoroughly and be sure you have all the ingredients.

3. If you want the best results, use the best products. Butter makes cakes with a better flavor and texture than any other shortening. Real vanilla is far superior to vanillin.

4. Check to be sure that you have cake pans that are the right size for baking the cake. Always keep your baking tins spotlessly clean.

5. Be accurate in your measurements. And don't assume that you can improve the cake by increasing the amount of an ingredient. Butter makes a cake rich, but too much butter can ruin it.

6. Place the cake pans in the center of the oven or space them so they get an even heat.

7. Don't trust entirely to cooking times given in recipes. Test the cakes for doneness. When a toothpick or cake tester comes out clean, the cake is done. Or you can test with your finger: Touch the cake lightly on top; if it springs back, it is done; if the impression of your finger remains, bake it a little longer. Do not overbake or the cake will be crusty and have poor texture.

BASIC TWO-EGG LAYER CAKE

This recipe is for two 8-inch cake tins.

½ cup of butter

1 cup of sugar

2 eggs, separated

1¾ cups of sifted all-purpose flour

½ teaspoon of salt

2 teaspoons of double-acting baking powder

⅔ cup of milk

1 teaspoon of genuine vanilla

Here is the step-by-step process for preparing the cake.

1. Remove the butter from the refrigerator about an hour ahead of time to give it a chance to soften.

2. Get out the cake pans. Butter them, sprinkle them lightly with flour and shake it around in the pans. Toss out excess flour. Or butter the pans and line the bottoms with buttered waxed paper or with cooking parchment.

3. Assemble the ingredients and utensils for mixing:

large bowl and wooden spoon, or electric mixer
small bowl for egg yolks
larger bowl for egg whites
eggbeater
flour sifter and bowl for dry ingredients

4. Preheat the oven at 350°.

5. Put the soft butter in a large bowl and cream it with a wooden spoon or put it in the electric mixer at low speed. Gradually add the sugar, creaming it into the butter by hand or in the mixer until it is fluffy.

6. Break the eggs and separate them, putting the yolks in a small bowl and the whites in a larger bowl. Beat the whites until they are stiff enough to stand in peaks when you lift out the beater, but not stiff enough to be dry.

7. Beat the yolks until lemon-colored, and then add the beaten yolks to the butter-sugar mixture, blending them in thoroughly.

8. Sift the flour and measure 1¾ cups. Then sift the measured flour, the baking powder and salt all together.

9. Add a little of these dry ingredients to the butter-egg yolk mixture and then add a little of the milk. Stir in each addition thoroughly. Keep adding the dry ingredients alternately with the milk until it is all beaten into the batter.

10. Add the vanilla and stir it in.

11. Finally, *fold* in the beaten egg whites very carefully. Do *not* use the electric mixer. Use a wooden spoon or rubber scraper and cut down through the batter to the bottom of the bowl. Then turn the spoon and scrape up against the side of the bowl, folding some of the batter over the mass of egg whites. Repeat this process until the egg whites have been evenly distributed throughout the batter.

12. Pour the batter into the greased cake pans and bake at 350° until done. Start testing for doneness (see basic rules, page 62) after 30 minutes.

13. When the cake is done, remove it from the pans and cool on a wire cake rack.

14. Do not frost until cool. For frosting recipes, see page 70.

FOUR-EGG CAKE

This recipe makes a three-layer, 9-inch cake or a sheet cake 8 by 12 inches. Bake the layers at 350° for 30 minutes. Bake the sheet cake at 350° for 40 minutes. The sheet may be split into two layers and frosted; or cut in half and frosted as a layer cake; or you may leave it whole, frost it and cut it in squares.

1 cup of butter

2 cups of sugar

4 eggs, separated

2 teaspoons of double-acting baking powder

2²/₃ cups of sifted all-purpose flour

¹/₂ teaspoon of salt

1 cup of milk

2¹/₂ teaspoons of vanilla

Mix according to the instructions for Two-Egg Cake (see page 62).

FUDGE NUT CAKE

This cake may be baked in two 9-inch pans or in an 8- by 12-inch oblong pan. Bake the layers in a 350° oven about 35 minutes. Bake the sheet cake about 50 to 55 minutes.

¹/₄ cup of butter

1¹/₂ cups of sugar

2 eggs, separated

4 ounces or squares of unsweetened chocolate

1³/₄ cups of sifted all-purpose flour

2 teaspoons of double-acting baking powder

¹/₂ teaspoon of salt

1¹/₂ cups of milk

2 teaspoons of vanilla

1 cup of chopped nuts

¹/₂ extra cup of sugar

Follow the mixing directions given for Basic Two-Egg Layer Cake (see page 62). Melt the chocolate over hot water and add it after you add the egg yolks. Add the chopped nuts with the last of the flour. Beat the ¹/₂ cup of sugar listed at the end of the ingredients into the beaten egg whites just before you fold them into the batter.

WHISKEY CAKE

This cake is moist and rich and keeps well. Wonderful for the holiday season. Bake it in a large loaf tin or in two 1-pound coffee tins.

1 pound of shelled walnuts
$^1/_2$ pound of seeded raisins
$1^1/_2$ cups of sifted all-purpose flour
1 teaspoon of double-acting baking powder
$^1/_4$ teaspoon of salt

$^1/_2$ cup of butter
$1^1/_8$ cups of sugar
3 eggs, separated
2 teaspoons of grated nutmeg
$^2/_3$ cup of bourbon whiskey

Remove the butter from the refrigerator ahead of time to let it soften. Grease the tins and line them with waxed paper; butter the paper. Preheat the oven at 325°.

Chop the nuts coarsely and cut the raisins in half. Sift the flour and measure $1^1/_2$ cups. Mix $^1/_2$ cup of the flour with the nuts and raisins. Sift the rest of the flour again with the baking powder and salt. Cream the butter and sugar together and add the 3 egg yolks, one at a time, to the butter-sugar mixture, beating well after each addition. Mix the nutmeg and whiskey together and add this liquid bit by bit, alternating with additions of the sifted dry ingredients. Add the nuts and raisins; finally beat the egg whites until stiff but not dry and *fold* them into the batter (see page 358).

Pour into the tins or loaf pan and let stand for a few minutes to settle. Bake at 325° for $1^1/_4$ hours. Remove the cake from the oven and let it stand in the pan or tins for 1 hour before taking it out.

I like to pour an extra half cup of whiskey over the cake when it is almost cool.

SPONGE CAKE

Few people make a plain sponge cake nowadays. This is a pity, for it is a very versatile cake, excellent served plain with fruit, surprisingly good when a little stale if moistened with rum or liqueur and topped with a rich custard sauce.

2 egg yolks
1 cup of sugar
³/₈ cup of hot water
Grated rind of 1 lemon
1 teaspoon of lemon juice
2 egg whites, beaten stiff but
   not dry

1 cup of all-purpose flour
1 teaspoon of double-acting
   baking powder
¹/₄ teaspoon of salt

Beat the egg yolks until thick and lemon-colored and gradually add ¹/₂ cup of the sugar, beating constantly. Add the hot water, lemon rind and juice and the rest of the sugar. *Fold* in the stiffly beaten egg whites thoroughly (see page 358). Sift the flour with the baking powder and salt and fold it into the batter until well mixed.

Butter and flour an 8- by 12-inch cake pan (see instructions under Basic Two-Egg Layer Cake, page 62) and pour in the batter. Bake in a 350° oven for about 25 minutes. Test for doneness (see instructions under basic rules, page 62).

ANGEL FOOD CAKE

This recipe is for a 9-inch tube pan.

1 cup of sifted cake flour
1¹/₂ cups of sugar
¹/₄ teaspoon of salt
1¹/₃ cups of egg whites
   (approx. 1 dozen eggs)

1¹/₃ teaspoons of cream of
   tartar
1¹/₂ teaspoons of vanilla or
   almond (I find almond
   best)

Sift the flour and measure. Then sift it four times with ¹/₄ cup of the sugar and the salt. Sift the rest of the sugar five times. Beat the egg whites in a large bowl using a rotary eggbeater. When they are foamy and white, but not stiff, add the cream of tartar. Continue beating until stiff enough to form peaks when you remove the beater. Do not let them get dry. They should be glossy and smooth. Sprinkle 2 tablespoons of sugar over the beaten egg whites and beat until just blended. Add the rest of the sugar, 2 tablespoons at a time, and beat in after each addition. Add the flavoring and beat this in.

Using a wooden spoon or rubber scraper, *fold* in the flour, sprinkling about ¹/₄ cup of the flour over the egg whites at a time. (For folding instructions, see page 358.) When all the flour is folded in thoroughly, pour the batter into an ungreased 9-inch tube pan and bake at 325° for 40 to 60 minutes or until delicately browned on top. When done, remove the cake from the oven and turn the pan upside down on a cake rack. Modern tube pans come with special legs at the top on which the pan can stand upside down. Let the cake cool in the pan for 1 hour. It should come out of its own accord. Otherwise, run a spatula around the edges and loosen it.

I prefer angel cake unfrosted. Do not cut it with a knife. Tear it with one of the special implements sold for this purpose or with your fingers. It is delicious toasted the next day.

CHOCOLATE ROLL

This delicate dessert is not a true cake. It is really a fallen soufflé.

6 eggs, separated	1 teaspoon of vanilla
1/2 cup of sugar	1 1/2 cups of heavy cream, whipped and sweetened
6 ounces of semi-sweet chocolate	Powdered sugar
3 tablespoons of strong coffee	Cocoa

Butter an 11- by 14-inch jelly roll pan, line it with waxed paper and butter the paper. Beat the egg yolks until light and lemon-colored and gradually beat in the sugar. Put the chocolate and coffee in the top of a double boiler over hot water and melt. Let cool slightly and then beat into the sugar and egg yolks. Beat in the vanilla. Beat the egg whites until stiff enough to form peaks when you remove the beater, but do not beat them dry. Fold them into the chocolate mixture.

Pour the batter into the greased pan and spread it evenly. Bake in a 350° oven for about 15 minutes or until a knife inserted into the batter comes out clean.

Remove from the oven, cover with a slightly damp towel and let stand for about 20 minutes. Meanwhile, arrange two 14-inch lengths of waxed paper on a worktable, side by side and slightly overlapping. Sprinkle paper with powdered sugar and cocoa. Run a spatula around the edges of the cake and invert it on the waxed paper; it should turn out easily. Carefully remove the paper in which it was baked. Spread the cake with sweetened whipped cream. Then, by lifting the edge of the waxed paper under the cake, get the end of the cake to fold inward; this starts the cake rolling. Continue lifting the waxed paper and roll the cake up gently and quickly and onto a large platter.

This makes 8 to 10 slices of elegant dessert.

OLD-FASHIONED GINGERBREAD

A cold winter evening is just the time to serve a rich homemade gingerbread, steaming hot and heaped with whipped cream. This is a true old-fashioned recipe.

1 cup of molasses	1 teaspoon of ginger
1/2 cup of butter	1 teaspoon of cinnamon
2 1/3 cups of all-purpose flour	1/4 teaspoon of ground cloves
Pinch of salt	
3/4 teaspoon of baking soda	1 cup of sour cream

Put the molasses and butter in a pan and heat until they boil. Sift the flour with the salt, soda, ginger, cinnamon and ground cloves. When the butter and molasses are slightly cooled add the sour cream and then stir in the spices and flour. Pour into a buttered pan and bake at 350° for about 40 minutes.

Cookies

BROWNIES

2 squares of unsweetened chocolate	1 cup of sifted all-purpose flour
1/4 cup of butter	1/2 teaspoon of double-acting baking powder
1 cup of sugar	
2 eggs, well beaten	1 cup of chopped walnuts
1/2 teaspoon of salt	1 teaspoon of vanilla

Put the chocolate and butter in the top of a double boiler over hot water and melt. Remove from the heat and add all the other ingredients, mixing them in thoroughly. Butter an 8-inch-square pan and pour the mixture into it. Bake at 350° for about 30 minutes. Cool and cut into squares. A good brownie is sticky and rich with chocolate. It should never be dry.

CHOCOLATE CHIP COOKIES

¾ cup of slightly softened butter

¾ cup granulated sugar

¾ cup firmly packed brown sugar

1 egg

1 teaspoon vanilla

3 tablespoons milk

2½ cups sifted all-purpose flour

1 teaspoon baking powder

¼ teaspoon salt

12-ounce package of semi-sweet chocolate bits

1 cup chopped walnuts, almonds, pecans, or filberts

Cream the butter and sugars together thoroughly, then beat in the egg, vanilla and milk. Sift the flour, baking powder and salt together. Stir into the batter. Add the chocolate bits and nuts. Place ½ teaspoons of the batter on a buttered or oiled baking sheet or pan, allowing an inch or so between portions. Bake in a 375° oven 8 to 12 minutes. Loosen with a spatula while quite warm and allow to cool on a rack.

PEANUT BUTTER COOKIES

½ cup butter

½ cup peanut butter

1 cup firmly packed brown sugar

1 egg

2 cups sifted all-purpose flour

¼ teaspoon salt

1 teaspoon vanilla

Cream the butter and peanut butter together. Beat in the sugar, then beat in the egg and vanilla. Sift the flour with the salt and mix with the batter to make a stiff dough. Shape into a long roll about 1 inch in diameter, and cut into one inch pieces. Form the pieces into balls and place 1 inch apart on greased cookie sheets. Press down the balls lightly with a fork to make a crisscross design. Bake at 375° 9 to 12 minutes or until delicately browned. Remove with a spatula while still warm and cool on a rack.

SCOTCH SHORTBREAD

³/₄ pound unsalted butter, slightly softened

1 cup granulated sugar

4 cups sifted all-purpose flour

Cream the butter well, gradually beat in the sugar, and continue beating until very light. Thoroughly mix in the flour to make a firm dough. Turn out on a floured board and knead until smooth. Place on an ungreased cookie sheet, pat out about ½ inch thick, and cut into pieces ½ inch wide and 3½ inches long. Or pat into 8-inch pie tins, and mark into wedges with a knife or fork. In either case prick the dough with a fork. Bake in a 300° oven about 30 minutes or until a light brown just around the edges. Cool slightly then transfer to a rack to finish cooling. Store in an airtight tin or plastic bag, and preferably age for a week in a cool place before eating.

Frostings

SEVEN-MINUTE ICING

This is a standard frosting, easy to make and good for almost any cake.

3 egg whites

³/₄ cup of sugar

Pinch of salt

6 tablespoons of light corn syrup

1 teaspoon of vanilla

Put the unbeaten egg whites, the sugar, corn syrup and salt in the upper part of a double boiler over hot water. Beat with a rotary eggbeater while you bring the water to a boil. Keep beating for 7 minutes, or until the mixture stands in soft mounds. Remove from the heat, beat in the vanilla and continue beating until the frosting stands in peaks and will hold its shape when spread.

CHOCOLATE FROSTING, HELEN EVANS BROWN

This amazing frosting was created by Helen Evans Brown and in my opinion is the best chocolate icing there is.

Melt 5 ounces of semi-sweet chocolate in the upper part of a double boiler over hot water. Stir in a pinch of salt and $\frac{1}{2}$ cup of sour cream. Blend until smooth and spread over top and sides of an 8-inch cake.

BUTTER FROSTING

$\frac{1}{4}$ cup of softened butter	$\frac{1}{4}$ cup of heavy cream
4 to 5 cups of sifted confectioner's sugar	Flavoring

Blend the butter and sugar together, then stir in the heavy cream. Flavor with any one of the following: 1 teaspoon of vanilla, $\frac{1}{2}$ teaspoon of almond, 1 tablespoon of instant coffee or 1 tablespoon of instant coffee mixed with Cognac; or substitute $\frac{1}{4}$ cup of maple syrup for the heavy cream.

Pies

As with cake mixes, pie crust and pie filling mixes have all but solved the pie problem for most cooks. But the best pies still are made with fresh ingredients, freshly mixed. Fresh butter makes the richest crust; fresh eggs, the finest fillings.

The next time you get hungry for that extra flaky, old-fashioned pie crust filled to bursting with juicy fruit or creamy custard, try making it yourself. It is not difficult.

PLAIN PASTRY FOR A TWO-CRUST PIE

I feel the best pastry is made with butter. Other fats that can be used are: margarine, vegetable shortening, lard, or half butter and half lard.

Handle the pastry as little as possible. Make it in a cool spot, using ice water and cold butter, and be sure your fingers are as cool as possible.

$2\frac{1}{2}$ cups of all-purpose flour, sifted	12 tablespoons of shortening
1 teaspoon of salt	3 to 4 tablespoons of ice water

Into a large bowl, or onto a marble slab, sift the flour and salt. Put the butter or other shortening (see above) in a hollow in the center of the flour and blend it in with your fingertips (or cut in with two knives or a pastry blender) until it is distributed through the flour and has a mealy consistency. Don't press it or knead; just flake it gently. When it is mealy, add about 3 to 4 tablespoons of ice water and work the mixture into a ball. If you need a little more water, add it, but be very careful not to add too much. The less water used, the better. The pastry should stick together but not be doughy. Roll the ball of pastry up in waxed paper and put it in the refrigerator to chill for 20 to 30 minutes.

To roll out: Divide the dough in half and put one half on a lightly floured board. Flour a rolling pin lightly and press it down into the center of the dough. Roll gently out toward the edge. Keep rolling gently from the center up to the edge, rotating the dough a quarter turn each time to shape it evenly into a circle. When it is large enough to fill the bottom and sides of the pie tin, roll it over the rolling pin and transfer it to the tin, unrolling it evenly over the bottom. Pat it down to fit the pan and trim off the edges, leaving a slight overhang to seal with the top crust.

Roll out the top crust in the same manner. After the pie is filled, place the top crust over the filling, press the edges of the top and bottom crust together with your fingers and trim off the excess dough with a sharp knife. Then, using the prongs of a fork or using your fingertips, flute or crimp the edge of the crust. Cut small slits in the top crust in two or three places.

Bake according to the recipe.

APPLE PIE

Much of the flavor of apple pie depends on the type of apples you use. Buy firm, juicy fruit, such as Greenings, Granny Smiths, Pippins or Gravensteins. Mealy apples are flat tasting when cooked. Allow 9 to 10 medium-sized apples for a pie.

Pastry dough	**1 cup of brown sugar**
9 to 10 apples	**Cinnamon**
Butter	**Salt**
1 cup of white sugar	

Prepare the pastry (see page 71) and line the bottom of a pie tin with a crust. Peel the apples and cut them in thin slices. Place a layer of sliced apples on the bottom crust, dot with butter, sprinkle with white and brown sugar and a little cinnamon and add a tiny pinch of salt. Repeat these layers until all the apples and sugar are used. The pie tin should be heaped up with apple slices.

Put on the top crust (see Plain Pastry instructions, page 71), seal the edges and gash the top crust in two or three places. Bake in a hot oven—450° to 500°—for 20 minutes. Reduce the heat to 400° for another 20 minutes, and then turn it down to 350° for a final 20 minutes, or until the crust is nicely browned and the apples cooked through.

Apple pie is best served warm. Serve it with heavy cream or whipped cream, or with a sharp cheese.

BLUEBERRY PIE

Pastry for 2 crusts (page 71)

3 to 4 cups of blueberries

Flour

Cinnamon

Butter

1 cup of maple syrup

Wash and pick over the blueberries. Prepare the pastry and line a pie tin. Fill with the blueberries, sprinkle them lightly with flour and a little cinnamon and dot with butter. Pour in the maple syrup. Top with the second crust (see instructions, page 72), seal the edges and gash the top of the crust. Bake as you do Apple Pie (above).

Serve warm with heavy cream or sour cream.

PEACH PIE

Pastry for 2 crusts (page 71)

8 to 9 ripe fresh peaches

Brown sugar

Bourbon

Cinnamon

Butter

Prepare the pastry and line a pie tin. Peel the peaches and halve them. Place the halves in the pie tin and fill the center of each with a tablespoon of brown sugar and a few drops of bourbon. Sprinkle lightly with cinnamon and dot well with butter. Put on the top crust, seal the edges and gash the top in two or three places. Bake according to instructions for Apple Pie (above). Serve with heavy cream or whipped cream.

RHUBARB PIE

Pastry for 2 crusts (page 71)

4 cups rhubarb cut into ³/₄-inch pieces

1¹/₂ cups sugar

4 tablespoons flour

¹/₄ teaspoon salt

1 teaspoon grated orange rind

1 tablespoon butter

Mix the rhubarb with the sugar, flour, salt and orange rind. Heap into a 9-inch pan lined with pastry. Dot with butter. Add the top pastry, trim the edges and crimp to seal the two crusts. Cut 3 or 4 small slits in the top crust. Bake at 450° 15 minutes, then reduce the heat to 350° and bake another 25 to 30 minutes. Serve warm or cold.

CHERRY PIE

Pastry for 2 crusts (page 71)

4 cups tart pitted cherries

1 to 1¹/₂ cups sugar

4 to 6 tablespoons flour

4 drops almond flavoring

1 tablespoon butter

Mix the cherries, sugar, flour, and almond flavoring. Heap into a 9-inch pan lined with pastry. Dot with butter. Add the top pastry, trim the edges, and crimp to seal the crusts. Cut 3 or 4 small steam vents in the top crust. Bake at 450° 15 minutes, reduce the heat to 350° and bake another 25 to 30 minutes. Cool on a rack and serve cold.

MINCE PIE

Pastry (page 71)

2 cups of prepared mincemeat

1 or 2 apples

³/₄ cup of seeded raisins

¹/₂ cup of Cognac

Butter

2 egg yolks, beaten

Buy the finest mincemeat available and doctor it up with 1 or 2 extra apples, peeled and chopped, the seeded raisins and ¹/₄ cup of Cognac. Taste for seasoning and add spices if necessary.

Prepare the crust according to instructions under Plain Pastry, and heap the mincemeat on the bottom crust. Dot liberally with butter and add another ¼ cup of Cognac. Cover with the top crust, seal and gash in two or three places. Brush the top crust with beaten egg yolks and bake according to directions for Apple Pie, above. Serve hot or cold.

VARIATIONS

Open-faced: For the top crust, cut the pastry dough into strips and lay them across the top in a lattice pattern.

Turnovers: Roll out a 6-inch circle of dough for each turnover. Place mincemeat filling on one half of dough, fold over the other half and crimp the edges. Slash the top in two or three places. Bake in a hot oven until pastry is browned.

CUSTARD PIE

½ Plain Pastry recipe (see page 71)

5 eggs

¾ cup of sugar

1 teaspoon of vanilla

Nutmeg

2½ cups of light cream or heavy cream and milk mixed

Prepare one half of the Plain Pastry and line a pie tin with it. Beat the eggs and then beat the sugar into them. Add the vanilla and a pinch of nutmeg and then beat in the cream, or milk and cream mixed. Pour this into the pie shell and bake in a 375° oven until the top is delicately browned and the center still a bit runny. The custard should be set around the edges but not in the center because the pie will continue cooking for a short time after it is removed from the oven. Test for doneness with a silver knife. If the knife comes out clean, the pie is done.

PUMPKIN PIE

1 Plain Pastry recipe (see page 71)

2 cups of strained, cooked pumpkin or squash

1 cup of brown sugar

1 cup of heavy cream

1 cup of milk

¼ cup of Cognac

6 eggs, lightly beaten

½ cup of finely shredded preserved ginger

2 teaspoons of cinnamon

¼ teaspoon of ground cloves

¼ teaspoon of salt

Prepare the pastry dough and line a pie tin with it. Mix all the ingredients with the strained pumpkin until well blended and pour into the pie shell. Bake in a 350° oven for about 45 minutes or until the filling is set around the edges but still a little runny in the center. (See Custard Pie, page 75.)

Serve warm or cool, plain or with whipped cream. Makes two 8-inch pies or one 9-inch pie.

Tarts and Rolls

RICH TART PASTRY

2 cups all-purpose flour (unsifted)

3 tablespoons of sugar

³/₄ cup of butter

1¹/₂ teaspoons of grated lemon rind

3 hard-cooked egg yolks, mashed

2 raw egg yolks

¹/₂ teaspoon of salt

Make a well in center of flour, working either on a table or in a bowl. Add all ingredients. The butter should not be ice-cold nor so soft that it is oily. Using fingertips, make a paste of center ingredients, gradually incorporating flour to make a firm, smooth ball of paste. Work as quickly as you can so the butter won't become greasy. When bowl or tabletop has been left clean, wrap the dough in waxed paper or aluminum foil and chill until firm enough to roll between sheets of waxed paper.

Note: To make pastry for quiche, hors d'oeuvre and meat pies, omit sugar and lemon rind from recipe. Pastry can be made in an electric mixer equipped with a flat paddle, combining all ingredients at once. For a more brittle, less crumbly pastry, use only egg whites.

PASTRY IN THE FOOD PROCESSOR

2 cups all-purpose flour

8 tablespoons unsalted butter, well chilled

¹/₄ teaspoon salt

2 tablespoons sugar (optional)

1 tablespoon lemon juice

2 eggs

Put the flour, butter, sugar (for dessert pastry only), and salt in the beaker of the food processor, and pulse for about 10 seconds until the mixture is granular and no large pieces of butter remain. Add the lemon juice and eggs, and process until a ball of dough forms, 10 to 15 seconds more. Sprinkle the surface with flour and wrap in plastic or waxed paper to chill. When firm but still workable roll out on a floured board to ¼ inch thick. Makes enough pastry for a one-crust 9-inch pie or tart.

CREAM CHEESE PASTRY

½ pound of cream cheese
Heavy cream to moisten
½ teaspoon of salt
¼ pound of butter

¼ cup of vegetable shortening
2¾ cups all-purpose flour (unsifted)

Follow instructions for Rich Tart Pastry (page 76).

LEMON PIE

The Pastry

1 large egg yolk
2 tablespoons of ice water
1 tablespoon of lemon juice
Pinch salt

1 stick (½ cup) of butter
1½ cups of sifted all-purpose flour
2 tablespoons of sugar

Beat yolk lightly and add ice water, lemon juice and salt. Cut or work butter into flour, then add, along with sugar, to the egg mixture. Work ingredients together until they form a soft ball. Chill for ½ hour and pat into a flan ring or a 9-inch tin. Place a piece of foil inside shell and fill with beans or rice to weight it down. Bake at 350° for 25 to 30 minutes. Remove beans or rice and save to use for this purpose again.

The Filling

6 egg yolks
1½ cups of sugar
Grated rind of 1 lemon
½ cup of lemon juice
3 tablespoons of butter

4 tablespoons of cornstarch
¼ teaspoon of salt
1½ cups of boiling water

Beat egg yolks well, add remaining ingredients except boiling water, and beat again thoroughly. Combine with boiling water and pour into top of double boiler. Cook over hot water until mixture thickens, and allow to cook for 5 to 10 minutes longer over simmering water. Pour into baked shell. Top with meringue.

The Meringue

3 egg whites

1 teaspoon of cream of tartar

Pinch of salt

6 tablespoons of sugar

Beat egg whites till they form soft peaks. Add cream of tartar and salt and continue beating till whites are stiff but not dry. Add sugar, a little at a time, beating it in well. Spread meringue over the pie, being certain to cover the surface completely, including the edge of the crust. If you are deft with the pastry tube, you may pipe the meringue over the pie, using a number 6 rosette tube.

Bake at 350° for 15 to 18 minutes or until the meringue is lightly browned.

STRAWBERRY TART

Rich Tart Pastry (see page 76)

1 egg yolk, beaten

1-pound jar currant jelly

1 tablespoon kirsch

2 pints ripe strawberries

½ cup heavy cream

Fit the rolled out pastry in a 9-inch flan ring on a baking sheet or a tart pan with a removable bottom. Line with foil and fill with dried beans or rice to weight it down during baking. Bake at 425° 18 to 20 minutes. Remove the foil and beans (save the beans for another time). Brush with the beaten yolk and bake for another two minutes. Allow to cool.

Place the currant jelly in a heavy-bottomed sauce pan, and cook over moderate heat until melted and just at the boiling point. Stir in the kirsch, remove from the heat and allow to cool for a few minutes. Brush the bottom of the crust with 2 tablespoons of the jelly. Arrange the berries nicely in the shell, and brush with the remaining melted jelly. Whip the cream, and flavor with another tablespoon of kirsch, if you like. Serve it with the tart.

NUTTED LEMON ROLL

Spoon lemon curd on Sponge Roll (see below). Cut into small squares. Roll very tightly. Dip each end into lemon curd and finally into chopped pistachio nuts.

LEMON CURD (Lemon Butter)

Melt ¼ pound of butter, and add the grated rind of 1 lemon, the juice of 3 large lemons, ¼ teaspoon of salt, and 1½ cups of sugar. Cook over hot water with the yolks of 3 eggs and 3 whole eggs beaten together, whisking constantly until the mixture is shiny and thick. Cool.

SPONGE ROLL OR SPONGE LAYER

4 eggs
¼ cup of sugar
¼ cup of all-purpose flour
¼ cup of cornstarch

½ teaspoon of vanilla
½ teaspoon of grated lemon rind

Separate eggs. Beat egg whites to soft peaks, gradually add sugar and continue beating until stiff. Beat egg yolks slightly. Stir 1 cup of egg whites into egg yolks. Pour mixture over remaining egg whites. Add flour and cornstarch, which have been sifted together. Add the vanilla and lemon rind. Fold the mixture together. Pour into an 11- by 16-inch pan lined with buttered waxed paper. Bake in a hot oven (400°) 10 minutes.

LEMON CREAM PIE OR TARTLETS

Combine equal parts lemon curd and whipped cream. Spoon into baked pie shell or tart shells. Garnish with chopped pistachio nuts.

STRAWBERRY CREAM ROLL

1 sponge roll (see above)	1 pint of sliced, sugared
1½ cups of heavy cream, whipped	strawberries
3 tablespoons of sugar	Powdered sugar
1 teaspoon of vanilla or kirsch	

Trim sponge roll. Spread with flavored whipped cream. Dot with sliced strawberries and roll. Sprinkle with powdered sugar. Serve with Raspberry Sauce.

Raspberry Sauce

1 package of frozen raspberries	Sugar (optional)
	Crème de cassis

Purée the raspberries. Add sugar if desired. Flavor with crème de cassis.

Puddings

Puddings can be either hearty or light and elegant deserts. They are generally not as complicated or time-consuming to prepare as pies or cakes. Many can be whipped up in a few minutes, and all can be dolled up to impress guests. Here are some standards that I regard as old favorites:

CRÈME BRÛLÉE (Serves 4)

This rich dessert is an elegant classic, fit for a grand dinner party.

1 pint of heavy cream	Dash of vanilla
5 eggs	½ cup of light brown sugar
5 tablespoons of sugar	

Put the cream in the top part of a double boiler over hot water and heat until it reaches the boiling point. Beat the eggs lightly, and then beat in the sugar. Flavor with a touch of vanilla. Slowly add the hot cream to the egg mixture, beating with a wooden spoon constantly. Return the cream and eggs to the top of the double boiler and cook, stirring constantly, until the mixture coats the spoon with a thin film. Do not overcook or the eggs will curdle. Pour into a heat-proof serving dish and cool for 6 to 8 hours. When ready to serve, sprinkle the top of the crème with brown sugar in an even layer and run under the broiler flame for just a minute to glaze the sugar. Or use a salamander—a special French utensil that is heated red-hot and then held over the sugar to glaze it. Cool before serving.

VARIATION

With chestnuts: Buy canned whole chestnuts put up in syrup. Drain the chestnuts. Then cover them with dark rum. Prepare the Crème Brûlée as above and dot with the rum-soaked chestnuts just before serving.

BAKED CUSTARD PUDDING (Serves 4)

5 eggs
³/₄ cup of sugar
2 teaspoons of vanilla or 1 teaspoon scraped vanilla bean

2 cups of milk or half milk and half cream

Beat the eggs until light and lemon-colored and then beat in the sugar and vanilla. Beat in the milk, or milk and cream mixed, and pour into a glass casserole or pudding dish. Sprinkle lightly with sugar and bake at 350° for about 35 to 40 minutes. The custard should be not quite set in the center. It continues to cook for a minute or two after taken from the oven. (See Custard Pie, page 75.) Do not overcook or it will separate and turn watery.

Custard may be baked in individual molds. These will cook in a few minutes less.

Serve chilled with cream or whipped cream.

VARIATIONS

Spiced custard: Add a pinch of ground cloves and ½ teaspoon of nutmeg or mace to the egg-milk mixture before you cook it.

Caramel custard: Combine 1 cup of sugar and ½ cup of water in a heavy skillet and cook until the sugar turns syrupy and light brown. Pour this into the bottom of the casserole or pudding dish and swirl it around to coat the dish well. Pour the custard mix into the caramel lining and bake as above. Unmold on a plate and serve with a topping of caramel and whipped cream.

CHOCOLATE MOUSSE (Serves 4 to 6)

6 ounces of semi-sweet
chocolate

1 tablespoon of powdered
coffee

3 tablespoons of butter

6 eggs, separated

$1/2$ cup of heavy cream

5 tablespoons of sugar

Melt the chocolate with the coffee in the upper part of a double boiler over hot (not boiling) water. Add the butter and stir until melted. Beat the egg yolks until very light, add a little of the chocolate mixture and blend with a wire whisk. Then add the rest of the chocolate and beat over hot water for a few minutes until smooth. Cool. Whip the cream and add the sugar. Then beat the egg whites until very stiff. Fold the whipped cream and egg whites into the chocolate mixture. Chill.

STEAMED FIG PUDDING (Serves 4 to 6)

1 cup of beef suet

$1/2$ pound of dried figs

3 cups of bread crumbs,
grated

$1/2$ cup of milk

3 beaten eggs

1 cup of sugar

Chop the suet and figs well and rub them together with a wooden spoon or grind together in a food processor. Soak the grated bread crumbs in the milk and add to the suet-fig mixture. Add the beaten eggs and sugar and blend thoroughly. Pour into a mold or into 1-pound coffee tins, cover tightly and place on a rack over boiling water in a kettle. Cover and steam for 3 hours, adding water if needed.

Unmold and serve with Hard Sauce, Brandy Sauce or Brown Sugar Sauce, pages 355–357.

VARIATIONS

Steamed Date Pudding: Instead of the figs, use 1 cup of chopped dates and $1/2$ cup of chopped walnuts.

Steamed Prune Pudding: Instead of the figs, use $1/2$ pound of pitted chopped prunes and $1/2$ cup of chopped walnuts, and flavor with $1/4$ cup of dry sherry.

Steamed Raisin Pudding: Instead of the figs, use $1/2$ pound of sultana raisins soaked in $1/4$ cup of Cognac, and add $1/2$ cup of whole toasted, blanched almonds.

DIPLOMAT PUDDING

Ladyfingers
Cognac and water (or dry
 sherry and water)

Apricot or raspberry jam

Dip ladyfingers in a mixture of Cognac, or sherry, and water, and line a mold with them. Spread with jam and add a layer of dipped ladyfingers. Alternate layers of jam and ladyfingers until the mold is full, finishing with ladyfingers: Pour ½ cup of Cognac or sherry over the contents of the mold, cover with two thicknesses of foil and weight down. I find a plate arranged on top and weighted with heavy canned goods does the trick. Chill the weighted mold overnight or for 24 hours if possible.

Unmold and serve with whipped cream or Custard Sauce (pages 355–356).

RICE PUDDING

I am not a Rice Pudding fan myself, but there are many people who think highly of it. Here are two versions:

POOR MAN'S RICE PUDDING (Serves 4 to 6)

1 quart of milk
½ cup of rice
½ cup of molasses
Pinch of salt

1 teaspoon of vanilla
3 tablespoons of melted
 butter

Mix the milk, rice, molasses, salt and vanilla and pour into a baking dish. Bake at 250° for 3 hours, stirring several times during the first hour. Add the butter the last time you stir it.

Serve with warm or cold cream.

RICE CUSTARD PUDDING (Serves 4 to 6)

2½ cups of cooked rice
1 cup of sugar
½ cup of sultana raisins
1 teaspoon of vanilla

5 eggs
2 cups of rich milk
Pinch of salt
Cinnamon

Mix the rice, $^1\!/_2$ cup of the sugar, the raisins and vanilla. Beat the eggs and add the milk, the remaining $^1\!/_2$ cup of sugar and a pinch of salt. Add the rice and raisin mixture to the milk and eggs. Pour into a buttered baking dish and bake at 350° for 35 to 40 minutes or until the custard is set. Remove from the oven and sprinkle with cinnamon. Serve cold with heavy cream or whipped cream.

VARIATION

Cook in individual custard cups. These will be done in about 25 minutes.

Note: Do not overcook the custard or it may be watery. (See suggestions under Custard Pie, page 75.)

INDIAN PUDDING (Serves 6)

$^1\!/_4$ **cup of cornmeal (water-ground meal, if possible)**

$4^2\!/_3$ **cups of milk**

4 tablespoons of butter

1 cup of New Orleans molasses

$^1\!/_2$ **teaspoon of cinnamon**

$^1\!/_2$ **teaspoon of ginger**

2 well-beaten eggs

Blend the cornmeal with 1 cup of the milk. Heat 3 cups of milk in the top of a double boiler over hot water and stir in the milk and cornmeal mixture. Cook and stir until smooth. Continue cooking for 25 minutes. Add the butter, molasses and spices and stir in the 2 beaten eggs. Pour into a buttered casserole and pour the remaining $^2\!/_3$ cup of milk over the top. Bake in a 350° oven for 1 hour.

Serve hot with heavy cream or ice cream.

BREAD AND BUTTER PUDDING (Serves 4)

6 slices of stale bread

Butter

Sugar

Cinnamon

$^1\!/_2$ **cup of brown sugar**

$^1\!/_2$ **cup of seedless raisins**

4 eggs

2 cups of milk

2 tablespoons of white sugar

1 teaspoon of vanilla

Cut the crusts from the bread and toast the slices lightly. Butter them well, sprinkle with sugar and cinnamon and form into sandwiches. Cut these into long, finger-shaped pieces and arrange them in a well-buttered casserole. Sprinkle with the brown sugar and raisins.

Beat the eggs and add the milk, white sugar and vanilla. Pour this custard over the bread and place in a pan filled with 1 inch of hot water. Bake in a 375° oven until the custard is set.

Serve hot with heavy cream.

Crêpes

Sweet

⅞ cup of all-purpose flour	2 tablespoons of Cognac
1 tablespoon of sugar	1 teaspoon of vanilla
3 eggs	⅛ teaspoon of salt
2 tablespoons of melted butter	About 1½ cups of milk

Unsweetened

⅞ cup of all-purpose flour	2 tablespoons of Cognac
3 eggs	¼ teaspoon of salt
2 tablespoons of melted butter	About 1½ cups of milk

Sift dry ingredients together and add eggs one at a time, mixing well, until there are no lumps (a mixer at low speed is excellent). Add flavorings and melted butter. Gradually stir in milk and mix until the batter is the consistency of light cream. Let batter rest an hour or two before baking.

To bake, heat a 6-inch crêpe pan well and butter it. Pour in about 1½ tablespoons of the batter, and tip the pan so it covers the entire surface. Pour any excess batter back in the bowl. Cook crêpe until it shakes loose from the bottom of pan. Turn with fingers or with spatula and brown lightly on reverse side. If not using immediately, crêpes may be kept for several days in the refrigerator or for a month in the freezer.

CHOCOLATE CRÊPES

Stack about 14 to 16 crêpes as you bake them, sprinkling a small amount of grated chocolate on each crêpe. Keep warm. When they are completely stacked, dress with hot chocolate sauce and serve in wedges with whipped cream, sweetened to taste and spiked with Cognac. Garnish with chopped pistachio nuts.

Chocolate Sauce

In a double boiler over medium heat melt 12 ounces of chocolate chips and 2 squares of bitter chocolate. Add 1 tablespoon of instant coffee dissolved in 3. tablespoons of hot water. Stir until smooth, and blend in 1 cup of heavy cream and 2 tablespoons of Cognac.

CRÊPES SUZETTE

12 small lumps of sugar
²/₃ cup of Cognac
¹/₄ pound of butter
Juice of an orange

2 tablespoons of grated orange zest
¹/₃ cup of Grand Marnier
18 crêpes, folded in quarters

It is best to use a crêpe suzette pan and an alcohol burner or an electric skillet for this dish. Heat the skillet to about 325°. Place the cubes of sugar in the dry pan; and when they begin to melt down, add half the Cognac and ignite. As the flame dies down, stir in the butter and blend well to make a smooth syrup. Add the orange juice, the rind and the Grand Marnier. When the mixture begins to bubble and boil, add folded crêpes and turn them several times in the sauce. Finally, add the second dosage of Cognac, flaming, and spoon the sauce over the crêpes. Serve at once.

Eggs and Breakfast Meats

The Egg

Samuel Butler once said that a chicken was only an egg's way of making another egg. Which came first in the order of creation is not important here. What concerns us is that the egg usually comes first in the day's schedule, and also first in the beginning attempts to cook. It takes a rough beating in the process.

You have only to look at an egg to realize it is a delicate thing and must be treated with care. It figures more prominently in our diet than almost any other single food. It is eaten in various ways at breakfast, makes many a fine luncheon dish, such as a soufflé or omelet, and goes into innumerable desserts, such as pies, cakes, puddings, sauces, and soufflés. It is used in salads, sandwiches, stuffings, batters, pancakes and breads.

During World War II when eggs were rationed in Britain, the greatest treat a guest could bring his host was a new-laid egg nestled in a padded box. If you have to do without eggs, you fully realize how important they are.

First, the selection of eggs: Fresh eggs are what you want. Cold-storage eggs simply do not taste as good. In fact, some people dislike them thoroughly. They are satisfactory for such things as cakes and puddings; but for boiled, poached, scrambled or fried eggs and for such egg dishes as omelets, you should use the freshest eggs you can get. Where do you find them? In most cities, fine food shops have eggs delivered regularly from nearby poultry farms. If you live near the countryside you can probably find a local farmer who will keep you supplied. Eggs sold in the average market, though not necessarily cold storage, may have been shipped some distance and refrigerated for some time. Eggs deteriorate in flavor easily and if not strictly fresh will be tasteless.

To test an egg for freshness: Put it in a bowl of cold water. If it sinks, it is fresh.

Grading of eggs: Eggs are graded according to size and quality, grade A being the largest and freshest. Grade B is cheaper, but you do not get as much egg.

Color in eggs: The color of the shell or the yolk has no effect on the quality of the egg.

Storing eggs: Put eggs in the refrigerator as soon as you buy them; they go stale if they stand at room temperature too long.

If you are using the whites only in a recipe, put the yolks in a shallow bowl and cover them with cold water. Store in the refrigerator. They may be added later to scrambled eggs or used in soft custards and puddings.

If you are using the yolks only, put the whites in a bowl and cover tightly with plastic or foil. These can be added to soufflés or used for meringue.

Special cooking utensils for eggs: Eggs and certain metals have a sad effect on each other. Do not boil eggs in an aluminum pan; they will darken it. Glass or enamel is best. If you are cooking an egg dish, such as a pie filling or soft custard, and the pan is aluminum and the spoon you use is metal, the egg mixture is apt to turn a peculiar shade of gray-green. This is very unappetizing. To be safe, always use a wooden spoon when you stir eggs.

General cooking suggestions for eggs: It is better to have eggs at room temperature when you cook them. If they have just come from the refrigerator, run warm water on them for a minute or so. If you have to boil eggs at refrigerator temperature, pierce the large end with a needle, and there will be no cracks in the shell when the egg is cooked (unless it was cracked to start with).

Always cook eggs slowly. High heat ruins them. This even applies to boiling eggs. Do not overcook eggs; they become tough and flavorless. A hard-cooked egg should be watched carefully or it will be tough. Do not boil sauces after egg has been added; they curdle.

Boiled Eggs

Eggs should be at room temperature when they go on the stove, so take them out of the refrigerator some time in advance, or put the cold egg into warm water for a minute or so. If you must use an icy-cold egg, add $\frac{1}{2}$ minute to the boiling time.

Fill a pan (not aluminum) with enough water to cover the eggs thoroughly. Bring the water to a rolling boil and lower the eggs into it gently, using a spoon. Turn the flame down so that the water is just barely bubbly. Otherwise the eggs will bang against the side of the pan and the shells may break. Eggs boiled more gently seem to taste better.

The classic 3-minute egg of forty years ago—the white coagulated but still on the soft side and the yolk runny—is now a $3\frac{1}{2}$-minute egg, due to the larger size of the eggs produced today. A 4-minute egg has a firm white and runny yolk. A hard-cooked egg is boiled for 10 to 12 minutes.

Remove eggs from the water at once, or they will go on cooking. Rinse them under the cold water tap for a brief second so you can handle them. (Hold them in a spoon while you do this.) Then break them into bowls, add a good dab of butter and let each person season his own to taste. Or you can serve them English fashion in egg cups, the large end up.

If you are hard-cooking eggs, put them in cold water the minute they are cooked. Don't put them in the refrigerator until they are cold. They will look better when opened, if given this treatment.

Poached Eggs

A friend once reported seeing the following sign in a restaurant: "We reserve the right to refuse to poach eggs for anyone"!

Many people who are experienced cooks shy away from this simple job. Their problem is usually how to keep the whites from trailing off in ragged streamers through the water. Here's how you do it:

1 or 2 eggs per person
Water to cover
$\frac{1}{2}$ teaspoon of salt

$\frac{1}{2}$ teaspoon of vinegar or lemon juice

Use a shallow saucepan or skillet. It is easier to slip the eggs into such a pan. Put in enough water to cover the eggs, add the salt and lemon juice (or vinegar) and bring just to a boil. Meanwhile, break each egg into a saucer or soup bowl, then slip, one at a time, into the boiling water. The vinegar or lemon juice will help the whites coagulate, but the real secret of keeping the egg compact lies in the amount of "boil" in the water. Never put the eggs into rapidly boiling water. The rolling liquid will whip the white away before it can set.

There are several ways to avoid this. You can bring the water just barely to the boil and then slip the eggs in. Turn the flame down and let them simmer gently. If you wish to be safer, bring the water to a bubbling boil, then take the pan from the fire and slip each egg in as the bubbling dies down. Let them stand for 1 second, then return them to the flame and cook them very gently until done. A third method favored by some is the whirlpool method. When the water barely begins to boil, stir it with a spoon until a funnel-shaped whirlpool is formed in the center. Into this drop each egg. Lower the flame and simmer gently. I prefer either of the first two methods.

If the water doesn't quite cover the top of the egg, spoon some of the hot liquid over it as it cooks. An egg will poach to firm white and soft yolk in about 2½ minutes, but you can readily tell by looking. When the white is all white and firm the egg is done. Remove the eggs with a slotted or perforated spoon, draining them thoroughly before you serve them on toast slices. There is nothing less appetizing than a watery poached egg on a soggy piece of toast.

To poach eggs hard, cook them for 4½ minutes. These are often served cold in aspic, or as garnish for salad platters. If you are going to use them for this purpose, trim off the ragged edges.

WAYS TO SERVE POACHED EGGS

With Corned Beef Hash: Brown corned beef hash (see pages 216–217). Top each serving of hash with one poached egg.

Eggs Benedict: Allow 1 English muffin and 2 poached eggs per serving. Toast the split muffins, top each half with a slice of sautéed or boiled ham. Then place a poached egg on top of the ham and cover with Hollandaise Sauce (pages 351–352).

Eggs Italian: For 4 servings use 2 large tomatoes and 8 poached eggs. Cut the tomatoes into 8 slices (4 from each one). Heat 2 tablespoons of olive oil in a large skillet and add 1 minced clove of garlic. Sauté the tomato slices in the hot oil, seasoning to taste with salt, pepper and a little basil.

Top each tomato slice with a hot poached egg, sprinkle with grated Parmesan cheese and run under the broiler to brown.

Eggs Mornay: Allow 2 eggs per serving, and arrange the poached eggs in a baking dish. Cover with Sauce Mornay (page 350), sprinkle with grated Swiss cheese and run under the broiler to brown.

Eggs in Noodle Nests: For 4 servings, sauté ½ pound of fresh mushrooms in 4 tablespoons of butter until just done. (If the mushrooms are small, leave them whole; if large, slice them.) Boil 8 ounces of fine noodles in salted water until barely tender. Drain thoroughly, mix with the sautéed mushrooms and season to taste with salt and freshly ground black pepper. Arrange into 4 nests on serving plates and place a poached egg in the center of each nest. Sprinkle liberally with chopped parsley.

Eggs Florentine: For 4 servings, cook 1 package of frozen chopped spinach. Drain thoroughly, season to taste with salt and freshly ground black pepper and blend in 2 tablespoons of butter. Spread the spinach in a shallow baking dish and top it with 8 poached eggs. Cover with Sauce Mornay (page 350), sprinkle with grated Parmesan cheese and run under the broiler to brown.

Fried Eggs

How often have you been served fried eggs swimming in lukewarm grease and staring up at you with glazed orange eyes? It's a heartbreaking sight and one that can be avoided. Here's how:

1 or 2 eggs per person	**Salt and pepper to taste**
1 tablespoon of ham or bacon fat per egg (for butter, see below)	

You will have better luck if you use a heavy skillet. Lightweight metals get red-hot and eggs are not fond of too much heat. Melt the fat and have it hot but not bubbling. If you cook the eggs too fast the whites will be brown around the edges and tasteless. If you cook them too slowly, they will be leathery. You want moderate, even heat. Drop each egg into the fat and as it begins to set, spoon some of the hot fat over it. This will give the yolks a nice film. Baste them often until they have cooked nicely on top. When the whites are firm and the yolk has a film, season them to taste with salt and pepper and lift them out gently with a slotted spatula. Be sure to drain off the fat.

If you want your eggs "over," turn them just before they have finished cooking on top, and give them a very brief minute on the other side.

FRIED EGGS IN BUTTER

In a heavy skillet, melt 1 tablespoon of butter for each egg. Heat it over a moderate flame until hot, but do not let the butter turn color. Drop the eggs in and proceed as above. Season to taste with salt and pepper just before they are done, and for an added touch of elegance, top each egg with a spoonful of heavy cream. Continue cooking just until the cream heats through. Do not drain these eggs. The rich buttery quality adds to their tastiness. Serve them on crisp pieces of toast with the cream and butter poured over the top.

Scrambled Eggs

The secret to perfect fluffy scrambled eggs is low heat and plenty of butter. They can be cooked in a double boiler over hot water or in a skillet. The double boiler is safer.

2 eggs per person plus 1 for the pan

1 scant tablespoon of butter for each egg

Salt and pepper to taste

1 tablespoon of water or cream for each egg

Heat water in the bottom of the double boiler until it is bubbly. Add the butter to the top section and let it melt and get hot. Break the eggs in a bowl, season to taste with salt and pepper and add 1 tablespoon of water or cream for each egg. Water will give you fluffier eggs; cream will give you richer eggs. Beat the eggs slightly (don't whip them too thoroughly), using a fork, a wire whisk or an eggbeater. When the butter is hot, pour the eggs into the pan and let them set for a minute or two. Then start stirring, using a fork or, if you prefer, a wooden spoon. Stir the cooked eggs away from the sides and bottom of the pan toward the center. Keep stirring until the eggs are well mixed and soft but not too runny. Remove them from the fire before they are too set, for they will go on cooking with their own heat. Dish up quickly before they get hard.

SCRAMBLED EGGS IN THE SKILLET

If you are using a skillet, melt the butter over a medium flame. Do not let the butter burn or turn color. It should be hot, but not sizzling. Proceed as above, but watch the eggs carefully; if they seem to be cooking too fast, turn the flame down.

SCRAMBLED EGGS WITH VARIOUS SEASONINGS

Like omelets, scrambled eggs lend themselves to a variety of seasonings and sauces. Here are some suggestions:

With herbs: Always use fresh herbs with eggs if possible; they are much tastier. Chives, parsley, chervil and tarragon go best. They can be used in combination or separately.

A word of warning about herbs is necessary. Because a little adds zest do not think that a lot makes the food even better. They must be used with discretion. They range from the very bland to the very sharp. Parsley can be used by the tablespoonful; tarragon by pinches.

For 9 scrambled eggs (4 servings) you might add 4 tablespoons of parsley, 3 teaspoons of chives, 2 teaspoons of chervil and a very scant teaspoon of tarragon. If you are using the tarragon alone or in combination with only one of the other herbs you can increase the amount a little, but be sure you like the flavor of it first.

Chop the herbs very fine and add to the eggs before cooking or right after you pour the eggs into the pan. Serve herbed eggs with a sprinkling of chopped parsley on top.

With curry: Add 1 teaspoon of curry powder (or more if you're very fond of it) to 9 eggs (4 servings) before scrambling.

With ham: For 9 eggs (4 servings) use 1 cup of chopped, ground or finely cut cooked ham. Heat the ham in the butter before you add the eggs. Pour the eggs over the ham and mix during cooking.

With mushrooms: For 9 eggs (4 servings) sauté 6 medium-sized sliced mushrooms in butter. Add the sautéed mushrooms to the egg mixture while it is cooking.

With cheese: Add grated Parmesan, cheddar, Swiss or Gruyère cheese to the scrambled eggs. The amount you use will depend on your taste for cheese, but allow at least a tablespoon per serving. If you add the cheese to the eggs before they are cooked it will be blended all through. If you add cheese while the eggs are cooking, you will have streaks of melted cheese in the egg mixture. Either way is delicious.

With onions: For 9 eggs (4 servings) chop 4 little green onions (scallions) very fine and sauté them lightly in butter. Add them to the eggs while they are scrambling.

With smoked salmon: For 9 eggs (4 servings) cut 4 thin slices of smoked salmon into tiny strips. Heat these gently in the butter in which you are going to cook the eggs. Add the eggs and scramble. Do not salt the eggs until the last minute. The salmon may provide enough. Just before you serve, add a dash of lemon juice. Dish up on toast and top with chopped parsley.

With tomato: For 9 eggs (4 servings) peel (see page 447), seed and chop 2 ripe tomatoes. Cut up 4 green onions (scallions) and sauté them gently in 2 tablespoons of butter until just soft. Do not let them brown. Add the tomatoes and 1 tablespoon of fresh chopped basil. Let this mixture cook down and blend for 4 or 5 minutes. Salt and pepper to taste. Mix 9 eggs but omit the seasonings and liquid. Pour the eggs over the tomato mixture, blend and scramble. Just before they are done add 6 finely chopped ripe olives. Serve with a sprinkling of grated Parmesan cheese.

Omelets

There are four types of omelets: plain, fluffy, French and Italian. The first two are easy to make and can be combined with a great variety of sauces and flavorings to make excellent breakfast, luncheon or supper dishes. The French omelet is probably the most elegant egg dish ever invented. It is very difficult to make and calls for a special pan and long practice. I can only say that the cook who works hard to achieve the necessary dexterity will find the results extremely satisfying. A perfect French omelet is heavenly eating. The Italian omelet, or Frittata, is open-faced, requires slow cooking, and is an extremely versatile dish.

Plain Omelet

It is possible to cook a large omelet for 2 or 3 persons, but you will find that omelets are tastier if they are cooked individually in a skillet 8 or 9 inches in diameter. The pan should have rounded sides and be heavy, made of iron, cast aluminum or tin-lined copper. If possible, never use it for any other purpose. Clean it by wiping it with a paper towel—you can rub off stubborn spots with a little salt—and never use soap and water on it. Better still, use a heavy non-stick pan.

2 eggs (per person)   Scant ½ teaspoon of salt
4 teaspoons of water or milk   2 tablespoons of butter
(optional)

Break the eggs in a bowl, add the milk, or water if you like a softer mixture, and the salt. Beat the eggs lightly. Melt the butter in the skillet and
let it get bubbly hot but not smoking or brown. Pour in the egg mixture
and almost immediately start loosening the edges of the mixture with a
spatula, lifting up the eggs where they have set to let the uncooked top
part run underneath. When the omelet is mostly cooked but still creamy
and not hard on top, slip the spatula under one edge and roll it over, folding it as you slide it out on a hot plate. Serve at once.

Omelets can be varied by adding sauces or other foods just before you
fold them. Flavorings or foods are also sometimes cooked with the omelet.
Here are some suggestions:

Mushroom Omelet: Fold sautéed or creamed mushrooms into the omelet.

Curried Spanish Omelet: Make a hot curry sauce (page 354) and fold
it into the omelet. You can add tuna, crab, lobster, chicken or any meat
you like to the sauce before you fold it in.

Omelet with Tomato Sauce: Fold a tomato sauce (page 352) into the
omelet.

Cheese Omelet: Sprinkle the top of the omelet with grated Parmesan
cheese, grated sharp cheddar or grated Gruyère a minute before it finishes
cooking.

Chicken Omelet: Fold creamed chicken or chicken hash into the omelet.

Dried Beef Omelet: Fold creamed dried beef into the omelet.

Creamed Fish Omelet: Fold any creamed fish into the omelet.

Vegetable Omelet: Fold any buttered green vegetable—asparagus,
spinach, broccoli—into the omelet.

Onion Omelet: Sauté tiny chopped green onions in plenty of butter and
add them to the egg mixture before you cook the omelet.

Omelet Fines Herbes: Mix finely chopped parsley, chives and chervil
with the egg mixture before you cook it.

Watercress Omelet: Mix finely chopped watercress with the egg mixture and cook it.

Country Omelet: Fry chopped bacon until crisp and add chopped cooked potato and thin onion rings. Sauté the potato and onion until done. Pour the egg mixture over this in the skillet and cook as for an omelet.

FLUFFY OMELET (Serves 4)

This omelet is cooked in a large, heavy skillet that can be transferred to the oven. It is similar to a soufflé and can be used as a dessert with a sweet sauce.

4 eggs	**2 tablespoons of butter**
³/₄ teaspoon of salt	**4 teaspoons of milk**

Separate the eggs. Beat the yolks with the milk and salt. Beat the whites until stiff but not dry and fold them into the yolks gently. Melt butter in the heavy skillet. Pour eggs into skillet and cook slowly over low heat for about 5 minutes, or until the omelet has puffed up and is brown on the bottom. Transfer to a 400° oven to finish browning on top and cook through. This should take only about 8 to 10 minutes. Cut in wedges and serve from the skillet. This omelet benefits by being served with a sauce, such as a tomato sauce (page 352).

VARIATIONS

Cheese Fluffy Omelet: Serve with a cheese sauce (page 350).

Dessert Fluffy Omelet: Omit the salt and add 1 tablespoon of sugar to the omelet mixture. When it is cooked, sprinkle the top with confectioner's sugar and serve with melted jam or jelly as a sauce.

FRENCH OMELET

It is absolutely necessary to use individual heavy omelet skillets for this dish. (See Plain Omelet, page 94.) Before you tackle the job, you should practice the motions you must use, for it takes dexterity and few people can do it on the first try. Perhaps you remember the old parlor game in which you patted your head with one hand while you rubbed your stomach with the other. It is a difficult job to keep each hand doing a different motion. The trick with omelets is to keep the left hand shaking the pan gently back and forth while the right hand whirls a fork in circles. Try this over and over until you can do it easily.

3 large eggs (for each omelet)	Pinch of salt
1½ tablespoons of cold water	1 good-sized tablespoon of butter

First heat the pan over a medium flame. Break the eggs into a bowl, add the water and salt and beat them with a fork until they are thoroughly mixed. Do not use an eggbeater; it will froth the eggs too much. When the pan is hot enough to sizzle the butter without burning it, add the butter and let swirl around until melted and piping hot. Lift the pan from the heat and pour the egg mixture in quickly. Now is the time you use your exercise. Lower the pan to the heat and start shaking it back and forth with your left hand while you stir the eggs with the fork in your right hand. Stir the eggs in wide circular sweeps, and do it rather quickly. Keep this up for about a half minute. Then let the egg mixture settle quietly to set on the bottom for a brief second or so. Tilt the pan and roll the omelet out, starting it away from the edge on one side with a spatula or fork. Let it roll over itself onto a hot platter.

As with a plain omelet, the French omelet should still be moist and soft on top when you roll it out of the pan. It will finish cooking with its own heat. A true French omelet is never flat or firm but always soft.

FRITTATA (Serves 6)

The frittata is an Italian omelet that, like the Fluffy Omelet, is cooked both on top of the stove and in the oven. It lends itself to endless variations, and, served with a salad, makes a substantial luncheon or supper dish. Here is one version:

6 extra-large eggs	5 tablespoons grated Parmesan
1 cup onions, thinly sliced	4 tablespoons butter
2 garlic cloves, finely chopped	1 tablespoon finely chopped parsley
⅓ cup olive	1 large fresh basil leaf, cut in strips
Salt	
Freshly ground black pepper	
3 small zucchini, sliced very thin crosswise	

Sauté the onion and garlic in the olive oil until translucent. Do not brown. Add the zucchini, and cook for about 4 minutes. Sprinkle with salt and pepper, drain off the oil, and transfer to a bowl.

Beat the eggs with ½ teaspoon of salt and ½ teaspoon of pepper, and add 4 tablespoons of the Parmesan cheese and the onion-zucchini mixture. In a heavy 10-inch skillet heat the butter until it is hot and bubbly but not browning and pour in the egg mixture. Sprinkle the chopped parsley over it, and lower the heat. Cook until the bottom has set and the top is still somewhat runny. Sprinkle with the remaining Parmesan, and run under a broiler for half a minute or so until the top has just set. Do not brown.

Loosen the edges of the frittata with a spatula or knife. Slide onto a platter. This omelet can be eaten hot, at room temperature or even cold. Cut into wedges and serve.

Breakfast Meats

Traditional breakfast meats, such as bacon or ham, are usually smoked. But a fine crisp pork chop, a tender lamb chop or a good piece of steak will seldom be refused by a hungry male. For ways to prepare these and other regular meat dishes, see the Meat chapter.

BACON

The best bacon is country-cured and bought by the slab. It may be a little extra trouble to slice it and cut off the rind, but the rind is a dividend. It can be used to flavor legumes, soups and vegetable dishes. If you can't get slab bacon in your area, buy the leanest sliced bacon you can find. Allow 4 to 6 slices per person and put the bacon in a cold skillet over a medium flame. Pour off the fat as it accumulates, if you like your bacon very crisp. Turn often to cook evenly on both sides. When the slices are brown and crisp, remove them from the skillet and drain on absorbent paper.

FRIED HAM SLICE

If you are using a country-cured ham slice (Virginia ham, Kentucky ham), it should be cut from a ham that has already been soaked and cooked. Otherwise use a slice of tenderized ham for frying. Have it cut about $\frac{1}{2}$ inch thick. Slash the fat around the sides in several places and use a bit of the fat to grease the skillet. Put the slice in the greased skillet and place it over a low flame. Cook slowly until brown on the bottom, then turn and finish cooking on the other side.

BROILED HAM SLICE

This method is more satisfactory than frying. There is less danger that the ham will dry out. Use precooked, country-cured or tenderized ham and ask the butcher to cut it 1 to $1\frac{1}{2}$ inches thick. Slash the fat around the edges and arrange the slice on a greased broiling rack. Broil under a medium flame until brown and cooked on top. Turn and finish broiling on the other side.

VARIATION

Brush canned pineapple slices with a little bacon or ham fat and broil them with the ham slice. When you turn the pineapple, sprinkle a little brown sugar on the top and finish broiling and glazing. Serve with the ham. Or cook apple rings in the same way.

CANADIAN BACON

Canadian bacon is very lean and comes in a long, round roll. Buy it sliced or buy a piece and slice it yourself. Allow 4 to 6 thin slices per person. Melt a little butter in a skillet, add the slices and cook until browned on both sides.

BAKED CANADIAN BACON (Serves 6 to 10)

This is an excellent choice for a large Sunday brunch. It simplifies the cooking and a 3-pound piece of baked Canadian bacon will serve as many as 10 persons easily if you also serve eggs.

3-pound piece of Canadian bacon   Pepper
Bacon slices (if necessary)   Dry mustard

Arrange the Canadian bacon roll in a baking dish, fat side up. (If the roll does not have a good layer of fat on one side, put strips of regular bacon on the top.) Rub the top with coarsely ground black pepper and a little dry mustard. Bake in a 325° oven for about 45 minutes, or until hot and cooked through. Serve in thin slices.

LINK SAUSAGES

Allow 4 tiny sausages or 2 larger sausages per person. Puncture each one with a fork and place them in a skillet. Add water to cover and bring to a boil. Lower the flame and simmer the sausages for about 5 minutes. Then drain off the water. (This method reduces the shrinkage.) Return the skillet to the flame and cook the sausages slowly, turning them to brown evenly. Drain off the excess fat as it accumulates.

SAUSAGE MEAT PATTIES

1 pound of pork, ground   **1 teaspoon of thyme**
1 teaspoon of salt   **$^1/_2$ teaspoon of basil**
1 teaspoon of pepper

Sausage meat comes ready-prepared and is sold by the pound, but you will have better results if you ask your butcher to grind the fresh pork for you and then season it yourself. Order lean pork ground with 20% fat included. To one pound of ground pork add salt, coarsely ground black pepper and thyme and basil to taste (about 1 teaspoon of thyme and $^1/_2$ teaspoon of basil). Blend and shape into patties. Melt a little bacon fat in a skillet, add the patties and cook slowly, turning to brown evenly on both sides. Be sure to cook them thoroughly. Pork must be well done.

ITALIAN SAUSAGES

These used to be available only in Italian shops, but most markets stock them now. They come either sweet or hot. Take your pick and cook according to directions for Link Sausages (above).

BROILED VEAL OR LAMB KIDNEYS

Broiled kidneys with bacon is special breakfast fare for guests.

For VEAL KIDNEYS, see page 242. For LAMB KIDNEYS, see page 263.

SAUTÉED CALF'S LIVER

Liver and bacon make an excellent Sunday brunch. See recipe, page 240.

CORNED BEEF HASH

By far the best corned beef hash is homemade (page 216), but if you do use the canned variety, melt some butter or bacon fat in a skillet, add the hash and press it down with a spatula. Cook slowly until thoroughly heated through and crusty on the bottom. If you like the brown crust mixed through the hash, turn it occasionally.

Serve corned beef hash plain or topped with a poached or fried egg.

CORNED BEEF PATTIES

Form the corned beef hash into patties and fry in butter or bacon fat until cooked through and browned on both sides. Serve with Hashed Brown Potatoes and Scrambled Eggs.

CREAMED DRIED BEEF (Serves 4)

4 tablespoons of butter	**2 cups of milk and cream, mixed**
4 tablespoons of flour	
Pepper	**¹/₄ pound of dried beef**

Prepare a white sauce with the butter, flour and milk and cream, mixed (page 349). When it is smooth and thick, add the dried beef, pulled apart into small pieces. Blend thoroughly and serve over toast or toasted muffins. Sprinkle the top with freshly ground black pepper.

Fish and Shellfish

Fish

We have an abundance of fish in this country—fish from two oceans, from the Gulf of Mexico, and from many rivers and lakes—but we are not nearly so enthusiastic about fish as Europeans. To many of us, fish means only deep-fried shrimp or canned tuna. Our neglect of fish is a sad state of affairs, for few foods are tastier than fresh fish broiled gently until golden brown and served up with lemon, butter and parsley. Add to this a potato dressed with parsley butter, a green salad and a bottle of dry white wine, and you have a most elegant meal.

I think there are two reasons for the American attitude toward fish. First, many people have never had fish well prepared. Too often it is over-cooked, dry and tasteless. Second, many American cooks believe fish is difficult to prepare and are afraid to try. Actually broiling a fish fillet is easier than broiling hamburger. You don't even have to turn it.

Fish cooks quickly and is done the minute you can flake it easily with a fork or toothpick. *Never* overcook it. It should be moist and tender, with a delicate texture. Fish can be served simply, merely dressed with lemon butter and chopped parsley, or it can be enhanced with a great variety of other flavorings and sauces: tomato, green pepper, onion, garlic, mush-room, cheese, wine, cream, egg, dill, tarragon.

Buying fish: Allow ½ pound of fillets or steaks per person. If you are buying whole fish with the head and tail left on, allow 1 pound.

When you buy steaks and fillets, look for those with firm flesh and a sweet odor. When you buy whole fish, look for moist skin and shiny scales tight to the skin. The eyes should be bright and clear and the gills pink to red and fresh-looking. The flesh should be firm. Test it by pressing with your finger. It should spring back. There should be no strong or unpleasant odor.

Preparing fish: Steaks and fillets are ready to cook. Whole fish sold in the markets comes already cleaned. The only requirement is that you should wash it well and scale it. Large center cuts of fish must also be scaled. When you scale fish, hold the end nearest the tail and scrape toward the head with the blade of a knife, removing all loose scales. Then rinse the fish well.

If you have a fisherman in the family and must clean the fish yourself, here is the way to do it: First, scale the fish. Next, remove the fins with a sharp, pointed knife; cut around each fin, loosening it thoroughly so you can take it out "by the roots." Then clean the fish by slitting from the vent on the underside near the tail up the length of the belly. Scoop out the insides, entrails, stomach and all, and be sure to remove any blood clots. Rinse thoroughly under cold running water. If you intend to cook the fish without the head and tail, cut these portions off with a very sharp knife, severing the head just back of the gills. You will find, however, that fish cooked with the head left on is moister and tastier.

Storing fish: Fish should be used as soon as possible because it does not keep well. It can be stored for a short time (overnight, for example) wrapped in foil or in a covered dish in the refrigerator.

Frozen fish: If you buy frozen fish, keep it frozen in the freezer compartment of the refrigerator until the day you are ready to cook it. Then remove it from the freezer and place it on one of the refrigerator shelves. Allow it to thaw enough so that you can separate the pieces. If thawed at room temperature it tends to get flabby.

Broiled Fish

Fillets, steaks and small whole fish can be broiled. Whole fish (if very small) can be broiled with the heads and tails intact. If you like fish split for broiling, ask the fish dealer to cut off the heads and tails and cut the fish open so that they will lie flat.

BROILED FISH FILLETS (Serves 4)

4 large or 8 small fillets
6 tablespoons of butter
Salt and pepper
Melted butter

4 tablespoons of chopped parsley
Lemon wedges

Remove the broiling pan from the broiler and line it with foil. (This is not absolutely necessary, but it makes the cleaning job much easier, and it is also easier to remove the fillets from the broiler.) Put the pan back in the broiler and turn on the heat. Let the broiler heat for 10 minutes before cooking.

When ready to cook, remove the broiling pan and spread it liberally with butter. Arrange the fillets in the pan, sprinkle them with salt and pepper and dot them with butter. Broil them, basting once or twice with the butter in the pan, or adding more butter if necessary. Most fillets cook in about 5 to 8 minutes. If they are unusually thick, cook for 10 minutes per inch of thickness. Do not turn the fish. Test for doneness with a fork or toothpick. The fish is done when it flakes easily.

Serve the fillets right from the broiler pan or slip the whole foil lining, with the fish on top, onto a platter. Serve with additional melted butter to which you have added chopped parsley, and lemon wedges.

Traditional accompaniments for fish are boiled potatoes dressed with parsley butter, or oven-fried potatoes, and a green, either cooked or in a salad (cooked spinach, for example, or a good romaine and onion salad dressed with oil and vinegar).

VARIATIONS

With crusty top: If you like a very crusty top on your broiled fillets, dust them lightly with flour before cooking.

Amandine: A few minutes before the fish is done, add a sprinkling of chopped, toasted almonds. Baste with melted butter mixed with dry white wine.

With wine: Baste the fish with melted butter, dry white wine and a bit of chopped chives.

With mushrooms: Sauté mushrooms in butter (allow about 2 mushrooms per person) and top the fillets with these and the juices from the mushroom pan.

Cheesed: A few minutes before the fish is done, sprinkle with grated Parmesan cheese.

With tomato: Sauté 2 onions and ½ green pepper (for 4 persons) in butter or olive oil until just soft. Add 2 tomatoes, peeled, seeded and chopped, and cook down. Season to taste with salt and pepper. A few minutes before the fish is done, spread each fillet with a little of this mixture and top with a sprinkling of grated Parmesan or Switzerland Swiss cheese.

With shrimp sauce: Make a Rich Cream Sauce (see page 349) and add 8 good-sized, chopped, cooked shrimp to the sauce. A few minutes before the fish is done, spread each fillet with a little of this sauce and sprinkle with grated Parmesan cheese.

Mornay: A few minutes before the fish is done, spread each fillet with a little Sauce Mornay (see page 350).

BROILED FISH STEAKS

Fish steaks are broiled according to the directions for Broiled Fish Fillets (page 104). Allow 1 fish steak per person. Most fish steaks will need no turning during the cooking, but if they are very thick—more than an inch—cook for 10 minutes per inch of thickness, and turn them midway in the cooking, using a spatula or pancake turner. Baste the turned steaks with plenty of melted butter and finish cooking. Test for doneness with a fork or toothpick.

Any of the variations given for Broiled Fish Fillets can be used for fish steaks.

BROILED WHOLE FISH

If you broil the whole fish with the head and tail intact and without splitting, dust the outside with a little flour to give a crisp finish to the skin. Proceed as for Broiled Fish Fillets (page 104), turning the fish midway in the cooking. Brush the turned fish with melted butter and cook until done. Test with a fork or toothpick.

Larger whole fish should be broiled on a greased broiling rack. Line the broiler pan with foil and place it under the rack to catch the drippings.

Serve broiled whole fish with parsley butter and lemon wedges.

BROILED SPLIT FISH

Broil whole split fish as you do Broiled Fish Fillets (page 104), placing them skin side down on the broiler pan. Cook without turning. They should be done in 5 to 8 minutes. If unusually thick, cook 10 minutes per inch of thickness. Test with a fork or toothpick. Serve with parsley butter and lemon wedges.

Sautéed Fish

This method of cooking is especially suited to small whole fish, such as small trout, smelt and butterfish. Fillets or steaks may be cooked in the same manner, but they are better if broiled.

SAUTÉED WHOLE FISH MEUNIÈRE (Serves 4)

4 to 8 small whole fish
4 to 6 tablespoons of butter and olive oil mixed
Milk
Flour

Salt and pepper
Chopped parsley
Lemon wedges

Clean the fish (or have the fish dealer do this) and leave the heads and tails on if you wish. Melt the mixed butter and oil in a large, heavy skillet. When it is piping hot, dip each whole fish in milk and then in flour and place it in the pan. Following the rule of 10 minutes per inch of thickness, cook the fish over a medium flame until they are nicely browned on the bottom. Then, working carefully with a spatula or pancake turner, turn each fish over and finish cooking until brown on the other side. Add more butter and oil to the skillet if necessary. Cook only until brown and done when tested with a fork or toothpick. Do not let them dry out. Season with salt and pepper.

Remove the fish to hot plates or a hot platter, add a little more butter to the pan and toss 4 tablespoons of chopped parsley in the melted fat. Pour this over the fish and garnish with lemon wedges.

SAUTÉED FISH FILLETS MEUNIÈRE (Serves 4)

4 fish fillets
Flour
4 tablespoons of butter

Salt and pepper
Lemon juice
Chopped parsley

Dredge the fillets with flour. Melt the butter in a skillet and brown the fillets on both sides. Turn them gently with a spatula or pancake turner, being careful not to break them. Cook until they are just done and flaky when tested with a fork or toothpick. Season with salt and pepper. Remove to a hot platter. Add lemon juice and a good sprinkling of chopped parsley to the pan juices; stir and pour over the fish.

SAUTÉED FISH NIÇOISE

Proceed as for Sautéed Whole Fish Meunière (see page 106) but add 1 onion, peeled and cut into thin slices, to the pan while the fish are cooking. When the fish are done, remove them to a hot platter and add 2 ripe tomatoes, peeled, seeded and chopped, to the onion in the skillet. Sprinkle with a tiny pinch of basil (or a few fresh basil leaves, if available) and cook over a high heat until soft. Add ½ cup of dry white wine, blend and pour over the fish.

Baked Fish

A good-sized fish—4 to 8 pounds—baked whole and brought to the table on a well-garnished platter is an elegant sight to see. Baking is also a suitable method for small whole fish, for center cuts of large fish and for steaks or fillets.

Bake fish in a hot (400° to 450°) oven and do not overcook. Follow the rule of cooking for 10 minutes per inch of thickness, measuring at the thickest point. Test for doneness with a fork or toothpick.

BAKED FISH FILLETS OR STEAKS (Serves 4)

4 large fish fillets or 4 fish steaks	Salt and pepper
Butter	Parsley
Flour	Lemon wedges

Turn on the oven and heat it to 450°. Line a shallow baking pan with foil and put it to heat in the oven. You need not use the foil, but it makes cleaning easier. When the pan is hot, brush it well with butter, arrange the fillets or steaks in the pan, sprinkle them lightly with flour, salt and pepper and dot with butter. Cook the fish for 10 minutes per inch of thickness, basting several times with melted butter, until tender when tested with a fork. Serve with chopped parsley, additional butter if necessary, and lemon wedges.

VARIATIONS

Herbed: In the bottom of the baking pan put a good layer of chopped parsley and chopped chives. Arrange the fish on top of the herbs. Proceed as above.

With wine: Baste the fish with dry white wine or dry vermouth mixed with melted butter.

Use any of the variations suggested for Broiled Fish Fillets, pages 104–105.

FISH FILLETS OR STEAKS EN PAPILLOTES

Allow 1 large fillet or 1 steak per person. For each piece of fish tear off a piece of aluminum cooking foil large enough to wrap the fish. Butter the foil, place the fillet or steak on it, season to taste with salt and pepper and dot with butter. Fold the foil over the top and double the edges together to make a tight case. Fold up the ends of the foil. Arrange these foil packages on a baking sheet and bake the fish in a 425° oven for 18 minutes. Then open one of the foil packages and test the fish for doneness with a toothpick or fork. If it is not yet done, roll it up again and continue cooking for a few more minutes.

VARIATIONS

Browned: If you like a brown finish on top, after the fish is cooked, open each foil case and fold it back to expose the top of the fish. Run under the broiler flame for about 1 minute to brown a bit.

Herbed: Top each piece of fish with a teaspoon of grated onion and a tablespoon of chopped parsley before baking.

Cheesed: Top each fillet with 1 tablespoon of heavy cream and a sprinkling of grated Parmesan cheese before baking.

Italian: Top each fillet or steak with a teaspoon of grated onion, a slice of tomato and a little grated cheese before baking.

BAKED SMALL WHOLE FISH

Follow the directions for Baked Fish Fillets (see page 107). Do not turn the fish during cooking. Baste frequently.

BAKED STUFFED WHOLE FISH

For 4 persons buy a whole fish weighing 4 to 6 pounds and have the fish dealer remove the head and tail, if you wish. Good whole fish for baking are salmon, bluefish, sea trout, striped bass, salmon trout, small red snapper, or any other fish of like size.

Some people stuff fish with a bread crumbs and herb stuffing, but I feel it is an uninteresting combination. If you prefer this type of stuffing, use the one suggested in the Poultry chapter, page 305. For my taste, a flavorful vegetable stuffing has more zest and goes better with fish. For this use 2 to 3 onions, peeled and cut in thin slices, 1 small green pepper cut in thin rings, a few sprigs of parsley and 1 sliced tomato.

Wash the fish and scale it (see Preparing Fish, page 103). Set the oven for 450° and preheat a baking dish lined with foil. Use heavy foil or a double layer. This will enable you to lift out and transfer the fish to a platter.

While the oven is heating, stuff the fish with the cut vegetables, and season the stuffing with a little salt and pepper. Add dots of butter, using about 2 tablespoons. Secure the stuffing with small skewers or fasten the fish with toothpicks. When the oven is hot, butter or oil the foil in the baking pan, put the fish in the pan and rub it well with butter. Strip the top with 2 or 3 slices of bacon and bake, allowing 10 minutes per inch of thickness. Baste frequently with melted butter. Test for doneness with a fork or toothpick. The fish is done when it flakes easily.

Remove the cooked fish, foil and all, to a platter and serve with Parsley Butter, Lemon Butter or Hollandaise Sauce.

VARIATIONS

With wine: Baste the fish with dry white wine, using about 1 cup of wine during the cooking.

Herbed: Stuff the fish with chopped green onions, chopped parsley and green pepper rings. Put a layer of chopped parsley and chives in the bottom of the baking dish and surround the fish with sliced tomatoes. Baste with dry white wine mixed with melted butter, and serve the fish with the sauce from the baking pan.

Using fish steaks: Substitute 2 large fish steaks for the fish and place the stuffing between the steaks, arranging them in the baking dish sandwich-fashion.

BAKED CENTER SLICE OF FISH

Allow ½ to ¾ pound of fish per person and bake stuffed, according to directions for Baked Stuffed Whole Fish (see page 109); or bake without stuffing, basting frequently with melted butter. Serve with an Egg Sauce or Hollandaise Sauce.

Poached Fish

This method of preparing fish has certain advantages. Poached fish is not fattening; it is equally good hot or cold; it can be served with various sauces; and the broth from the fish can be used as a base for fish sauces, soups or aspics.

You may poach whole fish or fillets, steaks or center cuts. The procedure is the same. Use either salted water or court bouillon (see below) for liquid and do not let the fish boil. Simmer it gently until it flakes easily when tested with a fork or toothpick. This will take 10 minutes per inch of thickness, measuring at the thickest point.

COURT BOUILLON

The richest bouillons are made with fish trimmings (fish heads and bones). Ask your fish dealer to give you some. If you prefer, you can omit the trimmings.

Fish trimmings	**4 to 6 peppercorns**
1 cup of dry white wine	**½ bay leaf**
1 quart of water	**Pinch of thyme or**
2 sprigs of parsley	**tarragon**
1 onion stuck with 2 cloves	**Slice of lemon**
1 teaspoon of salt	

Put all ingredients together in a kettle and bring to a boil. Lower the heat and simmer for 20 to 30 minutes. Strain.

VARIATIONS

With vermouth: Omit the fish trimmings and substitute dry vermouth for half of the wine.

With garlic: Add 1 clove of garlic.

POACHED FISH FILLETS (Serves 4)

4 large or 8 small fish fillets	**Parmesan cheese**
Court Bouillon to cover	**2 cups of Rich Cream Sauce**

Use a shallow pan, such as a skillet, and into it put enough Court Bouillon (see above) to cover the fillets. Bring this to a boil, add the fillets, and let them simmer gently. Do not boil the broth after the fish is added. Fillets should cook in about 5 minutes. If thick, cook for 10 minutes per inch of thickness. Test for doneness with a fork or toothpick.

Lift the cooked fillets from the broth very gently and arrange them on a hot, oven-proof serving dish. Turn up the heat under the bouillon and boil rapidly to reduce to 1 cup. Make 2 cups of Rich Cream Sauce (double the recipe on page 349), using the cup of bouillon and 1 cup of cream for liquid. Pour this sauce over the fish fillets, sprinkle lightly with grated Parmesan cheese and run under the broiler for a minute to brown a little.

VARIATIONS

With wine sauce: Cook the fillets in a liquid of $1/2$ dry white wine and $1/2$ water. Add a pinch of salt, a pinch of tarragon and a sliced onion. Strain the broth before using it to make the sauce.

With seafood sauce: Add chopped, cooked shrimp, crabmeat or lobster meat to the sauce.

With mushroom sauce: Add sautéed mushrooms to the sauce.

With curry sauce: Make a Cream Curry Sauce with the fish broth and cream (see pages 350 and 354).

With egg sauce: Make an Egg Sauce with the broth and cream (see page 348).

Mornay: Make a Sauce Mornay with the broth and cream (see page 350).

Niçoise: While the fillets are poaching, sauté 1 chopped clove of garlic and 1 onion in 2 tablespoons of butter or olive oil until just soft. Add 2 large tomatoes, peeled, seeded and chopped, and a pinch of basil. Cook down. When the fillets are done, remove them to a hot, oven-proof serving dish and cook the broth down to 1 cup. Add the broth to the sautéed vegetables, blend thoroughly and thicken with 3 tablespoons of tomato paste. Taste for seasoning and spread over the fish fillets. Sprinkle with grated Parmesan cheese and glaze slightly in the broiler.

COLD POACHED FISH FILLETS

Prepare as for Poached Fish Fillets (page 111) and when the fillets are cooked remove them to a platter and set aside to cool. Reduce the broth to 1 cup over a high flame. Clarify it with egg white and eggshell (see Consommé, page 364). Dissolve 1 envelope of unflavored gelatin in ¼ cup of cold water and stir into the hot broth until melted. Set this aside to cool until slightly thickened but still runny. Combine with ½ cup of mayonnaise and chill until firm enough to spread as an icing. Do not let it get too firm. Ice the fillets with this sauce and decorate with sliced hardcooked eggs, strips of pimiento, green pepper rings, olives, capers, cold cooked shrimp, or any garnish you choose. Refrigerate to firm the sauce.

VARIATION

Let the jellied broth chill until it is firm enough to spread and still hold its shape. Arrange garnishes on top of the fillets: hardcooked egg slices, sliced stuffed olives, capers, cooked shrimp, or any decorations you prefer. Brush with the jelly until thoroughly covered. Chill and serve with a plain mayonnaise to which you have added chopped fresh dill to taste; or serve with Green Mayonnaise (see page 345).

POACHED FISH STEAKS—Follow the recipes for Poached Fish Fillets (page 111).

POACHED CENTER SLICE OF FISH

To poach a large center slice of fish, you will need a big kettle or fish poacher. In this put enough Court Bouillon (see page 110) to cover the fish, and bring it to a boil. Wrap the fish in cheesecloth, leaving long ends of the cloth to hang out of the kettle. Use the long ends as handles to lower the fish into the broth and to remove it when it is done. Put the fish in the boiling broth and simmer—do not boil. Allow 10 minutes per inch of thickness. After the fish has cooked, lift it from the broth and gently unwrap it until you can pry into the cavity and test at the center of the backbone. If it is not yet done at the center, wrap it again and return it to the broth for a short time.

When the fish is done, remove it from the broth and roll it very gently onto a platter as you remove the cheesecloth; if you do this deftly, you will be able to remove the skin with the cheesecloth. Otherwise, skin the fish after it is unwrapped. Set it aside to cool.

Reduce the broth over a high flame until it measures about 1½ cups. Use this broth with cream added to make a Rich Cream Sauce (see page 349). The amount of sauce you need depends on the amount of fish. Figure about 3 cups of sauce for a 4- to 5-pound center cut. Serve the sauce separately or pour it over the fish and garnish with sliced hard-cooked eggs, capers and chopped parsley.

VARIATIONS

With Dill Sauce: Make a Dill Sauce to serve with the fish (see page 350).

With Caper Sauce: Make a Caper Sauce to serve with the fish (see page 350).

Mornay: Make a Mornay Sauce to serve with the fish (see page 350).

COLD POACHED CENTER CUT OF FISH

Poach the fish as above and when it is removed to the platter, prepare the sauce according to directions for Cold Poached Fish Fillets (see page 112), increasing the amount of sauce according to the size of the fish.

POACHED WHOLE FISH

Follow directions for Poached Center Slice of Fish (see above), and when it is cooked, remove the skin just down to the tail and up to the head, leaving these intact.

Fish Casseroles

SCALLOPED TUNA (Serves 4)

2 cans of tuna chunks
1½ cups of coarse cracker
    crumbs
1 cup of chopped celery
2 cloves of garlic, chopped
2 large onions, chopped

1 green pepper, seeded and
    chopped
½ cup of chopped parsley
Salt and pepper
½ cup of melted butter
2 eggs, lightly beaten

Roll out crackers with a rolling pin until they are coarse crumbs. Combine with the tuna chunks and the chopped vegetables. Season with salt and pepper and mix with the melted butter and beaten eggs. Pour into a buttered casserole and top with bits of butter. Bake in a 375° oven for 30 minutes.

SCALLOPED SALMON

Prepare as for Scalloped Tuna, but substitute canned salmon for the tuna in the recipe. Be sure you remove all skin and bone from the salmon and flake it before you mix it with the other ingredients.

Shellfish

The most popular kinds of shellfish—shrimp, lobster and crab—are often sold already cooked. This does save work, but it is wiser to prepare your own for two good reasons. First, shellfish is always better when you buy it fresh and cook it and eat it at once. When you keep it too long on ice after cooking, it loses some of its delicate flavor and is never as juicy. Second, most fish dealers cook shellfish too long; the result is a tough, dry, tasteless dish. Once you take the trouble to cook your own shrimp, lobster and crab, you'll never again buy the ready-cooked product.

When you buy uncooked shellfish, remember these points. Crab and lobster must be alive and kicking. Clams and oysters in the shell should be tightly closed. Avoid damaged shells and any that are partly open. All shellfish should be kept by the fish dealer on beds of ice and sold from the ice. Do not try to keep shellfish long before using it. Buy it at the last minute and cook immediately.

Clams

There are many varieties of clams available along our coastlines, and each region has its own specialty. When you buy them, tell the fish dealer how you wish to prepare them, and he will recommend the right kind. For all cooking methods except steaming it is wise to buy ready-shucked (shelled) clams. You will save yourself the hard job of prying the shells open with a knife.

Allow 1 quart of shucked clams for 4 persons. If you are steaming clams, 1 quart of clams in the shell will serve only one true clam lover, but will be enough for two with less enthusiasm.

If you like raw clams on the half shell, fish dealers will prepare these for you.

CLAMS ON THE HALF SHELL

For this dish you need small clams—littlenecks or cherrystones. Tell your fish dealer how you wish to serve them and he will remove half of the shell for you. Serve 6 clams per person and arrange the shells on beds of ice. Some people insist on eating these morsels with catsup or cocktail sauce. They are much better eaten simply with lemon juice, freshly ground black pepper and a little horseradish, if you like.

STEAMED CLAMS

Allow $\frac{1}{2}$ to 1 quart of unshucked (unshelled) clams per person. Tell the fish dealer you wish to steam them and he will recommend the right type of clam. New Englanders demand a soft-shell clam, but small, hard-shell clams can be cooked in this manner if you prefer. Be sure the clams are all tightly closed in their shells. Avoid clams with open or damaged shells; this means the tiny animal inside is dead. Clams must be alive when they are cooked.

Wash and scrub the clams well and rinse them several times to get rid of the sand. Place them in a large kettle and put about ½ inch of water in the bottom. Cover the kettle tightly and cook just until the clam shells steam open.

Remove the steamed clams and discard any with unopened shells. Serve with bowls of the broth from the kettle and bowls of melted butter for dunking the clams as they are removed from the shells.

VARIATION

À la Marinière: Put the clams in the kettle and add dry white wine, pouring in enough wine to make about ½ inch in the bottom of the kettle. Add 1 tablespoon of butter for each serving and 1 peeled onion, 2 sprigs of parsley, a pinch of thyme, a bay leaf and a few peppercorns. Steam as above. Strain the broth and serve it with the clams.

BAKED CLAMS (Serves 4)

24 clams on the half shell	**Chopped garlic**
Chopped chives	**Bacon**
Chopped parsley	**Rock salt**

Order clams on the half shell from the fish dealer. In the bottom of several pie tins put a layer of rock salt. Place the tins in the oven and heat to 425°. Meanwhile, top each clam with a little chopped chive, chopped parsley, chopped garlic and a piece of sliced bacon. When the oven is hot and the pie tins are thoroughly heated, arrange the clams in their shells on the beds of rock salt. Bake at 425° just until the bacon is crisp.

VARIATIONS

Broiled: These clams may be broiled instead of baked. Heat the broiler well and heat the tins of rock salt before you arrange the clams. Broil for 4 minutes.

Crumbed: Top each clam with a small spoonful of Herb Butter (see page 354) and a sprinkling of Buttered Crumbs (see page 53).

SAUTÉED CLAMS (Serves 4 to 6)

1 quart of shucked clams (littlenecks)	Paprika
1/4 pound of butter	Chopped parsley
Salt and pepper	Buttered toast

Drain the clams and trim off the tough little necks. Melt the butter in a large skillet and when it is bubbly add the clams. Cook just until the edges curl and the clams are hot through and plumped up. Season with salt, pepper and paprika and add chopped parsley. Dish up on buttered toast.

VARIATIONS

Pungent: Add 1 tablespoon of Worcestershire sauce to the pan.

With onion: Sauté a few chopped green onions in the pan before you add the clams.

Herbed: Sprinkle the clams with a little tarragon and chopped chives as they cook.

PAN-FRIED CLAMS

Follow directions for Sautéed Clams (above), but dip each clam in beaten egg and roll in crumbs before sautéing.

VARIATION

Razor Clams: Dip shucked, cleaned razor clams in egg, then in crumbs, and brown in butter on both sides. Season to taste with salt and pepper and serve with lemon wedges.

SCALLOPED CLAMS (Serves 4)

2 cans of minced clams or 2 cups of freshly steamed clams, minced	Salt and pepper
	Paprika
Butter	1 large or 2 small onions
3/4 cup of fine toast crumbs	1/2 cup of chopped parsley
3/4 cup of cracker crumbs	1/2 cup of heavy cream

Melt ½ cup of butter and blend with the toast crumbs and cracker crumbs. Add salt, pepper and paprika to taste (about 1 teaspoon each of salt and pepper and 1½ teaspoons of paprika). Peel the onion and chop very fine or grate. Mix ⅔ of the crumbs with the minced clams, the onion and the parsley and put in a well-buttered casserole. Top with the rest of the crumbs, dot liberally with butter and pour the cream over all. Bake in a 375° oven for 20 to 25 minutes, or until brown, bubbly and well blended.

VARIATION

Mix grated Parmesan cheese with the crumbs on top of the casserole.

CLAM HASH (Serves 4)

2 medium onions	**Salt and pepper**
6 tablespoons of butter	**6 bacon slices**
1½ cups of diced cooked potatoes	**4 tablespoons of grated Parmesan cheese**
2 cups of minced clams, canned or freshly steamed	

Peel the onions and chop them very fine. Melt the butter in a large skillet and add the chopped onion to sauté gently until soft. Mix the diced potato, the drained minced clams and salt and pepper to taste. Add to the onions and press down with a spatula. Cook for about 10 minutes or until a brown crust forms on the bottom. Meanwhile fry the bacon until crisp and then crumble it. When the hash is brown on the bottom, turn it with the spatula, mixing some of the crust throughout. Press down again and let cook for a few minutes. Top with the grated cheese, sprinkle with the bacon bits and cover tightly for a minute to let the cheese melt.

CLAM SAUCE

A rich clam sauce may be served over spaghetti, noodles or rice. For recipe, see page 295.

CLAM CHOWDER—See page 373.

CLAM SOUFFLÉ—See page 361.

Crab

There are two general types of crabs available in our markets: hard-shell and soft-shell. Actually, a soft-shell crab is one that has shed its shell and not yet grown a new one. These are sold in eastern markets, cleaned and ready for cooking, and are cooked and eaten whole. The smaller they are, the better. The number of crabs per serving depends on their size.

In some areas of the Pacific Coast, hard-shell crabs are sold whole and ready-cooked. Cooked crabmeat, picked from the shell, is also available in the Pacific Coast region, and this is the most common way to sell crab in the East. One pound serves 4 persons.

If you are fortunate enough to be able to buy hard-shell crab fresh-caught and uncooked, this is the way to prepare it. Plunge the live crab (it must be alive) into boiling, salted water to cover and boil for 8 minutes per pound. Remove from the water and cool.

To clean whole, cooked, hard-shell crab: Break off the claws. Pull off the back and remove all spongy parts underneath. Turn the crab over and you will find a small apron-shaped section on the underside. Pull off the apron and split the body in two. Leave the crab in the shell if you wish to serve it cold with mayonnaise, or pick out the meat from the body and from the legs. Crack the shell of the legs with a nutcracker and remove the meat with a small fork or pick.

CRACKED CRAB WITH MAYONNAISE

Buy whole cooked or uncooked hard-shell crabs, allowing 1 per person unless they are the exceptionally large crabs from the Pacific Northwest. In that case, one crab will probably serve two persons.

If the crabs are uncooked, cook and clean according to the directions above, but leave the crab in the shell. Crack the claws so that meat may be easily extracted, and break the bodies into halves or quarters. Arrange the cracked crab on a bed of ice and serve with lemon wedges and mayonnaise for dipping. Give each person a pick or small fork for extracting the crabmeat.

SAUTÉED CRABMEAT (Serves 4)

1 pound of crabmeat	**Chopped parsley**
4 tablespoons of butter	**Lemon wedges**
Salt and pepper	

Heat the butter until it bubbles and add the crabmeat. Toss it about in the pan until it is heated through and lightly browned. Season to taste with salt and pepper and sprinkle with chopped parsley. Serve with lemon wedges.

VARIATIONS

With almonds and cream: Add ½ cup chopped toasted almonds to the pan. When the crab is cooked arrange it on pieces of buttered toast. Add 4 tablespoons of heavy cream to the pan and 4 tablespoons of chopped parsley. Heat and pour over the crab.

With wine: After the crab is cooked, rinse the pan with ¼ cup of dry white wine. Pour this over the crabmeat.

With mushrooms: Sauté ½ pound of mushrooms and add these to the pan with the crab. Rinse the pan with ¼ cup of cream.

Herbed: A minute before the crab is done, add 2 tablespoons of chopped chives and 2 tablespoons of chopped parsley to the pan. Stir these herbs in with the crabmeat.

CRABMEAT MORNAY (Serves 4)

1 pound of crabmeat	**Buttered crumbs**
Sauce Mornay (page 350)	**Butter**
Grated Parmesan cheese	

Follow instructions for making Sauce Mornay, but double the recipe. You will need 2 cups of sauce. Add the crabmeat; heap into a buttered casserole or into individual ramekins. Top with grated Parmesan cheese and buttered crumbs and bake in a 425° oven for 15 minutes or until brown and bubbly.

VARIATIONS

Creamed, with mushrooms: Substitute Rich Cream Sauce (page 349) for the Sauce Mornay and add ½ pound of sautéed mushrooms to the mixture.

With Madeira Sauce: Substitute Rich Cream Sauce and add ¼ cup of dry sherry or Madeira to the sauce.

With Curry Sauce: Make a Cream Curry Sauce (page 350) and fold the crabmeat into the sauce with ½ cup of chopped toasted almonds. Serve on rice and accompany with a good chutney.

CURRIED CRABMEAT (Serves 4)

1 pound of crabmeat	Chutney
Curry Sauce (see page 354)	Chopped toasted almonds
Cooked rice	

Prepare the regular Curry Sauce. Add the crabmeat and heat through. Serve on rice and accompany with chutney and chopped toasted almonds.

CRAB MARTINIQUAIS (Serves 6)

6 strips of bacon	1/3 cup of dark rum
2 medium onions, finely chopped	1/2 cup of white wine
	Salt and pepper
1 clove of garlic, finely chopped	1 tablespoon of chili powder
1/2 pound of ham cut in strips	1 pound of crabmeat
	1/3 cup of chopped parsley
1/2 cup of chopped, seeded, peeled tomatoes	1/3 cup of heavy cream

Cook the bacon in a heavy skillet over high heat. When just barely crisp, remove and cut rather coarsely. Add the onion and garlic to bacon fat and let them just wilt. Add the ham and chopped tomatoes, and flambé with heated rum. Pour white wine over, and season to taste with salt, pepper and the chili powder. Cook for 10 to 15 minutes to blend well. Add the crabmeat and parsley, and cook until just heated through. Stir in the heavy cream, and cook for 2 to 3 minutes.

Serve with rice or fried toast.

SAUTÉED SOFT-SHELL CRABS (Serves 4)

8 crabs (depending on size of crabs)	Salt and pepper
	Chopped parsley
Flour	Lemon wedges
8 tablespoons of butter	

Dip the crabs in flour and brown them in the hot butter on both sides until they are crisp and done. Season to taste with salt and pepper as they cook. Arrange on a hot platter and pour the pan juices over them. Sprinkle with chopped parsley and surround with lemon wedges.

BROILED SOFT-SHELL CRABS (Serves 4)

8 to 12 soft-shell crabs	**$1/4$ cup of chopped parsley**
Flour	**$1/4$ cup of chopped chives**
Butter	**Salt and pepper**

Heat the broiler and line the broiler pan with foil. This saves cleaning time and trouble. Dip the crabs in flour and arrange them on the broiler pan. Blend 8 tablespoons of soft butter with the parsley and chives and put a good dab of it on top of each crab, saving half of it for the other side of the crabs. Broil for 4 minutes, basting with melted butter. Season to taste with salt and pepper and turn the crabs to finish cooking. Dab the crabs again with the herbed butter and baste as they finish cooking. Give them about 3 to 4 minutes on the second side. Serve with the sauces from the broiling pan poured over them.

WEST COAST CRAB CAKES (Serves 4)

1 pound crabmeat	**$1/2$ teaspoon freshly ground black pepper**
1 pound cooked flaked fish	
8 water chestnuts, finely chopped	**Flour**
	5 tablespoons oil
6 to 8 green onions, finely sliced	**2 tablespoons chopped fresh coriander**
2 egg yolks	**Soy Sauce**
$1/2$ teaspoon salt	

Blend the crabmeat with the fish, water chestnuts, green onions, egg yolks, and salt and pepper. Form into 8 balls, place on a plate and refrigerate for about an hour to firm up. When ready to cook, heat the oil in a large skillet. Lightly flour the crab balls and place in the skillet. Flatten each ball with a spatula. Sauté gently, turning once, until a delicate brown on both sides. Drain on paper towels. Sprinkle with the coriander and serve with soy sauce.

DEVILED CRAB (Serves 4)

1 pound of crabmeat

4 tablespoons of butter

³/₄ cup of finely chopped onion

2 tablespoons of finely chopped green pepper

2 cups of Rich Cream Sauce (see page 349)

2 tablespoons of finely chopped parsley

1 teaspoon of dry mustard

Few grains of cayenne

Buttered crumbs

Melt the butter in a skillet, add the chopped onion and chopped green pepper and sauté gently until soft. Do not brown. When done, mix with the Rich Cream Sauce and add the chopped parsley, the dry mustard and a dash of cayenne. Fold in the crabmeat. Heap the mixture in individual serving shells or ramekins and top with buttered crumbs. Bake in a 425° oven for 10 to 15 minutes or until brown and bubbly.

CRAB SALAD—See Basic Seafood Salad, page 342.

Lobster

We have both well-known types of lobster in this country: the large-clawed variety, which we call Maine lobster; and the spiny or rock lobster. The Maine lobster, as its name implies, is native to the New England coast area. Spiny lobsters live in more southern waters.

You can buy whole lobster, cooked or uncooked, or prepared lobster meat. Whole, uncooked lobster must be alive. Allow a 1¹/₂- to 2-pound lobster per person. Some people will settle for a 1-pound lobster, but they are not great lobster eaters. When you buy lobster meat, allow 1 pound for 4 persons.

BOILED LOBSTER

Allow a 1½-pound lobster for each person. In a large kettle put enough water to cover the lobsters and add 1 tablespoon of salt for each quart of water. Bring to a rolling boil. Grab the live lobsters, one at a time, back of their heads just behind the powerful pincers. Be careful not to let the claws or pincers reach you. Plunge them into the boiling water headfirst. Cover and simmer for 5 minutes for the first pound and 3 additional minutes for each additional pound. A 1½-pound lobster will cook in about 8 to 10 minutes. A 2-pound lobster will take 11 to 12 minutes.

Remove the cooked lobster from the water and put it on a board or worktable on its back. Using a heavy, sharp knife and a mallet or hammer, split the lobster in half the long way, from head to tail. Remove the stomach and the intestinal tract, but do not discard the green liver or any reddish deposit. This latter is lobster roe and is called "coral." Crack the claws with a nutcracker so that the meat will come out easily.

Serve boiled, hot lobster with plenty of melted butter and lemon wedges. Or let it cool and serve it with mayonnaise, Green Mayonnaise or Rémoulade Sauce (page 345).

BROILED LOBSTER

Allow a 1½- to 2-pound lobster for each person. Have your fish dealer split and clean them for you (but you must cook them very soon after) or do it yourself. To clean: place the live lobster on a work board or table and using a heavy, sharp knife and mallet, insert the point of the knife between the body and tail shells and drive it through to sever the spinal cord. When the lobster stops moving, turn it over on its back and split it lengthwise from head to tail, cutting it into two parts. Remove the stomach and intestinal tract but leave the grayish-colored liver and the roe, or "coral," if there is any. Brush the flesh of each half with plenty of melted butter and broil in a heated broiler for 12 to 15 minutes. Baste frequently with additional butter as the lobster cooks or it will dry out. Season to taste with salt and pepper and serve with melted butter and lemon wedges.

SAUTÉED LOBSTER MEAT—See Sautéed Crabmeat, page 119.

LOBSTER MORNAY—See Crabmeat Mornay, page 120.

CURRIED LOBSTER—See Curried Crabmeat, page 121.

LOBSTER SALAD—See Basic Seafood Salad, page 342.

LOBSTER À L'AMÉRICAINE (Serves 4)

This is a famous, classic seafood dish served in Paris and in outstanding French restaurants in New York. It's not easy to prepare but the finished product is elegant.

2 2-pound live lobsters

²/₃ cup of olive oil

4 tablespoons of butter

1 medium onion, finely chopped

6 shallots or small green onions, finely chopped

1 clove of garlic, finely chopped

8 medium-sized ripe tomatoes, peeled, seeded and chopped

4 tablespoons of chopped parsley

1½ tablespoons of chopped fresh, or 1½ teaspoons of dried, tarragon

1½ teaspoons of thyme

1 bay leaf

2 cups of dry white wine

4 tablespoons of tomato purée

Salt, pepper, cayenne

⅓ cup of Cognac

Kill the lobsters, and then split and clean according to directions under Broiled Lobster (see page 124). Then remove the claws and cut the tails in sections, cutting through where the shells are jointed. Wash well.

Heat the olive oil in a very large kettle and when hot add the pieces of lobster in shell. Toss them about in the hot oil, using a pair of tongs, until the shells are colored red and the lobster meat is seared. Remove the lobster pieces to a hot platter and add the butter to the oil in the kettle. Sauté the onion, shallots and garlic in the hot butter and oil until lightly colored. Add the tomatoes to the onion mixture. Then add the parsley, tarragon, thyme, bay leaf and wine, and simmer gently for 30 minutes. Add the tomato purée and season to taste with salt, pepper and cayenne. Pour the Cognac over the lobster pieces and ignite to blaze. Then return the lobster to the kettle to cook in the sauce, cover tightly and simmer for 20 minutes. Serve over rice.

LOBSTER FRA DIAVOLO (Serves 4)

2 2-pound live lobsters
½ cup of olive oil
4 tablespoons of chopped
    parsley (Italian parsley, if
    available)
1½ teaspoons of oregano
Pinch of cloves
Pinch of mace

Salt and pepper
1 medium onion, finely
    chopped
1 clove of garlic, finely
    chopped
2½ cups of canned
    tomatoes
⅓ cup of Cognac

Prepare the lobsters as for Lobster à l'Américaine (see page 125). Heat the olive oil in a large kettle and add the lobster pieces. Using tongs, toss them about in the hot oil until the shells are red and the meat seared. Lower the heat and let the lobster simmer gently for about 10 minutes. Add the rest of the ingredients, except the Cognac, and mix. Cover the kettle and cook for about 15 minutes, stirring frequently to be sure the flavorings blend.

Place the lobster in the center of a large heat-proof platter and surround it with mounds of rice. Pour the sauce over the lobster and pour Cognac over this. Ignite and blaze.

LOBSTER NEWBURG (Serves 4)

2 2-pound live lobsters
4 tablespoons of butter
4 tablespoons of olive oil
Salt and pepper
1 cup of dry white wine

⅓ cup of Cognac
2 cups of heavy cream
⅔ cup of bouillon (fish or
    meat stock)
Beurre Manié (page 348)

Prepare the lobster as for Lobster à l'Américaine (page 125). Heat the butter and oil together in a large kettle and add the lobster pieces. Using tongs, toss them about until the shells turn red and the meat is seared. Season to taste with salt and pepper. When the shells are red, remove the lobster pieces and put them on a hot platter. Add the wine and Cognac to the kettle and boil it rapidly until it is reduced to half its volume. Add the cream and the bouillon—any court bouillon in which you have cooked fish or shellfish, or a meat bouillon. This latter can be made with hot water and a bouillon cube. Add the lobster pieces, cover the kettle and simmer gently for 30 minutes.

Remove the lobster and take the meat out of the shell. Place the meat in a deep dish. Let the sauce cook down a bit and thicken with the Beurre Manié. Taste for seasonings and pour over the lobster.

VARIATION

Quick Lobster Newburg can be made by adding cooked lobster meat to Rich Cream Sauce (page 349) flavored with Cognac.

LOBSTER THERMIDOR (Serves 4)

2 2-pound live lobsters

Olive oil

Salt and pepper

1 cup of dry white wine

1 cup of bouillon (fish or meat)

2 tablespoons of chopped green onion

2 tablespoons of chopped fresh, or 2 teaspoons of dried, tarragon

3 cups of Rich Cream Sauce (page 349)

1 teaspoon of dry mustard

Grated Parmesan cheese

Melted butter

Kill the lobsters, split in half and clean as for Broiled Lobster (page 124). Season each half with salt and pepper and brush with olive oil. Place in a 425° oven and bake, basting frequently with additional olive oil, for 15 minutes. Remove from the oven and let cool until the lobster can be handled. Then remove the meat from the shell, keeping the shells intact. Crack the claws and extract the meat.

Put the wine in a skillet and add the bouillon, the chopped onion and tarragon and cook this down rapidly until it is almost a glaze or paste. Add it to the Rich Cream Sauce and heat through. Stir in the mustard and taste for seasoning. Dice the lobster meat and add this to the hot sauce to heat through. Heap the mixture in the lobster shells, sprinkle the tops with grated Parmesan cheese and brush with melted butter. Run under the broiler a minute to brown.

DEVILED LOBSTER

Follow directions for Deviled Crab (page 123), substituting cooked lobster meat for the crabmeat.

Oysters

Oysters vary in size, flavor, saltiness and texture. Even oysters from the same small bay can be entirely different if they come from different oyster beds. If you are not familiar with the oysters in your area, ask the advice of your fish dealer when you buy, or try the various kinds available and decide which you like best.

Like clams, oysters are sold shucked, by the pint or quart; or in the shell or on the half shell, by the dozen. When buying, follow the instructions given for clams (page 115).

OYSTERS ON THE HALF SHELL—See Clams on the Half Shell, page 115.

BROILED OYSTERS—See variation under Baked Clams, page 116.

DEVILS ON HORSEBACK

Drain shucked oysters and marinate them in dry white wine flavored with grated garlic and a little freshly ground black pepper. Let them soak for about 1 hour. Drain the oysters and wrap each one in a thin slice of bacon. Broil just until the bacon is crisp.

SAUTÉED OYSTERS—Follow directions for Sautéed Clams, page 117.

BAKED OYSTERS—Follow the recipes given for Baked Clams, page 116.

OYSTERS ROCKEFELLER (Serves 4)

24 oysters on the half shell	**2 cups of watercress**
¹/₂ pound of butter	**¹/₃ cup of fine bread crumbs**
¹/₄ cup of chopped shallot (or green onion)	**¹/₃ cup of Pernod**
¹/₄ cup of chopped fennel	**Salt, pepper and cayenne**
¹/₂ cup of chopped parsley	**Rock salt**
1 teaspoon of chervil	

Melt 3 tablespoons of the butter in a skillet and add the shallot, fennel, parsley, chervil; sauté gently for a few minutes. Add the watercress and let it wilt. Put this mixture in an electric blender with the rest of the butter, the bread crumbs and the Pernod and blend thoroughly. Season to taste with salt, pepper and cayenne. Arrange the oysters on beds of rock salt in pie tins. Dampen the salt slightly. Top each oyster with a spoonful of the butter and herb mixture. Bake in a 475° oven for about 4 minutes or until the butter-herb mixture has melted down and the oysters are hot through.

OYSTERS CASINO (Serves 4)

24 oysters on the half shell
8 to 12 slices of bacon
¹/₂ cup of butter
¹/₃ cup of chopped green pepper
2 tablespoons of chopped chives

4 tablespoons of chopped parsley
Lemon juice
Rock salt

Place strips of bacon in a cold skillet and put them over low heat. Cook just until transparent. Cut each strip into halves or thirds. You will need one piece of bacon to top each oyster. To the skillet add 2 tablespoons of the butter, and heat. Add the chopped green pepper and cook gently until barely soft. Mix the green pepper with the chives and parsley and blend thoroughly with the rest of the butter.

Arrange the oysters on beds of rock salt (put the rock salt in pie tins or a long, shallow baking tin) and dampen the salt slightly. Top each oyster with a spoonful of the butter mixture and then a piece of bacon and a few drops of lemon juice. Cook in a 450° oven until the bacon is crisp and the oysters are thoroughly heated.

SCALLOPED OYSTERS

Chop oysters fine and substitute for the minced clams in Scalloped Clams (page 117).

OYSTER PAN ROAST (Serves 4)

For this dish the oysters are cooked in a skillet in plenty of butter. It is more like poaching than frying.

1 quart of oysters	**Lemon juice**
³/₄ cup of butter (or more)	**Fried toast**
Salt, pepper and cayenne	**Chopped parsley**

Melt the butter in a skillet, drain the oysters and add them to the hot butter. Season to taste with salt, freshly ground black pepper and a dash of cayenne. The oysters take only a very short time to cook. They will plump up and get puffy. At that point they are done. Give them a dash or so of lemon juice and dish up on fried toast. Top with parsley.

To make fried toast: Cut the crusts from thin slices of bread. Dip the bread in plenty of melted butter and brown on both sides in a skillet. Add more butter to the skillet if the bread is too dry. It should be buttery and crisp.

VARIATIONS

With white wine: Add a dash of dry white wine to the pan juices and pour over the oysters.

With green onion and green pepper: Mix sautéed green onions and chopped green pepper to the oysters when you dish them up.

With garlic: Cook a minced clove of garlic in the butter for a few minutes before you add the oysters. Add a dash of Worcestershire sauce and 1 teaspoon of dry mustard at the last minute.

PAN-FRIED OYSTERS—See Pan-Fried Clams, page 117.

OYSTER STEW (Serves 4)

1¹/₂ pints of oysters and their liquor	**1 pint of cream**
4 tablespoons of butter	**Salt, pepper and cayenne**
¹/₂ pint of milk	

Drain the liquor from the oysters and heat it with the milk and cream. While it is cooking, heat 4 bowls and add 1 tablespoon of butter to each bowl to melt. Season the hot cream and oyster liquor with salt, pepper and cayenne and add the oysters. Let it come just to the boiling point but do not boil. When steaming hot pour into the bowls and serve with toasted French bread.

Scallops

In most areas in this country the scallop is shelled and only the small, round muscle is sold. The muscle of the deep sea scallop is about 1½ inches long and 1 to 1½ inches round. In some regions, tiny bay scallop muscles are available. These morsels are about ⅓ the size of the muscle of the sea scallop. They are exceptionally tender and delicate in flavor. One pound of either variety will serve 2 persons with big appetites and 3 with average capacity.

BROILED SCALLOPS

Dry the scallops well (they tend to be watery) and place them on a greased pie tin or baking dish. Season to taste with salt and pepper and brush with melted butter. Heat the broiler and place the baking dish under the flame. Broil sea scallops for about 5 minutes and bay scallops about 3 minutes.

BROILED MARINATED SCALLOPS (Serves 4 to 6)

Use the larger sea scallops for this dish.

2 pounds of sea scallops
½ cup of olive oil
½ cup of dry white wine
1 minced clove of garlic

1 teaspoon of dried tarragon
Salt and pepper
½ cup of chopped parsley

Wash the scallops. Mix the rest of the ingredients, place in a deep bowl and add the scallops. Soak them for 2 hours, turning occasionally to be sure they are thoroughly bathed. When ready to cook, arrange the scallops on small skewers and broil in the oven or over charcoal, about 2 inches from the flame. Turn frequently to broil the scallops on all sides. They will be cooked in about 5 minutes.

These marinated scallops can be served as an appetizer or as a main course.

VARIATION

Oriental: Substitute dry sherry for the white wine in the marinade and season with soy sauce and grated fresh ginger instead of salt and pepper.

SAUTÉED SCALLOPS

This is by far the best way to cook the tiny bay scallops. It seems to preserve their delicate flavor.

1½ pounds of bay scallops (or sea scallops)	**Salt and pepper**
Flour	**Chopped parsley**
4 tablespoons of butter	**Lemon wedges**
2 tablespoons of olive oil	

Wash the scallops and dry them on absorbent towels. Heat the butter and oil in a large skillet. Roll the scallops in flour and sauté them in the hot fat quickly, turning them on all sides. Don't overcook. Bay scallops will be done in a minute or two; sea scallops take a little longer. Season to taste at the last and serve with a dusting of chopped parsley and a garnish of lemon wedges.

VARIATIONS

Herbed: Add ¼ cup of chopped chives and ½ cup of chopped parsley to the pan as the scallops are cooking. When the scallops are done, season to taste with salt and pepper, and remove them to a hot platter. Rinse the pan with ½ cup of dry white wine and pour over the cooked scallops.

With garlic: Sauté 1 minced clove of garlic with the scallops. When they are cooked, season, remove them to a hot platter and add ½ cup of chopped parsley, 2 peeled, seeded and chopped tomatoes and ½ cup of dry vermouth to the pan. Cook quickly until thoroughly heated and blended. Pour over the scallops.

Provençale: Sauté 1 minced clove of garlic with the scallops, season, and toss with ½ cup of parsley.

SCALLOPS WITH CURRY

1½ pounds of scallops
4 tablespoons of butter
1 minced clove of garlic
1 chopped onion
Flour
Salt and pepper

1 tablespoon of curry
  powder
½ cup of dry vermouth
2 cups of Rich Cream Sauce
  (page 349)

Melt the butter and sauté the garlic and onion gently. Wash and dry the scallops, roll them in flour seasoned with salt and pepper, and sauté them, turning to brown on all sides. When they are browned but not dry, sprinkle with the curry powder and add the vermouth. Cook up for a minute or two and add to the hot Rich Cream Sauce.

Serve on rice and accompany with chutney and toasted chopped almonds.

POACHED SCALLOPS, MORNAY (Serves 4)

1½ pounds of scallops
Dry white wine and water
1 onion, peeled
Parsley

Tarragon
Sauce Mornay (page 350)
Grated Parmesan cheese
Buttered crumbs

In a skillet put enough wine and water to cover the scallops. Add the onion, 3 sprigs of parsley and a pinch of tarragon. Bring to a boil. Add the scallops and simmer until just done. This will take from 3 to 4 minutes for sea scallops and only a minute or so for bay scallops. Drain the scallops and return the liquid to the pan. Reduce it over a high flame until it measures ¾ cup.

Using the reduced broth for part of the liquid, make double the recipe for Sauce Mornay. Add the cooked scallops to the sauce, heap in an oven-proof serving dish or in individual ramekins and top with grated Parmesan cheese and buttered crumbs. Place in a hot oven (450°) for a few minutes to brown, or run under the broiler flame.

VARIATIONS

With creamed mushrooms: Using the reduced broth for part of the liquid, make double the recipe for Rich Cream Sauce (page 349) and add the cooked scallops and ½ pound of sautéed mushrooms. Top with buttered crumbs and brown under the broiler.

With crabmeat: Using the reduced broth as part of the liquid, make double the recipe for Rich Cream Sauce (page 349). Add the scallops and ½ cup of crabmeat. Heap in individual ramekins and place 1 crab leg on top of each ramekin. Sprinkle with grated Parmesan cheese and brown under the broiler flame or in a very hot oven.

COLD POACHED SCALLOPS

Poach scallops according to directions for Poached Scallops Mornay (page 133). Drain and cool. Arrange the cold scallops on a bed of romaine and top with mayonnaise, Green Mayonnaise or Rémoulade Sauce. Garnish with chopped parsley, sliced hardcooked egg and olives.

COQUILLES ST. JACQUES

1½ pounds of scallops	⅓ cup of water
½ cup each of white wine and water, mixed	Juice of 1 lemon
7 tablespoons of butter	½ teaspoon of salt
2 sprigs of parsley	½ teaspoon of pepper
1 small onion, peeled	2 tablespoons of flour
1 bay leaf	4 egg yolks
Pinch of thyme	1 cup of heavy cream
½ pound of mushrooms, chopped	Grated Parmesan cheese
	Buttered crumbs

Place the wine and water mixture, 2 tablespoons of the butter, the parsley, onion and bay leaf in a shallow pan and bring to a boil. Rinse the scallops and add them to the wine, lower the heat and simmer gently for 4 to 5 minutes, or until the scallops are just tender and done. Remove them from the pan, strain the broth and save.

Melt 2 more tablespoons of butter. Chop the mushrooms and add them to the hot butter. Add the water, lemon juice, salt and pepper and cook for 5 minutes. Drain the mushrooms, saving the liquid. Mix the mushroom liquid with the strained wine broth and put over a low flame. Make a Beurre Manié (see page 348) with the remaining 3 tablespoons of butter and 2 tablespoons of flour. Slowly add it to the liquid, stirring it in with a wooden spoon. Continue cooking and stirring until the mixture is smooth and thick. Taste for seasoning and add the scallops, finely chopped, to blend with the sauce. Set aside to cool a little.

Beat the egg yolks with the cream and stir into the cooled sauce. Place over hot water and continue stirring and cooking over hot water (not boiling water) until the mixture is thoroughly smooth and thickened. Add the mushrooms. Heap into individual ramekins, top with grated Parmesan cheese and buttered crumbs and run under the broiler flame to brown.

SEVICHE

1 pound bay scallops
Juice of 4 to 5 limes or lemons
¹/₄ cup olive oil
1 large clove of garlic, finely chopped
2 tablespoons finely chopped green onions

2 tablespoons finely chopped green chilies
2 tablespoons chopped parsley
1 teaspoon salt
Dash of Tabasco
Fresh coriander, chopped

Place the scallops in a bowl and pour the juice over them. They should be completely covered. Let them stand in the refrigerator for 3 to 4 hours so the juice can "cook" them. Drain well, and toss with the olive oil, garlic, onions, chilies, parsley, salt and Tabasco. Arrange in a serving dish lined with lettuce, and garnish with chopped coriander. This can be served as an hors d'oeuvre (provide small skewers or toothpicks) or as a first course at dinner.

Shrimp

Most of the shrimp sold in this country are the large variety from the Gulf, though the tiny Pacific shrimp are available in the Far West. Shrimp are sold raw (green) in the shell, cooked in the shell, or cooked and shelled. I have yet to eat a ready-cooked shrimp that was not overdone, dry and tasteless, and this shellfish is so easy to prepare yourself that it seems unnecessary to depend on the fish dealer to do the cooking.

One pound of unshelled raw shrimp will serve 2 persons amply for a main course, and 4 persons for appetizers.

Cleaning shrimp: Shrimp can be shelled and cleaned before or after cooking. Either way, the method is the same. Peel off the shell (it comes off easily), rinse off the grit and with a sharp-pointed knife remove the black vein down the back. If you plan to serve the shrimp as appetizers to be eaten with the fingers, leave on the tails. This makes them easier to handle.

BOILED (POACHED) SHRIMP

Cook the shrimp (shelled or unshelled) in one of the Court Bouillons on page 110. Or prepare the following broth: In a kettle put enough water to cover the shrimp and add 1 thick slice of lemon, 3 sprigs of parsley, 1 peeled onion, 3 or 4 peppercorns and 1 teaspoon of salt. Bring to a boil and add the shrimp. Let them simmer until they turn pink and are cooked through. Shrimp cook in 3 to 5 minutes, depending on their size. Do not cook over 6 minutes.

COLD POACHED SHRIMP

Poach shrimp according to directions above. Drain and cool. If you have cooked them in the shell, remove shells and clean. Serve these shrimp chilled, with mayonnaise, Green Mayonnaise, Rémoulade Sauce, Tartar Sauce or Vinaigrette Sauce.

SHRIMP DE JONGHE (Serves 4)

2 pounds of shrimp, cooked	1 teaspoon of tarragon
2 cloves of garlic	1 teaspoon of salt
1/4 pound of butter	1/2 teaspoon of pepper
2 tablespoons of chopped parsley	Pinch of mace
1 teaspoon of chopped chervil	Pinch of nutmeg
	3/4 cup of fine bread crumbs
2 tablespoons of chopped green onion	1/2 cup of dry sherry

Peel the garlic and mash it with a fork. Work it into the butter and gradually add the rest of the herbs and seasonings. Finally work in the crumbs and sherry.

Arrange the cooked shrimp in buttered, individual ramekins and top with the butter-herb mixture. Bake in a 450° oven for 5 to 8 minutes, or just until thoroughly hot and bubbly. Or run under the broiler flame for 2 to 3 minutes.

BROILED SHRIMP, ITALIAN STYLE (Serves 4)

2 pounds of shrimp	1 teaspoon of salt
1/2 cup of olive oil	1 teaspoon of dry mustard
2 cloves of garlic	1 teaspoon of oregano
1/4 pound of prosciutto	1 teaspoon of black pepper
1/2 cup of red wine	Chopped parsley (Italian
1 cup of tomato purée	parsley, if possible)

Heat the olive oil. Peel and chop the garlic and add it to the hot oil to sauté. Let it soften but not brown. Cut the ham in shreds, add to the oil and garlic and cook for 1 or 2 minutes. Then add the wine, tomato purée, salt, mustard, oregano and pepper. Blend thoroughly and heat through.

Shell the shrimp but leave the tails on. Remove the black veins along the backs and rinse the shrimp to clean off all grit. Place the shrimp in a shallow pan large enough for them all to lie flat in the pan. Mix a handful of chopped parsley with the sauce and pour it over the shrimp. Marinate for several hours. Broil under a broiler flame in the same pan without draining off the sauce. Baste with the sauce in the pan during the broiling. The shrimp will cook in about 7 to 9 minutes.

JAMBALAYA WITH SHRIMP (Serves 4)

2 pounds of shrimp	2 cups of canned tomatoes
4 tablespoons of butter or bacon fat	Salt and pepper
2 tablespoons of flour	1 teaspoon of oregano or basil
3 onions, chopped	2 cups of uncooked rice
1 clove of garlic, chopped	3 cups of broth or fish stock
1/4 cup of cooked ham	

Melt the butter or fat in a heavy kettle with a tight lid. Blend the flour into the hot fat and add the peeled and chopped onions and garlic. Cut the ham in strips and add it to the onion mixture. Cook slowly until the onion is soft. Add the canned tomatoes and cook them for a few minutes to blend and thicken. Season to taste with salt and pepper and add oregano or basil. Add the rice and pour over it boiling broth or stock to cover 1 inch above the rice. Use fish stock (see Court Bouillon, page 110) or meat broth. You can make a broth with boiling water and bouillon cubes. Cover the kettle tightly and lower the heat to simmer. Let the rice and seasonings cook slowly. Shell the shrimp and remove the black veins along the backs. Rinse to wash out all grit. The shrimp should be added about 8 minutes before the rice is done. If the mixture gets too dry before the rice cooks, add more broth.

VARIATION

Mexican Shrimp with Rice: Add 2 teaspoons (or more, to taste) of chili powder to the seasonings.

ORIENTAL SHRIMP CURRY (Serves 4)

2 pounds of shrimp

2 pounds of ripe tomatoes

4 tablespoons of olive oil

2 cloves of garlic, chopped

2 medium onions, chopped

¹/₂ cup of tomato purée

Salt to taste

1 tablespoon of curry (or 2 tablespoons, if you like it hot)

¹/₂ cup of dry white wine or dry sherry

Peel the tomatoes (see page 447) and remove the seed sections. Chop the tomatoes very fine. Heat the olive oil and add the onions and garlic. Cook until soft but not brown. Add the tomatoes, cover and simmer gently over very low heat for ³/₄ hour. Add the tomato purée and salt to taste. Cover again and simmer gently for another 15 minutes. Add the curry to taste, cook to blend for a minute or two and then put through a strainer.

Shell the shrimp and remove the black veins along the backs. Rinse well to wash off the grit. Return the sauce to the stove and thin down to the desired consistency with dry white wine or dry sherry. Heat to the boiling point and add the shelled shrimp. Simmer for about 5 minutes.

Serve with rice, French-fried onion rings, chopped salted peanuts, a good chutney and sliced bananas dressed with olive oil and a little wine vinegar.

SHRIMP MORNAY (Serves 4)

2 pounds of shrimp
2 cups of Sauce Mornay
(page 350)
Butter

Buttered crumbs
Grated Parmesan cheese

Prepare the shrimp according to instructions on Boiled (Poached) Shrimp, page 136. Make Sauce Mornay, doubling the recipe. Heap the shrimp in buttered serving shells or individual ramekins. Top with the sauce and sprinkle with buttered crumbs and grated Parmesan cheese. Run under the broiler flame to brown.

SHRIMP AND MUSHROOMS IN SHELLS (Serves 4)

2 pounds of shrimp
1/2 pound of mushrooms
4 tablespoons of butter
Buttered crumbs

2 cups of Rich Cream Sauce
(page 349)
Grated Parmesan cheese

Prepare the shrimp according to instructions on Boiled (Poached) Shrimp, page 136. After the shrimp are removed from the broth, reduce it over a high flame until it measures 1/2 to 3/4 cup. Strain. Using this broth as part of the liquid, prepare double the recipe for Rich Cream Sauce. Sauté the mushrooms in the butter. Heap the cooked shrimp and mushrooms in individual oven-proof serving dishes or in shells. Top with the sauce and sprinkle with buttered crumbs and grated cheese. Run under the broiler flame to brown.

VARIATIONS

Herbed: Add sautéed, chopped green onions and chopped parsley to the shrimp mixture.
With Madeira: Add 1/4 cup of Madeira or dry sherry to the sauce.

CURRIED SHRIMP

Add cooked shrimp to the regular Curry Sauce on page 354 and serve with rice and chutney.

HERBED SHRIMP (Serves 4)

2 pounds of shrimp
¹/₄ pound of butter (soft)
1 minced clove of garlic
1 tablespoon of chopped chives
1 teaspoon of dried tarragon

1 tablespoon of chopped parsley
¹/₂ teaspoon of salt
¹/₂ teaspoon of black pepper
¹/₂ cup of fine bread crumbs
¹/₂ cup of dry white wine

Prepare the shrimp according to directions for Boiled (Poached) Shrimp (page 136). Shell and clean. Arrange the shrimp in buttered, individual baking dishes. Blend the softened butter with the garlic, chives, parsley, tarragon, salt, pepper and bread crumbs. Spread this over the shrimp and pour a little wine over each dish. Run under the broiler flame for a few minutes until brown and bubbly.

BROILED SHRIMP (Serves 4 to 6)

2 pounds of large shrimp
1 cup of olive oil
2 minced cloves of garlic
1 teaspoon of tarragon

1 cup of dry white wine
Salt and black pepper
Handful of chopped parsley

With kitchen scissors, slit the shell of each shrimp down the back and remove the black vein, but leave the shell on. Mix the rest of the ingredients and put them in a bowl. Add the shrimp and let them soak, turning frequently, for several hours. Arrange on a rack and grill in the broiler or over charcoal for 4 to 5 minutes, turning to cook on both sides.

VARIATION

Substitute either of the marinades suggested for scallops, pages 131–132.

Note: For instructions on making a charcoal fire, see pages 183–184.

TEMPURA (Serves 4)

2 pounds of shrimp
2 eggs, separated
³/₄ cup of beer
1 tablespoon of peanut oil
1 tablespoon of soy sauce

1 cup of cornstarch
1 teaspoon of dry mustard
   or ginger
Flour
Oil for deep-fat fryer

Shell the shrimp and remove the black vein, but leave the tails on. Heat the oil in the deep-fat fryer to 365°. Meanwhile, make the batter: Beat the egg yolks with the beer, oil, and the soy sauce. Sift the cornstarch and measure 1 cup. Add this to the beaten egg yolk mixture and add the mustard or ginger. Blend well. Beat the egg whites until stiff and fold them into the rest of the batter.

Dip shrimp into plain flour and then into the batter. Cook, a few at a time, in the deep-fryer basket for 4 minutes and drain on absorbent paper. Be sure to recheck the temperature of the oil before adding another basket of shrimp.

Serve Tempura with soy sauce, mustard and grated radish. Or serve with any hot sauce you choose: Sauce Diable (page 351), Barbecue Sauce (page 353), Curry Dip or Chili Dip (see page 27).

SHRIMP SALAD—See Basic Seafood Salad, page 342.

FRUIT

Ripe fresh fruit is a delight to the eye and to the taste buds. A cornucopia spilling out red apples, blooming peaches and pears and luscious grapes is a symbol of plenty. A delicate porcelain épergne laden with plums and apricots is an elegant centerpiece.

Fruit achieves its ultimate when you serve it in its natural state accompanied by cheese. There is no finer way to end an elaborate dinner. Select your handsomest bowl, fill it with ripe apples, pears, peaches, plums, grapes—any fruit or combination of fruits you choose. Provide individual fruit knives so each person can pare and cut his own, and with the fruit serve a fine dessert cheese, such as Camembert or Brie from France. An ideal dish for a hot summer afternoon is a bowl of fruit with cheese and a bottle of chilled white wine: a Riesling or a good dryish Moselle from Germany.

The best fruit buy is always the local product in season. The most delicate, such as berries, should be picked dead ripe and eaten just as soon as possible. No fruit benefits from being picked green. Peaches and pears that are picked green may become attractive to look at, but they never develop to the juicy, sweet stage of tree-ripened fruit. Hothouse fruit is beautiful, it's true, but seldom has the rich flavor of the garden variety. In general, when you buy fruit, taste is the primary consideration, then appearance.

Certain fresh fruits combine exceptionally well in fruit compotes, make delicious sauces for ice creams, and can be stewed, poached or baked. Here are suggestions on ways to use the most popular varieties of fruit available in our markets.

Apples

There are many varieties of apples sold across the country: some are especially suited to cooking; others are meant solely for eating; and a few are good for both purposes. The well-known Delicious apple, famed for its attractive appearance, is a beautiful addition to the fruit bowl, but it is not satisfactory for cooking; its bland, sweet taste is too flat. Apples usually called "greenings" are available in all areas for general cooking purposes. As their name implies, they are green-skinned and if tart enough and flavorful are a fine choice for applesauce, pies and other apple desserts. The MacIntosh and the Winesap are red-skinned apples with a tart, crisp tang, good for eating and for cooking. Rome Beauties are large, colorful apples usually recommended for baking, but if you prefer a smaller baking apple, the MacIntosh is just as tasty.

In some parts of the country, you may find Gravensteins or Spitzenbergs; both apples I remember from my early days in the Pacific Northwest. They have greenish skins with red streaks, and their crispness and real apple flavor make them delicious for both eating raw and cooking.

When buying apples for eating or baking, allow one apple per person. If you plan to make applesauce, you will need about 1½ apples per person, or even 2, if they are exceptionally small.

APPLESAUCE (Serves 4)

6 medium-sized apples	**Pinch of salt**
½ cup of water	**⅓ to ½ cup of sugar**

Cut the apples in quarters, peel them and core them. As you peel them, put the apple quarters in a bowl of cold water to keep them from turning brown. When they are all peeled and cored, cut them into slices and put them in a saucepan with ½ cup of water and a tiny pinch of salt. Cover and simmer gently until the apples are almost soft. Then add sugar to taste. Apples vary so in tartness that it is difficult to tell you just how much sugar you will need. You must add a little at a time, tasting to find out how sweet the sauce is. After it is sweetened enough, continue simmering for a few minutes to melt the sugar thoroughly and cook down the sauce.

With lemon: If the apples are not tart enough, add just a dash of lemon juice to them as they cook.

Spiced: Add your favorite spice to taste. Good choices are cinnamon, nutmeg, ground cloves or mace.

Strained: If you like a very fine, smooth sauce, put the applesauce through a fine sieve or foodmill after it has cooked.

Applesauce and horseradish: This is excellent served with pork dishes. Simply add horseradish to taste and blend into the sauce.

BAKED APPLES

1 apple per person
Sugar
Water

1 tablespoon of butter per apple

Wash the apples and remove the cores with an apple corer. Peel the skin down from the top for about 1½ inches. Arrange the apples in a baking dish in ½ inch of water and fill the cavities with sugar. Top each with 1 tablespoon of butter. Bake in a 350° oven for one half hour to an hour or until the apples are tender. Baste once or twice with the juices in the pan.

VARIATIONS

Spiced: Add your favorite spice to the cavities along with the sugar. Cinnamon, nutmeg, ground cloves or mace are all good.

With brown sugar: Use brown sugar instead of white.

With maple sugar: Use maple sugar, or omit sugar and baste with maple syrup.

With sherry: Baste the apples with a little dry sherry during the baking and serve with a custard sauce (page 355) flavored with sherry.

Flamed: Bake the apples in an oven-proof serving dish. When they are done, pour heated rum, Cognac or Grand Marnier over them, ignite them and bring to the table blazing. Serve with custard sauce or whipped cream.

FRIED APPLE RINGS

Wash and core apples but do not peel. Cut them in ½-inch slices and sauté in butter until brown on both sides. Serve with pork dishes.

GLAZED APPLE RINGS

Cook as for Fried Apple Rings (see above), but sprinkle the apples with a little sugar as they are sautéing. Let the sugar blend with the butter and glaze the apple rings slightly.

Apricots

This delicate fruit is in season all too short a time. Like the peach, it must be really ripe to be sweet and juicy. Eat it plain, or peel it and serve it with cream or in combination with other fruits.

To peel apricots easily, put them in boiling water for a minute or two. Allow 3 to 4 apricots per serving.

APRICOTS WITH CREAM

Peel and slice apricots and serve them with sugar and heavy cream.

APRICOTS WITH LIQUEUR

Peel and slice apricots and pour your favorite liqueur over them, allowing 1 jigger of liqueur per serving. Try Grand Marnier, kirsch, Cognac, Cointreau or Triple Sec.

APRICOTS COMBINED WITH OTHER FRUIT

Combine apricots with strawberries and pineapple; strawberries and banana; grapes and strawberries; pineapple; or peaches and plums.

POACHED APRICOTS (Serves 4)

12 apricots	**1 cup of water**
1 cup of sugar	**Dash of lemon juice**

Peel the apricots and leave them whole or halve them, but do not discard the pits. Bring the sugar and water to a boil, and boil for 4 or 5 minutes. Add the apricots, pits and a dash of lemon juice. Poach gently (do not boil) just until the fruit is cooked through. This will take 8 or 10 minutes. Spoon the liquid over the fruit occasionally and turn the apricots once during the cooking. Remove the apricots and cook the liquid down a bit. Pour it over the fruit and serve warm or cold. You may serve this with whipped cream or a custard sauce, if you wish.

VARIATIONS

With liqueur: After the apricots are cooked add 2 jiggers of your favorite liqueur. Try Cognac, Grand Marnier or kirsch.

Flamed: Arrange the apricots in a flame-proof serving dish while they are still hot. Pour heated liqueur over them and ignite. Bring to the table blazing.

APRICOTS WITH ICE CREAM

Serve poached apricots (above) with any of the suggested flavorings, or serve plain over vanilla ice cream.

VARIATIONS

Flamed: Spoon flamed apricots over vanilla ice cream.

With raspberry syrup: For each person, arrange two halves of poached apricots on a plate, top these with a scoop of ice cream and pour a little raspberry syrup over all.

POACHED DRIED APRICOTS

1 pound dried apricots	**1½ cups water**
1½ cups sugar	

Put the apricots in a small pan, cover with water, and let soak for an hour or so. Then bring to a boil and drain. In another pan combine the sugar and water, and bring to a boil. Add the apricots and simmer for about 15 minutes over low heat. Cool and then chill in the refrigerator. Serve with heavy cream. These can also be puréed for apricot sauce, filling or sherbet.

Bananas

The best bananas are ripe bananas. It should be unnecessary to make such a statement, but strangely enough, many people serve the fruit while it still has a green tinge at the tip of the skin. Ripe bananas have yellow skins, flecked or streaked with dark brown. Allow one banana per person.

BANANAS COMBINED WITH OTHER FRUITS

Sliced bananas and cream is a popular dish, but try the fruit in some of these suggested combinations: Combine bananas with strawberries or raspberries; orange slices, grapefruit sections or pineapple cubes; grapefruit sections and melon balls; grapefruit sections and strawberries; or pineapple cubes and strawberries.

Bananas turn dark if the slices are exposed to the air for long. If you are mixing a fruit compote ahead of time, either wait until the last minute to add the bananas, or sprinkle the slices with a little lemon or lime juice to keep them from turning.

BAKED BANANAS (Serves 4)

4 bananas

4 tablespoons of butter

4 tablespoons of brown sugar

2 teaspoons of lemon or lime juice

Peel the bananas and cut them in half the long way. Arrange them in a shallow baking dish greased with butter. Sprinkle the banana halves with a little brown sugar and a bit of lemon or lime juice and dot liberally with butter. Bake in a 350° oven for 10 to 15 minutes, or until the bananas are cooked through but not mushy.

VARIATIONS

Broiled: Broil the bananas instead of baking them.

Flamed with rum: Cook the bananas in a flame-proof serving dish. When they are done, pour 3 ounces of dark rum over them, ignite and bring them to the table flaming.

Flamed with Cognac: Substitute Cognac for the rum in the previous variation.

BANANA CREAM FREEZE (Serves 4)

This is an excellent way to use up overripe bananas.

2 very ripe bananas
$1/2$ cup of sugar
2 tablespoons of lemon juice
$1/2$ pint of whipping cream
Pinch of salt

Mash the bananas with a fork, sprinkle them with the lemon juice and $1/2$ cup of sugar. Whip the cream until firm and stiff, but not buttery, and beat in the pinch of salt as you whip. Blend the bananas with the sugar and lemon juice, and fold this mixture through the whipped cream. Pour into an ice-cube tray or any container that will fit into the freezer section of your refrigerator. Freeze until fairly firm but not hard. Do not stir.

Blackberries

Dead-ripe blackberries are a rare treat. Their rich flavor is entirely different from that of any other berry. If you live in areas where the wild berries grow, by all means take a jaunt to the woodlands and pick a batch. Scratches and snagged clothes are worth the delight that is in store for you when you eat the wild fruit. Try them plain in plenty of heavy cream or in any of the following ways.

BLACKBERRIES COMBINED WITH OTHER FRUITS

Combine fresh blackberries with raspberries; mix them with strawberries; or sprinkle fresh blackberries over sliced ripe peaches.

BLACKBERRIES WITH ICE CREAM

Fresh crushed blackberries sugared to taste and poured over vanilla ice cream are delicious.

STEWED BLACKBERRIES (Serves 4)

1 quart of blackberries	**1 cup of water**
1 cup of sugar	**Pinch of salt**

Wash the blackberries and pick them over, discarding any that are mushy or greenish. Bring the sugar, water and salt to a boil and cook for 4 or 5 minutes. Add the berries and simmer gently until they are just barely cooked. Do not overcook or the berries will be mushy. They should take about 8 to 10 minutes. Serve warm or cold with cream.

VARIATIONS

With custard sauce: Serve with custard sauce (page 355).

With ice cream: Serve over ice cream.

With other fruit: Serve in combination with other stewed or poached fruit.

BLACKBERRY CREAM FREEZE

1 pint of blackberries	**¹/₂ pint of whipping cream**
Sugar to taste	**Pinch of salt**

Wash the berries, crush them gently with a fork and sugar to taste. Whip the cream with a pinch of salt added until it is firm but not buttery. Fold in the crushed berries and turn into an ice-cube tray or any container that will fit into the freezing compartment of your refrigerator. Freeze until firm but not hard.

Blueberries

These dark, plump berries have a bland but distinctive flavor. Although in the East blueberry muffins and blueberry pie are very popular, this delicate fruit is at its best when eaten fresh with plenty of heavy cream. Or try it in combination with other fruits.

BLUEBERRIES COMBINED WITH OTHER FRUITS

Heap blueberries over sliced fresh peaches; combine them with strawberries or raspberries; or with apricots and pineapple cubes.

BLUEBERRIES WITH CUSTARD SAUCE

Make a Creamy Custard Sauce (page 356) and flavor it with Cognac or Grand Marnier. Serve over blueberries.

BLUEBERRIES AND PEACHES WITH ICE CREAM

Slice fresh peaches and crush them lightly to extract some juice. Sugar to taste and combine with blueberries. Serve over vanilla ice cream.

Boysenberries

This berry is a comparatively new hybrid. It is not available in all sections of the country, but if you live in the Far West you will often see it in the markets. It has a tart tang and is more tasty cooked than fresh. In pies and tarts it is elegant.

STEWED BOYSENBERRIES

Follow the directions for Stewed Blackberries (page 149). Serve with heavy cream, whipped cream, custard sauce or ice cream.

Cherries

There are several varieties of cherries sold in the markets. By far the handsomest, and probably the most popular, is the Bing, a dark red juicy cherry that is excellent fresh or cooked. The Lambert is a dark red cherry well known in the Northwest. It is also excellent for eating or cooking. The Royal Anne has a yellow skin with reddish tinges. Its flavor is more delicate, but it can be used in any way suggested for the red cherries. For 4 persons, buy 1 to 1½ pounds.

FRESH CHERRIES

An elegant way to serve fresh cherries is to heap them whole, with stems intact, in individual glass dishes. Serve small bowls of ice water with the cherries so each person can dip the fruit as he eats it.

POACHED CHERRIES (Serves 4)

1 to 1½ pounds of red cherries

½ cup of sugar

1 cup of water

Pinch of salt

Wash the cherries, stem them and remove the pits. This can be done by using a cherry pitter, or by cutting the cherries in half. Bring the sugar, water and pinch of salt to a boil and boil for several minutes. Add the cherries and simmer gently until they are just done. Serve warm or cold with whipped cream, ice cream or custard sauce.

VARIATION

Flavor the cooked cherries with 3 ounces of kirsch, Cognac or Grand Marnier.

CHERRIES JUBILEE

Cook cherries as for Poached Cherries (page 151). Heap the hot cherries and juice in a flame-proof dish, add ½ cup of slightly heated kirsch, Cognac or Grand Marnier and ignite. Serve plain or spoon over vanilla ice cream.

Figs

Many people living in the more northern areas of the country think all figs come dried or canned. If you have never had the pleasure of feasting on fresh figs, watch for shipments from California and Florida. The fresh fig is a luxury in northern markets, it is true, but a luxury that is well worth the extra expense.

Figs come in two colors: purple-skinned and white-skinned. They are both delicious. Buy them fully ripe but firm and not mushy. Allow 2 or 3 figs per person.

FRESH FIGS WITH CREAM

Peel the figs carefully, being sure you do not crush them. The skin will peel off very easily if the fig is ripe. Slice and sugar only slightly. Figs are quite sweet. Serve with heavy cream.

Gooseberries

The tart green gooseberry is beginning to be a scarce item in our markets, possibly because it must be cooked to be eaten. To those of us who grew up when early summer meant gooseberry season and mouth-watering gooseberry fool and jam and tarts, its disappearance is a tragic loss. Cooked gooseberries have an elegant flavor.

The berries should be firm and a pale, delicate green. Avoid those that are the least bit soft. One quart of gooseberries will serve 4 persons amply and sometimes 5 or 6.

POACHED GOOSEBERRIES (Serves 4)

1 quart of gooseberries   **1¹/₂ cups of sugar**
1¹/₂ cups of water

Wash the gooseberries and remove the blossoms. Pick the stems off and discard any berries that are soft. Bring the sugar and water to a boil and cook for a few minutes. Add the gooseberries and simmer them in the hot liquid gently until they are just cooked through. Do not let them get soft and mushy. Stir occasionally to be sure they cook evenly. Taste for sweetness just before they finish cooking and add more sugar if necessary.

GOOSEBERRY FOOL (Serves 4)

This recipe is very old, for Gooseberry Fool was a delicacy centuries ago.

1 pint of gooseberries   **Whipping cream**
Sugar
A few tablespoons of water

Wash and sort the gooseberries as for Poached Gooseberries (see above). Put them in a saucepan with ¹/₄ cup of sugar and a few tablespoons of water. Cook very gently until the gooseberries are thoroughly done and soft enough to mash. Put them through a sieve or food mill and add sugar to taste. Whip the cream until thick but not buttery and fold the gooseberry purée through it. Chill for several hours.

VARIATION

Substitute milk for ¹/₂ of the cream. Do not whip the cream, simply mix it with the milk and blend both into the gooseberry purée. This makes a less rich and less thick concoction, but the flavor is equally delicious.

Grapefruit

This large yellow-skinned citrus fruit is usually eaten at breakfast, but its refreshing sharp flavor is an excellent addition to many fruit compotes, and a broiled grapefruit half is a fine choice for a light dessert.

Grapefruit, like other citrus fruit, is at its peak in the winter months. There are two general types available: thick-skinned and thin-skinned. Thick-skinned grapefruit tend to be pulpy and sour. Thin-skinned are juicy and far better in flavor. Heft them in your hand and select those that are heaviest; they will be sweeter and juicier. The pulp or meat of grapefruit can be either pale yellow or pink. Both are delicious. One grapefruit of average size will serve 2 persons.

GRAPEFRUIT IN COMBINATION WITH OTHER FRUITS

Combine grapefruit with bananas; strawberries and bananas; bananas and melon balls; raspberries or strawberries and melon balls; seedless white grapes and melon balls; or pineapple cubes and orange slices.

BROILED GRAPEFRUIT HALVES

Allow 1 half grapefruit per person. Cut the grapefruit in half and loosen the sections with a sharp knife. Arrange on a baking sheet and sprinkle with brown sugar, maple sugar or strained honey. Dot liberally with butter and broil under the broiler flame until the grapefruit is brown and bubbly and hot through.

VARIATION

Add a spoonful of sherry or rum to each grapefruit half.

Grapes

There are many varieties of eating grapes to pick from. Among my favorites is the Muscat, a green grape with a rather spicy flavor. It is even better when it has turned brownish and begun to shrivel. Then it becomes mellow and rich. The Malaga is another green table grape with a fine flavor; and the Lady Finger is the elegant long, thin green grape so beautiful in a fruit display. The Tokay is a delicious red grape; and the dark purple Ribier lends an attractive color contrast. Of course the Thompson seedless, the small sweet green grape, is always popular and is the best choice for fruit compotes. Any of the other varieties may be used in compotes, but they must be halved and seeded.

Some people enjoy the Concord, the dark purple grape with the slipskin. This is the native American variety with the definite grapy flavor used widely for making grape juice.

If you are arranging a bowl of grapes or grapes in combination with other fruits, a selection of two or three different varieties makes a pleasant picture and gives guests a chance to try different flavors.

GRAPES COMBINED WITH OTHER FRUITS

Combine grapes with melon balls and grapefruit sections; melon balls, strawberries and grapefruit sections; or grapefruit sections and raspberries or strawberries.

Melons

A chilled melon is one of the most refreshing feasts on a hot summer day. Fortunately we have a large supply and a great variety all through the hot weather. Watermelon and cantaloupe need no introduction. The honeydew, the Persian and the casaba (a late summer and fall melon) are more expensive, more delicate in flavor and considered by some people to be more elegant. The Cranshaw and the Christmas melon arrive late in the fall and hold into winter months.

There are several ways to detect the ripeness of a melon. Watermelons are generally thumped. They should give a hollow sound, not a dull thud. Cantaloupes give off a delicious aroma when ripe. Sniff them and look at the skin to see if the green between the webbing has turned a grayish color. The honeydew when ripe has turned to a creamy yellow and has a faint sweet smell. You can also test it by pressing gently on the stem end. A ripe melon will give a little. A ripe casaba is bright yellow and also has "give" at the stem end. Cranshaw, Persian and Christmas melons can be tested in the same way. If you are not sure, rely on the judgment of the grocer. Then you can return the melon if it's green.

You must judge how much you need by the size of the melon. They vary greatly.

PLAIN MELON

Serve slices of melon with lime wedges or lemon wedges, and be sure to have salt available. Some people like a sprinkle of it on this fruit.

MELON BALLS COMBINED WITH OTHER FRUIT

Combine melon balls with grapefruit sections; raspberries or strawberries; seedless grapes and grapefruit sections; seedless grapes and bananas; or strawberries and pineapple.

MELON BALLS WITH LIQUEUR

Mix two or three varieties of melon balls and add the liqueur of your choice. Try Grand Marnier, kirsch, Cognac, Cointreau or Benedictine.

MELON WITH LIME OR LEMON ICE

Serve melon slices (honeydew or casaba are best) topped with a scoop of lemon or lime ice.

MELON SURPRISE

This can be made with watermelon or any of the larger melons, such as casaba, Persian or a large honeydew. Place the melon on the side that will balance best and hold it steady. Cut a large slice from the top side and scoop out the seeds. Cut out the flesh with a melon-ball cutter, being sure to get nicely rounded melon balls. Put the melon balls in a bowl and combine them with any other fruits you choose. Flavor to taste with sugar and add Cognac, Grand Marnier, Cointreau or dark rum. Mix well and heap back in the melon shell. Chill and serve.

VARIATIONS

With champagne: Omit the liqueur. Heap the fruit back in the melon shell and pour in all the champagne it will hold.

With white wine: Omit the liqueur. Heap the fruit in the melon shell and add dry white wine.

Peaches

Many of the peaches on the market today are picked green and shipped a great distance. They are beautiful to look at, but the texture is woody and they have no juice. Buy local peaches in season. They may not be as handsome, but they will have a rich, juicy peach flavor if they have been tree-ripened. Clingstones have an exceptionally good taste, but many people shun them because they are a little messy to slice. Don't let that stop you. Another of my favorites is the pale peach with the white meat inside. It is delicious.

The peach is a most versatile fruit. It can be eaten plain, sliced with cream, combined with other fruit or cooked in almost any way. Allow one average peach per person, or two if the peaches are very small.

PEACHES COMBINED WITH OTHER FRUITS

Combine sliced fresh peaches with any of the following: blueberries, sliced plums, fresh raspberries, apricots, strawberries, or any combination of these fruits.

PEACHES WITH LIQUEUR

Flavor sliced fresh peaches with Cognac, Grand Marnier, Cointreau, kirsch or dark rum. Allow about 1 ounce of liqueur per serving.

VARIATION

Combine peaches with other fruit and flavor with liqueur.

BROILED PEACH HALVES

Halve peaches and peel them. Arrange them on a greased baking sheet and sprinkle lightly with brown sugar or maple sugar. Dot liberally with butter and broil until sizzling on top and soft through, but not mushy. Serve with whipped cream flavored with vanilla and sugar.

Flamed with bourbon: Omit the whipped cream and arrange the peaches in a hot serving dish. Pour slightly heated bourbon over them (allowing about 1 ounce to a serving) and ignite. Carry to the table blazing.

BAKED PEACHES 1

Follow directions for Baked Bananas (page 147) and blaze the peaches with bourbon just before serving.

BAKED PEACHES 2 (Serves 4)

4 peaches	**³/₄ cup of water**
³/₄ cup of sugar	**3 ounces of bourbon**

Bring the sugar and water to a boil and cook for 5 minutes. Meanwhile, peel the peaches but leave them whole. Arrange them in a baking dish and pour the hot syrup over them. Bake in a 350° oven, basting with the juices in the pan frequently, for about 30 minutes, or until the peaches are tender when tested with a fork. Remove from the oven and cool slightly. Add the bourbon to the peaches and juice and let them stand in this mixture, turning them occasionally to be sure they are evenly bathed. Serve cold.

POACHED PEACHES (Serves 4)

4 peaches	**1 inch of vanilla bean or 1 teaspoon of vanilla extract**
1 cup of sugar	
1 cup of water	

Peel and halve the peaches. Combine the sugar and water and add the vanilla bean or extract. Bring this to a boil and cook for 5 minutes. Add the peach halves and poach gently, spooning the hot liquid over them and turning them once during the cooking. When they are tender but not mushy, take the pan from the stove and let the peaches cool in the syrup. Serve plain or with custard sauce or whipped cream.

With liqueur: After the peaches are cooked, flavor them with Cognac, bourbon or kirsch, allowing 1 ounce of liqueur per serving.

Orange-flavored: Omit the vanilla bean and add two good-sized strips or orange peel to the syrup. Flavor the peaches with Grand Marnier or Cointreau. Serve plain or with a custard sauce flavored with Grand Marnier or Cointreau.

PEACH SHORTCAKE

Make shortcake (page 46) and serve sliced peaches over it sugared to taste. Top with whipped cream.

PEACH MELBA

Serve poached peach halves (page 158) topped with vanilla ice cream and raspberry syrup.

Pears

Like peaches, pears are best when they are picked ripe. If they are very green, they will never develop a juicy, sweet taste. Bartletts, on the market in the summer, are good both raw and cooked. The Comice, Bosc and Anjou that arrive in the fall are also good for both purposes but they are exceptionally tasty served plain with a fine cheese. Allow 1 pear per person.

PEARS WITH CREAM

If you have never tried sliced pears with sugar and cream, you have a treat coming. Select ripe, juicy pears, peel them and cut into very thin slices. Sugar lightly and serve with plenty of heavy cream.

BAKED PEARS (Serves 4)

4 pears

1 cup of brown sugar

³/₄ cup of water

4 cloves

A bit of ground cinnamon

Wash the pears but do not peel them. You may cut them in half and core them or leave them whole. Heat the sugar and water to the boiling point and cook for 5 minutes. Arrange the pears in a baking dish, stick each one with a clove and add just a touch of cinnamon. Pour the syrup over the pears and bake in a 350° oven, basting frequently with the syrup, for 20 to 30 minutes, or until the fruit is tender but not mushy. Serve plain, hot or cold. Or serve with cream.

VARIATIONS

With Cognac: When the pears are cooked, flavor them with Cognac.

With ginger: Omit the cinnamon and add a few slivers of candied ginger to the baking dish.

POACHED PEARS (Serves 4)

4 pears

³/₄ cup of water

³/₄ cup of sugar

1 inch of vanilla bean or 1 teaspoon of vanilla extract

Peel the pears, halve them and cut out the cores. Stand in cold water to keep them from turning dark. Heat the water, sugar and vanilla bean or extract to the boiling point and cook for 5 minutes. Add the pear halves and poach gently, spooning the liquid over them from time to time and turning them once during the cooking. They should be tender in about 15 minutes. Do not overcook or the pears will be mushy. Cool them in the syrup and serve plain or with whipped cream or custard sauce.

VARIATIONS

With Cognac: Flavor the pears with Cognac after they are cooked.

Orange-flavored: Omit the vanilla bean and add 2 strips of orange peel to the syrup. When the pears are done, flavor with Grand Marnier or Cointreau.

With ginger: Omit the vanilla bean and add a few slivers of candied or preserved ginger to the syrup.

Flamed: Transfer the hot pears to a flame-proof serving dish and pour 3 ounces of slightly heated Cognac, Grand Marnier or kirsch over them. Ignite and carry to the table blazing.

PEAR MELBA

Serve poached pears topped with vanilla ice cream and crushed raspberries or raspberry syrup.

PEAR HÉLÈNE

Serve poached pears topped with vanilla ice cream and hot chocolate sauce.

Pineapple

Fresh pineapple is delicious if dead ripe, but if not ripe it is much too tart to eat uncooked. Test for ripeness by smell (it should have a strong pineapple odor); by pulling at one of the leaves at the top (it should pull out easily); and by color (a ripe pineapple has deep orange skin, not greenish). Pineapples come in various sizes. Tiny ones will serve 2 or 3 persons. Average-sized pineapples of 2 pounds will serve 4 to 6 persons, and the huge variety will easily serve 8.

PLAIN FRESH PINEAPPLE

Cut off the top and peel the pineapple, being careful to remove the prickly eyes. Cut the fruit in slices or fingers, cubes or wedges, removing the woody core section as you prepare it. Sugar to taste and chill.

VARIATION

With liqueur: Add 1 ounce per serving of Cognac, Grand Marnier or dark rum to the pineapple and let it mellow for at least an hour.

PINEAPPLE COMBINED WITH OTHER FRUITS

Combine fresh pineapple cubes with any of the following: strawberries, raspberries, bananas, strawberries and bananas, apricots, or grapefruit sections and bananas.

PINEAPPLE SURPRISE

Select a large pineapple and place it on its side. If it will not stay steady, cut a thin slice off the lower side to balance it. Cut a rather thick slice from the top side, leaving the leaves intact. With a sharp knife cut out the flesh, leaving a shell about 1 inch thick. Cube the pineapple and combine it with any other fruit you choose. Flavor to taste with sugar, and add Cognac, Grand Marnier, kirsch or dark rum. Heap the fruit back in the pineapple shell and chill.

VARIATION

With ice cream: Fill the pineapple shell with vanilla ice cream. As a topping for the ice cream, serve the fruit cut in cubes and flavored with sugar and rum.

BROILED PINEAPPLE SLICES

Cut a whole pineapple through, skin and all, into $1/2$-inch slices. Peel the slices and cut out the prickly eyes. Arrange the pineapple slices on a buttered baking sheet, sprinkle with brown sugar and dot heavily with butter. Broil until brown and bubbly. Allow about 3 slices per serving.

VARIATION

Flamed with rum: Arrange the cooked slices in a flame-proof serving dish and pour 3 ounces of rum over them while they are still hot. Ignite the rum and bring the fruit to the table blazing.

SAUTÉED PINEAPPLE

Sauté fingers or slices of fresh pineapple in hot butter. Add a sprinkling of brown sugar after you turn the pineapple. Serve plain or flavored with a little rum.

Plums

There are three general varieties of plums available in most markets during the summer months: the large dark plum, the large bright red plum and the small Italian prune plum. The red plum, though attractive, seems to have the least flavor. Ripe, juicy Italian prunes and the dark plump plums are fine additions to the fruit bowl and excellent with certain other fruits in compotes. Both poach well and make tasty tarts and pies. The green-gage plum, a beautiful plum with a delicate green skin, is unusually good if you can find a ripe one. This is difficult.

The plum is one fruit that should not be firm when you buy it. A ripe, juicy plum is soft, but not mushy. One pound will serve about 4 persons.

PLUMS COMBINED WITH OTHER FRUITS

Peel the plums and halve them or slice them. Combine with any of the following fruits: peaches, bananas and grapes; apricots and peaches; or grapefruit sections and bananas.

POACHED PLUMS (Serves 4)

1 pound of Italian prune plums	1 inch of vanilla bean or 1 teaspoon of vanilla extract
1 cup of sugar	
1 cup of water	Pinch of cinnamon

Wash the prunes and halve them, but do not peel. Remove the pits. Boil the sugar, water, vanilla bean or extract and cinnamon for 5 minutes. Add the prune halves and poach gently until just tender, spooning the liquid over them occasionally and turning them once during the cooking.

VARIATION

Substitute the large purple plums and poach them whole. Flavor after cooking with Cognac or kirsch.

BAKED PRUNE PLUMS (Serves 4)

1 pound of Italian prune plums	**Butter**
1 cup of brown sugar	**Cinnamon**
³/₄ cup of water	

Prepare the prunes as for Poached Plums (see page 163). Boil the sugar and water together for 5 minutes. Arrange the prunes in a baking dish, dot with butter and sprinkle with a bit of cinnamon. Pour the syrup over them and bake in a 350° oven for about 15 to 20 minutes, or until tender when pierced with a fork.

Raspberries

To many people, the raspberry is the most elegant of all berries. The best way to enjoy them is to get them in season, dead ripe, and eat them with sugar and plenty of heavy cream. They combine well with other fruits and can be stewed, but to me stewing them seems a waste.

They are sold by the pint and quart. One quart will serve 4 persons.

RASPBERRIES WITH LIQUEUR

Arrange the berries in a bowl. Sugar lightly and flavor with kirsch, Cognac or Grand Marnier. If you can find a French brandy called Eau de Vie de Framboise, buy it and pour a little over the raspberries. This brandy is made from the berry itself and combines with it beautifully.

RASPBERRIES IN COMBINATION WITH OTHER FRUITS

Combine raspberries with any of the following: fresh peaches, apricots, bananas, pineapple, or other berries.

RASPBERRY CREAM FREEZE (Serves 4)

1 pint of raspberries	**¹/₂ pint of whipping cream**
Sugar to taste	

Wash the berries, crush them lightly and flavor to taste with sugar. Whip the cream until stiff but not buttery and fold in the berries. Turn into an ice tray or a container that will fit into the freezing compartment of your refrigerator and freeze until firm but not hard.

Rhubarb

This red stalk is not a true fruit, since it is the stem of a green leafy plant. Like the gooseberry, it must be cooked, though years ago people used to gnaw on it to aid digestion—a severe remedy, for raw rhubarb is extremely tart. This very tartness gives the fruit its refreshing flavor when cooked, and it is delightful stewed, baked or put in a pie.

It comes early, before other summer fruits are on the market. Look for the brightest red stalks; those that are greenish are older and tougher. A pound will serve 4 persons.

BAKED RHUBARB (Serves 4)

1 pound of rhubarb   **1 cup of brown sugar**

Wash the rhubarb and cut it into 2-inch pieces. If the skin is too tough to cut, pull it off, stripping it down the length of the stalk. Add the sugar and mix lightly. Turn into a casserole, cover and bake in a 350° oven for 30 to 45 minutes, or until the rhubarb is tender.

VARIATION

Use half rhubarb and half fresh strawberries.

STEWED RHUBARB (Serves 4)

1 pound of rhubarb   **A few tablespoons of water**
1 cup of sugar

Prepare the rhubarb as for baking (see above) and cut it into 1-inch lengths. Place in a saucepan over very low heat with a few tablespoons of water (it will get watery as it cooks) and the sugar. Cook gently, covered, until just tender and juicy. This will take 20 to 25 minutes.

POACHED RHUBARB (Serves 4)

1 pound of rhubarb   **1 cup of water**
2 cups of sugar

Prepare as for Stewed Rhubarb (see page 165). Boil the sugar and water together for 5 minutes and add the rhubarb. Cover the pan and cook gently until the rhubarb is tender. Cool uncovered.

VARIATION

Use half strawberries and half rhubarb.

Strawberries

Strawberries, bright red and dripping with juice, are wonderful any way you serve them. Buy the local berries when you can; those picked green and shipped from far away are not as juicy and sweet. It's wise to peek under the berries on top of the box. I find the best are placed on top, and underneath they may be green or moldy. One quart will serve 4 persons.

The strawberry is a low-growing plant and the berries are sometimes covered with soil and grit. Wash them well. Remove hulls.

PLAIN STRAWBERRIES

This is an attractive way to serve berries if they are large and perfect. Wash them well, being sure that all grit is removed. In the center of each plate put a small mound of powdered sugar. Arrange berries around it with their stems pointing out to the edge of the plate. To eat, pick the berries up by their stems, dip in the sugar and nibble.

STRAWBERRIES WITH CREAM

Fresh strawberries lightly sugared and served with plenty of heavy cream are delicious. But here is a way to make this dish even more elegant: Wash the strawberries and hull them. Arrange them in a bowl and sprinkle with sugar to taste. Add a little Cognac, kirsch or Grand Marnier and let them stand to mellow. When you are ready to serve, cover the berries with a thick layer of whipped cream.

STRAWBERRIES COMBINED WITH OTHER FRUITS

Strawberries combine well with almost any other fruit. Try them with other berries, peaches or apricots, pineapple, grapefruit sections and bananas, or grapefruit sections and grapes; or poach them with rhubarb (see Rhubarb, page 166).

STRAWBERRIES WITH ICE CREAM

Plain, crushed strawberries are a perfect topping for vanilla ice cream, but if you would like a change try this: Wash the berries and hull them. Cut them in rather thick slices. Then cover them with sugar (use about 1½ cups for a quart of strawberries) and let them stand for 1 or 2 hours. Place the berries in a saucepan and bring them slowly to a boil. Cook for 1 minute only. Cool and serve over vanilla ice cream, or serve with a rich custard sauce.

STRAWBERRY SHORTCAKE

Wash, hull and crush slightly 1 quart of strawberries (for 4 persons). Make a shortcake (page 46). Sugar the berries to taste and serve them on the shortcake. Top with whipped cream or pass plenty of unwhipped heavy cream.

STRAWBERRY CREAM FREEZE

Follow directions for Raspberry Cream Freeze (page 164), substituting strawberries for the raspberries.

GRAIN DISHES

In some parts of the world, grains are cooked in water or broth and eaten with the main meal, as we would a vegetable. Like pastas, such dishes tend to have a bland flavor and take well to seasonings and flavorings. With rich sauces, or with the addition of bits of meat and vegetable, they can even serve as a main course at luncheon or supper.

Rice

Rice comes to the market in several forms. There is the old-fashioned polished, uncooked rice, of which the long-grained variety is best. Converted rice and Minute Rice are both specially processed and come with clear and simple cooking instructions on the packages. Brown rice, which many people prefer because it is the whole, unpolished grain, is cooked in the same way as the polished rice, but it takes a longer time.

BOILED RICE (Serves 4)

1 cup of polished long-grain rice   **1 tablespoon of salt**

2 quarts of water

Wash the rice thoroughly in a pan of cold water. Pour off the water and repeat. Continue washing in fresh water until the water runs clear and not cloudy. This is to rid the rice of excess starch. Four washings should be ample. Put water (2 quarts) and salt in a large kettle and bring to a rolling boil. Add the rice a little at a time, being sure that the water never stops boiling. Continue boiling uncovered until the rice is done. This will take about 15 minutes. Do not overcook or the rice will be mushy. Drain the cooked rice thoroughly and return it to the kettle. Dry it out over a very low heat on top of the stove or in a very low oven. Stir it occasionally with a fork as it dries to fluff it up. The drying should take only a few minutes. If you let it stand over heat for too long, it will be parched.

STEAMED RICE (Serves 4)

1 cup of rice	**Water or stock**
Butter	**$\frac{1}{2}$ teaspoon of salt**

Wash the rice as for Boiled Rice (page 168) and put it with the salt into a heavy skillet lightly greased with butter. Pour over it enough water or stock to cover the rice and come $1\frac{1}{2}$ inches above it. Cover tightly and bring to a rapid boil very quickly. Lower the heat and let the rice cook very slowly until all the liquid is absorbed. This should take about 15 to 20 minutes.

VARIATIONS

With chicken broth: Use chicken broth for the water or stock, and serve the rice with a chicken dinner.

With almonds: Steam the rice in a rich broth and toss it with toasted buttered almonds when it is cooked. Add a generous amount of melted butter.

With mushrooms: Mix the steamed rice with mushrooms sautéed in butter.

With bacon and onion: Mix the steamed rice with bacon bits and sautéed onions.

PILAF (Serves 4)

1 cup of uncooked rice	**Stock, broth or bouillon**
4 tablespoons of butter	**(about 2 cups)**
1 small onion, finely chopped	

Wash the rice (see Boiled Rice) and drain. Brown the onion lightly in the butter and add the rice. Cook it in the butter over low heat for about 4 to 5 minutes, stirring it often to let it brown evenly. It should be just lightly colored. Heat the liquid to the boiling point and pour it over the rice until it is a good 1½ inches above. Cover the pan tightly and bake in a 350° oven for 25 to 30 minutes, or until all the liquid is absorbed. Serve with plenty of butter.

Note: This can be cooked on top of the stove over very low heat.

VARIATIONS

With mushrooms: Sauté ½ pound of sliced mushrooms with the sliced onion and cook them with the rice.

With green pepper: Sauté 1 green pepper cut in strips with the onion and cook with the rice.

With herbs: Add a pinch of thyme or oregano to the broth.

With nuts: Add blanched slivered almonds or filberts to sauté with the onion.

Saffron rice: Add a pinch of saffron to the rice.

RISOTTO

This Italian rice dish, when done properly, has a creamy consistency while the grains of rice remain firm at the center. This is achieved by cooking the rice in an open pan and stirring in meat or fish broth at intervals. Since this method requires more liquid than is normally used to steam rice, the broth should be undersalted, and preferably homemade. It should also be kept hot while it is being added to the rice.

1 small onion, peeled and finely chopped

6 tablespoons of butter

1½ cups of rice, preferably Italian Arborio

3 to 4 cups of chicken or beef broth

½ cup of grated Parmesan cheese

Sauté the onion in the butter in a heavy saucepan until it is beginning to color. Stir in the rice thoroughly so that each grain is coated with butter. Then, using medium-high heat, pour 1 cup of hot broth into the rice, and stir in with a fork. Allow the rice to nearly absorb the broth, stirring it from time to time, before adding another cup. When the rice begins to soften, add the broth in smaller quantities so you can bring it to exactly the right consistency. This should take about 25 to 30 minutes. No additional salt should be needed if the broth is seasoned. Stir in the Parmesan cheese and serve immediately.

VARIATIONS

With shellfish: Use fish broth instead of chicken or beef, and when the risotto is done, gently stir in 2 cups of cooked shellfish: scallops, shrimp, lobster, crab, clams or mussels, in any combination. Do not add cheese.

With chicken: Use chicken broth, and when the risotto is done, gently stir in 2 cups of cubed cooked chicken breast and Parmesan cheese.

With vegetables: Use either chicken or beef broth, and when the risotto is done, gently stir in 2 cups of cooked peas, finely cut cooked green beans, or crisply cooked asparagus tips, and Parmesan cheese.

FRIED RICE (Serves 4)

2 cups of cooked rice	**Soy sauce**
4 strips of bacon or an equal amount of ham	**Pepper**
3 eggs	

Cut the bacon or ham into small bits and fry. If the ham is not fatty, use a little extra bacon fat or a little oil. When the meat is done and crisp, remove it from the pan and add the rice. Fry it in the fat for a few minutes, until it is lightly colored and hot through. Take the pan from the stove and add 3 raw eggs and the meat bits. Return to the heat and cook, stirring well, until the eggs are all mixed through and cooked. Season with soy sauce and freshly ground black pepper.

VARIATIONS

With mushrooms: Fry ½ pound of sliced fresh mushrooms with the meat. Remove the mushrooms and the meat, and fry the rice. Finish according to the recipe above, adding the mushrooms to the mixture with the eggs and meat.

With onion and green pepper: Fry onions and green pepper strips with the meat.

With leftover meat: Add bits of any leftover meat to the mixture as it finishes cooking.

With seafood: Omit the bacon or ham, and fry the rice in oil with chopped cooked shrimp or lobster, or crab flakes. Proceed as above.

RICE | 171

Cook brown rice in any of the ways suggested for white rice, allowing 8 to 10 minutes extra cooking time.

Wild Rice

This is not a true rice but a type of wild grain growing in marshy areas. It is difficult to harvest and there is not too much available. Consequently it is very costly, but the fine nutty flavor of wild rice makes the extra expense bearable on special occasions. Cook 1 cup for 4 persons.

To boil: Wash 1 cup of wild rice and slowly add it to 4 cups of boiling, salted water. Do not let the water stop boiling. Cook for 20 to 25 minutes, or until the rice is done but not mushy. Drain and serve with plenty of butter.

Variations

With mushrooms: Mix with sautéed mushrooms, using about ½ pound of mushrooms for 4 servings.

With ham or bacon: Mix with bits of cooked ham or bacon bits.

Kasha

Kasha is buckwheat groats, a popular dish in eastern Mediterranean countries. This recipe will serve 4 persons.

KASHA (Serves 4)

1 cup of buckwheat groats	2 cups of stock or broth
1 egg	4 to 6 tablespoons of butter
Salt	

Heat a heavy skillet with a tight-fitting lid. Add the groats and stir in the raw egg vigorously. Continue cooking and stirring until it is thoroughly blended and cooked dry. Add the stock or broth and salt to taste, cover, lower the heat and simmer very gently for about a half hour, or until the groats are cooked and the broth is absorbed. Mix with plenty of butter.

Barley

BARLEY CASSEROLE (Serves 4)

Most people think of barley as something that goes into a soup. Fine pearly barley makes an excellent casserole dish.

1 cup of pearl barley

1 large onion

½ pound of mushrooms

4 to 5 tablespoons of butter

2 cups of broth (meat or chicken)

Peel the onion and chop it. Wipe the mushrooms with a damp cloth and slice them. Melt the butter and sauté the onions and mushrooms until soft. Add the barley and brown it lightly. Pour into a buttered casserole. Before you pour the broth over the barley, taste it for seasoning. If it has enough, the casserole will need no additional salt or pepper. For broth use any stock from meat or chicken (see Soup chapter) or use canned meat broth, consommé or chicken broth. Or make broth with hot water and bouillon cubes. (You will need about 3 cubes for the 2 cups of liquid.) Pour 1 cup of the broth over the barley in the casserole and cover. Bake in a 350° oven for 25 to 30 minutes and then uncover and add the second cup of broth. Continue cooking until the liquid is absorbed and the barley done, about another 30 minutes.

VARIATIONS

Amandine: When you add the second cup of broth, sprinkle the top of the casserole with toasted almonds.

With chicken livers: Sauté ½ pound of chicken livers in butter very gently until just done. Add to the casserole.

Herbed: Sauté ¼ cup of finely chopped green onions and ½ cup of finely chopped celery. Add these and ½ cup of chopped parsley and ½ cup of toasted almonds to the casserole in place of the sautéed onion and mush-rooms.

With mushroom garnish: While the barley is baking, sauté an additional half pound of mushrooms in butter. Cook them whole. Let the mush-rooms cook down until they are very rich—almost black. Mix with plenty of whole toasted almonds and serve the casserole with the mushroom-al-mond mixture spread over the top. This is excellent with a poultry din-ner (chicken, turkey, duck or feathered game).

Cornmeal

This is one of America's contributions in the field of food. Italians are very fond of cornmeal and have devised some interesting ways to prepare it. Try to find water-ground cornmeal. It has a fine, rich flavor and is best for all purposes. There are small water mills still operating in the East and South, and their products are packaged and sold in the finest food shops across the country. If you cannot find water-ground meal in your area, many mills will ship directly to you.

POLENTA (Serves 4)

1½ cups of cornmeal　　　　　**1 teaspoon of salt**
4½ cups of water

In a very heavy saucepan, bring the water and salt to a boil. Slowly add the cornmeal, stirring constantly to be sure it does not lump. You must add it just a bit at a time. Continue cooking and stirring until the mix-ture is smooth and thick. Pour it into a mold, or line a sieve or strainer with cloth and pour it into that. Steam over hot water, covered, for 1 hour, or until the cornmeal has become a firm loaf.

Serve cut in slices with plenty of butter, salt, pepper and, if you like, grated Parmesan cheese.

Note: If you use quick-cooking cornmeal, follow the directions on the package, and serve as directed above.

VARIATIONS

With sauce: Serve with any of the tomato sauces, cheese sauces, or spaghetti sauces suggested in the Sauce or Pasta chapters.

With cheese: Cut into slices, brush liberally with melted butter and sprinkle with cheese. Run under the broiler to brown.

GNOCCHI (Serves 4)

1 cup of cornmeal	**6 tablespoons of butter**
3 cups of water	**½ cup of grated Parmesan**
½ teaspoon of salt	**cheese**

Cook as for Polenta (page 174), and as soon as the cornmeal is smooth and thick, remove from the heat. Stir in 2 tablespoons of butter and ¼ cup of grated cheese, and blend thoroughly. Pour the mixture into a shallow buttered pan, and spread it evenly to make a layer about ½ inch thick. Allow to cool.

Cut into 1½-inch squares or rounds and arrange, slightly overlapping, in a buttered baking dish. Melt the remaining butter and pour over the gnocchi. Sprinkle with the rest of the cheese. Bake in a 350° oven for 15 minutes, or until lightly brown and bubbly, or run under a broiler for a few minutes to heat through and brown.

Serve with meat dishes, particularly chicken, veal, ham, pork or sausage.

SPOONBREAD—See page 48.

MEAT

"Heaven sends us good meat, but the devil sends cooks," so people said in the eighteenth century. Let's face the fact that being a good cook means, first of all, being able to cook meat well. Meat is the main attraction at any major meal, and if it is not good, no amount of tasty salad, vegetable or dessert is going to appease the dissatisfied family or guests.

Before you can cook meat, you must buy it. Knowing how to select the best quality and the right cut is half the answer to having fine results on your table.

Beef

Beef is the most popular meat among Americans. It is pictured in color advertisements as bright cherry red with creamy white fat. That is how it looks when it is freshly cut. The outside of a well-aged piece of beef, however, may be dark red and even greenish with mold. When cut, the inside is still bright red and fresh-looking. Beef lovers generally prefer aged meat. It is tenderer and has more flavor. Properly aged beef has lost the watery fluid in the aging process, with the result that while it costs more, there is less shrinkage in cooking. Most butchers age beef only 2 to 3 weeks: a few fine butcher shops keep theirs hung for perhaps 3 months. If you like truly aged beef with the rich beefy flavor, you will hunt up such a shop.

Avoid, if you can, buying already packaged meats. They tend to lose their juice and flavor as they stand in their plastic wrappers. You will also find that some stores make up packages with the best cuts on top, and when you get them home and open them, the pieces of meat underneath are inferior.

Beef comes in several grades, selected and approved by U.S. government inspectors and identified by the government stamp on the outside fat. Look for the purple mark on the fat; read it and you will know the grade of meat.

Grades of Beef

Prime: Beef so stamped is hard to find, as much of it is bought by leading hotels and restaurants, but the finer butcher shops carry it. Prime beef comes from the heaviest steers and is fatty, with streaks of fat running through the lean. (This streaking is termed "marbling.")

Choice: This is the grade most generally sold throughout the country. Not as heavy nor as fatty as *prime,* but still excellent beef.

Good: This grade is acceptable for long-, slow-cooking dishes such as pot roasts or stews. Steaks from *good* grade beef need to be tenderized or marinated in a vinegar or wine liquid before cooking. Otherwise they will be tough.

Commercial and Utility grades of beef are generally reserved for commercial use only.

Cuts of Beef

STEAKS

Porterhouse: This is probably the choicest cut since it includes the filet and loin (or contrafilet). It is also the most expensive and obviously a cut for special or party occasions. It should be cut thick—at least 2 inches, and if possible, 3 or 4 inches.

T-bone: This is actually a porterhouse cut from the small end of the loin. Being not as large around, it is a good choice if you wish to serve individual steaks. It is as expensive as the porterhouse and should also be cut thick.

Tenderloin: This is the filet from the loin. It is the tenderest but not necessarily the most flavorful portion of the beef. A whole tenderloin weighs from 3 to 6 pounds and if rolled and wrapped in fat (barded) may be cooked in one piece. Various individual slices of tenderloin are known as "filet mignon," "châteaubriand" and "tournedos." It is the most expensive cut by weight, but since there is no bone and no fat, the actual cost is no greater than for a fine porterhouse.

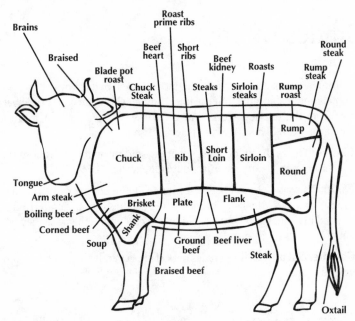

Sirloin: This steak is cut from the high part of the loin. It is flavorful and less expensive than the porterhouse, but there is often a large amount of waste because of the high percentage of bone. A whole sirloin cut several inches thick makes an excellent meal for a large group. Top sirloin, sometimes called "club steak" or "Delmonico steak," is a boneless cut from the end of the loin. It is not as choice as a fine sirloin or porterhouse. "Strip" or "boneless loin," also known as the "New York cut" in the West (but not in New York), is really a porterhouse with the filet and sometimes the bone removed.

Rib Steak: This is also called "entrecôte" or "club steak." It can be delicious if not too fat. It should be cut from the first few ribs and is even better if the bone is left in. It is excellent broiled. To carve, cut out the bone and slice the meat diagonally.

Rump Steak: This cut is less well known, but if from the best grade of beef it can be an excellent choice. It is boneless and therefore less expensive in the long run. It should be cut about 3 inches thick.

Chuck Steak: If your butcher carries prime beef, a chuck steak will be tender. Otherwise it should be marinated or tenderized before cooking.

Flank Steak: This is often called "London broil." It is the triangular piece on the underside below the loin. The major problem with flank steak is its texture. The meat comes in long, fibrous strips, but if cooked properly and carved on the bias in very thin slices, it is flavorful.

Skirt Steak: This formerly overlooked cut—a narrow strip from the plate—has become much sought after and as expensive as the top grade steaks. It has a stringy texture similar to that of flank steak, though it is richer in flavor. It is sometimes rolled up and broiled but is usually broiled flat. It takes well to marinating.

Minute Steak: This is a small steak of about 6 ounces, usually cut from the strip or the sirloin. It will take more than a minute to cook—timing depends on its thickness—and can be treated like any larger steak, though it really needs only salt and pepper.

ROASTS

Rib roast: This is the finest of beef roasts. There is a good deal of waste because of the bones, and if you have prime beef, there will also be a large amount of fat. Actually a fine large steak is a more economical buy, but there are times when a savory roast is just the thing. The first 3 ribs are the best. Have the butcher remove the chine bone and cut the rib bones short. A rolled rib roast saves you the trouble of wrestling with bones and fat, but it is not so magnificent in appearance as the standing rib roast. The Spencer roast is found in some parts of the country. This, too, is a rib roast removed from the bones. A whole Spencer roast is excellent for roasting on a spit for a large party.

Sirloin roast: This is the famous English roast of beef. It is more expensive but probably just as economical in the long run as there is less waste. A fine sirloin is very flavorful and, some people contend, far better than the rib roast.

Rump roast: If from prime beef, this cut can be a very tasty roast. If not prime, it should be treated as a pot roast for best results.

POT ROASTS, BRAISED DISHES

Rump, chuck, eye of round or *bottom round, brisket* and *shoulder (or arm)* are all good cuts for long, slow cooking. The brisket usually has a great deal of fat attached to it. Cut this off or have the butcher do it for you.

BOILED BEEF

Brisket: This is the choice cut for boiling. The fatty quality is an asset in this process. Fat can be cut away after cooking when the meat is arranged on the platter.

Flank: Another good cut for boiling, but the texture is probably less pleasing than that of brisket.

Short Ribs: A good choice for boiling if they are very meaty. There is more waste in this cut, since there is so much bone, but the broth from the boiling will be richer.

Rump: This, too, makes good boiling beef but is not as flavorful as the brisket or short ribs.

BEEF STEW

For stews and other dishes calling for cut-up pieces of beef, use round steak or top-grade chuck cut in 1½- to 2-inch squares. There is less waste in these than in some other cuts.

SWISS STEAK

For this dish and others like it, such as rolled beef, use lean round or chuck steak.

HAMBURGER

Do not buy ready-ground meat that is simply labeled "hamburger." This is scrap meat with a high percentage of fat and gristle ground with it. You save no money, for it only cooks away. The best buy, because it is the leanest, is top round. Some people, who like a little more fat, choose sirloin or chuck. If possible, select the piece of meat and have it ground to order.

Amounts to Buy

Many people will tell you that 1 pound of boneless beef will serve 4 people. These are small servings indeed, and few hungry men would be satisfied. About ⅓ pound of lean boneless beef makes a medium serving, and ½ pound is more generous. When the beef has a small amount of bone, allow at least ½ pound per serving. If it has a large amount of bone, allow more. The butcher can usually help you judge how far the piece of beef you buy will go.

Care and Storage of Beef

Do not store fresh beef in your refrigerator for more than 2 or 3 days. If possible, buy it just before you cook it. Of course, you can keep it much longer in a deep freeze. Beef should be room temperature when cooked, so remember to take it out of the refrigerator several hours before preparing it. Do not keep ground beef over 24 hours. It is very perishable. Store all raw beef loosely wrapped. If it comes packaged in plastic, remove the packaging and wrap it lightly in waxed paper.

Store cooked beef in a tightly covered container or tightly wrapped in foil. Uncovered cooked beef will dry out in the refrigerator and will sometimes lose its flavor.

Steak

The argument concerning the best method for cooking a steak rages constantly up and down the land. One befuddled New York hostess held what she termed a "Steak Tasting." She invited four friends with definite opinions on the subject and had each one prepare a steak in his or her favorite way. Then guests tasted and voted. One steak was pan-broiled; one was broiled under a gas flame; one was broiled with electricity; and one was sautéed and served up with a sauce. Most of the guests preferred the first—the pan-broiled.

Here are the basic ways to prepare steak, and the good and bad points of each.

Pan-Broiled: If properly done, this method will give you a juicy, flavorful result. It takes a deft hand, good judgment and strong eyes, for it is a smoky process.

Heat a large, heavy skillet—stainless steel, cast aluminum or steel and copper are best. An iron skillet will do, but not as well. Be sure the steak is trimmed of all excess fat. (This helps cut down the smoke problem.) When the skillet is very hot, add a thin layer of salt and spread it over the bottom evenly. Place the steak (and one about 1½ inches thick is best for this method) on the salt and brown it very quickly. Turn and brown the other side. Lower the flame and cook for about 6 minutes before turning again. Then cook the second side for another 4 or 5 minutes. This should give you a rare steak, but never take a chance. Test with a sharp knife near the bone. It's the only way you can see the color in the middle. Some people say you should never cut into a steak and should never turn it more than once while cooking. But if the steak has been well seared at the start it will hold its juices through one more turning; and cutting into it is necessary if you want to be sure of its state of doneness.

It is difficult to give exact timings for cooking steaks to the rare stage, the medium stage or the well-done stage. Cooking time depends on the type of heat, the stove itself, the type of skillet, the thickness of the steak and even on your definition of the terms "rare," "medium" and "well-done." Eight minutes to a side for rare steak is at best a guess; allow ten minutes, about, for medium; and longer for well-done, of course.

When your pan-broiled steak is done to your satisfaction, remove it to a hot platter. It should not need salt, but you may add a generous grinding of fresh black pepper and a good smear of butter, if you like. Steak cooked this way is covered with a delicious crunchy brown crust and needs no special seasoning or sauce.

Broiled Under Gas Flame: Some people insist on broiling steak quickly under a hot gas flame. I feel that with gas a longer, slower cooking gives a better result. If you have a thermometer for your broiler, heat it to 350°. Otherwise, heat the broiler, and then reduce the flame so that it is not roaring high. (A little more than a medium flame should be about right.) Grease the rack with a little of the fat trimmed from the steak. Be sure your steak is at least an inch thick for this process, and 1½ to 3 inches is even better. Slash the fat on the steak in several places, then arrange the steak on the broiler rack and place it about 3 inches from the flame. Allow 4 to 5 minutes cooking on the first side before turning. (This is for a 1½- to 2-inch steak.) Cook for another 5 to 6 minutes, and then test for doneness by cutting near the bone with a sharp knife. This length of time should give you a rare steak. For medium or well-done, cook longer before turning. The outside should be well browned by the time the steak is done. If not, raise the heat for the last few minutes. Remove the steak to a hot platter, season to taste with salt and freshly ground black pepper and add a smearing of butter, if you wish.

Note: If your steak is much more than 2 inches thick, it is best to sear it well on both sides under a high flame, before reducing the heat to cook it through. Allow more time.

Broiled with Electricity: This method is excellent from one standpoint. It gives even, well-controlled heat; but it is difficult to get a good brown crust with electricity. I find that by the time the steak is well browned on the outside, it is much too well done inside for my taste. Follow the instructions for broiling with gas.

Sautéed Steak: Many Americans think it is a crime to sauté a steak, yet French and Italians get excellent results with this method. The classic French Steak au Poivre, which is sautéed, is a magnificent dish, and many cuts—such as tenderloin, filet mignon, tournedos—are much better cooked gently in hot butter than broiled. They need the added lubrication.

Do not try to cook too thick a steak by this method. It is best for minute steaks about ½ inch thick (these come from the loin or sirloin), for slices of tenderloin cut 1 to 1½ inches thick, and for any other steak not over 1½ inches. Heat a large skillet and add enough butter or olive oil to put a good film of grease over the bottom. (If the meat has no fat, you may need to add more during the cooking.) When the grease is hot, put in the steak, or steaks, and sear them on the bottom. Lower the flame and cook gently. Turn and sear the other side. If the steak is small and thin—about ½ inch—a minute or so to a side is plenty of time. A thicker steak, say 1½ inches, will take 4 or 5 minutes cooking on each side.

Remove to a hot platter and season to taste with salt and pepper. Many people like to rinse out the skillet in which the steak has cooked with a little liquor (Cognac, bourbon, dry vermouth or red wine), and pour it over the meat as a sauce. To do this: Add 1 tablespoon of liquid for each serving to the skillet, blend with the pan juices and heat through. Pour it over the steaks.

Broiled Over Charcoal: This method has rapidly become one of the American male's favorite ways of preparing steak. If you have the proper equipment and the proper place to do it, it can be great fun and fine eating at the same time.

First about the fire. For most steaks you will need 35 to 40 pieces of charcoal. Heap them in your grill in a pyramid, or put them in your fire-lighter. Add 4 or 5 pieces of charcoal or briquets that have been soaking in a can of charcoal lighter or paint thinner for several hours. Light the fire and let the charcoal burn down until it is covered with white ash. Spread the ashy-colored charcoal around on the surface of the grill in an area large enough to heat the steak. Grease the rack and place the steak about 4 to 5 inches above the coals. A 2-inch steak will cook to the rare stage with about 5 to 6 minutes on each side. If you like a very crusty outside, move the coals closer to the meat for the last minute or so.

Try to cook the steak with only one turning, if possible, and use tongs when you do turn it. If the coals catch fire from the dripping fat and flame up, simply spray some water on them. Not too much, of course, or you will put them out entirely. One of the fine spray bottles used for sprinkling clothes is just the right answer.

When the steak is done, remove it to a hot platter and season it with salt and freshly ground black pepper.

Carving the large steak: If you are grilling a large steak for several people, place it on a hot platter or on a wooden carving board. With a sharp knife, cut the bone out completely. (Don't throw it away; it's wonderful to gnaw on.) Then slice diagonally across the steak in long strips. This gives each person a chance at all parts of the meat.

Steak Recipes

PLAIN STEAK (Serves 4)

4 to 6 pounds of sirloin or porterhouse or 4 T-bone steaks

Salt

Freshly ground black pepper

3 or 4 tablespoons of butter

Sauce, if desired

Pan-broil, broil in the oven or charcoal-broil (see instructions pages 182–184) to suit your taste. Place on a hot platter, season to taste with salt and freshly ground black pepper and add a good smearing of butter.

With a sharp knife, remove the bone and carve the steak diagonally in long strips. Serve with Béarnaise Sauce, Sauce Diable, Wine Merchant's Sauce, mustard or horseradish. If you insist on serving catsup, heat it first.

Suggested accompaniments: sautéed potatoes or Lyonnaise Potatoes, sliced tomatoes and raw onions dressed with oil and vinegar and seasoned with a dash of oregano.

Note: Leftover steak is delicious served in thin slices on toast. A tasty breakfast dish.

STEAK AU POIVRE (Serves 4)

Traditionally, this dish is sautéed. It can be broiled if you wish.

4 pounds of sirloin or porterhouse at least 1½ inches thick	**Salt**
	1 jigger of Cognac or whiskey
4 teaspoons of black peppercorns	

Roll the peppercorns with a rolling pin until they are crushed (or put them through a coarse grinder). Place the steak on a worktable and sprinkle half the crushed peppercorns on top of it. With the heel of your hand, press the pepper into the flesh of the meat firmly. Turn the steak over, and press the rest of the pepper into the other side.

Heat a heavy skillet and grease it lightly with some of the fat trimmed from the steak. Cook the steak according to directions for sautéing or panbroiling (pages 182–183), and when done to suit your taste, remove it to a hot platter and season with salt. Add Cognac or whiskey to the skillet, swirl it around in the pan to gather up the juices, and pour it over the steak.

VARIATION

With sour cream: Cook as directed above. Remove the steak from the skillet, and put it on a flame-proof platter. Pour a jigger of Cognac or whiskey over it and ignite it. Add a few drops of liquor to the skillet and 1 cup of sour cream. Blend and heat just to the boiling point. Season to taste with salt and serve in a sauceboat with the steak.

Suggested accompaniments: Baked potato dressed with butter, chopped parsley and crumbled bacon.

RIB STEAK (Serves 4)

2 to 4 rib steaks (depending on size)	**Pepper**
	Sauce, if desired
Salt	

Rib steaks vary in size; a small one will serve one person and a large one will serve two. The first five ribs are the tastiest. Broil them by your favorite method (see instructions pages 182–184). Remove to a hot platter and season to taste.

Serve with any of the sauces suggested above for sirloin or porterhouse. Rib steak is especially good with Bordelaise Sauce.

Suggested accompaniments: Slices of Poached Marrow (page 223), Oven-fried Potatoes or French-fried Potatoes and French-fried Parsley.

French-fried Parsley: Drop sprigs of parsley, a few at a time, into deep hot fat. The parsley will cook in a few seconds—at the most a half minute. Remove it at once and drain on absorbent paper. It should be crisp but not too shriveled.

RUMP STEAK FLAMANDE (Serves 4)

2- to 3-pound rump steak	**2 tablespoons of rosemary leaves**
Salt	

Let the steak stand at room temperature for some time, until it gets rather soft. Two or three hours should do. About 30 minutes before you plan to cook it, press dried rosemary leaves into the flesh of the steak on both sides, using about 1 tablespoon on each side. Press the herb in firmly with the heel of your hand so that it sticks in the meat. Broil according to your favorite method (pages 182–184) and serve on a hot platter. Season with salt and add a smearing of butter, if you like. The charred rosemary leaves on the outside of the steak give it an unusual and pleasing taste.

Suggested accompaniments: Very crisp Home-fried Potatoes and fresh asparagus with melted butter.

TENDERLOIN OR FILET (Serves 4)

4 tenderloin or filet steaks cut 2½ inches thick	**Butter**
Salt	**Sauce, if desired**
Pepper	

One tenderloin steak serves one person. These steaks may be broiled, but since they have practically no fat, they are better pan-broiled or sautéed. If you plan to broil them, have the butcher bard them with beef fat, salt pork or bacon. Cook them according to directions above, place them on hot plates and season to taste with salt, pepper and butter. Serve with Béarnaise Sauce, Sauce Diable or Bordelaise Sauce.

Suggested accompaniments: Baked potatoes and sautéed mushrooms.

TENDERLOIN STEAK, VERA CRUZ FASHION (Serves 4)

4 filets	Salt
Butter	Pepper
1 dozen mushrooms	8 ounces of rum
4 slices of pineapple	

Prepare the steak as for Tenderloin, page 186. While the steak is cooking, melt 2 tablespoons of butter in a small skillet and sauté 1 dozen medium-sized mushrooms until brown and tender. In another skillet melt 1 tablespoon of butter and sauté 4 slices of canned or fresh pineapple until slightly browned on both sides.

When the steak is done, salt and pepper to taste, arrange 1 pineapple slice on each plate, top it with an individual steak, and add 3 mushrooms as garnish. Pour 2 ounces of rum over each serving and ignite. Bring to the table flaming.

Suggested accompaniments: Sautéed eggplant is an excellent contrast for this unusual steak dish.

WHOLE BROILED TENDERLOIN (Serves 6 to 12)

Whole tenderloin 3 to 6 pounds (allow ½ to ¾ pound per person)	Salt
	Pepper
Melted butter or beef fat	

This is a very simple way to serve a large number of people. It is expensive, but then you do get all lean beef—no fat, no bones. Have the butcher tie it for you.

Broil it under gas or electricity or over charcoal according to directions on page 183. Use a meat thermometer, inserting it in the thickest part of the tenderloin. Broil the meat slowly, brushing it often with melted butter or beef fat and turning it to be sure it is evenly cooked all around. When the meat thermometer registers 120°, it should be done to the rare stage. Remove the filet to a hot platter, season to taste and cut in serving slices. Pass Béarnaise Sauce if you like.

Suggested accompaniments: A party menu built around a whole broiled tenderloin might include baked potatoes, with a large tray of dressings for the potatoes, such as whipped butter, rosemary butter, sour cream, crumbled bacon, grated cheese, chopped chives or little green onions, chopped parsley, chopped pimientos; a good tossed salad with plain oil and vinegar dressing, hot French bread or rolls, fresh fruit, cheese and a good dry red wine.

FILET MIGNON (Serves 4)

4 filets mignons	**Pepper**
2 tablespoons of butter	**4 pieces of crisp toast**
Salt	

The Filet Mignon comes from the end of the tenderloin. It is small, and hence the name mignon, which means tiny or petite. It is flattened out and rolled with a bacon or pork strip. (The butcher does this job; you don't.) It is best when sautéed quickly in butter (page 183) and served on crisp toast. Season to taste after cooking.

Suggested accompaniments: Potatoes Anna and buttered asparagus.

VARIATIONS

With white wine: Cook as above. When the filets are done, remove them to hot plates. To the pan add ⅓ cup of dry white wine or dry vermouth, 1 tablespoon of chopped or 1 teaspoon of dried tarragon, salt and pepper to taste and 1 tablespoon of butter. Blend and heat through and pour over the filets.

Suggested accompaniments: Fresh green beans, dressed with plenty of butter, and hot French bread.

Filet Mignon Rossini: This is an elegant party dish. Prepare the filets as in the basic recipe and while they are cooking, sauté 4 mushroom caps in 1 tablespoon of butter until they are brown and tender. Stuff each mushroom cap with mousse of foie gras (this comes in tins).

Arrange the cooked filets on slices of crisp toast. Season to taste with salt and pepper and top each filet with a stuffed mushroom cap. Crown this in turn with half a ripe olive.

Suggested accompaniments: For an elegant party dinner, start with smoked salmon, or a fine clear soup. Follow with the filets, shoestring potatoes, glazed tiny white onions, hot French bread, ice cream, fresh (or frozen) peaches, cheese and Cognac.

Filet Mignon Provençale: Prepare filets as in the basic recipe and while they are cooking, sauté or grill (broil) 4 thick onion slices. Sauté 4 to 6 chopped mushrooms in 1 tablespoon of butter at the same time. When the filets are done, place each one on a grilled onion slice, season to taste with salt and pepper and top with sautéed mushrooms.

Suggested accompaniments: Tomato slices, grilled with chopped garlic and parsley, and boiled parsley potatoes.

RUMP STEAK (Serves 4)

3 to 4 pounds of prime grade rump	**Pepper**
Salt	**Butter**

Buy a thick cut of rump—3 to 4 inches thick—and broil it whole by any of the methods listed (pages 182–184). It should broil very slowly so the heat can penetrate to the center and the outside get brown and crusty. A thick piece of rump will take 45 minutes to an hour to reach the rare stage. Turn it several times during the broiling to be sure it cooks evenly. Remove it to a hot platter, season to taste with salt and freshly ground black pepper and a good dab of butter. Slice thin.

Suggested accompaniments: French-fried potatoes, sliced tomatoes, onions and cucumbers, toasted French bread and cheese.

Note: This is delicious cold the next day.

STEAK SANDWICHES

Rump steak	**French bread**
Salt	**Rosemary Butter or Garlic Butter**
Pepper	
Butter	

Cook a rump steak on your outdoor charcoal grill (page 183). Split a loaf of French bread the long way and toast each half. Butter the bread well. Arrange thin slices of the meat on the bottom half of the bread and cover with the top half. Slice through in pieces for hearty steak sandwiches. If you like, butter the bread with Garlic Butter or Rosemary Butter (pages 354–355).

Suggested accompaniments: A bowl of radishes, onions and celery and a bowl of heated potato chips. Fruit and ice cream for dessert.

LONDON BROIL (Serves 4)

3-pound flank steak   **Salt and pepper**

Many people insist that flank steak must be cooked by a long, slow process. This well-known dish calls for *broiling* flank steak and is delicious if properly served. The secret is in the carving.

This is the one exception to the rule that you must always cook meat at room temperature. Flank steak should be at refrigerator temperature, so take it out at the last minute. Remove the tough membrane on the outside. You will need the help of a sharp knife for this.

Broil it quickly by gas, electricity or charcoal (pages 182–184), allowing about 5 minutes on each side. Season to taste with salt and pepper and remove it to a hot platter or carving board. Now comes the tricky part. With a very sharp knife held at an angle, slice diagonally through to the bottom. This cuts across the tough fibers of the flank. The slices should be very thin and the meat should be rare inside. Otherwise it will be tough.

Serve the hot slices of steak on hot toasted and buttered French bread.

Suggested accompaniments: French-fried onion rings and plain boiled potatoes in their jackets.

VARIATION

Orientale: Combine ½ cup of soy sauce with ¾ cup of dry vermouth or dry red wine, a 1-inch piece of fresh ginger grated (or candied ginger finely chopped), 3 cloves of garlic chopped and a handful of chopped parsley. Pour this mixture into the bottom of a deep platter or dish large enough to hold the steak. Marinate the steak in this sauce for several hours, turning it occasionally. Then broil as above, brushing it during the cooking with the marinade. Do not season the steak after cooking.

Suggested accompaniments: Buttered rice and spinach.

COSTATA ALLA PIZZAIOLA (Serves 4)

This Italian steak dish, typical of Naples, can be made with flank, tenderized round steak, or rib steak.

3 pounds of steak

1/2 cup of olive oil

3 cloves of garlic, finely chopped

1/2 cup of chopped green onions

1   can of solid-pack tomatoes

1 can of Italian tomato paste

1 teaspoon of oregano

Salt and pepper

Olive oil or butter

First, prepare the sauce: Heat the 1/2 cup of olive oil in a skillet and add the chopped garlic and the chopped green onions. Sauté until limp. Add the can of tomatoes, tomato paste, oregano and salt and pepper to taste. Simmer slowly for 1 hour.

Sauté the steak in olive oil or butter (see page 183) and when it is done to your taste, remove it to a hot platter and pour the sauce over it.

Suggested accompaniments: Fettucine Alfredo and a salad of orange and onion rings, dressed with oil and vinegar and garnished with green pepper strips.

Roast Beef

Preparation of the roast: Wipe the roast with a damp cloth and dry it well. You may rub it with salt and pepper before cooking, or season it halfway through the roasting. There are those who claim that salting at the start draws out the juices, but I have often done it and still had a juicy roast. It is certainly easier to salt before cooking. Stand the meat in an un-covered roasting pan, or any baking pan deep enough to hold the drip-pings. If you have a rack that fits in the pan, put it in and place the meat on top of the rack. This is not absolutely necessary, but if there is a great deal of fat on the roast, it will keep the meat from sizzling in the drip-pings.

The only way to be absolutely sure of the state of doneness of a roast is to use a meat thermometer. Buy one that registers from 0° to 220°. This is the best. Insert the thermometer in the fleshiest part of the roast, or test during cooking.

Roasting Methods: There are two methods for roasting beef. The first method: Heat the oven to 425° to 450°. Cook the meat at this tempera-ture for 30 minutes, or until it is well seared. Lower the temperature to

325° and continue cooking until done to your taste. Do not baste roast beef.

The second method: Heat the oven to 325° and roast the meat at this temperature until done to your taste. Do not baste. This method takes slightly longer.

Cooking Time: When using a meat thermometer, remove the roast when it registers 120° to 125° if you like rare beef. Then let the meat stand for 15 to 20 minutes before carving. It will continue to cook after being removed from the oven, the juices will settle and the texture will be firmer. If you like medium-rare beef, cook until the thermometer registers 130°; for medium, cook to 140°; and for well-done, cook to 150°.

If you have no thermometer, use the following tables:

For First Method (Searing)

Rare beef	12 to 14 minutes per pound
Medium-rare beef	14 to 15 minutes per pound

Note: The smaller the roast, the longer the time per pound.

For Second Method (325°)

Rare beef	15 to 17 minutes per pound
Medium-rare beef	17 to 20 minutes per pound

If you are not using a thermometer, check the state of doneness by cutting next to the bone with a sharp knife.

Roast Recipes

STANDING RIBS OF BEEF (Serves 4)

5-pound rib roast	**Pepper**
Salt	**10 medium-sized potatoes**

This is the most popular beef roast. The larger it is, the tastier; a three-rib roast is about the smallest desirable size. Remember, the first three ribs are the best. A five-rib roast is an elegant dish, and for a large party, a 7- or 8-rib roast is a magnificent sight to see, if your oven is big enough to hold it. Allow at least 1 pound of rib roast per person. Cold beef is no problem.

Have the butcher cut off the short ribs, and use them for dinner the next day. Then have him remove the feather bone and chine bone (this makes carving easier), but don't have the ribs cracked. The roast should be tied for the oven and an extra piece of suet put on the end for lubrication.

Be sure to let the meat stand out of the refrigerator for several hours before cooking. Then wipe it off, season it and stand it on the rib bones in the roasting pan. Cook according to instructions on page 191.

One hour before the roast is done, arrange peeled and halved potatoes around it in the pan and let them cook and brown in the fat and drippings. Baste them occasionally, and turn them over when they have cooked about ½ hour.

BEEF GRAVY

3 tablespoons of drippings	Pepper
3 tablespoons of flour	Glace de Viande or
1½ cups of liquid (stock or milk)	commercial sauce browner
Salt	

Roast beef is best served plain with the pan juices and perhaps a little horseradish or mustard. If you insist on having a thick beef gravy, here is the recipe: In a skillet blend the drippings from the roast with the flour. Cook and stir until lightly browned. Gradually add the heated liquid. This can be beef stock, or 1½ cups of hot water blended with 2 bouillon cubes, or milk. Stir constantly while adding the liquid, and continue stirring and cooking until the mixture is smooth and thick. Season to taste with salt and freshly ground black pepper. Add a few drops of glace de viande or sauce browner, if you like a darker gravy.

The classic accompaniment for roast beef is Yorkshire Pudding. It is crisp and puffy and flavored with beef drippings. Here is the recipe:

YORKSHIRE PUDDING

2 eggs, beaten	Salt
1 cup of milk	Beef drippings
Scant cup of flour	

Beat the eggs until light and fluffy. Gradually beat in the flour and milk. Add a good pinch of salt and 2 tablespoons of the beef drippings from the roast. Heat a baking pan or ring mold in the oven and pour ¼ cup of beef drippings over the bottom of the pan. Pour in the mixture and bake in a 450° oven for 10 minutes. Then reduce the heat and cook at 350° for 10 to 15 minutes longer, or until puffy and delicately browned. This can be done after the roast is removed from the oven and while it is standing to let the juices settle.

Serve the pudding cut in squares.

VARIATION

In muffin tins: Some people like to cook the pudding in individual muffin tins. Heat the tins, add a spoonful of drippings to each one and fill to ⅓ full with the pudding mixture. These will cook faster—in about 15 minutes, but they are less like pudding and more like popovers.

Suggested accompaniments: With your beef roast, browned potatoes and Yorkshire Pudding you might serve Rosemary Butter (see under Herb Butter, page 354). It is a delicious seasoning for all three. Also serve sautéed or baked onions, mashed yellow turnips, or Brussels sprouts.

BONED AND ROLLED BEEF ROAST—Follow instructions for the rib roast, page 192.

LEFTOVER BEEF ROAST

Why leftover beef should ever be a problem I cannot understand. There is nothing better than cold roast, sliced paper thin and served with mustard, chutney or pickled walnuts (these can be found in almost any food specialty shop). Meat to be served cold should be removed from the refrigerator an hour or so before eating to allow it to return to room temperature. Icy-cold meat has no flavor.

Suggested accompaniments: Fried potatoes (if there are any left from the roast beef dinner, use these and brown them in beef drippings) and coleslaw or a green salad with sliced raw mushrooms added to it.

For hot dishes with leftover roast beef:

Deviled Beef Slices: Beat 2 eggs until light and frothy. Pour fine bread crumbs into a shallow dish. Slice the beef in rather thick pieces, dip each one into the egg and then roll in the crumbs. Melt butter or beef drippings in a skillet and cook the beef slices until the crumbs are crusty and brown and the meat is hot through. Serve with Sauce Diable (page 351).

Deviled Beef Bones: If a little of the meat is left on the rib bones by the carver, these may be cooked in the same manner as Deviled Beef Slices (see page 194). Serve with Sauce Diable.

VARIATION

Broil the bones under a low flame until crispy and brown. Serve with Sauce Diable (page 351).

SIRLOIN ROAST—Cook as you do the standing rib roast, page 192.

RUMP ROAST

This is less expensive than rib or sirloin roast. It will not be as tender, but a prime quality rump roast has an excellent flavor. Wipe it off with a damp cloth, season it with salt and freshly ground black pepper, and rub it with a little dried rosemary, if you like the flavor. Follow the general directions for cooking roast beef (pages 191–192). Do not baste.

Serve the rump roast with the accompaniments suggested for rib roast.

Pot Roasts, Braised Beef, Stews

The best cuts for this type of cooking are round and rump. Brisket, chuck and shoulder (or arm) are also good. If you are cooking the meat in one large piece—a pot roast, for example—have it rolled and tied. It will carve more easily. If you like a rich sauce, ask the butcher for extra bones to cook with the meat. A veal knuckle is exceptionally good. Allow $3/4$ to 1 pound of meat per person, and don't be afraid of leftovers. Cold pot roast or braised beef is tasty.

Pot-roasting or braising is especially adapted to the less tender cuts of beef or to the less expensive grades. The long, slow cooking process breaks down the fibers of the meat and tenderizes it. The basic method is very simple: Use a deep, heavy pot with a tight cover. In this heat fat or oil, and then sear the meat on all sides over high heat. Add seasonings and some liquid, cover the pot, and simmer very gently over low heat for a long time—as much as several hours. Sometimes vegetables are added when the meat is partly cooked, and a sauce may be made from the juices.

PLAIN POT ROAST (Serves 4)

4 pounds of rump, chuck or round

Salt

Freshly ground black pepper

Flour

4 tablespoons of butter, beef fat or bacon fat

1 clove of garlic

1 onion

2 cloves

1 bay leaf

1 stalk of celery

1 cup of liquid (water, wine, beef broth, or tomato juice)

Buy a 4-pound piece of chuck, rump or bottom round and have the butcher bard it (tie it wrapped in a piece of suet). Heat the butter, beef fat or bacon fat in a deep pot that has a tight-fitting lid. Wipe the meat with a damp cloth, rub it with salt and freshly ground black pepper and roll it in flour. (Sprinkle flour on a piece of waxed paper or on a platter and roll the roast in it until all sides are floured.) When the fat is melted and hot, put the meat in the pot and sear it well, turning it to brown on all sides. Add the garlic, the peeled onion with the cloves stuck into it, the bay leaf and the stalk of celery. Add the liquid—water, wine, beef stock (which can be made from hot water and 1 bouillon cube) or tomato juice. Put the lid on the pot and lower the flame so the meat will simmer gently. The liquid should not boil. Simmer for 25 minutes per pound and turn the meat over once or twice while it is cooking. Add more liquid if the juices evaporate too much. When done, the meat should be thoroughly tender but not stringy or mushy.

If you like a thickened sauce, rub a little soft butter and flour together with your fingers. Keep adding flour until you can roll the mixture into tiny balls the size of green peas. This is *Beurre Manié*. Remove the meat to a hot platter and sprinkle the balls of butter and flour over the surface of the liquid in the pot, stirring constantly until the liquid is smooth and thickened to your taste. About 1½ tablespoons of flour will thicken 1 cup of liquid. Pour the sauce over the meat.

Suggested accompaniments: Arrange boiled potatoes and onions around the meat on the platter and serve with buttered spinach and dill pickles.

YANKEE POT ROAST (Serves 4)

4 pounds of beef	1 teaspoon of dried thyme
Salt	1 stalk of celery
Pepper	1 cup of liquid
Flour	6 small onions, peeled
4 tablespoons of fat	6 to 8 carrots, peeled
2 cloves of garlic	3 turnips, peeled
1 bay leaf	

Start as for the Plain Pot Roast. After the meat is seared, add the garlic, bay leaf, dried thyme, stalk of celery and liquid (water, wine, beef stock or tomato juice). Simmer for 1 hour. Remove the lid and add the onions, carrots and turnips. Salt and pepper the vegetables, put the lid back on and continue simmering until the vegetables are tender and the meat is done.

Remove the meat to a hot platter and surround it with the vegetables. Skim the excess fat from the liquid in the kettle and add more broth or other liquid to make enough for sauce. Thicken with balls of butter and flour kneaded together (see Beurre Manié page 348) and serve separately in a sauceboat.

Suggested accompaniments: Potato pancakes and green salad or sliced tomatoes. Fruit flavored with Cognac or liqueur is an excellent dessert.

BRAISED BEEF, ITALIAN STYLE (Serves 4)

5 pounds of rump, larded	Parsley
3 cloves of garlic	Stalk of celery
Salt	1 cup of tomato juice
Pepper	1 cup of Italian tomato purée
Flour	
4 tablespoons of olive oil	$\frac{1}{2}$ teaspoon of dried basil or 1 tablespoon of chopped fresh basil
2 large onions, coarsely chopped	
2 carrots, sliced	$\frac{1}{2}$ cup of ripe olives
1 teaspoon of oregano	

Buy a 5-pound piece of rump and have the butcher lard it (run strips of salt pork deep into the flesh). This will help to tenderize the meat and give it a richer flavor.

Wipe the meat with a damp cloth. Peel the garlic and cut it into small slivers. With a sharp knife make small gashes in the flesh of the meat and insert a piece of garlic in each gash. Rub the meat well with salt and pepper and roll it in flour (see Plain Pot Roast, page 196). Heat the olive oil in a deep pot and sear the meat quickly, turning it to brown on all sides. Add the onions, the carrots, the oregano, 1 sprig of parsley, and the celery and tomato juice. Cover the pot tightly and simmer over low heat for 2 hours.

Remove the cover and add the tomato purée and dried or fresh basil. Cover again and simmer for another 30 minutes or until the meat is tender. Put the pot roast on a hot platter. Skim the fat from the sauce and add to it ¼ cup of chopped parsley and ½ cup of ripe olives. Heat through and pour into a sauceboat.

Suggested accompaniments: Plain pasta; a salad of escarole and romaine dressed with olive oil and wine vinegar; hot Italian bread; fresh fruit and cheese.

VARIATION

Substitute a dry red wine for the tomato juice as liquid.

HUNGARIAN POT ROAST (Serves 4)

5 pounds of rump	**2 carrots**
4 tablespoons of olive oil or beef fat	**1 teaspoon of oregano**
	Parsley
3 cloves of garlic	**Stalk of celery**
Salt	**1 cup of beef broth**
Pepper	**Paprika**
Flour	**1 cup of sour cream**
2 onions	

Prepare as for Braised Beef, Italian Style (page 197), but substitute beef broth for the tomato juice. You can make this with hot water and a bouillon cube. After the meat, seasonings and broth have simmered for 2 hours, remove the cover and add 1 tablespoon of Hungarian paprika and more broth if needed. Cover again and simmer until tender.

Remove the meat to a hot platter. Skim the fat from the sauce, add 1 teaspoon of paprika, salt (if needed) and 1 cup of sour cream. Cook and stir until hot through, but do not boil or the cream will curdle. Pour into a sauceboat.

Suggested accompaniments: Buttered noodles, sprinkled with poppy seed, and braised cabbage. Spaetzle (page 236) is also an excellent choice.

SAUERBRATEN (Serves 4)

4 pounds of round, rump or chuck	**3 allspice berries**
1 cup of wine vinegar	**3 cloves**
½ cup of cider vinegar	**1 tablespoon of crushed peppercorns**
½ cup of dry red wine	**1 tablespoon of salt**
2 onions, peeled and sliced	**8 tablespoons of butter**
2 carrots, peeled and sliced	**Flour**
1 stalk of celery, finely chopped	**1 tablespoon of sugar**
Handful of parsley	**⅔ cup of crumbled gingersnaps**
1 bay leaf	

Preparing this famous German dish is a long process, but the results are delicious. Buy a 4-pound piece of round, rump or chuck and have it tied. Wipe it with a damp cloth. Make a marinade by combining the wine vinegar, cider vinegar, red wine, onions, carrots, celery, parsley, bay leaf, allspice berries, cloves, crushed peppercorns (use a rolling pin or a coarse grinder) and salt. Mix well and pour into a deep bowl. Place the meat in this mixture, cover it and put it in the refrigerator for 3 days to soak. Turn it several times to be sure the whole of the meat is well bathed.

When you are ready to cook the meat, remove it from the marinade and wipe it dry. Pour the marinade into a pan and heat it. Meanwhile, melt 4 tablespoons of the butter in a deep pot and sear the meat. Sprinkle the meat lightly with flour while it is searing and turn it to brown on all sides. When it is brown, pour the hot marinade over it, cover it tightly, lower the heat and simmer gently for 2½ to 3 hours, or until the meat is tender. Then pour the liquid off the meat and set the pot with the meat aside. Skim the fat from the liquid and strain the broth. Melt 4 more tablespoons of butter in a skillet and blend in 4 tablespoons of flour and the sugar. Cook slowly until the flour and sugar have browned slightly. Gradually add the strained marinade, stirring constantly, and continue cooking and stirring until it is thickened and smooth. Pour this sauce over the meat in the pot, add the gingersnaps and return the meat to the fire. Cover and simmer for 30 minutes.

Suggested accompaniments: Traditionally Sauerbraten is served with dumplings. Personally I prefer boiled potatoes or noodles.

BRAISED BEEF, BORDEAUX FASHION (Serves 4)

This is a French peasant dish from the Bordeaux region in France, and I first ate it there with the local pickers during grape harvest time. The cook prepared five meals a day for fifty hungry field hands. This was one of her specialties:

4 to 5 pounds of brisket	**1 sprig of parsley**
6 tablespoons of beef fat	**1½ cups of broth**
1 teaspoon of salt	**12 to 14 carrots, peeled**
1 teaspoon of pepper	**1 onion, stuck with 2 cloves**
1 bay leaf	**8 to 10 potatoes, peeled**
1 teaspoon of thyme	

Buy a 4- to 5-pound brisket of beef and have the butcher remove some of the excess fat, but take the fat home to use for browning the meat. Wipe the meat with a damp cloth. Melt about 6 tablespoons of the beef fat in a deep pot and sear the meat well on all sides in the hot fat. Add the salt, freshly ground black pepper, bay leaf, thyme, parsley and beef broth or bouillon made with hot water and bouillon cubes. Cover the pot tightly, lower the flame, and simmer slowly for 1½ hours. Remove the cover and add the carrots and the onion stuck with cloves. Cover again and simmer until the carrots are done and the meat tender.

While the meat is finishing, boil the potatoes. Serve the meat sliced on a platter and surrounded by the carrots and potatoes. Pass a bowl of the broth to be eaten with the meat.

Suggested accompaniments: Hot French bread is especially good when dunked in this broth. Also serve a good green salad, a dry red wine, and fruit and cheese for dessert. You will have an unusual, hearty and tasty party menu.

BRAISED BEEF À LA MODE (Serves 4 to 6)

This combination pot roast and boiled-beef dish is another French specialty. It is excellent for a cold luncheon or buffet platter since it jellies nicely. (See end of recipe.)

5 to 6 pounds of rump, sirloin or round, larded and tied	**4 tablespoons of butter**
2 pounds of veal neck	**Salt**
1 calf's foot or veal knuckle	**Pepper**
Water	**¼ cup of Cognac or whiskey**
1 onion, stuck with 2 cloves	**12 small white onions, peeled**
1 sprig of parsley	**12 carrots, peeled**
1 teaspoon of dried thyme	**1 or 2 turnips, peeled**
1 stalk of celery	

Buy 5 to 6 pounds of rump, top sirloin or bottom round. Have the butcher lard it for you and tie it.

First make a broth with the veal neck and the knuckle or calf's foot: Put them in a deep pot and add 2 quarts of water, the onion stuck with cloves, and the parsley, thyme and celery. Cover and simmer slowly for ½ hour. Add 1 tablespoon of salt and continue simmering for 1½ hours.

Wipe the beef with a damp cloth. Heat the butter in a deep pot and sear the meat, browning it quickly on all sides. Salt and pepper it to taste—about 1 teaspoon of each—and pour over it the slightly warmed Cognac or whiskey. Ignite the liquor with a match and let it burn until the flame dies down. Add the bones from the broth and enough of the broth to cover ¾ of the beef. Cover tightly and simmer slowly for 2½ hours. Take off the cover and add the peeled onions, carrots and turnips. Cover again and continue simmering until the vegetables are tender and the meat is done.

Serve as you do Braised Beef, Bordeaux Fashion (see page 200).

VARIATION

Cold Braised Beef, à la Mode: To serve the above dish cold, remove the meat from the broth when it is done and trim off the ragged edges and excess fat. Turn the flame up under the broth and cook it uncovered at a brisk boil until it has reduced to 2 or 3 cups at the most. Then strain it through a linen napkin or several layers of cheesecloth.

Dissolve 1 envelope of unflavored gelatin in ½ cup of cold water and then stir it into 1 cup of boiling strained broth. Add the rest of the broth.

Rinse a deep mold in cold water and in the bottom of it arrange a layer of sliced stuffed olives, sliced hard-cooked eggs and sliced cooked carrots from the meat dish. You may arrange the beef on top of this in one piece or slice it and arrange the slices in neat rows. Over all pour the broth. Let it cool and then place it in the refrigerator to jelly.

When you are ready to serve, unmold the jellied meat onto a platter and garnish it with pickles, sliced hard-cooked eggs, olives and parsley.

Suggested accompaniments: potato salad, sliced tomatoes, garlic bread, a bottle of rosé wine and, for dessert, a baked custard with rum-soaked chestnuts.

Note: You can make Cold Beef à la Mode in individual molds for individual servings. Unmold on serving plates on a bed of greens for an attractive luncheon dish.

SWISS STEAK, OR BRAISED BEEF (Serves 4)

3 pounds of round steak	**3 tablespoons of butter, beef fat or bacon fat**
Flour	
2 cloves of garlic	**2 onions, peeled and sliced**
1 teaspoon of salt	**1 to 1½ cups broth, water or wine**
1 teaspoon of pepper	

The best cut for this steady favorite is round steak. Buy 3 pounds and have it cut thick. Then have it cut into 2-inch squares (or do this yourself). Or you can cook it whole. The process is the same. Sprinkle one side of the meat with plenty of flour, a half teaspoon of salt and a half teaspoon of pepper. Then scatter 1 finely cut clove of garlic over it. With a mallet or the edge of a heavy plate pound the seasonings into the steak, flattening it slightly. Turn the steak over, add the same amount of seasonings on the other side, and pound these in.

In a heavy skillet melt the butter, beef fat or bacon fat. Brown the meat on all sides in the hot fat and add the onions to brown at the same time. When all the meat is thoroughly browned add the broth, wine or water.

You can make the broth with hot water and bouillon cubes. Cover the skillet tightly, lower the heat and simmer for 1½ to 2 hours, or until the meat is tender and the broth thick and rich. Or you can put the skillet in the oven (if it is oven-proof) and bake it at 325° for 1½ to 2 hours.

Suggested accompaniments: Plain boiled potatoes dressed with chopped parsley and butter, scalloped tomatoes and a cucumber salad. If you cook the meat in the oven, you might cook Apple Betty at the same time for dessert.

VARIATIONS

With beer: Prepare the steak as above. When you brown it, add 1½ pounds of onions, peeled and sliced. Instead of the broth, add 1 pint of beer, cover and simmer as above. This is a version of Carbonnade Flamande, a favorite Belgian dish.

With red wine: Prepare the steak as for Swiss Steak, above. In place of butter, try out (cook until crisp) 3 slices of salt pork, chopped, in a skillet and brown the meat in the fat from this. Add 6 onions, peeled and sliced, and brown. Pour over this 1½ cups of red wine and add 1 bay leaf and 1 teaspoon of dried thyme. Cover and simmer as above.

Suggested accompaniments: boiled potatoes and braised carrots.

Hungarian style: Prepare as for Swiss Steak, above, but pound 2 tablespoons of Hungarian paprika into the steak along with the flour and other seasonings. Brown in fat, add 1½ cups of broth, cover and simmer as for Swiss Steak. Remove the meat to a hot platter and add to the broth 1 teaspoon of paprika and 1 cup of sour cream. Heat through, but do not boil. Pour over the steak.

Suggested accompaniments: This is especially good served with buttered Spaetzle (page 236).

Mexicaine: Prepare as for Swiss Steak, above. While the steak is browning add 1 cup of finely chopped onion to the pan and brown with the meat. When the meat is browned, add 1 cup of tomato sauce, ½ cup of broth and 1½ tablespoons of chili powder. Cover and simmer as above. Taste for seasoning. You may like more chili powder.

Suggested accompaniments: Polenta (page 174), chopped raw onions and additional chili sauce.

LES OISEAUX SANS TÊTES (Serves 6)

Translated literally "birds without heads," this is a good party dish, attractive, tasty and actually not difficult to do.

12 pieces of round steak ³/₈
   inch thick and 5 to 6
   inches square

1 large onion, chopped

Butter

6 mushrooms, finely
   chopped

¹/₂ teaspoon of thyme

1 teaspoon of salt

1 teaspoon of pepper

1 clove of garlic, chopped

3 tablespoons of chopped
   parsley

1¹/₂ cups of bread crumbs

1 egg, beaten

¹/₄ cup of melted butter

12 thin slices of ham

4 to 6 tablespoons of fat

Flour

1¹/₂ cups of broth or wine

Make a stuffing first: Brown the onion in 4 tablespoons of butter. Add the chopped mushrooms, thyme, salt, freshly ground black pepper, chopped cloves of garlic, chopped parsley, and fine bread crumbs. Beat the egg and add to the mixture with enough melted butter to moisten the stuffing (about ¹/₄ cup). Spread out the pieces of steak and place on each one a thin slice of ham. Then add a little stuffing, roll up, jelly-roll fashion, and tie securely with string.

In a large skillet melt 4 to 6 tablespoons of butter or beef fat. Roll each "bird" in flour and then brown in the hot fat, turning to sear all sides. When all the "birds" are brown, add 1¹/₂ cups of broth or red wine, cover tightly, lower the flame and simmer slowly for 1¹/₂ to 2 hours. Turn the "birds" often during the simmering to be sure they cook evenly and stay moist. Add more liquid if necessary. Serve with pan juices.

If you like a richer sauce, add 1 cup of sour cream to the pan juices after the "birds" are removed to a hot platter. Blend and heat through, but do not let it boil.

Suggested accompaniments: sautéed potatoes and string beans with bacon.

VARIATION

Omit the ham and use a strip of bacon and 2 anchovy fillets. Also, reduce the amount of salt.

BRAISED SHORT RIBS (Serves 4)

This cut is apt to be quite fat. Look for the leanest you can find. Allow about 1 pound per person, and even more is not extravagant, for short ribs are mostly bone.

4 to 6 pounds of ribs	**2 cloves of garlic**
Flour	**1 bay leaf**
Salt and pepper	**1 cup of liquid (water, broth**
1 onion, stuck with 2 cloves	**or wine)**

Wipe the ribs with a damp cloth and put them in a baking pan with a cover. Sprinkle them lightly with flour and season with salt and pepper. Heat the oven to 450° and roast the ribs for 25 minutes, basting every few minutes with the melting fat in the pan. Then lower the oven temperature to 325° and while it is cooling down, remove the pan and pour off the excess fat. Add the onion stuck with cloves, garlic, bay leaf and liquid (water, beef broth or red wine). Cover the pan and return it to the oven. Continue cooking for 1½ hours.

Remove the ribs to a hot platter and serve the pan juices separately. If you like a thicker sauce, place the pan over a flame and stir in small balls of butter and flour kneaded together (see Beurre Manié, page 348). Continue stirring and cooking until thick and smooth.

Suggested accompaniments: baked potatoes and puréed broccoli.

VARIATIONS

Chinese fashion: Make a marinade for the ribs by mixing 1½ cups of red wine, ¾ cup of soy sauce, 3 finely chopped cloves of garlic, 1 teaspoon of rosemary and 1 tablespoon of chopped fresh or candied ginger. Place this in a deep bowl and soak the ribs in the mixture for 4 to 6 hours. Turn them frequently so they will be thoroughly bathed.

Remove them from the liquid, dry them with paper towels. Melt 4 tablespoons of fat in an oven-proof pan, sprinkle the ribs with flour and brown them on all sides in the hot fat. Add the marinade and bake as above in a 325° oven. Remove the cover for the last ½ hour of baking to give the ribs a glaze.

Suggested accompaniments: steamed rice, petits pois or Chinese snow peas, toasted French bread. For dessert, try baked pears with a soft custard sauce.

BEEFSTEAK AND KIDNEY PIE (Serves 8)

This classic English dish is an excellent choice for an elegant buffet party. The following recipe will serve 8 persons generously.

3 pounds of round steak
3 tablespoons of flour
1 teaspoon of salt
1 teaspoon of black pepper
Thyme
4 tablespoons of chopped suet
1 onion stuck with 2 cloves

Water or bouillon
3 or 4 veal kidneys
3 tablespoons of butter
2 onions, sliced
¹/₄ cup of chopped parsley
Pastry dough
1 egg, lightly beaten

Cut the round steak into strips about 3 inches long and 1¹/₂ inches wide. In a paper sack, put the flour, salt, freshly ground black pepper and a teaspoon of thyme. Add the pieces of meat and shake well. This gives the round steak an even coating of flour and seasonings.

Melt the finely chopped suet, and when it is crisp and the fat is hot, brown the meat in it very quickly. Add the onion stuck with cloves, another pinch of thyme and just enough water or bouillon to cover the meat. Reduce the heat, cover the pan and simmer until tender. This will take about 1¹/₂ hours.

While the steak is simmering, clean 3 or 4 veal kidneys and cut them into neat slices. Peel and slice 2 onions. In a skillet, melt 3 tablespoons of butter and brown the kidney slices. Add the onion slices and cook until they are soft and yellow, but do not let them brown.

Select a 2- to 2¹/₂-quart casserole or baking dish and in the center place a tall cup upside down to hold up the crust. Arrange the steak, kidneys and onions in layers in the casserole. Blend together the broth from the steak and the juices from the skillet in which you cooked the kidneys and onions, taste for seasoning (the juices may need a little more salt, pepper or thyme) and pour over the meat in the casserole. The liquid should come to within an inch of the top. If there is not enough, add a little stock or vegetable juice. If you like a thicker sauce, add small balls of butter and flour kneaded together. (Take some soft butter and rub flour into it with your fingertips. Roll it into balls about the size of tiny green peas.) Finally add chopped parsley. Top the dish with a rich pastry dough (see page 76) or rich biscuit dough (see page 45). Brush the top of the dough with beaten egg to give color to the crust. If you like, you can make a little extra pastry dough and cut leaves, rosettes or other designs from it. Arrange these on top of the crust in a decorative pattern.

If you use a pastry dough top, bake in a 450° oven for 10 minutes and then reduce the heat to 350° for another 15 to 20 minutes. For biscuit dough, bake at 425° for 15 to 18 minutes.

VARIATIONS

With mushrooms: If you do not like kidneys, substitute 1 pound of mushrooms sautéed lightly in butter. Or use half mushrooms and half kidneys in the pie. Mushrooms give it a very rich flavor.

With rosemary: Substitute rosemary for the thyme in the recipe.

With mashed potatoes: Put a 1-inch layer of mashed potatoes in the bottom of the casserole, spread it with butter and sprinkle with flour. Then proceed as above. This is a slightly richer pie, and the potatoes absorb some of the juice.

BEEFSTEAK AND KIDNEY PUDDING (Serves 4 to 6)

This is another famous English beef recipe and it makes hearty eating on a cold winter night. Suet crust is an old-fashioned delight too seldom seen these days.

3 cups of flour	**½ pound of mushrooms, sliced**
1½ cups of very finely chopped suet	**1 teaspoon of salt**
Ice water	**1 teaspoon of black pepper**
2 pounds of rump or round steak	**1 teaspoon of rosemary**
3 veal kidneys	**2 tablespoons of chopped parsley**
3 onions, sliced	**Water or stock**

First, prepare the suet crust by blending the flour with the chopped suet. The suet must be very fine—almost powdery. Add just enough ice water to make a stiff paste. Roll one half of the dough out on a floured board into a circle large enough to line a deep bowl. (Or you can roll the dough between sheets of plastic wrap.) Line the bowl with the rolled-out dough.

Cut the beef into 2-inch squares and roll them well in flour. Clean and slice the kidneys, peel and slice the onions, then slice the mushrooms. Arrange the steak, kidneys, onions and mushrooms in the bowl in layers and season each layer with a little salt, freshly ground black pepper, rosemary and chopped parsley. When you finish, the bowl should be heaped full, almost overflowing. Then fill up to 2 inches below the top with water or stock. Roll out the rest of the dough and cover the bowl with it, moistening the edges of the crust and sealing it down over the bowl.

Take a cloth large enough to cover the bowl completely, dip it in hot water and wring it out. Then flour it well. Wrap the bowl in this and tie it securely. Or use the more modern method and wrap the bowl thoroughly in foil. Just be certain it is fastened so the bowl will be watertight.

Fill a large kettle with enough water to come within an inch of the top of the bowl. Bring it to a boil and lower the bowl into the boiling water. Boil for 4 hours, watching to be sure there is enough water to surround the bowl.

Remove the pudding from the water and take off the cloth or foil. Slash the crust to let the steam escape. Serve it piping hot from the bowl in which it was steamed, and with it serve mashed potatoes and braised Brussels sprouts.

LEFTOVER MEAT PIE (Serves 4)

You can use almost any leftover beef for this recipe: roast, steak, boiled beef, pot roast or stew. It is also good when made with leftover veal, lamb or pork.

2 to 2¹/₂ cups of cooked meat	**Leftover gravy or canned beef gravy**
2 onions, sliced	**Biscuit dough**
7 tablespoons of butter	**¹/₄ cup of chopped parsley**
¹/₂ pound of mushrooms	

Cut the meat into bite-size pieces. Peel and slice the onions and sauté them in 4 tablespoons of butter. Sauté the mushrooms in 3 tablespoons of butter. In a casserole, arrange layers of the meat, onions and mushrooms and over all pour enough leftover gravy or canned beef gravy to come within 1 inch of the top of the casserole. Cover with rich biscuit dough (see page 45) in which you have blended the chopped parsley. Bake at

425° for 15 minutes. Reduce the heat to 325° and bake for another 15 minutes or until the pie is heated through and the crust is cooked.

OXTAIL RAGOUT (Serves 4)

This dish has a gelatinous quality that many people find very tasty. Serve it informally to guests who aren't afraid to use their fingers, for the best of the meat clings to the bones and must be nibbled off. Allow 1 pound per person and a little extra for the pot.

2 oxtails	1 onion stuck with 2 cloves
Flour	1 teaspoon of thyme
Salt	2 cups of tomato juice
Pepper	2 cups of water
4 tablespoons of butter or beef fat	4 turnips
	4 to 6 leeks
8 to 10 carrots	
2 cloves of garlic	

When you buy the oxtails, have the butcher cut them into sections. In a paper sack put some flour seasoned with salt and pepper and add the oxtail sections. Shake them well to coat them evenly with the seasoned flour. Melt butter or beef fat and when it is hot, brown the pieces of oxtail on all sides. Then add 2 carrots, the garlic, onion stuck with cloves, thyme, 1 teaspoon of salt, 1 teaspoon of freshly ground black pepper, and the tomato juice and water. Bring this to a boil, cover the pan, lower the heat and simmer for 3 to 4 hours.

Peel the remaining carrots and cut them in half; peel and quarter the turnips; and wash the leeks thoroughly, being careful to get all the grit out of them. Add these to the ragout and continue cooking for another 45 minutes to an hour.

I prefer this dish unthickened, but if you like a thicker sauce, add pea-sized balls of butter and flour kneaded together and stir these in until the juice is thick and smooth.

Serve Oxtail Ragout with boiled or baked potatoes, tiny white onions browned in butter and cooked until just tender, and hot garlic French bread. A beet and hard-cooked egg salad is a good addition to the menu. For dessert try hot apple pie.

HUNGARIAN GOULASH (Serves 4 to 6)

3 pounds of top round
3 tablespoons of flour
1 teaspoon of salt
1 teaspoon of pepper
2 teaspoons of paprika

4 tablespoons of lard or butter
1 cup of tomato purée
1 cup of stock or water

Have the meat cut into 2-inch cubes or do it yourself. In a paper bag put the flour, salt, freshly ground black pepper and paprika. Add the meat cubes and shake them thoroughly to get them evenly coated with the mixture. Heat lard or butter and brown the meat cubes quickly on all sides. Add tomato purée and stock or water. Cover the pan and bake in a 350° oven for 2 to 3 hours or until the meat is tender and the flavorings are well blended and mellowed.

Serve with plain boiled potatoes or buttered noodles. A crisp green, such as broccoli, braised lettuce or braised celery goes well with this goulash, and pickles are an appropriate addition. For dessert serve cinnamon-flavored baked apples with heavy cream.

BEEF STEW (Serves 4)

This is the favorite of many cooks. It's easy to prepare for a large number of people; it can be stretched; it can be prepared in advance and reheated; it can continue cooking or be kept hot awaiting late arrivals; and it can be dressed up.

Allow ½ pound of beef per person and be sure it is lean. Too much fat makes a greasy stew. Round steak or lean chuck are best. Have it cut in cubes of 1½ to 2 inches.

2 pounds of lean beef in cubes
Beef fat, butter or bacon fat
Flour
Salt and pepper
1 clove of garlic
1 teaspoon of thyme

2½ to 3 cups of stock or bouillon
Few sprigs of parsley
Few celery leaves
1 onion
1 bay leaf

Roll the meat cubes in flour seasoned with salt and pepper. Melt the beef fat, bacon fat or butter (or mix butter and beef or bacon fat) in a heavy kettle or Dutch oven. Start with about 2 tablespoons of fat and keep adding as you need it. When the fat is hot but not burning add the peeled clove of garlic and brown the meat cubes, sprinkling them with a bit of thyme as they brown. When the meat is browned on all sides, add enough stock or bouillon (this can be made with boiling water and bouillon cubes) to cover the beef. This will take about 2½ to 3 cups of liquid. Bring to a boil, put a tight lid on the kettle, reduce the heat and simmer gently for 1½ to 2 hours, or until the meat is tender. Degrease the sauce.

If you like a thicker sauce, remove the meat cubes when they are tender and add pea-sized balls of butter and flour kneaded together. Stir these in until the sauce is thick and smooth. Return the meat cubes to the pan to reheat. Serve with rice, noodles or mashed potatoes.

VARIATIONS

With vegetables: Add any vegetables you like to the stew about 45 minutes before the meat is done. You may add small peeled white onions, potatoes peeled and halved, carrots peeled and left whole or cut in half lengthwise, stalks of celery, green beans cut lengthwise, or frozen green peas (add these during the last 15 minutes of cooking).

With dumplings: Top the stew with dumplings. Make a dumpling dough (page 46) and add 4 tablespoons of chopped parsley to the flour when you mix the dumplings. Drop spoonfuls of this mixture over the surface of the stew a few minutes before serving time. Be sure to space the dumplings 2 to 3 inches apart. They swell during cooking. Cover tightly and continue simmering for 15 to 20 minutes.

With mushrooms: Brown ½ pound of mushrooms with the meat and use red wine for half of the liquid. Serve sprinkled with plenty of chopped green parsley.

With tomato: Brown with the meat 1 green pepper cut in strips and 2 onions, peeled and sliced. Substitute basil for the thyme. Halfway through the cooking, add 3 to 4 fresh tomatoes, peeled, seeded and chopped. Serve garnished with chopped parsley and accompanied by rice mixed with chopped ripe olives and chopped pimiento.

BEEF STROGANOFF (Serves 4)

There are many different versions of this dish. Beware of those that specify long cooking. Beef Stroganoff is much better when prepared quickly a few minutes before it is eaten and is one of the specialties that is fun to do at the table if you have an electric skillet or chafing dish.

1¹/₂ pounds of filet of beef	**A-1 sauce or Worcestershire sauce**
6 tablespoons of butter	
Olive oil	**1¹/₂ cups of sour cream**
2 tablespoons of chopped green onions	**Salt**
	Pepper
¹/₄ cup of white wine of vermouth	**Chopped parsley**

Ask the butcher to cut the meat into very thin slices. You can try it yourself, but it is difficult to do a neat job.

Melt 4 tablespoons of the butter in the pan and get it as hot as you can without burning. If you add just a bit of olive oil to the butter it helps prevent it from turning brown. Sauté the beef slices in the hot fat very quickly. When they are delicately browned on both sides and done (this takes only a minute or two) remove them to a hot platter. Add remaining butter and the chopped green onions and cook for a minute. Then add white wine or vermouth, a dash or two of A-1 sauce or Worcestershire sauce and the sour cream. Stir well and heat through, but do not boil or the sour cream will curdle. Salt to taste and pour the sauce over the beef. Top with a sprinkling of freshly ground black pepper and chopped parsley. Serve with rice.

VARIATION

Add 3 tablespoons of chili sauce to the sauce.

Boiled Beef

Many countries have a version of this simple classic dish and all are delectable, for good boiled beef is one of the most satisfying of foods. To be good, it must be prepared with care and attention. The best cut for boiled beef is the brisket, and short ribs are the next choice. You may also use the rump and shin. Just be sure to get as lean a piece as possible. Boiled beef is equally delicious cold, so be generous when you buy. Leftovers are never a problem.

BOILED BEEF (Serves 6)

4 to 5 pounds of lean
  brisket
Salt
Pepper
Rosemary or thyme
1 onion stuck with 2 cloves
3 to 4 leeks

3 to 4 carrots
1 stalk of celery
1 sprig of parsley
Water
Cabbage, potatoes, carrots
  or turnips

Rub the brisket with salt, freshly ground black pepper and a little rosemary or thyme. Place it in a large kettle with the onion stuck with cloves, leeks, carrots, celery, parsley and water to cover. Bring it to a boil and boil for 5 minutes. Then skim off any scum that may gather on the surface, add 1 tablespoon of salt, cover, lower the heat and simmer. Cook the beef for about 2 or 2½ hours or until it is tender. After 2 hours' cooking, you may add any additional vegetables you like. Potatoes, turnips, more carrots, a cabbage cut in quarters—any or all of these are good. Continue cooking until the vegetables are done and the meat is tender.

Remove the brisket to a hot platter, surround it with the vegetables and serve with sharp horseradish or with Mustard Sauce. You can serve the broth first as a soup course, if you like, and then follow it with the meat and vegetables. After this have a good salad of crisp greens dressed with oil and vinegar. Blueberry pie with plenty of heavy cream is a fine choice for dessert.

COLD BOILED BEEF

This is fine eating but even better when pressed. To do this, remove the boiled beef from the broth and put it in a deep bowl or pan. Cover with foil and top with a plate or platter. On this pile heavy items to weight the meat down. An electric iron or heavy tins of food will do. Let the meat cool at room temperature and then put it in the refrigerator to chill while it is still weighted. It will press into a firm piece of meat that can be cut into neat, even slices.

Serve cold boiled beef with potato salad and a hot vegetable, such as string beans with almonds.

POT AU FEU (Serves 6)

This is the French version of the boiled beef dinner.

3 pounds of lean brisket
1 piece of salt pork
1 onion stuck with 2 cloves
4 to 5 leeks, well washed
1 stalk of celery
9 carrots, peeled
1 turnip, peeled
Sprig of parsley
Water
1 teaspoon of dried or a
    sprig of fresh thyme

1 tablespoon of salt
1 4-pound roasting chicken
6 potatoes, scrubbed
1 head of cabbage,
    quartered
18 to 20 tiny white onions
3 tablespoons of butter
1 teaspoon of sugar

This recipe will serve 6 persons amply. In a large pot put the brisket, the salt pork, the onion stuck with cloves, the leeks, the celery, 3 carrots, the turnip, parsley and either a teaspoon of dried thyme or a sprig of fresh thyme. Add enough water to cover and bring it to a boil. Add 1 tablespoon of salt, cover, lower the heat and simmer 2 hours. Then add the chicken, whole and trussed. Continue cooking until the meat and chicken are tender; this will take about 1 more hour. One half hour before serving add potatoes with their skins left on, a quartered head of cabbage and 6 carrots. Continue cooking until the vegetables are tender.

Meanwhile, brown tiny white onions in butter and let them cook until soft, shaking the pan so they will cook evenly. Add a little sugar to give them a nice brown glaze.

Serve this Pot au Feu in the French manner in large soup plates, giving each person some broth, meat, vegetables and onions. Traditional accompaniments are coarse salt (kosher or Malden salt), sour pickles, horseradish and plenty of crusty French bread. Crisp celery is a nice contrast, and for dessert try an Apple Charlotte.

BEEF SALAD

Combine broken pieces of romaine, sliced hard-cooked eggs, onion rings, thin slices of boiled beef, sliced cold cooked potato and quartered tomatoes and capers. Toss with a French dressing and sprinkle with chopped parsley. With hot rolls or cornbread this makes a good summer lunch or supper.

VARIATION

Cold beef platter: Arrange leaves of romaine or Boston lettuce on a platter. Add sliced cooked potatoes that have marinated in oil and vinegar, sliced tomatoes, quartered hard-cooked eggs and slices of cold boiled beef. Serve with French (vinaigrette) dressing, mayonnaise, sliced pickles and horseradish on the side. A very appetizing summer buffet dish.

Corned Beef

Corned beef is a much neglected dish. If it's good, it's fine eating; if it's poor, it's not worth the bother. Many cooks have poor results because they think corned beef needs no attention. It has to be watched carefully. If underdone, it is tough; if overdone, it is mushy, unappetizing in appearance and tasteless.

The choice cuts of corned beef are the brisket and the rump. You will find variation in the flavor of corned beef. This comes from the curing process; some is more highly spiced than others. Ask your butcher for advice.

NEW ENGLAND BOILED DINNER (Serves 6)

4 to 5 pounds of corned brisket or boned rump	6 onions
1 clove of garlic, slivered	6 turnips
1 onion stuck with 2 cloves	1 head of cabbage, quartered
8 carrots	6 potatoes, cooked separately
Water	

Wash the meat well and let it soak in cold water for an hour before you cook it. Then slash it in several places and insert slivers of garlic. Place the beef in a large pot, add 2 carrots and an onion stuck with cloves and cover with cold water. Bring to a boil, skim off any scum that has formed, lower the heat and simmer for 2½ to 3 hours or until the corned beef is tender but not mushy. After 2 hours test it constantly with a sharp fork.

During the last hour, add 6 carrots, the onions and the turnips. Twenty minutes before you are ready to serve, add a quartered head of cabbage.

Arrange the cooked corned beef on a hot platter and surround it with the vegetables. Serve with baked or boiled potatoes and a variety of good mustards and pickles. For dessert—a freshly made chocolate cake and plenty of hot coffee.

VARIATIONS

With salt pork: Add a piece of salt pork to the pot when you are cooking the beef. Then cook the vegetables separately. Serve mustard sauce for the meat and plenty of butter for the vegetables.

With corned pork or tongue: Cook the corned beef with corned pork or corned tongue. Cook the vegetables separately and serve as above.

COLD CORNED BEEF

Cut paper-thin slices of cold cooked corned beef and trim off all the fat. Arrange the meat slices on a platter and serve with a selection of mustards, coleslaw, raw onion rings and thinly sliced pickles. Toasted sesame rolls and plenty of cold beer go well with this buffet lunch or supper. Finish with a chilled fruit compote and small cakes.

CORNED BEEF HASH (Serves 4)

If you are a corned beef hash fan, buy an extra pound of corned beef when you plan to cook it for dinner. You can make far better hash than you can buy in cans.

1 pound of cooked corned beef	Pinch of ginger
3 boiled potatoes, chopped	Pinch of allspice
1 small onion, chopped	4 tablespoons of beef fat
$1/_2$ teaspoon of salt	Cream or water
$1/_2$ teaspoon of pepper	

Chop the cooked corned beef coarsely and chop the cooked potatoes and the raw onion. Combine all together and season with salt, freshly ground black pepper, ginger and allspice. Heat the beef fat in a skillet, add the hash and press it down with a spatula or pancake turner. Let it cook slowly, mixing it well with a fork for the first few minutes. Then press it down again and continue cooking over a low heat. Add a little boiling water or hot cream and let this cook dry. There should be a nice crust on the bottom of the hash. If you like, you can dot the top with butter and run it under the broiler flame for a few minutes to brown a bit. Using a pancake turner, fold the hash over and roll it out on a hot platter, crusty side up. Serve with poached or fried eggs. The traditional accompaniments are coleslaw and chili sauce. For dessert, I suggest baked Indian Pudding with ice cream.

CORNED BEEF IN CASSEROLE (Serves 4)

2 cans of corned beef hash

2 onions, chopped fine

1 clove of garlic, chopped fine

1 green pepper, seeded and cut into thin strips

6 tablespoons of butter

1 teaspoon of dry mustard

1 tablespoon of Worcestershire sauce

6 tablespoons of chopped parsley

Grated cheese

Buttered crumbs

Melt the butter in a skillet and sauté the onion, garlic and green pepper until just soft. Mix with the corned beef hash, the dry mustard and Worcestershire sauce. Butter a casserole and put a layer of the corned beef mixture in the bottom. Sprinkle with the chopped parsley and top with the rest of the corned beef mixture. Sprinkle with buttered crumbs mixed with grated Parmesan, Switzerland Swiss or cheddar cheese and bake in a 400° oven for 25 to 30 minutes or until brown and bubbly.

Chopped Beef

HAMBURGER

Although it was originally a German dish, chopped beef or hamburger steak—or, as the French called it, "Bifteck Hambourgeoise"—has become one of the most popular foods in America. Many children arrive at the age of maturity unaware that there is any other cut of beef.

The best hamburger is about 80% lean and 20% fat. If you like your beef ground to order, ask the butcher to grind top round, bottom round or sirloin tip and to add a small amount of beef suet when he grinds. Most of the beef already ground is pretty well fatted.

Ground beef should be treated carefully, refrigerated immediately and thoroughly wrapped in foil or plastic. For dinner, estimate ½ pound of ground beef per person. Some people may eat more, some less. For hamburger on a bun or hamburger sandwiches, a 4-ounce patty is an ample serving.

Hamburger is best when it is lightly handled. Form the cakes with your hands without pressing the meat too firmly. You may mix the meat with seasonings before forming into cakes, if you wish.

Aside from salt and pepper, suggested seasonings might be crumbled rosemary leaves, crumbled oregano, finely chopped garlic or onion, chopped chives, or finely chopped tomato.

BROILED HAMBURGERS

Form hamburgers into cakes of approximately 8 ounces each. Season to taste. Brush with butter or olive oil or melted beef fat. Broil over coals or in the oven broiler until nicely browned and crusted on both sides and cooked to your favorite degree of doneness on the inside. An 8-ounce hamburger should be approximately 1 inch thick. I find if you mold this type of hamburger into an oval, it is easier to handle and more attractive on the plate. A 1-inch-thick hamburger would take about 6 minutes on each side, for rare. Serve hamburger patties with crisp fried potatoes, potato chips, sliced beefsteak tomatoes or sliced onion. They make ideal indoor or outdoor food and are delicious served with cold beer.

PAN-BROILED HAMBURGERS

These same hamburgers may be pan-broiled on top of the stove. To my taste, they are even better when so prepared. Rub the skillet well with beef fat or add a mixture of butter and oil (about 1 tablespoon of each). The pan should be hot. Sear the meat quickly on both sides over a high heat and reduce the heat and cook, turning the meat once more until the hamburgers have achieved the desired state of doneness. Serve as for Broiled Hamburgers, above. You may add a drop or two of Worcestershire sauce, 2 or 3 tablespoons of red wine, a touch of Cognac or a spoonful of chili sauce to the pan when you remove the meat. Swirl around in pan and pour over the hot beef cakes.

Old-fashioned: Prepare hamburgers as above, remove to hot platter and smother with onion rings, which have been sautéed in butter and oil until soft and nicely browned. Season to taste with salt and pepper.

À Cheval: Top hamburger cakes with freshly fried eggs, one for each serving, and decorate each egg with 2 anchovy fillets.

Marseillaise: Press finely chopped garlic (approximately 3 cloves for 4 servings or more) into hamburger cakes. Sauté the cakes quickly in olive oil. Salt and pepper to taste and serve with sautéed eggplant.

Cheeseburger: Combine 2 pounds of chopped beef with a small amount of fat. Add 2 tablespoons of finely chopped onion, $\frac{1}{2}$ teaspoon of salt, 1 teaspoon of freshly ground black pepper, $\frac{2}{3}$ cup of grated sharp cheese, 1 teaspoon of Worcestershire sauce and a dash of Tabasco. Blend these ingredients well and form into cakes; either broil or pan-broil according to directions above.

Au Poivre: Roll hamburger cakes in freshly cracked black pepper and either broil or sauté as above. Salt to taste, rinse the pan with $\frac{1}{3}$ cup Cognac and pour over the steaks. Serve with crisp sautéed potatoes.

With mushrooms: Prepare the hamburgers as above and serve heaped with mushrooms sautéed in butter and seasoned with salt and pepper, chopped chives and chopped parsley. Rinse the pan with $\frac{1}{3}$ cup of dry vermouth or white wine and pour over the hamburgers.

HAMBURGER SANDWICH

The traditional hamburger is a 4-ounce cake broiled or pan-broiled to the required state of doneness and served on a heated, toasted, buttered bun. There is nothing as unappetizing as a cold hamburger bun with a hot hamburger.

VARIATIONS

The California Hamburger: Cook hamburger as above. On the bottom half of each toasted, buttered bun place a slice of raw onion, brush with a dab of mayonnaise, add the cooked hamburger and top with a slice of thin ripe tomato, hamburger relish, sliced dill pickle and the top half of the buttered bun. Serve with additional relish, mustard and chili sauce, if you wish, but heat the chili sauce before serving, because cold sauce is not inviting with hot food.

Cheeseburger: Form hamburgers into very thin, 2-ounce cakes. Salt and pepper them and place a slice of cheese slightly smaller than the hamburger cake on half of the hamburgers. Top with the other halves and broil or pan-broil as above. Serve in buttered, toasted buns.

Farm Style: Combine 1½ pounds of ground beef with ½ cup of finely chopped green onions, ½ teaspoon of salt and 1 teaspoon of Worcestershire sauce. Form into cakes and wrap each one with a rasher of bacon. Broil and serve on buttered buns.

MEAT LOAF

There are many different kinds of meat loaf. Some of them are loose, sloppy and unappetizing; others, firm, well-textured and delicious, either hot or cold. This is my favorite meat loaf recipe:

2 pounds of ground beef	**1 crumbled bay leaf**
1 pound of ground pork	**½ teaspoon of crumbled thyme leaves**
2 garlic cloves, finely chopped	**1 teaspoon of freshly chopped green pepper**
1 fairly large onion, finely chopped	**½ cup of dry bread crumbs**
1 teaspoon of salt	**2 eggs**
1 teaspoon of freshly ground black pepper	**Bacon or salt pork**

Mix all ingredients except bacon thoroughly and knead with the fingers until the mixture is very thoroughly blended. Form into a long loaf or cake and press firmly. Arrange enough slices of bacon or salt pork on the bottom of a baking pan to hold the meat loaf. Brush the loaf with butter and cross with 2 to 4 additional slices of bacon. Roast at 325°, basting occasionally, for 1½ to 1¾ hours or until the meat loaf is cooked through.

Constant basting makes a moister loaf. If you serve this meat loaf hot, let it stand on a hot platter for 10 to 15 minutes before you carve it, to settle the juices. It is even more delicious when served at a temperature between warm and cold, with a salad. It is excellent served in thin slices the next day, and it makes superb sandwiches.

VARIATIONS

With hard-cooked eggs: Instead of forming this into a loaf, pat ½ of the meat into a cake and place it on the bacon strips for roasting. Place peeled hard-cooked eggs along the center of this cake and mold the remaining meat loaf mixture on top. In this way you serve a slice of egg in each slice of meat.

Ham Loaf: Use 1 pound of ground ham instead of ground pork and half the amount of salt in the mixture.

Tongue: Substitute 1 pound of ground beef tongue for the ham or pork mixture and add a little additional beef fat to the mixture.

Beef Kidney

BEEF KIDNEY STEW (Serves 4)

1 beef kidney	3 tablespoons of olive oil
3 tablespoons of vinegar	2 cloves of garlic, chopped
2 cups of water	½ cup of chopped onion
Flour	1 teaspoon of rosemary
Salt	1 bay leaf
Pepper	1 cup of red wine
4 tablespoons of butter	

Remove all the membrane from the kidney and soak the kidney in 2 cups of water with 3 tablespoons of vinegar for 2 hours. Then cut it into thin slices and dredge these in flour seasoned with salt and freshly ground black pepper. Heat butter and olive oil and sauté the kidney slices quickly, browning them on both sides. Add finely chopped garlic and onion, and continue cooking for 5 minutes. Then add the rosemary, the bay leaf and the red wine. Simmer for 15 minutes or until the kidney slices are tender. Serve with boiled potatoes.

Beef Tongue

SMOKED BEEF TONGUE

This elegant dish seems simple, but it does take time to prepare. Beef tongues weigh 3 to 4½ pounds each. Allow about ½ pound per person.

1 smoked beef tongue	2 cloves of garlic
1 onion stuck with 2 cloves	1 sprig of parsley
1 bay leaf	Water

Put the tongue in a large kettle and cover it with cold water. Bring this to a boil and boil for 5 minutes. Skim off any scum that comes to the top. Add the onion stuck with cloves and the bay leaf, garlic and parsley. Cover the pan, lower the heat and simmer gently until the tongue is tender. Allow about 50 minutes per pound.

When the tongue is done, remove it from the broth and carefully skin it. You will need a very sharp knife. Remove all the skin and trim it neatly; then return it to the broth to keep warm. Serve this tongue with caper-mustard sauce (capers added to mustard sauce), horseradish sauce or bottled beet and horseradish from the grocery or delicatessen. Chopped, buttered spinach and boiled potatoes are the vegetables generally served with smoked tongue, and they seem to go better with it than anything else, with the possible exception of beets with sour cream. When you cut the tongue, slice it as thin as possible.

BRAISED FRESH TONGUE

Fresh tongue is harder to find in the markets than smoked tongue, but it makes a delectable dish and is well worth shopping around for.

1 fresh beef tongue	1 teaspoon of dried or 1 tablespoon of fresh basil
Broth for the tongue (see Smoked Tongue page 221)	1 teaspoon of black pepper
4 tablespoons of butter	1 teaspoon of mustard
1 large onion	1 cup of sliced ripe olives
2 cloves of garlic	$1/4$ cup of capers
1 cup of tomato purée	$1/4$ cup of chopped parsley
1 teaspoon of salt	

Cook the fresh tongue as you do the smoked one. Skin it, trim off the root end and return it to the hot broth to keep warm.

Melt the butter in a skillet and sauté the chopped onion and garlic until just soft. Add tomato purée, dried or fresh basil, salt, freshly ground black pepper, dry mustard and blend all together thoroughly. Bring this to a boil. Remove the tongue from the broth and add it to the tomato sauce.

Let it cook over a low flame for 30 minutes, turning it often. Then add the sliced ripe olives, the capers and the chopped parsley.

Serve this tongue in tomato sauce with crusty sautéed potatoes and puréed spinach dressed with plenty of butter.

Beef Marrow

POACHED MARROW

Marrow is the soft center section of certain beef bones. Ask the butcher for marrow, and perhaps you can persuade him to extract the marrow for you. If not, have him saw through the bones cutting them into 1½-inch lengths. People who enjoy this delicacy can easily consume the marrow from 4 to 5 such pieces of bone. As garnish, allow 1 piece per person.

Take the marrow bones home and using a sharp pointed knife, pry out the soft center sections. In a skillet put enough water to cover the pieces of marrow and add 1 teaspoon of salt. Bring this to the boiling point and add the marrow. Poach it gently (do not boil) until it is translucent. Spoon out and serve on toast or serve as a garnish for meat dishes.

Veal

In France, Austria and Italy veal is extremely popular. In fact Italians think it is better than beef. Yet in this country it is the least sought after of all meats. I think our lack of interest in veal may be attributed to the quality of the meat. It is very difficult in our markets to get true milk-fed veal. This fine baby veal is so pale it is almost white; it is tender and delicate and also very expensive. Older veal, which is plentiful in the average butcher shop, needs longer cooking and extra seasoning to give it flavor. If there are Italian markets in your area you are likely to find they carry the best quality.

The leg of veal is considered by many to be the choicest cut, although fine loin chops can be equally good. From the leg come those delectable morsels known as scallopine of veal or veal scallops. The veal cutlet also comes from the leg.

Shoulder and breast of veal—more economical—can be delicious, especially stuffed and braised.

Butter is by far the best fat to use for cooking veal. It does not drown the delicate flavor of the meat. Some special recipes call for oil, and occasionally you may use bacon fat: for example, when the veal is stuffed with ham.

Don't rush veal. It should be cooked slowly and be thoroughly done.

Leg of Veal

ROAST LEG OF VEAL (Serves 6)

A 4-pound boneless roast cut from the leg will serve 6 persons. Have the butcher tie the roast firmly, and for tastier meat, ask him to lard it with salt pork strips.

4 pounds of boneless leg roast	**Salt and pepper**
	Tarragon or thyme
Salt pork, bacon or ham fat	**Melted butter**
2 cloves of garlic	**Dry vermouth**

Cover the roast with slices of salt pork, bacon or ham fat. Salt and pepper it to taste and rub it with a little tarragon or thyme. Arrange it in a roasting pan and insert a meat thermometer in the thickest part of the roast. Add 2 cloves of garlic to the pan and roast the meat at 325°, basting it often with melted butter and dry vermouth mixed with the pan juices. The roast is done when the meat thermometer registers 160° to 165°. This will take a little less than 2 hours.

If you like potatoes browned in the roasting pan with the meat, add them for the last hour of cooking. If not, serve the roast with sautéed potatoes, crisp and brown, and the pan juices, unthickened. A good accompaniment is creamed chopped spinach. Finish with a bowl of sliced oranges flavored with a little Cointreau and sprinkled with shredded coconut.

VARIATION

With anchovies: Cover the top of the veal roast with anchovy fillets and sprinkle with chopped garlic. Pour oil from the anchovies over the roast and then cover it with bacon slices. Roast as above, removing the bacon and anchovies just before the meat is done. The anchovies may be added to the pan juices. Do not salt the roast. There is plenty of salt in anchovies.

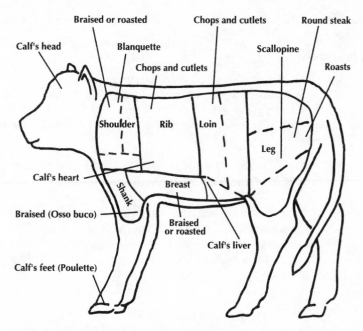

Braised or roasted · Chops and cutlets · Round steak · Calf's head · Blanquette · Scallopine · Chops and cutlets · Roasts · Shoulder · Rib · Loin · Leg · Calf's heart · Breast · Braised (Osso buco) · Shank · Braised or roasted · Calf's liver · Calf's feet (Poulette)

VITELLO TONNATO (VEAL WITH TUNA SAUCE) (Serves 6)

This classic Italian summer dish has many versions. Here is an interesting one from a former New York restaurant.

3¹/₂ pounds of rolled boneless leg of veal

2 large cas of tuna in olive oil

1 large, sliced onion

10 fillets of anchovy

¹/₂ sour pickle

2 cloves of garlic, peeled

4 stalks of celery

1 carrot, peeled and sliced

Thyme

Parsley

1 pint of white wine

1 cup of olive oil

In a heavy saucepan place the veal, the tuna and oil from the cans, and the rest of the ingredients. Bring to a boil. Cover the pan, lower the heat and simmer gently about 1¹/₂ hours or until the veal is tender.

Let the veal cool in the juices, then remove it to a platter and cut it in very thin slices.

Strain the juices from the pan through a very fine sieve and taste for seasoning. Serve the sliced meat with the cold sauce and with tiny gherkins. A cold rice salad mixed with finely cut vegetables and a French dressing goes well with this dish.

VARIATIONS

1. Mix the sauce with an equal amount of mayonnaise.
2. Cut cold roast or braised veal into thin slices. Make a sauce with 1 tablespoon of onion juice, 3 finely chopped anchovy fillets, 1 tin of tuna fish in olive oil, 1 cup of mayonnaise and 2 tablespoons of capers. Blend well and serve with the sliced veal.

SCALLOPINE OF VEAL (Scallops of Veal)

Scallops are small slices of veal cut from the leg. They must be cut very thin and then pounded to flatten them out. Most Italian and French butchers have a special metal pounder for this job. A pound of scallops of veal will serve 2 to 3 people amply, and sometimes even 4, depending on the size of the appetites.

PLAIN SCALLOPINE (Serves 2)

4 scallops, pounded thin ($^1/_2$ to $^3/_4$ pound)	**3 tablespoons of butter**
	Salt and pepper
Flour	**Lemon quarters**
1 tablespoon of olive oil	

Dust the scallops with flour, and sauté them quickly in the oil and butter, about 3 or 4 minutes a side. Season to taste with salt and freshly ground black pepper. Serve with lemon quarters. Also serve broiled tomatoes and pasta dressed with butter and grated cheese. This is a distinguished dinner that can be prepared in less than half an hour.

VARIATIONS

With crumbs and cheese: Cook as for plain scallops. When the scallops are done, remove them to a hot platter and add 3 more tablespoons of butter to the pan. When this is melted add 4 tablespoons of fine dry bread crumbs and 3 tablespoons of finely chopped parsley. Heat through and spread on the scallops. Sprinkle liberally with grated Parmesan cheese and paprika.

With mushrooms: Cook as for plain scallops, season to taste with salt and pepper, and transfer to a warm dish. Add extra butter to the pan, and sauté 1 cup of thinly sliced mushrooms until just tender. Add 2 tablespoons of chopped parsley and salt and pepper. Spread over the veal. Serve with sautéed potatoes and tiny peas cooked with onions and lettuce.

Alla Marsala: Cook scallops in the usual manner. When they are browned on both sides and almost done, add ¼ cup dry Marsala and let the wine cook down for a few minutes. Serve sprinkled with chopped parsley.

SCALLOPINE WITH TARRAGON (Serves 4)

8 scallops (1 to 1¼ pounds)	**Salt and pepper**
Flour	**½ cup of white wine or dry**
6 tablespoons of butter	**vermouth**
1 teaspoon of tarragon	

Dip the scallops in flour and sauté them about 3 or 4 minutes on each side in the butter until slightly browned. Transfer to a warm dish, and season to taste with salt and pepper. Add the dried tarragon (or 1 tablespoon of fresh tarragon) and white wine or dry vermouth to the pan. Cook for a few minutes until the liquid is reduced a little. Pour over the scallops. Serve with a rice pilaf, fresh string beans with almonds and toasted garlic bread.

VARIATION

Serve these tarragon scallops cold with a potato salad dressed with olive oil and wine vinegar.

SCALLOPS VIENNESE (WIENER SCHNITZEL) (Serves 4)

1½ pounds of veal scallops	**Flour**
Peanut oil or olive oil	**Fine, dry bread crumbs**
2 eggs	**Salt and pepper**

Pour 2 inches of oil in a deep skillet. Heat the oil to 375°, and while it is getting hot, beat the eggs lightly, and set out two bowls, one of flour, seasoned with salt and pepper, the other of fine dry bread crumbs. When the oil is bubbly, dip each scallop in flour, then in beaten egg and finally in crumbs and fry them quickly in the oil until golden brown on both sides. Arrange the cooked scallops on a hot platter and garnish with lemon quarters and chopped parsley. Serve with potatoes hashed in cream, buttered turnips, and a green salad.

Breaded Veal Cutlet is prepared in the same way. Substitute cutlet for the scallops (cutlet is also cut from the leg) and be sure to have the butcher slice the cutlet very thin.

With Parmesan cheese: Substitute grated Parmesan cheese for half of the dry bread crumbs and mix a little chopped parsley with it. Dip the scallops in the flour, then in the egg and finally in the cheese-crumbs-parsley mixture. Cook as above.

Holstein: Serve the scallops with a rolled anchovy and a fried egg on top of each one. With this scallop dish serve crisp fried potatoes and braised cabbage.

SCALLOPS WITH CREAM (Serves 6)

**6 large or 12 small scallops
(1½ to 2 pounds)**

4 tablespoons of flour

1 teaspoon of salt

1 teaspoon of pepper

1 teaspoon of paprika

6 tablespoons of butter

1 cup of heavy cream

Put the flour, salt, freshly ground black pepper and paprika in a paper sack. Add the scallops and shake them well to coat them with the mixture. Brown them on both sides in hot butter. It will probably be necessary to do them in 2 or 3 batches. Then cover the pan and cook slowly for 5 minutes, or until the meat is thoroughly tender. Add the heavy cream to the pan and let it cook down over low heat for 3 or 4 minutes. Taste for seasoning. Serve these scallops in cream with mashed potatoes liberally dressed with butter, tiny French peas cooked with onions, and a celery salad.

VARIATION

With sour cream: After the scallops are browned, add more paprika—a generous sprinkling—and cover the pan. When the meat is tender, remove it to a hot platter. Add 1 tablespoon of chili sauce and 1 cup of sour cream to the pan. Stir and heat through but do not let it boil or the cream will curdle. Taste for seasoning and pour the sauce over the scallops. Serve with Gnocchi (see page 175).

Shoulder of Veal

This cut may be roasted, but you will find it much tastier if you braise it and serve it with a rich sauce. The shoulder should be boned and rolled by the butcher. If you plan to stuff it, be sure to ask the butcher to cut a pocket in the meat for you.

BRAISED SHOULDER OF VEAL (Serves 4 to 6)

4 pounds of veal shoulder
and bones from the meat
2 cloves of garlic
3 to 4 tablespoons of butter
1 teaspoon of salt
1 teaspoon of pepper
1 cup of white wine or dry
vermouth

1 cup of broth or water
1 teaspoon of tarragon or
thyme
1 onion
1/2 bay leaf

Have the butcher bone, roll and tie the shoulder for you and ask him to give you the bones. Make small incisions in the meat with a sharp knife and insert slivers of garlic. Melt butter in a deep Dutch oven or casserole and brown the meat on all sides, turning it often with a fork or tongs. It should sizzle and spit to get a good brown color. Sprinkle with salt and freshly ground black pepper and add the white wine or dry vermouth, the broth or water, the bones, the tarragon or thyme, the onion and bay leaf. Cover with a tight lid. Lower the heat and simmer gently on top of the stove, or place in a 325° oven, and cook for 1 1/2 to 2 hours. Test the meat for tenderness and cook a little longer, if necessary.

Transfer the cooked shoulder to a hot platter, remove the strings and garnish the platter with tiny string beans cooked until tender and then tossed in hot butter, small new potatoes cooked in butter until golden brown, and a delicate dusting of chopped parsley.

Skim the excess fat from the juices in the pan and serve the broth separately as a sauce. If you prefer a thick sauce, brown 3 tablespoons of flour in 3 tablespoons of butter and add the pan juices. Continue stirring and cooking until the sauce is thickened and smooth. Taste for seasoning.

With glazed prunes: Use red wine and water for the liquid, and while the veal is simmering cook 1½ pounds of prunes in 1 cup of red wine and ½ cup of sugar until dry and glazed. Reserve a few of the glazed prunes for a garnish and add the rest to the meat pot a few minutes before the veal is done. Arrange the meat on a hot platter, decorate with the glazed prunes and serve the unthickened sauce separately.

With olives: Follow the first recipe and 15 minutes before the meat is done add 1½ cups of small Spanish olives. Garnish the shoulder with the olives and serve the strained sauce, thickened or not, separately.

Niçoise: Brown the meat in olive oil flavored with 2 chopped garlic cloves. Add 1 cup of tomato purée, 1 cup of broth or stock, 12 small white onions, ½ green pepper cut in strips, 2 tablespoons of chopped parsley and 1 teaspoon of oregano. Cover the pot and proceed as above. About 15 minutes before the veal is done, add 1 cup of ripe olives. Serve this with buttered pasta and sautéed eggplant.

In aspic: Braised shoulder of veal is delicious cold. Arrange neat slices of the meat in a shallow serving dish and pour the broth over these. Chill in the refrigerator. The broth will jell nicely, and the sliced meat in this rich aspic makes tasty eating on a hot summer day.

STUFFED VEAL SHOULDER (Serves 6)

5 to 6 pounds of boned shoulder of veal	**1 pound of ground pork**
2 cloves of garlic, chopped	**1½ cups of bread crumbs**
2 large onions, chopped	**1 egg**
4 tablespoons of butter	**Salt and pepper**
¼ cup of chopped parsley	**Fat (butter and oil or bacon fat)**
1 teaspoon of basil	**2 cups of white wine**

Be sure to ask the butcher to cut a pocket in the shoulder and give you the bones. Sauté the garlic and onions in butter until they are soft and lightly browned. Add the chopped parsley, the basil and the ground pork and cook gently for 10 minutes.

Mix the bread crumbs with an egg, lightly beaten, 1 teaspoon of salt and ½ teaspoon of freshly ground black pepper. Combine this with the pork and vegetables and blend well. Stuff the veal pocket with this mixture and sew it up or fasten it with skewers. Heat enough butter, oil or fat to just cover the bottom of a skillet and brown the veal shoulder on all sides, seasoning to taste with salt and pepper. Then add the white wine and the bones from the meat and proceed according to directions for Braised Shoulder of Veal (page 229). When the veal is done, remove it to a hot platter and surround it with buttered broccoli. Serve with buttered noodles lightly sprinkled with grated Parmesan cheese. Pass the sauce from the meat separately.

Breast of Veal

STUFFED BREAST OF VEAL (Serves 6)

This economical cut can be very tasty. Be sure to ask the butcher to cut a pocket in the large end of the meat.

5 to 6 pounds of breast of veal	**1½ cups of dry bread crumbs**
1 large onion	**1 teaspoon of thyme**
2 cloves of garlic	**2 eggs lightly beaten**
3 tablespoons of butter	**3 tablespoons of whiskey**
1 cup of ground ham	**¼ cup of chopped parsley**
1 cup of liver sausage	**Salt**
3 tablespoons of cream or milk	**Strips of bacon or salt pork**

Chop the onion and garlic and sauté them in hot butter. Add the ground ham and mix thoroughly. Mash the liver sausage and thin it with a little cream or milk. Combine the ham mixture with the liver sausage, dry bread crumbs, thyme, beaten eggs, whiskey, chopped parsley and salt to taste. (You will probably need only a pinch of salt as the ham and sausage will both have salt already.) Stuff the breast of veal with this mixture, put a layer or two of foil over the opening and fasten it to the meat on both sides with metal skewers.

Place the meat on a rack in a roasting pan, and top it with strips of bacon or salt pork. Bake at 325°, allowing 25 minutes per pound (stuffed weight). Or put a meat thermometer in the thickest part of the roast (do not let it touch a bone) and roast until the thermometer registers 165°.

Serve this special dish with glazed onions and baked potatoes dressed with sour cream, crumbled bacon and chopped parsley.

VARIATIONS

Alternate stuffing: Use the stuffing given under the recipe for Stuffed Veal Shoulder (page 230).

Cold Breast of Veal: Stuffed Breast of Veal chilled and served cold is a great treat on a hot summer day. If you plan to use it this way, change the stuffing and substitute 1½ cups of ground veal for the ham and add 1 cup of ground pork. Reduce the bread crumbs to ½ cup.

Veal Chops

A large thick loin chop will serve one person. Rib chops, though just as tasty, are smaller, and you may need to allow two for those with hearty appetites.

VEAL CHOPS WITH CREAM SAUCE (Serves 4)

4 loin chops ³⁄₄ to 1 inch thick	**Salt**
Flour	**Pepper**
4 to 6 tablespoons of butter	**1 cup of cream**

Dip the chops in flour and sauté them in hot butter until they are delicately browned on both sides. Cover the pan, reduce the heat, and simmer for 10 to 15 minutes or until the meat is done and tender. Salt and pepper the chops to taste and remove them to a hot platter.

Add 2 tablespoons of flour to the pan juices and blend and cook until lightly browned. Slowly stir in the cream; continue stirring and cooking until the sauce is thick and smooth. Taste for seasoning and add salt and pepper if needed. Serve the sauce with the chops. Mashed potatoes and braised lettuce are excellent accompaniments. Follow with an endive salad, a selection of cheeses and plenty of coffee.

VEAL CHOPS WITH SAUCE SOUBISE (Serves 4)

For the meat:

4 large loin chops or 4 to 6 rib chops ³/₄ to 1 inch thick	**Salt**
	Pepper
Flour	**Grated cheese**
Butter	

Flour the chops and sauté them in butter until nicely browned on both sides. Cover the pan, lower the heat and cook gently 10 to 15 minutes until they are cooked through and tender. Season lightly with salt and pepper. Remove the chops to an oven-proof serving dish and top each one with some of the sauce. Sprinkle with additional grated cheese and run under the broiler flame to melt the cheese and brown lightly. Serve with crisp home-fried potatoes, a salad of cucumbers and onions in French dressing and hot French bread. For dessert, serve Crème Brûlée.

For the sauce:

3 medium onions	**¹/₄ cup of heavy cream**
5 tablespoons of butter	**¹/₂ cup of grated Gruyère or Swiss cheese**
3 tablespoons of flour	
Nutmeg	**Salt**
1 cup of milk	**Pepper**

Chop the onions very fine and put them in a saucepan with 2 tablespoons of butter. Cover the pan and let the onions steam over very low heat until they are soft. Do not let them brown. While the onions are steaming make a Rich Cream Sauce: Melt 3 tablespoons of butter, add the flour and a dash of nutmeg and blend thoroughly. Gradually stir in 1 cup of milk and stir and cook until the mixture thickens. Add ¹/₄ cup of heavy cream and cook a few minutes longer. Then add the grated cheese and blend until it melts. Season to taste with salt and pepper. Add the steamed onions when they are done.

VEAL PARMIGIANA (Serves 4)

This popular veal dish is an American version of an Italian specialty. In Italy, Veal Parmigiana is chopped veal, rolled in flour, dipped in egg, then rolled in crumbs and cheese and sautéed in butter. It is served with additional cheese and chopped parsley. Here is the American version:

For the meat:

4 large veal chops ³/₄ to 1 inch thick

Flour

Salt and pepper

1 egg, lightly beaten

¹/₂ cup of dry bread crumbs

Grated Parmesan cheese

¹/₄ cup of chopped parsley

Olive oil

4 pieces of mozzarella cheese

Season some flour with salt and pepper. Mix the bread crumbs with ¹/₂ cup of grated cheese and the chopped parsley. Dip the chops in the flour, then in the beaten egg and finally in the crumbs-cheese-parsley mixture. Sauté them in hot olive oil until they are nicely browned on both sides. Reduce the heat, cover the pan and cook slowly for 10 minutes. Remove the chops to a flat oven-proof baking dish and sprinkle them liberally with more grated cheese. Spoon half the tomato sauce over the meat and top with slices of mozzarella. (If you can't find it in your area, use Muenster instead.) Cover with the rest of the tomato sauce and sprinkle with more grated cheese. Bake in a 350° oven for 20 minutes or until the cheese is melted and the sauce and meat are well blended. Perfect accompaniments for this rich dish are pasta dressed with oil and garlic, a huge salad of greens dressed with olive oil and wine vinegar, and some of the crisp bread sticks called *grissini*. I feel a simple red table wine is almost a must with this heavily sauced dish.

For the sauce:

3 cloves of garlic

1 medium onion

4 tablespoons of olive oil

1 teaspoon of basil

One 18-ounce can of Italian plum tomatoes

One 16-ounce can of tomato purée

1¹/₂ teaspoons of salt

1 teaspoon of pepper

Chop the garlic and onion and sauté them in hot olive oil untill soft. Add the basil, canned tomatoes, tomato purée, salt and pepper. Simmer this mixture for 30 minutes and then strain it through a sieve. Keep it hot over a pan of hot water or very low heat.

STUFFED VEAL CHOPS, ITALIAN STYLE (Serves 4)

For this unusual dish, you will need Italian prosciutto. The best is imported. It comes ready to eat and is sold cut in paper-thin slices. Besides being useful in many recipes, prosciutto is a delectable morsel served with fresh fruit for a first course.

4 rib chops ³/₄ to 1 inch thick cut with pockets in them

¹/₄ pound of sliced prosciutto

2 cloves of garlic, finely chopped

¹/₂ cup of fine dry bread crumbs

¹/₄ cup of chopped parsley

1 teaspoon of basil

3 tablespoons of melted butter

4 tablespoons of olive oil

Flour

2 medium onions, sliced

¹/₂ cup of dry vermouth

1 cup of tomato purée

Salt

Pepper

Cut the prosciutto into thin strips and mix with the garlic, bread crumbs, parsley, basil and melted butter. Stuff the chops with this mixture and fasten them with toothpicks or small metal skewers.

Heat the olive oil in a skillet, dust the chops in flour and brown them quickly in the hot oil. When they are browned on both sides, add the onions and the dry vermouth. Cover the pan and simmer gently for 25 minutes. Then turn the chops, cover the pan again and simmer for another 20 minutes. Remove the meat to a hot platter, add tomato purée to the pan juices and let it cook down for 4 or 5 minutes, stirring to blend the flavorings. Be careful not to let the sauce stick to the pan or burn. Season to taste with salt and pepper and serve with the stuffed chops. With these fine-tasting stuffed chops serve Polenta (page 174) and zucchini sautéed in olive oil and flavored with garlic and parsley.

Veal Sauté and Other Dishes

VEAL SAUTÉ (Serves 4)

In spite of its name, this is really a stew, and an elegant one. It is a fine choice for a buffet party. If you make an extra amount, you can freeze part of it and use it a week or two later.

2¹/₂ pounds of veal shoulder boned and cut into 2-inch cubes

Flour

Salt

Pepper

¹/₄ cup of olive oil

1 teaspoon of paprika

¹/₂ cup of chopped green onions

1 teaspoon of rosemary or thyme

1 cup of white wine or vermouth

¹/₂ cup of water

12 small white onions, peeled

3 carrots, peeled and sliced

Dredge the meat well with flour seasoned with salt and pepper and brown it on all sides in hot oil, sprinkling it with a little paprika as it cooks. When all the pieces of meat are well browned, add the chopped green onions, rosemary or thyme, white wine or vermouth and water. Cover the pan and simmer gently for 40 minutes. Then add the tiny white onions and carrots. Cover the pan again, simmer until the vegetables are tender and the meat cooked through. If you like a thick sauce, add pea-sized balls of butter and flour kneaded together. Sprinkle them into the stew and stir until the liquid becomes thick and smooth.

If you wish, you can give this dish a more festive touch by adding cooked frozen green peas just before you dish up the stew and topping it with a liberal sprinkling of Italian parsley.

With Veal Sauté serve *spaetzle*. Here is how they are made:

Spaetzle: Beat 3 eggs lightly and mix them with 3 cups of sifted flour and a generous ¹/₂ teaspoon of salt. You can do this job with your electric mixer. When this is well blended, gradually add 1 cup of milk and continue beating for about 4 minutes. Drop tiny balls of this dough from the end of a small spoon into briskly boiling water. The spaetzle are cooked when they rise to the surface. Drain and dry them on paper towels and sauté them quickly in hot butter.

VARIATIONS

With tomato: Follow the recipe on page 236, substituting 1 cup of tomato juice and ½ cup of tomato purée for the wine and water. Add 3 peeled, seeded and chopped tomatoes.

With green pepper: Sauté the veal cubes in the olive oil until brown, as above, omitting the paprika. Then add 12 small white onions, 3 green peppers, cut into thin strips, and 2 chopped pimientos, and continue sautéing for 15 minutes. Add ½ cup of white wine, cover and simmer for 45 minutes. Add another ½ cup of white wine and simmer until the veal is tender. Serve with rice pilaf.

BLANQUETTE OF VEAL (Serves 4)

This is a famous French dish. It looks elegant when it is brought to the table and makes a grand party specialty.

2½ pounds of veal shoulder cut into 2-inch cubes	8 tablespoons of butter
1 onion stuck with 2 cloves	Lemon juice
Salt	24 small white onions
¼ teaspoon of thyme	4 tablespoons of flour
½ teaspoon of pepper	Salt and pepper
Boiling water	2 egg yolks
15 to 18 mushrooms	½ cup of heavy cream

Place the meat cubes in a deep kettle with the onion stuck with cloves, 1 teaspoon of salt, thyme and freshly ground black pepper. Cover with boiling water, put a lid on the pan and simmer gently until the meat is tender. This will take about 1¼ to 1½ hours.

Meanwhile, remove the stems from the mushrooms and sauté the caps in 4 tablespoons of butter. Add a dash of lemon juice and salt, and cook them until they are just tender. Peel the onions and cook them in just enough salted water to cover until they are barely done. Do not let them get mushy or fall apart. They should be firm.

When the meat is tender, remove it to a hot platter and keep it warm. Let the broth from the meat cook down over a brisk flame for 5 minutes and then strain it. Add the liquid from the onions and any juice from the mushrooms. You will need 2 cups of stock. Add broth or consommé if you haven't enough. Melt 4 tablespoons of butter and blend in the flour. Gradually stir in the stock and continue stirring and cooking until it is smooth and thick. Season to taste with salt and pepper. Beat the egg yolks and mix them with the heavy cream. Add this to the sauce and stir until heated through, but do not let it boil or the eggs will curdle. Add a dash of lemon juice and pour the sauce over the meat. Surround this with the onions and mushrooms and serve with steamed rice.

OSSO BUCO (Serves 4)

4 pieces of veal shank, 2 inches thick

Flour

Salt

Pepper

4 tablespoons of olive oil

1 clove of garlic

$^1/_2$ cup of white wine

$^1/_2$ cup of tomato purée

1 anchovy fillet

3 tablespoons of chopped parsley

Grated rind of a lemon

Dredge the meat in flour seasoned with salt and pepper and brown in olive oil in a heavy pot. Add a finely chopped clove of garlic, white wine and tomato purée and cover the pot. Simmer for 1$^1/_2$ hours. Then add the finely chopped anchovy fillet, chopped parsley and grated lemon rind. Blend thoroughly and heat through. Serve with rice baked in chicken broth and colored with saffron (a very tiny pinch is ample). A green salad makes a nice contrast with this hearty dish. Finish with a light dessert—baked pears with cookies—and some coffee.

Veal Birds

There are many versions of this dish. Basically, they are all made of veal cutlet, sliced rather thin, spread with stuffing and rolled. The rolls are fastened or tied and then browned in butter or other fat. Liquid is added, the pan is covered and the rolls are cooked until tender over low heat or in the oven. Veal birds are usually served with rice or noodles. Sometimes cream or sour cream and herbs are added to the pan juices to make a sauce.

Here are several recipes:

VEAL BIRDS WITH SAUSAGE (Serves 6)

6 slices of veal	¹/₂ cup of broth or white wine
Flour	
³/₄ cup of sausage meat	1 onion stuck with 2 cloves
Pepper	1 additional bay leaf
2 bay leaves	Sprig of parsley
4 tablespoons of butter	1¹/₂ teaspoons of salt

The veal slices should be about 6 by 4 inches and fairly thin. Buy larger slices for people with hearty appetites. Spread the meat out on a table top or working surface and sprinkle the slices lightly with flour. In the center of each place a few spoonfuls of sausage meat. Add a little freshly ground black pepper and a bit of crumbled bay leaf, and roll the slices up. Fasten them with toothpicks or small metal skewers and brown quickly on all sides in hot butter. Add broth or white wine, the onion stuck with cloves, a bay leaf, a sprig of parsley and salt. Cover the pan and simmer gently for 1 hour or until the meat is tender. Turn the rolls once during the cooking.

Serve veal birds on buttered rice with apple slices sautéed in butter and glazed with a little sugar sprinkled over them. Sliced tomatoes and onions are a good choice for a salad course to follow.

VARIATION

With ham: Spread the veal slices with mustard and then add thin slices of ham. Sprinkle with a little rosemary and freshly ground black pepper and roll up and fasten with toothpicks or metal skewers. Cook as above. When the rolls are done, remove them to a hot platter and add 2 tablespoons of flour to the pan. Blend the flour with the pan juices and gradually stir in 1 cup of milk. Continue stirring and cooking until the sauce is smooth and thick. Season to taste with salt and pepper and serve with the rolls. Accompany this version of Veal Birds with Lyonnaise Potatoes.

Calf's Liver

This is one of the great meat delicacies, but it must be the best liver and perfectly cooked to rate this high standing. Some of the liver sold these days is frozen. It is not as good as freshly cut liver. Find a good butcher who keeps a supply of fresh calf's liver and will cut it to your order. One pound will serve 2 to 3 persons, or 4 if appetites are modest.

Liver needs little seasoning. It should be cooked quickly and is best when it is a little rare in the center and nicely browned on the outside. Buy paper-thin slices for quick sautéing and thickish steaks for broiling.

SAUTÉED LIVER (Serves 4)

1½ pounds of thinly sliced liver

3 tablespoons of butter

3 tablespoons of olive oil

Flour

Salt and pepper

½ cup of chopped green onion

½ cup of chopped parsley

Heat the butter and olive oil together (the oil will keep the butter from burning). Dip the liver slices in flour and sauté them quickly, allowing about 1 minute to each side. The slices should be crispy brown but pinkish in the center. Salt and pepper them to taste, sprinkle with chopped green onion and chopped parsley and serve with the pan juices poured over them. With sautéed liver, serve crisp bacon strips, English mustard and tiny new potatoes boiled with their skins on.

BROILED LIVER STEAK

1 or more thick slices of liver, allowing ⅓ to ½ pound per person

Butter

Salt and pepper

Ask the butcher to cut the liver 1½ to 2 inches thick. Brush well with melted butter and broil over charcoal or in the broiler, allowing 4 to 5 minutes for each side. The liver should be nicely browned on the outside and pink inside. Season to taste with salt and freshly ground black pepper and serve with Béarnaise Sauce, French-fried onions, sautéed potatoes and a good tossed salad with plenty of olive oil and wine vinegar dressing.

SWISS SOUR LIVER (Serves 4)

1 pound of liver	**¹/₂ cup of dry white wine**
Flour	**1 bay leaf**
6 tablespoons of butter	**1 cup of sour cream**
Salt and pepper	

Cut the liver into strips about 1 inch wide and 2 inches long and roll the strips in flour. Melt the butter in a skillet and when it is bubbly add the liver and sauté it quickly. This will only take a minute or so. Salt and pepper the liver to taste and remove to a hot platter. Add dry white wine, crumbled bay leaf and sour cream to the pan. Blend these thoroughly with the pan juices and heat through but do not boil or the sour cream will curdle. Return the liver to the sauce and reheat it for a minute. Serve with rice and a casserole of tomatoes and eggplant baked in the oven.

CALF'S LIVER VENETIAN STYLE

1 pound Calf's liver sliced very thin	**Salt**
2 cups onions, thinly sliced	**Freshly ground black pepper**
3 tablespoons olive oil	**1 tablespoon wine vinegar**

Trim the liver and cut into strips 1 inch wide. Set aside. Heat the oil in a large skillet and sauté the onions until cooked through and just beginning to color. Transfer to a bowl and keep warm. Add more oil to the skillet if needed, turn up the heat, and quickly sauté the liver strips, about a minute on each side. Season with salt and pepper. Add the onions to the pan, toss with the liver over medium heat, and stir in the vinegar. Serve at once with boiled new potatoes.

Veal Kidneys

These morsels are true gourmet fare, yet most Americans shun them. I suspect this is due to unfamiliarity. Try them with a good sauce, and I'm sure you'll be delightfully surprised.

One veal kidney will serve one person. If you plan to broil them, have part of the fat removed. For other cooking methods, all fat should be cut away.

BROILED VEAL KIDNEYS

1 kidney per person	**Salt**
Butter	**Pepper**

Ask the butcher to remove part of the fat, or do it yourself before you cook the kidneys. Also remove all the outer membrane. Cut each kidney in 3 or 4 slices and remove the white core. Brush the slices with melted butter and broil them close to the flame until the outside is nicely browned and the inside still pink and rare. Season to taste with salt and pepper.

Serve these broiled kidney slices with a good English mustard, some crisp watercress and French-fried potatoes.

KIDNEYS BLAZED WITH GIN (Serves 4)

4 kidneys without fat	**Juniper berries**
1 pint of water	**4 tablespoons of gin**
Juice of 1 lemon	**2 cups of cooked rice**
4 tablespoons of butter	**$^2/_3$ cup of heavy cream**
8 mushrooms	**Chopped parsley**
Salt and pepper	

Clean the kidneys and soak in the water and lemon juice (acidulated water) for 1 hour. Remove them and wipe them dry. Heat the butter and sauté the kidneys in it, turning them often so they will brown evenly. Add the mushrooms cut in thick slices and let them cook with the kidneys for a few minutes. Add salt and pepper to taste and a few crushed juniper berries. When the kidneys are brown on the outside and still pinkish rare in the center (test with a sharp knife to see how done they are), add the gin and light it to blaze the kidneys and juices in the pan. Arrange the kidneys on a bed of cooked rice. Add heavy cream to the pan and blend and heat through. Pour this over the kidneys and rice, and garnish with chopped parsley. Serve with crisp toasted bread and a beet and egg salad on a bed of romaine.

KIDNEYS IN RED WINE (Serves 4)

This is an excellent dish to prepare at the table in an electric skillet or chafing dish.

4 kidneys with fat removed	**Salt**
Milk	**Pepper**
6 tablespoons of butter	**2 cups of cooked rice**
¹/₂ cup of chopped green onions	**¹/₂ cup of red wine**
Chopped parsley	

Clean the kidneys, cut into thin slices and soak for 1 hour in milk. Melt the butter and sauté the chopped green onions and ¼ cup of chopped parsley for 3 minutes. Remove the kidney slices from the milk and dry them on a towel. Add them to the pan and cook quickly for 2 minutes, browning them on both sides. Salt and pepper them well and arrange them on a bed of cooked rice. Add the red wine to the pan and let it boil up quickly, blending it with the pan juices and onion and parsley. Pour this sauce over the kidneys and rice and sprinkle liberally with chopped parsley.

Lamb

Until recent years Americans always overcooked lamb. People shied away from lamb that was the least bit pink, despite the fact that this is a meat that is much better when served rare. A number of restaurants—

mostly French, to be sure—now serve fine roasted lamb that resembles good rare beef. Slowly we are breaking down the old custom of cooking it until it falls from the bones.

Young lamb is best, of course. Shop around in your community and see if you can find lamb that is genuinely young. The most likely markets are Greek and Italian.

Lamb is graded like beef—*prime, choice, good*. Naturally prime is the finest quality, but choice is excellent. Roasting cuts are the leg, the shoulder and the rack. The saddle, which is the double loin, is sometimes roasted for a grand dinner party. Another party cut is the baron of lamb, a combination of the saddle and two legs. This can be a practical cut if you are roasting on an outdoor electric spit. A crown roast of lamb is a double rack shaped into a crown. It is generally served with mushrooms, sausages or vegetables heaped in the center.

Leg of lamb: This is the most popular roast. It weighs from 3 pounds (from a tiny lamb) to 8 to 10 pounds (from heavy lamb). The fiber-like covering should be removed by the butcher. Some people think the shank bone should be removed, but I find carving easier if it is left in. If you are planning to roast the leg on a spit, have the butcher bone, roll and tie it for you.

Shoulder of lamb is a good buy for roasting or braising. Its flavor is often better than the leg. Be sure to have it boned and rolled or you will have a hard job carving it.

Lamb chops are cut from the loin, the rack and the shoulder. Loin chops are by far the best and should be cut thick—2 to 2½ inches. They should be broiled or pan-broiled just to the rare stage. The French, or rib, chops may be cut thick or as thin as you wish. These small morsels have only about two bites each on them. But they are tasty bites. If you want good-sized portions, ask the butcher to cut the chops three ribs thick, or even four, and grill them until they are crusty brown on the outside but rare in the center. Shoulder chops are popular pan-broiled and can be very tasty.

Lamb steaks are cut from the leg. If you have a small family buy a leg and have the butcher cut one or two thick steaks from it. Roast the rest of the leg for one meal and have another meal of lamb steaks.

Breast of lamb is good braised, barbecued or broiled to the crisp stage. When you buy this cut, look for the leanest you can find. It is apt to be fatty. There is little meat on the breast but the flavor is good.

Cold lamb is delicious if it is pink and juicy. Gray, flabby, cold lamb is thoroughly unappetizing.

Be sure you always serve hot lamb on hot, hot platters or plates. Lamb fat congeals easily and it is unattractive. It doesn't taste good either.

In place of the ever-present mint sauce or jelly, try a bottle of good red wine with lamb. This is the true complement to the meat.

Leg of Lamb

This is a delectable roast if done just to the rare, pink stage. The bone in the leg is large, so allow at least 1 pound per serving. Be sure the butcher removes the filmy covering on the outside of this cut. This transparent fiber is as tough as plastic.

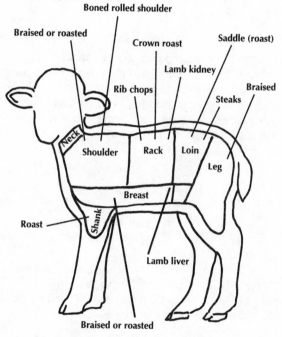

ROAST LEG OF LAMB (Serves 4)

5- to 6-pound leg of lamb	**Flour**
2 cloves of garlic	**Salt**

Wipe the meat with a damp cloth. Make about 6 or 8 gashes in the flesh and insert slivers of garlic. Rub with flour and let stand at room temperature for about 1 hour. Preheat the oven to 325°. Insert a meat thermometer in the thickest part of the meat without touching the bone. Arrange the leg of lamb in a roasting or baking pan, salt to taste, and roast, without basting, until the meat thermometer reaches 140°. If you remove the roast when it registers 140° and let it stand for a few minutes, it will continue to cook with its own heat. The lamb will take about 1¼ to 1¾ hours to cook, for medium-rare.

Serve with the pan juices and the following bean dish:

Soak 2 cups of dried beans overnight (unless you use quick-cooking beans). Cook them in salted water to cover with 1 onion stuck with 2 cloves, 2 crushed cloves of garlic and a bay leaf (see page 16). When tender, remove from the stove and drain well. Dress with plenty of butter, some fresh crushed garlic and a handful of chopped parsley.

With the roast lamb and beans serve plain watercress or crisp celery and a good bottle of red wine.

VARIATION

Baker's Style: Let the roast cook for ½ hour. Meanwhile, peel potatoes and cut them in halves or quarters. Boil them in salted water for 10 minutes. Drain thoroughly. After the meat has roasted for ½ hour, add the potatoes to the roasting pan, season them to taste with salt and freshly ground black pepper, dot them with butter and sprinkle with a little rosemary. Let them cook with the roast, turning them once and basting a bit with the pan juices.

STUFFED LEG OF LAMB

When you go to buy the lamb, take with you 2 or 3 peeled cloves of garlic and a few sprigs of fresh mint. Ask the butcher to bone the leg, put the garlic and mint in it and then roll and tie it. Or have him bone the leg, then take it home and finish the job yourself.

Roast this stuffed, boned leg according to the directions for Roast Leg of Lamb (page 245). Serve with the same bean dish and chopped spinach dressed with butter and a touch of nutmeg.

POLYNESIAN STUFFED LEG OF LAMB, ALBERT STOCKLI

A fine New York chef created this stuffing one night on the spur of the moment. It is unusual and unusually delicious.

Buy a boned leg. In the center put thick slices of avocado, strips of pimiento and slivers of garlic. Salt and pepper well and roll and tie tightly.

Roast according to directions for Roast Leg of Lamb (page 245). Serve this with rice pilaf.

VARIATION

Roast rack of lamb: For a small dinner for 2 persons, use a rack of lamb. Make a deep cut in the rack and insert the avocado, pimiento and garlic. Tie it firmly. Season with salt and pepper and roast at 375° for about 35 minutes, or until a meat thermometer inserted in the fleshy part registers 140°. Serve with crisp fried potatoes.

MARINATED LEG OF LAMB (Serves 4)

5-pound leg of lamb	2 teaspoons of oregano
2 cloves of garlic	2 teaspoons of salt
½ cup of olive oil	1 carrot, sliced
1 pint of red wine	3 sprigs of parsley
3 thickly sliced onions	
¼ teaspoon of ground cloves	

Wipe the leg with a damp cloth and insert slivers of garlic in the flesh. In a deep bowl mix the rest of the ingredients. Put the lamb in this marinade and set it in the refrigerator or a very cool place. Marinate it for 24 hours, turning frequently to be sure it is bathed on all sides.

Remove the meat from the marinade, arrange in a roasting or baking pan and insert a meat thermometer in the flesh, being sure it does not touch the bone. Roast in a 400° oven, basting often with the marinade, until the thermometer registers 140°. This will take about 1¼ hours. Remove the meat to a hot platter, degrease the juices in the pan, add 1 cup of the marinade and bring to a boil. Serve this sauce with the roast, and with it also serve sautéed potatoes, buttered turnips mixed with sautéed mushrooms, watercress and a good red wine. For dessert, cheese, fruit and more red wine.

BRAISED LEG OF LAMB (Serves 4)

5-pound leg of lamb	6 peeled turnips
Garlic	12 small, unpeeled potatoes
Flour	$\frac{1}{2}$ teaspoon of pepper
Salt	$\frac{1}{4}$ cup of chopped parsley
Butter	1 teaspoon of rosemary
8 small peeled onions	1 cup of consommé or
6 peeled carrots	bouillon

Prepare the leg for roasting according to instructions in Roast Leg of Lamb (page 245). Insert a meat thermometer in the fleshy part of the leg and place it in a large roasting pan with a cover. Brown, uncovered, in a hot (500°) oven, basting every few minutes with melted butter. This should take about 25 minutes. When the meat is well browned, add the onions, carrots, turnips and potatoes and sprinkle all with pepper, rosemary and chopped parsley. Pour in 1 cup of consommé (or 1 cup of boiling water mixed with 1 bouillon cube), cover the pan and reduce the heat to 300°. Cook until the meat thermometer registers 140° and the vegetables are tender. Serve with crisp French or Italian bread and an orange, onion and romaine salad.

BOILED LEG OF LAMB (Serves 4)

This old English dish is surprisingly good. It is juicy, tender and full of flavor.

5-pound leg of lamb	1 tablespoon of salt
2 cloves of garlic	1 onion stuck with 2 cloves
Rosemary	1 bay leaf
Water to cover	1 sliced carrot

Wipe the meat with a damp cloth and slash the flesh in several places. Insert slivers of garlic and rub the leg well with rosemary. Put it in a large kettle and cover with boiling water. Add the salt, the onion stuck with cloves, the bay leaf and sliced carrot. Cover the kettle and simmer gently for about 1½ hours. Then insert a meat thermometer in the fleshy part of the leg and see if it will register 140°. If not, remove the thermometer and cook for a few more minutes. Then test again. When the meat reaches

140°, remove it to a hot platter and surround it with mounds of cooked spinach. Serve with mashed potatoes and the following Caper Sauce:

Caper Sauce: Melt 3 tablespoons of butter and blend in 3 tablespoons of flour. Slowly add 1 cup of degreased lamb broth, stirring constantly to be sure it does not lump. When the mixture is thick and smooth, cook it for 4 more minutes and add ½ cup of cream beaten with 2 egg yolks. Do this gently or the egg will curdle. Never let the sauce boil. Add ¼ cup of capers and season to taste with salt and freshly ground black pepper.

Shoulder of Lamb

This cut is usually boned, rolled and tied. It has excellent flavor but not the firm texture of the leg meat. It can be cooked in any of the ways suggested for Leg of Lamb.

ROAST SHOULDER OF LAMB

Cook according to the directions for Roast Leg of Lamb (page 245). The meat thermometer should register 140° for medium-rare.

SPITTED SHOULDER OR LEG OF LAMB

The boned shoulder or a boned, rolled and tied leg may be spitted and cooked over charcoal or in an electric rotisserie. Insert a meat thermometer, rub the meat well with salt and pepper and oregano or rosemary. Balance it carefully on the spit and roast over charcoal or in the rotisserie until the thermometer registers 140° for medium-rare.

Serve with sautéed potatoes or baked potatoes.

BRAISED SHOULDER OF LAMB (Serves 4)

3-pound boned shoulder of lamb

2 cloves of garlic

Olive oil

1/2 cup of soy sauce (Japanese)

1/2 cup of sherry

1/4 cup of grated fresh ginger or 2 teaspoons of ground ginger

6 tablespoons of olive oil

2 onions stuck with cloves

Sprig of parsley

Wipe the boned and tied shoulder with a damp cloth and slash the flesh in several places. Insert slivers of garlic and rub the lamb well with olive oil. In a large bowl mix the soy sauce (Japanese soy sauce is best), the fresh or ground ginger and the sherry. Put the meat in this marinade and let it soak for 4 hours, turning occasionally. Remove the lamb, wipe it with paper towels and brown with 6 tablespoons of hot olive oil in a heavy kettle or Dutch oven. When it is browned on all sides, add the onion stuck with cloves, the parsley and the liquid in which the lamb marinated. Cover and simmer gently in a 300° oven for 2 hours. Remove the lamb to a hot platter and pour the degreased juices over it. Serve with steamed rice, braised cabbage (use Chinese cabbage for this, if you can get it) and tiny white onions glazed.

BRAISED SHOULDER OF LAMB, PERSIAN STYLE (Serves 4)

3-pound boned shoulder of lamb

2 cloves of garlic

4 tablespoons of olive oil

8 small white onions, peeled

4 peeled and seeded tomatoes or 1 can of solid pack tomatoes

1 teaspoon of thyme

1 1/2 teaspoons of salt

1 teaspoon of pepper

1 large eggplant or 2 small ones

Butter

Chopped parsley

Wipe the meat with a damp cloth and slash the flesh in several places. Insert slivers of garlic. Heat the olive oil in a large kettle and brown the lamb on all sides in the hot oil. Add the onions, tomatoes, thyme, salt, and freshly ground black pepper and cover the kettle. Simmer gently for 1 hour. Peel and cube the eggplant and add it to the top of the ingredients. Dot with butter, cover the kettle and simmer until the eggplant is tender.

Remove the lamb to a hot platter and surround it with the eggplant and onions. Degrease the sauce, then boil vigorously for 5 or 6 minutes to reduce it and pour it over the meat. Sprinkle lavishly with chopped parsley. With this serve a rice pilaf mixed with raisins and pine nuts.

BRAISED SHOULDER OF LAMB, TARRAGON (Serves 4)

3-pound shoulder of lamb, boned	Butter
	Olive oil
Tarragon	½ cup of white wine or vermouth
Salt and pepper	
Flour	

Wipe the meat with a damp cloth and make several gashes in the flesh. Push a few tarragon leaves into the gashes. Then rub the meat with tarragon, salt and flour. Melt 4 tablespoons of butter with 3 tablespoons of oil in a heavy kettle or Dutch oven. Brown the lamb shoulder on all sides in the hot fat. Insert a meat thermometer in the fleshiest part. Add 1 teaspoon of tarragon, 1 teaspoon of salt and 1 teaspoon of freshly ground black pepper. Pour the white wine or vermouth into the kettle, cover and roast in a 300° oven for 40 minutes. Remove the cover and continue roasting until the thermometer registers 140°.

Remove the meat to a hot platter, degrease the juices, and pour over the meat. Serve with tiny new potatoes and tiny French peas cooked with onion and mixed with bits of smoked ham and plenty of butter.

Breast of Lamb

This economical cut can be most tasty if it is not too fatty. Buy the leanest you can find. Because it is very bony, you must allow about 1 pound per person.

BARBECUED BREAST OF LAMB (Serves 4)

4 pounds of breast of lamb	Water to cover
1 onion, peeled	Mustard
1 bay leaf	Catsup
1 tablespoon of salt	Fine, dry bread crumbs

Leave the breast in one piece and put it in a kettle with the onion, bay leaf and salt. Cover with water and bring to a boil. Cover, lower the heat and simmer for 30 minutes, or until almost tender. Remove the lamb to a platter, cover with a plate or several layers of foil and weight the meat down by putting heavy objects (cans of food or an electric iron) on top. Let the meat cool. When it is cool, remove the weights and slip out all the bones you can.

Brush the meat well with mustard and then with catsup. Roll in fine crumbs and broil slowly in the oven or over charcoal until browned on one side; then turn to brown on the other side. Serve with Sauce Diable (page 351).

VARIATIONS

Breaded: After the lamb has simmered and been cooled, remove the bones and dip the meat in beaten egg and then in crumbs. Sauté in hot butter until brown on both sides. Serve with Sauce Soubise (page 350).

LAMB BREASTS, CHINESE STYLE (Serves 4)

2 to 3 breasts of very young lamb	2 tablespoons of finely chopped fresh or candied ginger
Soy sauce (Japanese variety)	$\frac{1}{2}$ cup of vermouth
2 cloves of chopped garlic	$\frac{1}{4}$ cup of olive or peanut oil

Brush the meat well with soy sauce and roll in the garlic and ginger. Arrange on a rack in a baking pan and roast in a 325° oven for 1½ hours, basting frequently with a mixture of the vermouth, oil and ¼ cup of soy sauce. If the breasts are not crisp enough, run them under the broiler for the last few minutes.

Serve with fried rice, buttered asparagus and garlic or herbed bread. Pass paper napkins.

Charcoal-Broiled: Broil these breasts of lamb over charcoal, basting frequently with the sauce. Cook them slowly to brown and crisp well and cook through.

Lamb Chops

Lamb chops are luxury fare. If you plan to have them, splurge and buy the best thick chops. Allow 1 large or 2 small chops per person. They should be at least 1½ inches thick, and even 2½ inches is not too much. Do not overcook them. They are best rare.

BROILED LAMB CHOPS

Here is a timetable for broiling chops. The time given is *total* broiling time.

1½-inch chops:
> 6 to 8 minutes for rare
> 8 to 10 minutes for medium-rare
> 10 to 13 minutes for well-done

2-inch chops:
> 9 to 12 minutes for rare
> 12 to 14 minutes for medium-rare
> 16 to 20 minutes for well-done

3-inch chops:
> 12 to 15 minutes for rare
> 15 to 18 minutes for medium-rare
> 20 to 25 minutes for well-done

Cook for half of time given on one side and then turn to finish cooking on the other side. Bring close to the heat for the last half minute to get a brown crust. If you are cooking very thick chops, turn the fat edge to the heat for a minute or two at the last to brown and cook crisp, but make sure it is not close enough to the heat to catch fire. Season to taste with salt and freshly ground black pepper.

ENGLISH LAMB CHOPS

These are double loin chops cut clear across the saddle. They are expensive and elegant. Ask the butcher to tie a kidney in the center and fasten the chop with a skewer. Allow 1 per person and grill according to the timetable on page 253. Serve with stuffed baked potatoes and coleslaw. Cold ale or beer is a fine accompaniment.

RIB OR FRENCH CHOPS

Have the butcher trim the chops and scrape the bone. He should give you little paper frills to add to the bone tips when you serve. Allow at least two chops for each person. Grill as you do loin chops (page 253). Serve on toast with a garnish of watercress and crisp potato chips.

VARIATION

Pan-broil the chops. Heat a skillet and add just a bit of butter. Cook the chops quickly, 2 or 3 minutes to a side, just until nicely browned. Season to taste.

BABY LAMB CHOPS

These are very tiny. One person can easily eat three of them. Have them cut about 1½ inches thick. Pan-fry them in a little butter, allowing about 1 teaspoon of butter for each chop. Sear them quickly on both sides and then reduce the heat to let them sauté slowly until cooked to the stage of doneness you prefer. Test by making a slight cut next to the bone. Season to taste with salt and pepper.

When the chops are done, remove them to a hot platter. Pour off any fat. Add 1 tablespoon of butter to the pan, 1 teaspoon of tarragon and 2 tablespoons of chopped parsley. Finally add 2 ounces of dry white wine or dry vermouth and heat and blend with the pan juices and herbs. Pour this over the meat.

ROAST RACK OF LAMB

The rack consists of one side of the rib chops, 6 to 7 in all, enough for two servings. Have the chine bone cut through so the chops can be carved without difficulty, and wrap foil around each rib end so it doesn't char in cooking. A rack should be roasted at a high temperature to the rare stage.

1 rack of lamb, well trimmed	**Salt**
1 clove of garlic, crushed	**Freshly ground black pepper**
1 teaspoon crumbled rosemary or thyme	

Set the oven to 450°. Rub the lamb with the garlic, rosemary or thyme, and salt and pepper. Place, fat side down, on a rack in a roasting pan. Roast for 15 minutes then turn it over to the bone side and roast another 5 minutes. Press the meat lightly with your fingers and a layer of paper towel. If it feels fairly firm, it is done. If not, continue cooking 5 to 7 minutes or until a meat thermometer registers 140°, for medium-rare. Let it rest for five minutes before carving. You can either cut down between the bones or in long slices parallel to the bone. Serve with broiled tomatoes.

Rack of Lamb Persillé: Trim most of the fat from the lamb. Mix 2 finely chopped garlic cloves with ¾ cup of fine fresh breadcrumbs, ½ cup of chopped parsley, and a sprinkling of salt and freshly ground black pepper. Rub the rack with butter, place in a shallow roasting pan, fat side down, and roast for 20 minutes at 450°. Reduce the heat to 400°, invert the lamb, and roast another 5 minutes. Remove from the oven and pat the crumb mixture on the fat side. Either return to the oven or place under a broiler to brown the crust.

Lamb Ragouts

A fine ragout—or stew, if you prefer—is meat braised slowly and gently in some liquid with a bit of seasoning added. It is an excellent way to prepare the less tender cuts, and if done well can be as elegant as a roast.

RAGOUT OF SPRING LAMB (Serves 6)

4¹/₂ to 5 pounds of lean
    shoulder or breast of
    lamb

Flour

6 to 8 tablespoons of beef
    fat or butter

12 small white peeled
    onions

2 or 3 peeled carrots

2 crushed cloves of garlic

1 leek

1 teaspoon of thyme or
    marjoram

1 bay leaf

Salt

Pepper

1¹/₂ to 2 cups of broth or
    water

12 tiny new potatoes,
    parboiled

¹/₄ cup of chopped parsley

Buy lean meat and have it cut into serving-size pieces. Don't let the butcher cut it into tiny cubes. The pieces should be big enough to look like meat when they are cooked. Flour the meat lightly and brown thoroughly on all sides in beef fat or butter. You will need quite a bit of fat to do this job—6 to 8 tablespoons or even more. When the meat is all browned, add the onions, carrots, garlic, leek, thyme or marjoram, bay leaf and salt and pepper to taste. Add enough broth or water to half cover the meat and vegetables, cover the pan and simmer gently for 45 minutes.

Remove the lamb, onions and carrots and put them in a casserole. Add the potatoes, which have been parboiled for 10 minutes in salted water. Skim the fat from the liquid in which the meat was cooked and strain the sauce through a sieve lined with a piece of fine linen to catch all the cloudy particles. Pour the strained sauce over the meat and vegetables and top with the chopped parsley. Cover and bake in a 350° oven for 45 minutes to an hour. Serve from the casserole. The only additions necessary to make this a fine dinner are a good green salad and toasted French bread. Thicken with Beurre Manié (page 348) if desired.

NAVARIN (FRENCH SPRING LAMB RAGOUT) (Serves 6)

4¹/₂ to 5 pounds of lean shoulder or breast of lamb

Flour

6 to 8 tablespoons of beef fat or butter

Salt and pepper

Broth or water

12 turnips, peeled and halved

12 small white onions, peeled

Butter

2 teaspoons of sugar

2 garlic cloves

4 carrots, peeled and cut in sticks (julienne)

1 or 2 leeks

12 small new potatoes

1 package of frozen peas

Have the meat cut into serving-size pieces. Flour lightly and brown thoroughly on all sides in 6 to 8, or more, tablespoons of fat. When the meat is browned, add salt and pepper to taste and enough broth or water to half cover the meat. Cover the pan and simmer gently for 45 minutes. While the meat is simmering sear the turnips and onions in butter, then turn the heat down and let them sauté gently, shaking the pan from time to time to cook them evenly. Sprinkle them with the sugar to glaze slightly.

Remove the meat to a casserole, add the turnips, onions, garlic, carrots, leeks and new potatoes with their skins on. Skim the fat from the liquid in which the meat was cooked and strain the sauce through a sieve lined with a piece of fine linen. Pour the strained sauce over the meat and vegetables and add broth, if necessary. Put a lid on the casserole and bake in a 350° oven for 1 hour. Add the frozen peas 15 minutes before the meat and vegetables are done. Thicken with Beurre Manié (page 348) if desired.

VARIATIONS

With rice: Omit the potatoes and add 1½ cups of washed rice 30 minutes before the casserole is done. At the same time add 1 cup of boiling broth or consommé.

Bretonne: Soak 2 cups of dry beans overnight and boil until tender. Add these in place of the potatoes. Or add canned kidney beans during the last half hour of cooking.

Italian: Omit the potatoes and substitute tomato purée for half of the broth. Add 1 teaspoon of oregano and several spoonfuls of chopped Italian parsley. Serve with buttered noodles.

Mexican: Omit the potatoes and substitute tomato purée for half of the broth. Flavor with 2 teaspoons of chili powder, or more, to taste. Add 1 cup of pitted ripe olives during the last half hour of cooking. Serve with Polenta (page 174).

Californian: Omit the potatoes and substitute tomato purée for half of the broth. Add 3 green peppers cut in strips and 1 cup of pitted ripe olives. Serve with garlic bread and a salad of avocado, orange and onion slices.

IRISH STEW (Serves 6)

This dish is actually a white ragout of mutton.

4 pounds of lean shoulder or breast of lamb	**1 stalk of celery**
6 medium potatoes, peeled	**3 sprigs of parsley**
6 medium onions, peeled	**1 bay leaf**
Salt and pepper	**1 teaspoon of thyme**
1 leek	**Water to cover**

Have the butcher cut the meat into serving-size pieces. In a large casserole arrange a layer of the meat and top with a layer of sliced potatoes and a layer of sliced onions. Season with salt and pepper and repeat the layers until the meat and vegetables are used up, ending with a layer of meat on top. Add the other seasonings and just enough water to cover. Put a lid on the casserole and bake in a 350° oven for 1½ hours or until the meat is tender.

Serve with hot biscuits or hot bread and a good green salad.

LAMB CURRY WITH RICE (Serves 6)

3 to 4 pounds of lean lamb shoulder
1 onion stuck with 2 cloves
1 bay leaf
1 crushed clove of garlic
Water or broth
Salt
2 large onions, chopped
2 large apples, chopped, unpeeled
6 tablespoons of butter

1 1/2 tablespoons of curry powder
1 teaspoon ground or 1 tablespoon grated fresh ginger
1 teaspoon of chili powder
1 teaspoon of pepper
1 tablespoon of tomato purée
Cornstarch or Beurre Manié (page 348)

Ask the butcher to cut the lamb into serving-size pieces. Put the meat in a saucepan with the onion stuck with cloves, the bay leaf and garlic, and season to taste with a little salt. Add just enough water or broth to cover, and bring to a boil. Put a lid on the pan, lower the heat and simmer gently for 45 minutes.

In the meantime, peel the onions and chop them, and chop the apples, leaving the peel on. Melt the butter and sauté the chopped onions and apples until tender. Sprinkle them with the curry powder, ginger, chili powder and pepper, and add the tomato purée.

Skim the fat from the broth in which the meat has cooked and add 1 cup of the broth to the apple and onion mixture. Cover the pan and simmer gently for 30 minutes. Taste for seasoning and add salt and more curry if necessary. Add another cup of broth and blend and heat through. Thicken with cornstarch or Beurre Manié. Add the meat and simmer for 1/2 hour, covered.

Serve with rice pilaf, crisp French-fried onions, chutney, toasted almonds, grated coconut, raisins soaked in Cognac and crisp, crumbled bacon. Other condiments that go well with curry dishes are Bombay duck (this comes in cans), chopped raw onions, chopped green pepper and chopped hard-cooked eggs.

Shish Kebab

These morsels are best when made with lean lamb from the shoulder or leg. Have the butcher cut the meat into $1\frac{1}{2}$- to 2-inch cubes. The meat can be marinated or not, as you wish (for marinades, see Marinated Shish Kebab below). Allow 5 or 6 cubes of meat per person and push these on individual skewers. The closer you pack the meat on the skewers, the rarer and juicier the result will be.

PLAIN SHISH KEBAB

Arrange the meat on skewers and brush with olive oil, lemon juice and salt and pepper to taste. Broil, turning often to brown evenly, until crusty brown on the outside and rare-pink in the center. Or broil to your favorite state of doneness. Serve with Rice Pilaf, Barley Casserole, or Kasha.

VARIATIONS

Herbed: Sprinkle the kebabs with oregano or rosemary.

With fruit or vegetables: Alternate the meat cubes with any of the fruits or vegetables listed below. When broiling kebabs with these additions, brush the fruit or vegetables frequently with oil or butter to keep them from charring:

Tomato quarters
Onion squares (not rounds, which will break into rings and fall off the skewers)
Squares of green pepper
Mushrooms
Tiny whole onions which have been parboiled for 5 or 10 minutes
Pineapple chunks
Orange slices with the skin left on, dipped in rosemary
Preserved kumquats

MARINATED SHISH KEBAB

Soak the lamb cubes for 4 to 24 hours in any of the following marinades:

1. 4 parts olive oil to 1 part lemon juice, seasoned with thyme, oregano, rosemary or tarragon.

2. 3 parts red wine to 1 part olive oil and 1 part lemon juice, seasoned with crushed garlic, thyme or oregano and freshly ground pepper.

3. 1 cup of soy sauce, ¼ cup of olive oil, ¼ cup of orange juice, 2 crushed cloves of garlic and grated fresh ginger.

Turn the meat pieces several times during the soaking. When ready to broil, wipe the meat with paper towels, arrange the cubes on skewers, brush with a little oil and lemon juice and cook as for Plain Shish Kebab (page 260).

SHASHLIK

This is the Russian version of Shish Kebab. Marinate the lamb cubes in the mixture listed below:

1 cup of oil	**Dill or bay leaves**
1 cup of red wine	**1 teaspoon of salt**
¼ cup of lemon and orange juice, mixed	**1 teaspoon of freshly ground black pepper**

Soak the meat for 24 hours, turning frequently. Arrange it on skewers and broil as you do Marinated Shish Kebab (see above).

Chopped Lamb

Chopped lamb can be rather dry, especially when it is made into patties. If prepared with plenty of lubrication it can be very good. Try these Near Eastern methods for best results.

NEAR EASTERN MEAT BALLS (Serves 4)

1½ pounds of ground lamb	**½ cup of chopped parsley**
2 cloves of garlic, minced	**Salt and pepper**
1 egg, lightly beaten	**Olive oil**
½ cup of pine nuts	

Mix the meat with the garlic, egg, pine nuts, parsley and salt and pepper to taste. Moisten with a little olive oil and form into tiny balls. Sauté in hot olive oil, shaking the pan briskly, until nicely brown on the outside but still pinkish rare in the middle. This will only take a few minutes.

Serve with rice and sautéed or broiled eggplant.

MOUSSAKA (Serves 4)

2 large or 3 medium eggplants	Salt and pepper
2 cloves of garlic	1 teaspoon of oregano
Olive oil	$1/2$ cup of chopped parsley
2 onions	$1 1/2$ pounds of ground lamb
$1/2$ cup of fine bread crumbs	2 eggs, lightly beaten
	$1/4$ cup of tomato paste

Cut the eggplants in quarters and peel the skin off each quarter in one section. Cut the meat of the eggplant into cubes and dust these with flour. Sauté in hot olive oil (about $1/4$ cup) with a minced clove of garlic. When they are all browned, remove half of the cubes and reserve them. Put the rest in a large mixing bowl with the finely chopped onions, the second clove of garlic, minced, the bread crumbs, salt and pepper to taste, oregano and the chopped parsley. Brown the ground lamb quickly in the pan in which you cooked the eggplant and add the meat to the 2 eggs, lightly beaten, and the tomato paste. Blend this in with the eggplant and crumb mixture.

Butter a large casserole and line it with the eggplant skin, purple side out. Arrange a layer of the plain eggplant cubes in the bottom, top with the meat mixture and add the rest of the plain cubes of eggplant. Dot with butter, cover and place in a pan of hot water. Bake in a 350° oven for 2 hours. Remove the casserole from the oven and let it stand for 10 minutes. Then turn it upside down to invert the contents on a large platter. Serve with rice pilaf and a tomato sauce (see pages 352–353).

Variations

With sliced eggplant: Cover the top of the casserole with sautéed eggplant slices.

With mushrooms and pine nuts: Add ½ pound of finely chopped mushrooms and ½ cup of pine nuts to the meat mixture.

With leftover lamb: Substitute ground leftover lamb for the fresh ground lamb.

Lamb Kidneys and Liver

These are highly prized delicacies and a fine choice for company breakfast, luncheon or late supper. They should be split and the white cord or membrane removed. Some people like to soak them in water with a little lemon juice or vinegar added, or in milk, for an hour or so before cooking. This is not necessary.

Cook kidneys quickly and serve them rare. They toughen when overcooked. Allow 2 or 3 kidneys per person.

BROILED KIDNEYS

Brush the split kidneys with melted butter or olive oil and broil very quickly under a hot flame until browned on the outside but still rare in the center. Season to taste with salt and pepper and serve with crisp bacon slices.

DEVILED KIDNEYS

Brush split kidneys with melted butter and English mustard. Broil quickly (see above) and serve with sauce Diable (page 351).

For English mustard: mix 1½ teaspoons of dry mustard with enough water or vinegar to make a smooth paste.

VARIATION

Breaded: Cook as for Deviled Kidneys and when the kidneys are broiled, dip them in melted butter, brush with more mustard and roll in fine bread or cracker crumbs. Return to the broiler to brown the crumbs. Serve with Sauce Diable (page 351) or with English mustard and crisp bacon strips.

KIDNEYS AND MUSHROOMS EN BROCHETTE

En brochette simply means broiled on skewers. Allow 2 kidneys and 4 large mushrooms per skewer and serve 1 skewer per person. Split the kidneys in half. Start each skewer with a mushroom, then add a kidney half, then another mushroom and so on until the skewer is full. If appetites are hearty, add another kidney to each skewer.

Brush the kidneys and mushrooms with melted butter and broil quickly, turning often to brown on all sides. Season to taste with salt and pepper and serve with boiled new potatoes and green beans dressed with plenty of butter and mixed with chopped almonds.

LAMB'S LIVER

This is as delicious as calf's liver and usually much less expensive. Prepare it according to any of the recipes for Calf's Liver (pages 240–241).

Mutton

Few Americans appreciate the fine dish that mutton can be, and nowadays it is hard to find. It is heavy meat and should be aged, just as beef is. Then cook it to the rare stage and you will have rich, juicy meat as tasty as any roast beef. Look for Canadian mutton when you buy; it is grown especially for the butcher market.

LEG OF MUTTON

Prepare according to the recipe for Roast Leg of Lamb (page 245) and be sure you cook it only to the rare stage (135° to 140° on the meat thermometer). Serve with mashed buttered turnips and roast potatoes.

ENGLISH MUTTON CHOPS

These huge chops should be cut at least 3 inches thick and 4 inches, if possible. Roast them in a 400° oven, basting them with the fat in the pan, for 20 minutes. Then put them in the broiler to brown to a crisp on both

sides. Season to taste with salt and pepper and serve with sautéed potatoes.

VARIATIONS

With tarragon: Baste the chops with a mixture of olive oil, lemon juice
and tarragon.

With thyme: Baste with consommé flavored with thyme.

With mushrooms: Serve with broiled mushrooms, broiled bacon and
crisp potatoes.

Pork

The French epicure Grimod de la Reynière once remarked that the pig
was the most encyclopedic of animals. Every part of the beast is edible,
he said, and every part is awfully good.

One thing to remember about pork is that it must cook thoroughly. To
kill trichinae, which may lurk in underdone pork, the meat should always
achieve a thermometer reading of at least 140°. To cook to the proper state
of doneness, allow a pork roast to reach an internal temperature of 160°
to 170°. Remove from the oven and let stand for a few minutes before carving.

The loin is the most popular roast of pork, though a fresh ham (leg)
can be just as good. Shoulder of pork roasts well but is even better braised.

There are three types of pork chops: loin, rib and shoulder. Loin chops
include part of the tenderloin and are the choicest. Rib chops are smaller
and not quite as tender, but are a good selection if you plan to braise them.
Shoulder chops are most economical but the flavor is less delicate. As with
pork roast, chops must be cooked thoroughly. Broiling is not wise, for
they tend to dry out before they reach the well-done stage.

The pork steak, which is cut from the fresh ham (leg), deserves to be
better known. It is excellent eating.

Spareribs, broiled or roasted, are one of the tastiest dishes among meats.
If you have an outdoor charcoal grill, by all means barbecue them.

Good pork is pinkish gray and the fat is white and waxy. When you
shop, avoid oversize pork. Meat from medium or small animals is usually firmer and better flavored.

Allow 1 pound per person for most pork cuts. Remember, bone and
fat take up part of the weight.

Loin of Pork

There are three cuts of pork that roast well: the loin, the fresh ham (leg), and the shoulder. Loin of pork is considered the choicest of the three and is certainly the easiest to cook. This portion of the pig includes the rib and loin section. The rib end contains delicate little chops; the loin end has loin chops and tenderloin. When you buy a loin roast, a center cut is most desirable, since it has the best of the ribs and tenderloin. The next best choice is a cut from the loin end.

The loin has a great deal of bone and you must allow about 1 pound per person. Ask the butcher to cut through the chine bone, which is attached to the rib and loin bones. This makes carving easier.

ROAST LOIN OF PORK (Serves 4)

4-pound loin roast	**Thyme**
Salt	**4 potatoes**
Pepper	

Be sure to have the butcher cut through the chine bone to make the roast easy to carve. Wipe the meat with a damp cloth and rub the fat side of the roast well with salt, pepper and thyme. Arrange it in a roasting or baking pan, fat side up. Insert a meat thermometer in the fleshiest part, but do not let it touch the bone. Roast, uncovered, in a 325° oven until the thermometer registers about 165°. This will take approximately 25 minutes per pound. Take the roast from the oven and let it stand a few minutes before carving. It will continue to cook with its own heat and the juices will settle.

If you like potatoes roasted with the meat, peel 4 potatoes and cut them in halves or quarters. Add them to the roasting pan about 45 minutes before the meat is done. Turn them once or twice during the cooking so they will brown evenly. Salt and pepper them as you turn them. Small white onions may be peeled and added to the roasting pan at the same time.

Serve roast pork with apple sauce or Glazed Apple Rings (page 145). Horseradish and mustard are both good with pork too. It is a rich meat and needs the contrast of sharp flavors.

VARIATIONS

With pan-roasted apples: Start the roast as above and 45 minutes before the meat is done add the potatoes, arranging them at one end of the

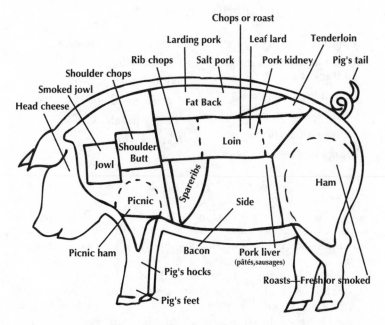

Chops or roast

Larding pork · Leaf lard · Tenderloin

Rib chops · Salt pork · Pork kidney · Pig's tail

Shoulder chops

Smoked jowl

Head cheese

Fat Back

Shoulder Butt · Loin

Jowl

Spareribs

Ham

Picnic · Side

Picnic ham · Bacon · Pork liver (pâtés, sausages)

Pig's hocks

Roasts—Fresh or smoked

Pig's feet

roasting pan. Arrange apple quarters at the other end and sprinkle them with a little sugar. Baste with the pan juices during the cooking.

Remove the roast to a hot platter and surround it with the apples and potatoes. Pour off all but 3 tablespoons of the fat in the roasting pan. Put the pan over heat on top of the stove and add 1½ cups of heavy cream and salt and pepper to taste. Cook and stir this into the 3 tablespoons of fat and scrape the bits of brown from the bottom and sides of the pan, blending it all together. Bring just to a boil. Serve this sauce with the meat.

With rosemary: Rub the roast with rosemary instead of thyme.

COLD ROAST LOIN OF PORK

Roast a loin of pork as above and let it cool to room temperature without chilling. Serve cut in thin slices with Mustard Mayonnaise (page 345), French Potato Salad (page 335) and Glazed Apple Rings (page 145).

CHOUCROUTE GARNIE (Serves 6)

3 pounds of loin of pork

Bacon or salt pork cut in
thick slices

4 pounds of sauerkraut

6 pig's feet or pig's knuckles

3 cloves of garlic

1 large piece of salt pork

2 teaspoons of pepper

Pinch of dill

White wine

1 garlic sausage

9 to 12 potatoes

6 knockwurst

This is an excellent hot buffet for a large group. It can be made the day before and is even better reheated.

Line a big kettle with strips of salt pork or bacon. Wash the sauerkraut and put it in the kettle. Wipe the loin with a damp cloth and add it along with the pig's feet or knuckles, the large piece of salt pork, the garlic, pepper and dill. Add just enough dry white wine to cover the ingredients. Put a lid on the kettle and simmer gently for 4 hours. Add the garlic sausage and cook another 15 minutes. Then add the knockwurst and cook 15 to 20 more minutes.

Meanwhile, boil the potatoes unpeeled. These will take about ½ hour, so put them on to cook when you add the garlic sausage to the sauerkraut mixture.

Arrange the sauerkraut in the center of a large platter. Surround it with the pig's feet, sliced salt pork, sliced loin of pork and sausages. Serve with the boiled potatoes.

VARIATIONS

You can make this dish with ham and salt pork or with chicken and pork.

Fresh Ham

Fresh ham is the uncured leg of pork. This cut varies in size from 5 to 6 pounds on up to 25 pounds. Allow 1 pound per person and if you cannot find a small enough fresh ham, buy a half ham. You may have leftover meat for the next day but it is excellent cold. Many butchers try to skin the leg for you. Don't let this happen. You are losing one of the best parts of the roast. The skin of the fresh ham, if properly cooked, is crisp and crunchy, a tasty tidbit to nibble on.

ROAST FRESH HAM (Serves 4 to 6)

6-pound leg of fresh pork
Salt and pepper

Thyme, oregano, or rosemary

Wipe the fresh ham with a damp cloth and score the skin. That is, slash it with a knife, crossing the slashes to make a diamond-shaped design. Rub the surface well with salt and pepper and thyme, oregano or rosemary, whichever you prefer. Place the ham in a roasting pan and insert a meat thermometer, being certain that it does not touch the bone. Roast in a 325° oven, without basting, for 25 to 30 minutes to the pound, or until the meat thermometer registers 165°. You may roast potatoes and onions with the meat, if you like. Peel the potatoes and onions and cut the potatoes into halves or quarters. Add the vegetables 45 minutes to an hour before the meat is done. Turn them once or twice during the cooking, season to taste with salt and pepper and baste with the juices in the pan.

Serve the fresh ham with the potatoes and onions, braised cabbage or sauerkraut, dill pickles and thinly sliced rye bread. Applesauce flavored with horseradish or Fried Apple Rings and horseradish, served separately, go well with this dish. A nice rosé, or good beer, is an excellent addition.

Carve the crisp skin from the roast in one big piece and break it up, allowing a small piece for each person. Carve the meat in very thin slices.

Shoulder of Pork

This cut should be boned, stuffed with garlic and parsley and then rolled and tied. A good butcher will do this for you. Italian butchers often have such roasts already made up. If you can't get it done this way, at least have the butcher bone the shoulder and roll and tie it, and when you get it home, unroll it, insert garlic and parsley and re-roll. Use 1 clove of garlic, chopped, and a few sprigs of parsley. Allow ½ to ¾ pound per person.

ROAST SHOULDER OF PORK (Serves 4)

3-pound shoulder of pork,   **Salt and pepper**
  boned and tied

Have the butcher stuff the roast with parsley and garlic, or do it yourself (see page 269). Rub with salt and pepper and arrange it in a roasting
pan. Roast as you do fresh ham (see page 269). Serve with the same accompaniments.

SHOULDER OF PORK, BAKER'S FASHION (Serves 4)

3-pound shoulder of pork,   **4 potatoes**
  boned and tied
                         4 onions
Garlic
                         Broth or consommé
Salt and pepper

Have the butcher bone, roll and tie the shoulder. Wipe the meat with
a damp cloth and slash the flesh in several places. Insert slivers of garlic.
Place the roast in a large casserole or deep baking pan and roast in a 325°
oven for 1½ hours. Add a layer of rather thickly sliced potatoes, salt and
pepper to taste, then a layer of sliced onions, and more salt and pepper
to taste. Top with another seasoned layer of potato slices and pour a little broth or consommé into the pan. Continue roasting for another hour,
basting frequently with the pan juices. When the shoulder and vegetables are cooked through, brown and bubbly, bring the casserole to the
table. Serve with Horseradish Sauce and baked apples.

BRAISED SHOULDER OF PORK (Serves 4)

3-pound shoulder of pork,
    boned and tied
Flour
Salt
Pepper
Paprika
Fat or oil
2 large onions stuck with 2
    cloves
2 carrots

1-inch piece of ginger or 1
    teaspoon of ground
    ginger
2 cups of tomato purée
1 teaspoon of oregano
1 bay leaf
12 small white onions,
    peeled
1½ pounds of fresh green
    beans, cut French style

Have the butcher bone the shoulder, stuff it with garlic and parsley and roll and tie it. Wipe the meat with a damp cloth and rub it with flour, salt, pepper and paprika. Heat bacon fat, pork fat or olive oil in a deep pot or Dutch oven and brown the meat in the hot fat on all sides. Reduce the heat and add the onions stuck with cloves, the carrots, a piece of green ginger or the ground ginger, tomato purée, oregano and bay leaf. Cover tightly and simmer for 1½ hours. Add the vegetables, cover the pot again and continue cooking for ½ hour or until the vegetables are done and the pork is tender.

Arrange the meat on a hot platter and surround it with the vegetables. Taste the sauce for seasoning and add more salt if needed. Pour the sauce over the meat and vegetables. Rice mixed with buttered almonds and ripe olives is excellent with this dish. Bake the rice in the oven (see Pilaf, page 169).

BOILED SHOULDER OF PORK, VIENNESE (Serves 4)

3-pound shoulder of pork
Garlic
Rosemary
Salt pork

3 pounds of sauerkraut
1 quart of beer
2 teaspoons of pepper
1 onion stuck with 2 cloves

Wipe the meat with a damp cloth and slash the flesh in several places. Insert slivers of garlic. Rub the shoulder with rosemary. Line a deep kettle with several slices of salt pork and place the meat on top. Add the sauerkraut, beer, pepper and onion stuck with cloves. Cover the kettle and simmer gently for 5 hours. Arrange the sauerkraut on a large platter and top with slices of the meat. Serve with boiled potatoes steamed dry, hot applesauce, plenty of crisp bread and cold beer. This dish is even better if cooked for 3 hours a day ahead of time and then finished the following day.

Spareribs

In my opinion, this is the most delicious cut of pork—and the most versatile. Just the thought of spareribs, broiled over charcoal or in the broiler and served with a pungent sauce makes me ravenously hungry.

Spareribs are fatty. They need slow cooking to melt off the excess fat and to absorb the seasonings. They are also bony, so allow at least 1 pound per person.

The following recipes are all suitable for outdoor cooking over charcoal or indoor cooking in an electric rotisserie or oven broiler. If you use a spit, lace the ribs on the spit, weaving them back and forth as if you were taking huge stitches with a big needle.

BROILED SPARERIBS (Serves 4)

4¹/₂ to 5 pounds of spareribs
Salt
Pepper
Rosemary
¹/₂ cup of honey

¹/₄ cup of lemon juice
¹/₄ cup of Worcestershire sauce
¹/₄ cup of sherry or Madeira

Wipe the meat with a damp cloth and cut the ribs into sections of 4 or 5 ribs each. Salt and pepper them and rub with rosemary. Broil them with a low heat (charcoal, electric rotisserie or oven broiler), turning frequently and brushing with a mixture of honey, lemon juice, Worcestershire sauce and sherry or Madeira. Cook them slowly until they are crisp and brown and thoroughly done. Serve with mashed potatoes, braised cabbage and a tomato salad with French dressing.

ROASTED SPARERIBS

Buy 1 pound of lean, meaty spareribs for each person. Sprinkle with salt and pepper and arrange on a rack in a baking pan. Roast in a 325°

oven for 1 hour, turning the ribs twice during the cooking. They should be well browned and crisp.

Serve with mashed potatoes and sauerkraut.

VARIATIONS

With honey and lemon: After the ribs have cooked 35 minutes, brush them with a mixture of honey and lemon juice ($\frac{1}{2}$ cup of honey to $\frac{1}{4}$ cup of juice).

With sauerkraut: In a large baking pan arrange a layer of peeled and sliced onions. Top this with a bed of sauerkraut and cover the sauerkraut with peeled, sliced apples. Arrange the spareribs on top and roast as above, turning the ribs twice during the cooking.

With soy sauce or honey: Season the ribs to taste and broil with a medium heat, turning them several times to cook on both sides. Brush them with soy sauce or honey when you turn them. Cook until they are very well done and very crisp.

PRECOOKED SPARERIBS (Serves 6)

This method takes a little more trouble, but the pre-cooking can be done a day or two in advance and the broiling time is reduced.

7 pounds of spareribs	**Water**
2 large onions stuck with cloves	**5 cloves of garlic**
	1 bottle of red wine
2 bay leaves	**$\frac{1}{4}$ cup of lemon juice**
1 teaspoon of salt	**$\frac{1}{2}$ cup of honey**
1 teaspoon of rosemary	
2 carrots	

Wipe the spareribs with a damp cloth and cut them into sections of 4 or 5 ribs each. Place them in a deep kettle with the onions and cloves, bay leaves, salt, rosemary, carrots and just enough water to cover. Bring to a boil and then reduce the heat. Cover and simmer gently for 35 minutes. Remove the ribs and allow the liquid to cool. Skim off the fat and add the garlic cloves and a bottle of red wine. Chianti or Barbera will do. Pour into a bowl or dish large enough to hold the ribs. Do not use a metal utensil unless it is stainless steel or enamel-coated. Marinate the ribs in this mixture for about 36 hours. Be sure to keep them in the refrigerator. When ready to cook, remove the ribs and broil them slowly over charcoal or in the oven. Turn them often and baste with a mixture of the honey and lemon juice.

Serve these spareribs with crisp potato chips, a huge bowl of coleslaw and some of the heated marinade for a sauce, if you like. Garlic bread goes well with these too.

ROASTED MARINATED SPARERIBS (Serves 4)

5 pounds of spareribs	**1¹/₂ teaspoons of oregano**
3 cloves of garlic, chopped	**¹/₂ cup of oil**
1 cup of consommé	**1 tablespoon of salt**
1 cup of tomato sauce	**¹/₂ cup of honey**
1 cup of red wine	**Dry mustard**
1 cup of orange juice	

Wipe the ribs with a damp cloth and leave them in large pieces. Place the garlic, consommé, tomato sauce, red wine, orange juice, oregano, oil and salt in a large deep dish or bowl. Marinate the ribs in this mixture for 24 to 36 hours, keeping them in the refrigerator. Turn them often to be sure they are evenly bathed. When ready to cook, remove the ribs and dry them on paper towels. Roast on a spit over charcoal (lacing them on the spit) according to general directions on page 272, or on a rack in a baking pan in the oven. They will take about ³/₄ of an hour in a 325° oven. If you roast these in the oven, be sure to pour off the fat from the bottom of the pan as it accumulates. Baste during cooking with a little of the marinade. After the ribs have cooked for 45 minutes, brush them with honey mixed with a little dry mustard (about 1 teaspoon) and increase the heat to 450° to give them a nice glaze.

While the spareribs are cooking, bring the marinade to a boil, lower the heat and simmer for 40 minutes. Serve this sauce with the ribs and with them also serve rice, a platter of sliced tomatoes and onions, dressed with oil and vinegar, and some good bread and butter. Finish with cheese and coffee.

Pork Steaks

These are cut from fresh ham (leg) and should be about ¾ to 1 inch thick. They are not too well known but make hearty and tasty eating.

BROILED PORK STEAK (Serves 4)

3 to 3½ pounds of pork steak	**Pepper**
Salt	

Wipe the meat with a damp cloth and broil very slowly to give the meat a chance to cook through thoroughly. Turn several times during the cooking. Allow about 10 to 15 minutes cooking on each side. Turn the heat up at the last to brown and crisp the outside. Season to taste with salt and pepper and serve with grilled or fried onions and garlic bread. A hearty cole slaw goes well with pork steaks.

VARIATION

Rub the steaks with thyme, rosemary or basil before broiling.

PORK STEAK AND SAUERKRAUT CASSEROLE (Serves 4)

3 to 3½ pounds of pork steak	**3 pounds of sauerkraut**
Flour	**4 onions, sliced**
Salt	**4 apples, sliced**
Pepper	**2 cloves of garlic**
3 tablespoons of bacon fat or butter	**White wine or vermouth**
	4 baking potatoes

Wipe the steak or steaks with a damp cloth and dust them with flour, salt and pepper. Heat bacon fat or butter and brown the meat on both sides. Wash the sauerkraut, peel and slice the onions, and peel, core and slice the apples.

In the bottom of a large casserole place a bed of sauerkraut. Add a layer of sliced onions, a layer of sliced apples and top with the pork steaks.

Sprinkle with freshly ground black pepper and 1 chopped clove of garlic. Add another layer of onions and apples and more sauerkraut. Add the second clove of garlic, chopped, more pepper and barely enough white wine or vermouth to cover the ingredients. Put a lid on the casserole and bake in a 300° oven for 3 hours. About 1 1/4 hours before the casserole is done, put 4 baking potatoes, well scrubbed and greased, in the oven to cook.

Serve this pork and sauerkraut casserole with the baked potatoes, some pungent pickles and a light, pleasant dessert, such as Crème Brûlée.

VARIATIONS

With loin chops: Substitute 4 thick loin pork chops for the steak. Serve with baked sweet potatoes.

With Fried Apple Rings: Omit the onions and apples. Serve with Fried Apple Rings, mashed potatoes, dressed with butter and chopped parsley, and an onion and avocado salad.

With cider: Substitute apple cider for the wine in the casserole.

With beer: Omit the apples and substitute beer for the wine in the casserole. Serve this casserole with horseradish mixed with apple sauce.

PORK ROLLS, POLISH FASHION (Serves 6)

6 thin slices of pork steak	Salt and pepper
1 large onion	Nutmeg
Butter	4 tablespoons of bacon fat or butter
1/4 cup of chopped parsley	
1 teaspoon of basil	Broth, beer or water
1/2 pound of ground pork or ham	2 teaspoons of flour
	1 1/2 cups of sour cream
1 1/2 cups of dry bread crumbs	1 tablespoon of paprika

First prepare a stuffing: Peel and chop the onion and sauté it in 4 tablespoons of butter until soft. Add 2 more tablespoons of butter and the chopped parsley and basil. Mix thoroughly. Combine this mixture with the ground pork or ham, the bread crumbs and 1/2 teaspoon each of salt and freshly ground black pepper. Omit the salt if you are using ham.

Wipe the pork slices with a damp cloth and sprinkle each one with a little salt, pepper and nutmeg. Put a mound of stuffing on each slice, roll it up and tie securely.

Melt bacon fat or butter in a skillet and brown the pork rolls on all sides. Reduce the heat and add 1 cup of broth, beer or water. Cover and simmer for about 45 minutes or until the meat is tender. Remove the pork rolls to a hot platter. Knead into small pellets 1 teaspoon of butter with the 2 teaspoons of flour and sprinkle this over the surface of the liquid in the pan. Stir the sauce and cook until smooth and thickened. Gradually add the sour cream, being careful not to let it boil or it will curdle. Add the paprika and taste for seasoning. Add salt and pepper if necessary. Pour the sauce over the pork rolls and serve with buttered noodles, chopped spinach dressed with tarragon butter and ice-cold beer.

Pork Chops

The choicest pork chops come from the loin or rib section. Shoulder chops are less expensive, but they are not the economical buy they seem because they have extra bone and fat.

A good thick loin chop is tops, and a fine rib chop runs it a close second. Ask the butcher to cut your chops 1 to 1½ inches thick. If you plan to stuff them, buy double-thick chops with pockets slit in them. Allow one chop per person.

Remember that all pork must be well done. Cook chops very slowly.

BROILED PORK CHOPS

A word of warning: This is not the best method for cooking pork chops, since pork needs slow cooking. Long broiling tends to dry them out and make them hard and tough. However, if you like broiled chops, cook them slowly, brushing with fat frequently during the broiling. Season to taste with salt and pepper during the last few minutes of broiling.

COUNTRY FRIED PORK CHOPS (Serves 4)

4 large or 8 small chops	Fine bread crumbs
4 strips of bacon	Salt
Flour	Pepper
1 or 2 beaten eggs	1 cup of cream

Wipe the chops with a damp cloth and slash the fat a bit around the edges to keep it from curling up during cooking. In a large skillet fry the bacon strips until crisp, then remove them to drain on absorbent paper. Dip the chops in flour, then in the lightly beaten egg and finally roll them in fine crumbs. Brown them quickly in the hot bacon fat, turning them with a spatula or pancake turner and being careful not to loosen the crumbs. When they are browned on both sides, season to taste with salt and freshly ground black pepper and add about ½ cup of cream. Reduce the heat, cover the pan and simmer gently for 20 to 25 minutes, or until the chops are tender.

Remove the meat to a hot platter, add a little more cream to the pan and stir it around, scraping off all the bits of brown from the skillet. Pour this sauce over the chops and top with crumbled bacon bits.

PORK CHOPS FLAMBÉ (Serve 4)

4 thick loin chops with pockets cut in them	1 egg
	Salt and pepper
Butter	¼ teaspoon of thyme
2 tablespoons of grated onion	Butter
	Water
½ cup of finely chopped mushrooms	¼ cup of Cognac
½ cup of fine bread crumbs	1 cup of sour cream

Melt 2 tablespoons of butter and sauté the onion and mushrooms. Add the crumbs and cook for about 5 minutes. Remove from stove, mix with ½ teaspoon of salt, ½ teaspoon of freshly ground black pepper and the thyme and blend with the egg. Stuff the chops with this mixture and fasten with small skewers or with toothpicks. Melt some butter in a heavy skillet with a tight lid and brown the chops quickly on both sides in the butter. When they are nicely browned, season with a little salt and pepper and add just enough water to cover the bottom of the pan—no more.

Put a lid on the skillet, lower the heat and cook the chops gently for about 40 to 45 minutes, turning them once or twice during the cooking. When they are tender, remove excess fat from the pan juices, pour Cognac over them and carefully ignite it to blaze. Remove the chops to a hot platter and add sour cream to the pan. Stir well to blend with the pan juices and heat through, but do not let it boil or it will curdle. Pour this sauce over the chops and serve with mashed potatoes and Fried Apple Rings.

DEVILED PORK CHOPS (Serves 4)

4 thick loin pork chops
Butter
Salt and pepper
Toasted bread crumbs
1 clove of garlic
1 teaspoon of dry mustard
1 tablespoon of Dijon mustard

1 tablespoon of Worcestershire sauce
1 can of beef gravy
Dash of cayenne
2 tablespoons of finely chopped pickles

Heat butter in a heavy skillet and brown the chops quickly on both sides. When they are browned, turn down the heat, cover the skillet and cook gently. Remove the cover after 18 to 20 minutes, salt and pepper the chops and press both sides into fine dry crumbs spread on a shallow dish. Return them to the skillet, dot with butter and put in a very hot oven (450°) for 10 minutes to brown well.

Meanwhile, peel and chop the garlic clove, blend it with 3 tablespoons of butter and cook over medium heat for a few minutes. Add the two mustards and the Worcestershire sauce and blend thoroughly. Stir in the beef gravy and heat. Season with salt, pepper and cayenne. Add the chopped pickles just before serving.

When the chops are browned, arrange them on a platter and serve with the hot devil sauce. Mashed potatoes and sautéed onions go well with this.

BRAISED PORK CHOPS (Serves 4)

4 thick loin pork chops   **1 cup hot water**
2 onions   **Bouillon cube**
Salt and pepper   **Chopped parsley**
Thyme
**2 stalks of celery with tops,
    diced**

Trim some fat from the edges of the chops and render the fat in a heavy skillet. Slash the remaining fat along the edges of the chops and wipe them with a damp cloth. When fat begins to collect in the pan, add the chops to brown well on both sides. Peel the onions, slice them and add to brown with the meat. Season to taste with salt, pepper and thyme. Transfer the browned chops and onions to a casserole and top with the finely diced celery and tops. Add 1 cup of hot water and 1 bouillon cube, cover tightly and bake in a 375° oven for 45 minutes. Uncover and continue baking for another 15 to 20 minutes to let the chops brown and the broth cook down. Sprinkle with chopped parsley during the last five minutes. Serve with baked potatoes and succotash.

VARIATIONS

With green pepper: Add a green pepper, sliced, to the casserole.

Au gratin: Sauté onion and green pepper with the meat and use half broth and half tomato juice for liquid. During the last 15 minutes of cooking, top the chops with grated Parmesan cheese and buttered crumbs.

SHOULDER CHOPS

Prepare shoulder chops in any of the ways suggested for loin chops.

COUNTRY PÂTÉ

2 pounds lean pork, coarsely
  chopped

2 pounds veal, finely
  chopped

1 pound pork liver, ground

1 pound fresh pork siding
  slices, finely diced

6 cloves of garlic, finely
  chopped

3 eggs

$^1/_4$ teaspoon nutmeg

$^1/_4$ teaspoon ginger

$^1/_3$ cup cognac or bourbon

1 tablespoon dried basil

1 tablespoon salt

$1^1/_2$ teaspoons freshly
  ground black pepper

Bacon or salt pork slices

Mix the meats together in a large bowl. Then add the garlic, eggs and seasonings, and blend thoroughly. Sauté a small piece quickly in butter to taste for salt. Line a 2½- or 3-quart baking dish or terrine with bacon or salt pork slices, and fill with the meat mixture. Arrange slices of bacon or salt pork over the top. Bake in a 325° oven for 2½ hours, covering loosely with foil for the first hour. Weight down the top and allow to cool completely before refrigerating. Serve directly from the dish or terrine.

Ham

Most hams sold in our markets have been cured by a special chemical process and "tenderized." That is, they are partly precooked and need no long soaking or boiling before you bake them.

Old-fashioned country-cured and aged hams: There are various types of country cures for ham: some give the meat a rich seasoning of herbs and spices; others a strong smoky or salty taste. These need soaking and boiling before baking; instructions for cooking are given below and you'll usually find directions printed on the ham wrapper. If there is no information attached to the ham, ask the dealer to tell you if it needs special preparation. Fine country-cured and aged hams include Virginia, Smithfield and Kentucky hams.

Some country-cured hams come ready to eat. They can be sliced very thin and eaten cold or heated through in the oven and then carved.

Hams range in size from 10 to 20 pounds, but if a whole ham is too large, you can buy a half. The butt end is meatier and easier to carve, but the shank is usually cheaper and just as tasty. Some people like to bake or broil a thick center slice of ham. This is an expensive way to buy the meat. If you want a center cut, buy a half ham and have the butcher cut a slice from the large end. Store the rest of the ham in your refrigerator (ham keeps well, since it is cured) and bake it a week or two later.

If you are looking for a very small ham roast, try smoked butt, smoked tenderloin or smoked shoulder of ham. These run from from 1½ to 3 pounds, and though the texture is not as even as the big ham, the flavor is excellent.

Allow about ½ pound of meat per person when buying a whole ham; if you are buying a piece of ham with a great deal of bone, for example the shank end, allow a good ¾ to 1 pound per person. Allow ⅓ to ½ pound per person of boneless ham.

Other hams: Canned hams, domestic and imported, offer a shortcut in preparation; they need only be heated through. Or serve them cold as they come from the can.

Several varieties of ready-to-eat hams are good eating as an hors d'oeuvre or snack food. Look for the highly seasoned Italian ham called prosciutto or for Westphalian ham. These should be sliced paper thin and served with thin slices of pumpernickel or rye bread. Prosciutto is especially good served with fruit. A favorite appetizer in many fine restaurants is a slice of chilled melon striped with thin slices of prosciutto.

To prepare aged hams: Scrub the ham well with a stiff brush, place it in a large kettle and cover with cold water. Soak overnight and if possible a little longer—about 18 hours altogether. Then drain off the water and add fresh water to cover. Put it on the stove and heat just until it simmers; do not let it boil. Simmer gently for 3½ hours. Turn off the heat and let the ham stand in the broth until it cools. Remove it from the kettle, peel off the rind, add any glaze you choose (see Baked Ham, below) and put in the oven until hot through and glazed (see instructions, Baked Aged Ham, page 284).

BAKED HAM (Tenderized)

Scrub the ham well with a stiff brush under running water. Pat it dry with paper towels and place it in a roasting pan skin and fat side up. Heat the oven to 300°, place the ham in the oven and roast uncovered and without basting. Allow about 20 minutes to the pound cooking time. Very large hams weighing over 15 pounds need only about 16 to 17 minutes per pound.

When the ham is done, remove it from the oven, and using a sharp knife or kitchen scissors, cut off the rind. Score the fat, if you wish, cutting it in long, diagonal slashes in one direction and then crossing these cuts with diagonal slashes in the opposite direction. This makes a diamond pattern in the fat. Push whole cloves into the fat at the corners of the diamond patterns. Mix 1 cup of brown sugar with 2 teaspoons of dry mustard and moisten with a little of the ham fat from the roasting pan. Spread this mixture over the top of the ham and return it to the oven. Increase the heat to 400° and cook until the sugar has glazed and the fat turned crisp.

VARIATIONS

With ground cloves: Omit the whole cloves and mix 1 teaspoon of ground cloves into the sugar-mustard spread.

With honey: Rub the fat with 2 teaspoons of dry mustard and spread strained honey over it.

With dry wine or cider: Remove the ham from the oven ³/₄ of an hour before it has finished cooking and remove the rind (see above). Score the fat and rub with a little brown sugar. Return the ham to the oven and cook for ³/₄ of an hour to 1 hour, basting every few minutes with dry Madeira, dry sherry, dry red wine, or apple cider. Use about 1 cup of the liquid for basting.

With pineapple: Remove the ham from the oven ³/₄ of an hour before it is done and take off the rind. Rub the fat with a little dry mustard and brown sugar and baste with pineapple juice. Cook for ¹/₂ hour. Arrange pineapple rings on the surface of the ham and brush them with honey. Return to the oven, increase the heat to 450° and cook until the pineapple is glazed.

With peaches and bourbon: Remove the ham from the oven ³/₄ of an hour before it is done and remove the rind. Rub the fat with a little brown sugar and dry mustard. Open a can of peach halves and mix ¹/₂ cup of bourbon in with the peach juice. Return the ham to the oven and cook for another ³/₄ of an hour to 1 hour, basting frequently with the peach juice and bourbon. While the ham finishes cooking, arrange the peach halves on a broiler pan, dot with butter and add a little brown sugar. Run under the broiler flame at the last minute to heat and brown. Arrange around the ham on the platter.

BAKED AGED HAM

Prepare ham by soaking and simmering (page 282). Cool in the liquid. Remove and pat dry with a paper towel and, using a sharp knife or kitchen scissors, cut off the rind. Place the ham in a roasting pan, fat side up, and prepare for glazing according to any of the directions given for tenderized ham (page 283). I suggest you use as little sugar as possible, for a fine aged ham needs no additional flavor. Place in a 300° oven and glaze slowly, giving the ham a chance to heat through. This will take about ¾ of an hour to 1 hour.

VARIATION

Crumbed: Place the soaked and boiled ham in a roasting pan without removing the rind. Bake at 300° for 1 hour. Remove from the oven and take off the rind. Mix 2 teaspoons of mustard with 4 teaspoons of paprika and ¾ cup of very fine dry bread crumbs. Add enough fat from the roasting pan to make a smooth paste. Spread this over the top of the ham and return to bake until the crumbs and seasonings are crisp and hot.

BAKED SMALL SMOKED BUTTS OR SHOULDERS

Since these small hams seldom have a fat surface to score and glaze, baste them with one of the wines or fruit juices suggested above for baked ham. Place the small ham in an open baking dish and cook at 300° for ½ hour; then begin basting. A 1½-pound ham will be done in 35 to 40 minutes; a 3-pound ham will take about 50 minutes to an hour.

BAKED HAM SLICE

Have the slice cut 1½ to 2 inches thick. Cut several gashes in the fat around the edge to keep the ham from curling up as it cooks. Place it in a shallow baking dish and bake for 15 minutes in a 350° oven. Glaze it with 1 teaspoon of dry mustard and 2 tablespoons of sugar mixed with a little ham fat. Spread this mixture on the ham slice and continue baking for another 20 or 25 minutes.

Use any of the variations suggested for baked ham.

GRILLED HAM SLICE WITH CREAM

Use a center-cut ham slice about 1 inch thick. Slash the fat around the edge to prevent the ham from curling. Heat the broiler and when it is hot, grease the broiler rack. Place the ham slice on the rack and broil for 10 to 15 minutes, or until the fat is browned and the ham sizzling. Turn and spread the top of the uncooked side with 1 teaspoon of dry mustard mixed with enough heavy cream to make a paste. Continue broiling until the slice is brown and bubbly on top. Sprinkle with fine bread crumbs mixed with paprika, and dribble a little more heavy cream over the top. Return to the broiler to brown the crumbs.

For other suggestions on grilled ham slice see Breakfast Meats, pages 98–99.

FRIED HAM

Ham slices may be fried if they are cut fairly thin—about ½ inch thick. Heat a heavy skillet and rub it with a little of the fat cut from the edge of the ham slice. Slash the fat on the slice to keep it from curling, and put the ham in the skillet. Cook rather slowly until browned on the bottom, and then turn and finish cooking until brown on the other side. The fat edges should be crisp.

You may fry apple slices or rings or pineapple rings in the pan with the ham slice, if you like. Glaze them during the last minute or two of cooking by sprinkling with a little brown sugar.

BOILED HAM

Ham boiled with vegetables makes an excellent boiled dinner. Use a small end of a whole ham or a small smoked shoulder or butt. Wash and scrub the ham well and place in a deep kettle with enough water to cover the meat. Bring to a boil, lower the heat and simmer gently allowing about 15 to 20 minutes per pound. About a half hour before the ham is done, add peeled potatoes, peeled onions, peeled carrots, a few stalks of celery and any other vegetables you like. Continue cooking until the meat and vegetables are tender. Serve the ham sliced on a large platter and surrounded with the vegetables. A good hot mustard goes well with this.

Be sure to save the ham broth to use in soup or a good bean or lentil casserole.

BACON AND SAUSAGE—See Breakfast Meats, pages 98–100.

| Pasta

The Italian term "pasta" covers the products known generally as spaghetti, macaroni and noodles, and these, in turn, come in countless shapes and sizes, with names such as linguine, capellini, fettuccine, cannelloni, penne and rigatoni. We used to rely solely on dried pastas, the best being imported from Italy, but today fresh pasta is widely available, and a variety of machines on the market make it possible to achieve excellent pasta in one's own kitchen. Below are recipes for both fresh white and green pasta.

Noodles, Macaroni, Spaghetti

HOMEMADE WHITE NOODLES (Serves 4)

2 large eggs
½ teaspoon of salt

1 to 1½ cups of flour

The amount of flour you will need is difficult to state exactly. Flour varies in consistency, and you will have to judge as you mix it in. Beat the eggs and salt together and add enough flour to make a stiff dough. Flour a board or the top of a worktable and turn the dough out onto it. Knead it, pressing in with your fingers and the heels of your palms and pushing down and away from yourself. Then fold the dough over and press again. Repeat this process for 8 to 10 minutes or until you have a smooth, firm dough. Cover with a dish towel and let stand for half an hour or more. Then flour a rolling pin and roll the dough out into a very, very thin sheet ⅛ inch thick. Let it stand to dry for 5 minutes. Cut into strips ⅛ to ½ inch wide.

Food processor method: Put 1½ cups of flour and the salt in the processor and blend for a second. Add the eggs and 1 tablespoon of olive or vegetable oil. Blend until the dough forms a ball, which should take only 10 to 15 seconds. Let rest, knead, and roll out, as in basic recipe.

To cook: Fresh noodles or dried noodles are both cooked the same way. Put several quarts of water in a large kettle. Add 1 tablespoon of salt and bring to a boil. Add the noodles. Start testing dried noodles after about 6 minutes; fresh noodles, as soon as they return to the boil. Drain thoroughly and serve dressed with plenty of butter, salt and freshly ground black pepper. You can also use any of the sauces listed for pasta (pages 290–295) or serve any of the following ways:

With butter and cheese (al Burro): Drain the noodles thoroughly and return them to the pan. Add 4 tablespoons of butter and ½ cup of grated Parmesan cheese. Shake the pan vigorously to mix well.

Fettuccine Alfredo: Use noodles about ¼ inch wide. Drain the cooked noodles and return them to the pan. Add 4 tablespoons of butter, ¼ cup of grated Parmesan cheese, ¼ cup of grated Switzerland Swiss or Gruyère cheese, ½ cup of heavy cream and a generous sprinkling of freshly ground black pepper. Shake vigorously to blend and then toss well with a fork.

Baked noodles in cheese sauce: Butter a casserole and put in the bottom a layer of cooked, drained noodles. Add Sauce Mornay or American Cheese Sauce (page 350). Repeat the layers until all the noodles are used. Top with buttered crumbs and bake in a 350° oven for about 20 minutes, or until the casserole is hot through, browned and bubbly.

HOMEMADE GREEN NOODLES (Serves 4)

½ cup of cooked spinach	½ teaspoon of salt
2 eggs	1 to 1½ cups of flour

Squeeze the spinach dry and chop very fine. Beat the eggs and salt together lightly and mix with the spinach. Add enough flour to make a stiff dough. Then proceed as for regular noodles (pages 287–288). Cook and serve green noodles as you would white noodles.

Food processor method: Blend the flour, spinach, salt and 1 tablespoon of olive oil for about 2 minutes. Add 1 whole egg and blend for another 8 or 10 seconds. Proceed as for regular noodles.

MACARONI

This hollow pasta comes in many shapes, all equally good. Select the one you prefer and cook in boiling salted water (enough to cover the pasta twice over) for 8 or 9 minutes. This gives you bitey pasta. If you like it softer, cook it to the stage of doneness you prefer. Serve plain, with butter and cheese, or with one of the Pasta Sauces, pages 290–295.

SPAGHETTI

Cook as you do macaroni (see above) and serve plain, buttered and sprinkled with grated Parmesan cheese, or serve with one of the Pasta Sauces, pages 290–295.

LASAGNA IMBOTTITA (STUFFED LASAGNA)

1 pound of lasagne, green or white	¼ cup of chopped parsley (Italian, if available)
Rich Meat Sauce (page 294)	1 pound of mozzarella cheese, sliced
1½ pounds of Italian sausage	Grated Parmesan or Romano cheese
4 hard-cooked eggs, sliced	
1 pound of ricotta cheese	

Broil or sauté the sausage until nicely browned on all sides and then drain off the fat. Slice into ¼-inch pieces.

Cook the lasagne in boiling, salted water until just tender but not mushy. Drain thoroughly. Butter a large baking dish (preferably a square one) and line the bottom with lasagne, overlapping them slightly. Add a layer of Rich Meat Sauce, a layer of the sausage slices, a layer of sliced eggs and then sprinkle with a little chopped parsley. Add another layer of lasagne, then a layer of ricotta, some sauce and a layer of sliced mozzarella, topped with a little chopped parsley. Continue these layers until all the ingredients are used, making the top layer of lasagne. Sprinkle well with grated Parmesan or Romano cheese and bake in a 350° oven for 25 minutes or until lightly browned on top and bubbling. Allow to stand for 10 minutes or so before serving.

This dish is even better heated up the second day.

VARIATIONS

With meat balls: Substitute tiny meat balls (recipe page 293) for the sausage.

With cheese only: Omit the sauce, eggs and sausage and make layers of lasagne, mozzarella, ricotta and Parmesan or Romano cheese. Dot each layer with butter.

Sauces for Pasta

GARLIC AND OIL (AGLIO E OLIO) (Serves 2)

½ cup of olive oil	Salt
2 cloves of garlic	Pepper

Peel the garlic and crush it slightly in a skillet. Add the oil and heat through, pressing the garlic cloves down occasionally with a fork to extract the juice. Season to taste with salt and freshly ground black pepper.

VARIATION

Add ½ to 1 teaspoon of basil.

MUSHROOM SAUCE (Serves 2)

½ pound of mushrooms	Pepper
3 tablespoons of olive oil	Lemon juice
Salt	

Slice the mushrooms thin and sauté them in the hot oil until soft. Season to taste with salt and pepper and add 2 tablespoons of lemon juice.

TUNA SAUCE (Serves 4)

1/4 pound of mushrooms
2 tablespoons of olive oil
2 cloves of garlic

2 cups of Tomato Sauce (page 353)
1 can of tuna

Slice the mushrooms, and mince the garlic. Sauté them in hot oil. Add the Tomato Sauce and flaked tuna, and heat thoroughly.

PESTO (Serves 4 to 6)

This classic Italian sauce was originally prepared with mortar and pestle. Nowadays it is more easily accomplished in a food processor or blender.

4 cups fresh basil leaves
1/2 cup parsley, preferably Italian
3 cloves garlic

1/2 cup pine nuts or walnuts
1/2 cup olive oil or more
1/2 cup Parmesan or pecorino cheese

Put all the ingredients except the cheese in a food processor or blender and process until a smooth paste, adding more oil if needed. Stir in the cheese and blend throughly.

BASIC MARINARA SAUCE

6 slices of bacon
1/4 cup of olive oil
3 onions
2 cloves of garlic
3 pounds of fresh tomatoes or one 33-ounce can of solid-pack tomatoes
3 anchovies

1 clove
Fresh or dried basil to taste
3 sprigs of parsley
Salt
Pepper

Cut the bacon into small pieces and fry until almost crisp. Add the olive oil and the peeled and chopped onions and garlic. Sauté until they are nicely colored and soft. Add the fresh tomatoes, unpeeled and unseeded, or the canned tomatoes, the anchovies, clove, basil, parsley, salt and pepper. Cook slowly until the tomatoes are cooked down and thickened. Strain through a fine strainer, or put in an electric blender to smooth. Return to the stove and simmer for another hour. Taste for seasoning and serve over hot pasta. Or use with any of the following additions:

With sausage: Cook 1½ pounds of Italian sausages in ½ cup of red wine until the wine is evaporated and the sausages are browned. Add to the sauce.

With shrimp: Five minutes before the sauce is done, add 1 pound of shelled raw shrimp and 1 teaspoon of tarragon. Finish cooking and serve over hot pasta.

With lobster: A few minutes before the sauce is done, add 1 pound of cooked or canned lobster meat and 1 teaspoon of tarragon. Heat through.

With shrimp and lobster: Five minutes before the sauce is done, add ½ pound of shelled raw shrimp and ½ pound of cooked lobster meat. Add 2 teaspoons of tarragon and finish cooking.

With fish: Add any cooked fish you choose.

With anchovy: A few minutes before the sauce is done add 6 anchovy fillets, 2 peeled and chopped cloves of garlic and ¼ cup of chopped parsley.

ITALIAN MEAT SAUCE

4 tablespoons of olive oil

4 tablespoons of butter

2 cloves of garlic, chopped

1 medium onion, chopped

1 pound of ground beef

½ pound of lean ground pork

1 carrot, grated

2 bay leaves

2 whole cloves

1 teaspoon of thyme

1 stalk of celery

1 33-ounce can of solid-pack tomatoes

Salt and pepper

1 cup of meat broth (or 1 cup of hot water plus 1 bouillon cube)

1 small can of Italian tomato paste

Heat the olive oil and butter and add the chopped garlic and onion. Sauté them gently until delicately browned and tender. Add the ground beef and pork; cook, stirring and tossing the meat about in the pan to keep it from caking. It should be loose and crumbly. When the meat is well browned, add the grated carrot, the bay leaves, the cloves, the thyme, the celery and canned tomatoes. Season to taste with salt and pepper and add the meat broth (or hot water and bouillon cube). Reduce the heat, cover and simmer gently for 2 hours, stirring occasionally. The sauce should be reduced and thickened. If not, cook uncovered for a little longer until it cooks down a bit. Put it through a fine strainer or food mill. Return it to the stove, taste for seasoning and add a can of Italian tomato paste. Cook gently for 15 minutes.

Serve over hot spaghetti, noodles or any pasta and pass grated Parmesan cheese or Romano cheese.

VARIATIONS

1. Do not strain the sauce but serve it with the bits of meat and vegetables in it.
2. Add meatballs to the sauce (see below).

MEATBALLS FOR ITALIAN MEAT SAUCE

1 pound of top round steak, ground	1 teaspoon of salt
½ pound of ground lean pork	Dash of red pepper
	¼ cup of chopped parsley
½ pound of ground veal	1 teaspoon of dried or 1 tablespoon of fresh basil
2 cloves of garlic, finely chopped	2 eggs
1 teaspoon of freshly ground black pepper	Butter and olive oil

Mix the ground meats together with all the seasonings and blend in two lightly beaten eggs. Form into small balls and brown them quickly in hot olive oil and butter mixed. Shake the meat balls around in the pan to cook them evenly and keep them round. When they are browned on the outside but not cooked through, add them to the Italian Meat Sauce and let them simmer in the sauce for ½ hour. Correct the seasoning.

RICH MEAT SAUCE

This heavy sauce takes all day to prepare, but the final result is outstandingly delicious.

1 pound of lean beef	1 onion stuck with 3 cloves
1 pound of pork shoulder	2 carrots
1 pound of veal neck	1 small turnip
Salt	2 stalks of celery
1 teaspoon of freshly ground black pepper	6 tablespoons of butter
4 garlic cloves, peeled and chopped	2 29-ounce cans of solid-pack tomatoes
1 bay leaf	1 teaspoon of dried or 1 tablespoon of fresh basil
1 teaspoon of dried basil	1 can of tomato paste

Place the meats in a large casserole, sprinkle with salt and pepper and add the garlic cloves, bay leaf, basil and onion stuck with cloves. Roast in a 450° oven until colored a deep golden brown. Remove the meat and put it in a deep kettle with the carrots, turnip, celery and water to cover. Bring this to a boil, lower the heat and simmer gently for 6 hours. Add more liquid during the cooking if necessary. When done, allow the meat and broth to cook and then skim the fat from the top. Remove the meat and chop it very fine. Reheat the broth and strain it. Add to the chopped meat.

Melt the butter in a skillet and add the solid-pack tomatoes. Mash them down well and add fresh or dried basil and 1 teaspoon of salt. Cook very slowly, uncovered, until the tomatoes have cooked down one third. Add the tomato paste, blend it in and taste for seasoning. Pour the tomato sauce through a strainer into the meat sauce and mix well. Heat over a very low flame for 1 hour. Serve on hot pasta and sprinkle with plenty of grated Parmesan or Romano cheese.

CLAM SAUCE

1 quart of unshelled clams	3 cloves of garlic
1 cup of dry white wine (or dry vermouth)	$\frac{1}{2}$ cup of chopped parsley (Italian parsley, if available)
1 medium onion	
1 carrot	$1\frac{1}{2}$ tablespoons of chopped fresh basil (or $1\frac{1}{2}$ teaspoons of dried basil)
1 stalk of celery	
$\frac{1}{2}$ cup of olive oil	Salt and pepper

Wash the clams well and remove all the grit. Place them in a deep kettle and add the wine. Peel the onion and carrot and cut in fine strips. Cut the celery in strips. Add the vegetables to the kettle, cover it tightly and heat. Steam until the clam shells open. Remove them from the kettle and discard any with unopened shells. Shell the rest of the clams and set them aside. Strain the broth in the kettle and return it to the stove to boil down. Let it reduce to one half its volume. Chop the clams.

Heat the olive oil in a skillet and peel and chop the garlic and add this to the oil. Add the parsley and basil and season to taste with salt and freshly ground black pepper. Let this simmer for a few minutes. Then add the reduced clam broth and finally the chopped clams. Pour over spaghetti or noodles and top with grated Parmesan cheese.

VARIATION

Add two or three spoonfuls of tomato purée and blend and heat thoroughly.

QUICK CLAM SAUCE

2 cans of minced clams (7 ounces each)	$\frac{1}{2}$ cup of chopped parsley (Italian, if available)
3 cloves of garlic	Grated Romano cheese
$\frac{1}{3}$ cup of olive oil	

Peel and chop the garlic and sauté it in $\frac{1}{4}$ cup of olive oil until just colored. Add the rest of the olive oil and the clam juice from the minced clams. Add $\frac{1}{4}$ cup of the chopped parsley and heat to the boiling point. Finally add the minced clams and heat thoroughly. Pour over hot noodles or spaghetti and sprinkle with the rest of the chopped parsley and grated Romano cheese.

POULTRY

Chicken, which used to be America's Sunday dinner "special," is now a favorite daily food; and turkey, the national preference for Thanksgiving and Christmas, is available the year round. Indeed, it would be impossible to plan menus in this country if poultry were suddenly unavailable. Even the most inexperienced or part-time cook will eventually have to face up to roasting a chicken or cooking a stuffed turkey.

Both chicken and turkey are at their best fresh-killed, and naturally if you can buy directly from the farmer you can be sure of getting a fresh product. However, scientifically bred birds from enormous farms throughout the country provide fresh poultry for most of our markets nowadays. Flavor has been sacrificed to uniformity, but we have gained readily available and more economical chickens and turkeys.

Chicken

Shopping for chicken means selecting the type best suited to the method of cooking you wish to use.

For broiling: Use young birds, 1½ to 2½ pounds. They should be firmly meated with a little fat on them. Avoid those that look too scrawny.

For frying or sautéing: Fryers can range up to 3½ pounds. Like broilers, they should be well meated.

For roasting: Select larger birds ranging from 3 to 5 pounds. But be sure the chicken is young, broad through the chest with a compact body. If the bird has yellowish, drawn-looking skin, or it has many long hairs, it probably is an older hen and suitable only for fricasseeing.

For fricasseeing and poaching: Use a fowl, which means an old hen. These weigh anywhere from 3 to 8 pounds. Though they are tough, unless fricasseed or poached, they do have fine flavor. They are seldom found these days, however.

For roasting for more than 4 persons: Select a capon if you are serving more than four people. These weigh up to 8 or 9 pounds and are tender and tasty.

Tiny chickens weighing only 1 pound are called squab chicken. They can be roasted whole or split and broiled. Serve 1 chicken per person.

Chicken Sauté

Many people confuse the terms "fry" and "sauté." Fried chicken is coated heavily with flour or batter and cooked in a great deal of fat. Sautéed chicken is seldom floured and is browned lightly in a small amount of fat, usually butter or olive oil. Then it is covered and cooked gently just to the tender, done stage. Any seasonings you choose are added halfway through the cooking to blend with the chicken and juices. The result is an elegant and delicate dish. Chicken sauté can be varied in many ways by the addition of a wide range of flavorings and seasonings.

BASIC CHICKEN SAUTÉ (Serves 4)

2 2-pound frying chickens	**¹/₂ cup of dry white wine**
6 tablespoons of butter	**Chopped parsley**
Salt and pepper	

Have the butcher disjoint the chicken. Wash it in lukewarm water and dry it on paper towels. Melt the butter in a heavy skillet or kettle with a tight-fitting lid. Brown the chicken pieces in the butter, turning them to color evenly. When they are all browned, season to taste with salt and a little freshly ground black pepper and cover tightly. Lower the flame and cook gently for about 5 to 8 minutes. Uncover and rearrange the chicken pieces, being sure they are all cooking evenly. Add half of the wine and re-cover. Cook for another 10 minutes. Uncover and move all the white meat sections to the top, balancing them on dark meat pieces. The dark meat takes longer to cook and during the last part should be at the bottom of the pan. Cover and finish cooking until the chicken is just tender, but still juicy and moist. This will take about 5 to 10 more minutes. Remove the chicken to a hot serving platter and add the rest of the white wine and 3 or 4 tablespoons of chopped parsley to the pan juices. Turn up the heat and stir the juices about until they boil up and blend. Pour over the chicken. This is particularly good served with a plain Rice Pilaf, cooked in chicken broth, and tiny green peas, French style. Serve a bottle of the same dry white wine you used in the cooking.

VARIATIONS

With broth: You may omit the wine and rinse the pan out with a little broth after the chicken is cooked.

With mushrooms: Add sliced mushrooms (about ¼ pound) to the pan when the chicken is half cooked and add more butter if necessary.

With green onions: Add chopped tiny green onions (about 6) to the pan when the chicken is half cooked.

With green pepper: Add minced green pepper and minced onion halfway through the cooking.

With chilies and olives: Add tiny canned green chilies, chopped (2 or 3), and ½ cup of green olives halfway through the cooking. Substitute a very dry Spanish sherry for the white wine.

With herbs: Add a mixture of chopped chives, chopped parsley and 1 teaspoon of thyme halfway through the cooking.

With rosemary: Add a good sprinkling of rosemary halfway through the cooking.

With garlic and tomato: Cook the chicken in olive oil and add a minced clove of garlic. Halfway through the cooking, add 6 small green onions, chopped, and 8 sliced mushrooms. Add the wine and continue cooking. Five minutes before the chicken is done, add 2 tomatoes, peeled, seeded and chopped.

With bacon and cream: Fry 6 slices of bacon until crisp. Remove them from the pan. Dust the chicken pieces lightly with flour and cook in the bacon fat. Follow directions for Chicken Sauté and halfway through the cooking add 1 onion sliced. Omit the wine. When the chicken is done, remove it to a hot platter and add ½ cup of heavy cream to the pan juices. Heat through and pour over the chicken. Top with crumbled bacon.

ITALIAN CHICKEN SAUTÉ (Serves 4)

Prepare 2 frying chickens for sautéing according to the recipe for Chicken Sauté. Heat ⅓ cup of olive oil in a heavy skillet and sauté the chicken pieces, browning them on all sides. Season to taste with salt and pepper, cover, reduce the heat and cook gently for 10 minutes. Add 1 minced clove of garlic, 1 minced onion and ½ cup of finely chopped prosciutto or Virginia ham. Pour ½ cup of dry red wine over the chicken, cover and cook for 5 minutes. Meanwhile, simmer 1 cup of Italian tomato purée with 1 teaspoon of dry basil. Cook for 5 minutes and add to the chicken sauté. Turn the chicken to bathe it in the sauce thoroughly. Cover and cook until the chicken is tender.

SAUTÉED CHICKEN, FLAMBÉ (Serves 4)

2 2-pound frying chickens	**2 egg yolks**
6 tablespoons of butter	**1 cup of cream**
Salt and pepper	**4 ounces of Cognac**
8 small green onions, chopped	

Prepare the chicken as for Basic Chicken Sauté (page 297) and sauté in butter until almost done. Season to taste with salt and pepper as it cooks. A few minutes before removing the chicken from the pan, add the green onions, coarsely chopped. When the chicken is cooked remove it to a hot, flame-proof platter and keep it hot.

Continue cooking the onions until soft, adding a little more butter if necessary. Beat the egg yolks, then beat the cream into them. Place the pan with the onions over hot water and slowly stir in the egg and cream mixture. Continue cooking and stir (using a wooden spoon) until thickened and smooth. Do not let it boil or the eggs may curdle. Season to taste, if necessary.

Pour the Cognac over the chicken and carefully ignite it to blaze. When the flame dies out, pour the sauce over all.

STUFFED CHICKEN BREASTS (Serves 4 to 6)

3 whole chicken breasts,
  boned and skinned

6 tablespoons butter

1/4 pound mushrooms, finely
  chopped

2 tablespoons shallots, finely
  chopped

Salt

Freshly ground black pepper

Flour

3 tablespoons peanut or
  olive oil

3/4 cup dry white wine or
  vermouth

Chopped parsley

Cut the chicken breasts in half, trim off any fat or bits of bone, and flatten between sheets of waxed paper or plastic wrap. Melt 3 tablespoons of butter in a small skillet, add the mushrooms and shallots, and cook over medium heat until the moisture evaporates and the mushrooms darken. Sprinkle with salt and pepper. (This is called "Duxelles.")

Place a tablespoon of the mushrooms on one half of each piece of chicken, and fold over the other half. Fasten with a toothpick. Lightly flour the stuffed chicken. Heat the oil and remaining butter in a large skillet, and sauté the chicken over medium heat, turning once, about 4 minutes on a side. When done, transfer to a warm dish, and deglaze the skillet with 1/2 cup of the wine for a minute. Lower the heat, add the chicken breasts, and cover. Cook for another 6 minutes, turning once. Season with salt and pepper and transfer again to a warm dish while you finish off the sauce. Remove excess fat from the pan juices, add the leftover wine, and heat quickly. Pour over the chicken breasts, sprinkle with chopped parsley and serve.

CURRY OF CHICKEN (Serves 4)

2 frying chickens

Water

Salt

1 medium eggplant

3 tablespoons of olive oil

2 medium onions

2 medium apples

2 tablespoons of curry
  powder

Cayenne

1 teaspoon of chopped
  garlic

1/2 teaspoon of ground
  ginger

Broth or white wine

10 tablespoons of butter

2 tablespoons of chutney

2 tablespoons of tomato
  purée

Put the neck, giblets and wing tips of the chicken in 2 cups of salted water and simmer gently for 1 hour. Peel and dice the eggplant and sauté in olive oil for 5 minutes. Add ½ cup of water and cover. Simmer gently for 40 minutes or until very soft. Peel and chop the onions and apples and sauté in 4 tablespoons of butter until soft. Add curry powder, salt to taste, a dash of cayenne, chopped garlic and ginger. Add 1 cup of the broth from the chicken giblets, cover and simmer gently for ½ hour.

Sauté the cut-up chicken according to directions for Basic Chicken Sauté (page 297), browning in 6 tablespoons of butter, seasoning to taste and then adding a bit of the chicken broth or white wine.

After the curry mixture has cooked for ½ hour, add the chutney, the tomato purée, the cooked eggplant and another cup of broth, and simmer ½ hour more. If the sauce is too thick dilute with a little broth or water. Taste for seasoning. Add the sautéed chicken pieces and heat through to blend with the sauce flavors. Let it all cook together for about 10 minutes.

Serve with chutney, grated coconut, chopped peanuts, chopped hard-cooked egg and raisins soaked in Cognac or whiskey.

Broiled Chicken

PLAIN BROILED CHICKEN

Allow ½ broiler per person. Ask your butcher to split the broilers and remove the backbones and necks. Wipe the chicken halves with a damp cloth, then rub them well with butter or oil. Preheat the broiler. Arrange the chicken bone side up on a greased rack 3 inches from the flame. Broil for 15 minutes. Season to taste with salt and pepper and turn. Brush with more butter and cook skin side to the heat for another 15 minutes, or until done. Test for doneness by puncturing the thigh joint with a fork. When the juice runs clear, not red, the chicken is cooked. Do not overcook chicken or it will be dry and tasteless. Season to taste on the skin side and serve with shoestring potatoes, peas and onions mixed, and hot French bread.

VARIATIONS

Charcoal-broiled: To broil over charcoal, place the chicken halves on a rack 3 to 4 inches from the coals. Cook according to the directions above, starting bone side first and finishing on the skin side.

With tarragon butter: Rub the chickens with Tarragon Butter (see Herb Butter, page 354) and baste with more Tarragon Butter during cooking.

With parsley: Melt butter and add plenty of chopped parsley. Pour this over the chicken halves as you serve them.

With herbs: Mix ½ cup of chopped parsley, ¼ cup of chopped chives and 1 tablespoon of dried tarragon. Blend this into 4 tablespoons of softened butter. Loosen the breast skin of the chicken halves and stuff a little of this mixture between the skin and the flesh. Broil as above, basting with butter frequently after you turn to cook the skin side.

Marinated Broilers: Mix the following marinade: to 1 cup of olive oil add ½ cup of white wine vinegar, 6 chopped green onions, 1 tablespoon of dried tarragon, 1 teaspoon of salt and 1 teaspoon of freshly ground black pepper. Soak the chicken halves in this mixture for 2 or 3 hours, turning them frequently to be sure they are well bathed. Broil as above, basting with the sauce during cooking.

Oriental Broilers: Soak the broiler halves in the following mixture: 1 cup of soy sauce, ½ cup of dry sherry, 1-inch piece of ginger grated (or 1 tablespoon of chopped, dried ginger), and 1 minced clove of garlic. Follow directions for Marinated Broilers, above.

With fruit juice: Substitute ½ cup of fruit juice (orange, pineapple) for the sherry in Oriental Broilers, above.

Barbecued: Marinate the chicken in Barbecue Sauce (page 353) and follow directions for Marinated Broilers, above.

Fried Chicken

OLD-FASHIONED FRIED CHICKEN (Serves 4)

1 4-pound chicken or two 2-pound chickens	**Bacon fat or butter and oil mixed**
Flour	**2 cups of milk and heavy cream mixed**
Salt and pepper	

Have the chicken cut into frying pieces. Wipe with a damp cloth and roll in flour seasoned with salt and freshly ground black pepper. Press the flour in firmly with your hands to be sure plenty of it clings to the chicken. Heat bacon fat or oil and butter mixed in a large heavy skillet. You will need plenty of fat; it should be about 1½ inches deep in the pan. When it is bubbly hot but not burning, add the chicken pieces and cook them on all sides until they are evenly browned.

Sprinkle with a little additional salt and pepper, cover, lower the heat and cook gently until the chicken is tender. Turn the chicken pieces several times during the cooking and at the last, move the pieces of white meat to the top. When the chicken is done, remove it to a hot platter and pour off all but 4 tablespoons of the fat. Blend 3 tablespoons of flour into the fat and slowly add the milk and cream mixed, stirring to be sure it does not lump. When the sauce is smooth and thick, season with salt and pepper and serve with the chicken. With this serve creamy mashed potatoes and buttered broccoli.

Roast Chicken

ROAST CHICKEN

When buying chicken for roasting, allow 1 pound per person. Roasting chickens generally run 3 to 4 pounds. If you want a larger bird, a wise choice is capon, which is cooked in the same way. These run 5 to 9 pounds and are delicious and tender.

Wash the bird and remove any pinfeathers. (You can use tweezers for this job.) Singe off any tiny hairs along the edges of the wings or on the legs. Rub the cavity of the chicken with the cut side of half a lemon, sprinkle it with salt and pepper, and add any flavors you wish—3 or 4 cloves of garlic, several sprigs of fresh tarragon or a handful of dry tarragon, a touch of rosemary, 2 or 3 small peeled onions, or several sprigs of parsley—plus 2 tablespoons of butter. Truss and tie the chicken.

To truss: First fold the wing tips back under the bird. Then take a long piece of white string, tie the leg tips together tightly and make a taut loop around the tail, leaving two fairly even ends of string. Now cross the string over the back of the bird, bring it over the wings to hold them firm against the body, and finally tie securely across the neck skin, which remains after the neck is removed.

Butter the chicken well, or lay strips of bacon across it. Turn on its side on a rack. (Also place giblets on rack.) Roast at 400° for 20 minutes. Turn to other side and again add bacon strips or baste with butter. Roast another 20 minutes. Place on its back and baste well. Roast for final 20 minutes. Salt and pepper. Check for doneness. (The legs should move easily.) If not sufficiently cooked to your taste, continue cooking. Do not overcook. A little pink at the joint will do no harm.

Serve chicken with degreased pan juices, crisp sautéed potatoes and a good salad.

For Cold Chicken: Allow cooked chicken to cool at room temperature. It should have just a touch of warmth and be crisp and fresh to the bite. I really prefer it this way.

VARIATIONS

With white wine: Baste with a mixture of dry white wine and melted butter.

Chicken Tarragon: Rub the chicken well with Tarragon Butter and put tarragon (at least one teaspoon) in the cavity, in place of thyme. Baste with Tarragon Butter during the roasting. Or baste with Tarragon Butter (see Herb Butter, page 354) mixed with dry white wine.

With green onions: Put 3 or 4 little green onions in the cavity with the parsley. Baste the chicken with Chive Butter (see Herb Butter, page 354) and white wine.

GIBLET SAUCE

Use the giblets and neck from the chicken to make this sauce. It is far better with chicken than the usual flour and water mixture called gravy.

Cover the giblets and the neck with $^2/_3$ water and $^1/_3$ dry white wine. Add 1 teaspoon of salt, 3 or 4 peppercorns, a sprig of parsley, 1 onion stuck with 2 cloves and 1 carrot. Bring to a boil and boil for 1 minute. Skim off the scum, cover the pan and lower the heat. Cook gently for 1 hour. Strain the broth and cook it down to 1 cup. Taste for seasoning. When the chicken is done, add the juices in the baking dish to the giblet broth and thicken, if you like, with Beurre Manié (page 348).

ROAST SQUAB CHICKEN

These tiny birds weigh only about 1 pound each. Serve one to a person. Prepare as you do roasting chicken and roast quickly in a 450° oven for 30 to 45 minutes, or just until tender. Use any of the seasonings suggested above for Roast Chicken.

CHICKEN ON THE SPIT

Prepare roasting or squab chicken as above. Spit the bird, running the spit through the center of the heaviest part to be sure it balances evenly. Spit larger chicken with the spit running through from head to tail. Spit tiny squab with the spit running through from side to side.

Use any of the seasonings or bastings suggested for Roast Chicken, (page 303) and cook over charcoal, allowing about 1½ hours for a 4-pound chicken, 1 hour for a 2½- to 3-pound chicken and 30 to 40 minutes for a small squab chicken. Baste during the cooking and test for doneness by moving the thigh up and down or puncturing the thigh joint with a fork. If the juice runs clear, not pink, the chicken is done.

ROAST STUFFED CHICKEN (Serves 4)

4-pound chicken	**¼ cup of chopped parsley**
Half a lemon	**1 teaspoon of thyme**
Butter	**Salt and pepper**
1 onion, chopped	**2½ cups of fine bread crumbs**
½ cup of chopped celery	

Wash and clean the bird (see Roast Chicken, page 303) and rub the cavity with the cut side of a half lemon.

To prepare the stuffing: Melt 6 tablespoons of butter in a skillet and add the chopped onion. Cook until just barely soft. Add the celery, parsley, thyme and 1 teaspoon each of salt and freshly ground black pepper. Mix with fine dry bread crumbs and add additional melted butter (about ¼ cup). The dressing should not be too dry. It should be rather moist with butter but not soggy. Stuff the chicken lightly and fasten the vent with metal skewers, or close it by folding a piece of foil into several thicknesses and tucking into the opening. Truss the bird (see page 303) and rub well with butter. Sprinkle lightly with salt and bake as for Roast Chicken, basting occasionally with melted butter or melted butter and white wine mixed.

Serve with Giblet Sauce (see page 304).

VARIATIONS

With mushrooms: Substitute chopped mushrooms for the celery and sauté them with the onion.

With nuts: Add ½ cup of chopped, blanched almonds or filberts and sauté them in the pan with the onion.

With sausage: Add 4 small link sausages, sautéed and chopped.

With ham: Add ½ cup of chopped, cooked ham.

Note: For larger or smaller chickens, allow a scant cup of stuffing for each pound the bird weighs.

Chicken Fricassee

PLAIN CHICKEN FRICASSEE (Serves 4)

For this dish, you can use a fowl. These older birds are mature and flavorful but need long cooking to tenderize. Otherwise use a roasting chicken. Have the butcher clean it and cut it into serving pieces as for frying.

4- to 5-pound fowl	**4 tablespoons of butter**
1 onion stuck with 2 cloves	**3 tablespoons of flour**
1 carrot	**³/₄ cup of heavy cream**
2 sprigs of parsley	**Lemon juice**
2 teaspoons of salt	

Wash the chicken pieces and put them in a large kettle with the onion, the carrot and the parsley. Add water to cover and bring slowly to a boil. Cover, lower the heat and simmer gently for 1 hour. Add 2 teaspoons of salt and continue cooking until the chicken is thoroughly tender but not mushy. The length of time depends on the age and toughness of the bird. It may take 15 more minutes; it may take another hour. Test at intervals with a fork. A roasting chicken will take about an hour.

When the chicken is done, remove it to a hot dish and keep warm in a very slow oven. Skim the fat from the broth and strain it. Then return it to the stove and cook down a little to make it richer. Melt the butter in a skillet, blend in the flour and gradually stir in 1½ cups of the chicken broth mixed with the cream. Add it slowly being sure the mixture does not lump. (For directions, see Roux, page 347.) Continue cooking and stirring until the sauce is thick and smooth. Arrange the chicken on a hot platter, add a dash or so of lemon juice to the sauce and pour it over the chicken. Garnish with chopped parsley and serve with rice or noodles.

CHICKEN PIE

Prepare a Plain Chicken Fricassee (see page 306). When the chicken is cooked, remove it from the broth and take it off the bones in large pieces. Arrange the meat in a casserole. Sauté ½ pound mushrooms in 4 tablespoons of butter and add these to the chicken meat. Make the sauce (see Chicken Fricassee) and pour over the chicken and mushrooms. Top with a pastry dough (see page 76) or rich biscuit dough (page 45) and bake in 450° oven for 15 to 20 minutes, or until the top crust or biscuit is brown and cooked through.

CHICKEN AND DUMPLINGS

Make a Plain Chicken Fricassee (page 306) and after the sauce is thickened, put spoonfuls of dumpling dough (page 46) over the surface. Be sure you space them a few inches apart, for dumplings puff out. Cover the pan and steam gently for about 15 minutes, or until the dumplings are light and cooked through. Arrange the chicken on a platter, surround with the dumplings and cover with the sauce.

CHICKEN SHORTBREAD

Make the Plain Chicken Fricassee on page 306 and when the chicken is done take the meat from the bones. Finish the sauce and return the chicken meat to the pan with the sauce. Add ½ pound of mushrooms sautéed in butter. Serve this creamed chicken over biscuit (page 45) or cornbread.

BROWN FRICASSEE (Serves 4)

4-pound roasting chicken cut in serving pieces	**Chicken stock or broth to cover**
Flour	**Pinch of thyme**
Salt and pepper	**1 bay leaf**
6 tablespoons of butter	**½ to ¾ cup of cream**
1 onion, chopped	

Use a roasting chicken for this dish and have the butcher cut it up as for frying. Wipe the chicken pieces with a damp cloth and roll in flour seasoned with salt and pepper. Melt 6 tablespoons of butter in a heavy kettle, such as a Dutch oven, and brown the chicken pieces on all sides. Add the chopped onion and let it color slightly. Pour over this enough chicken stock or broth to cover. (You can make this by cooking the chicken giblets and neck—see Giblet Sauce, page 304—and adding the giblet broth to chicken bouillon cubes dissolved in hot water.) Add a bay leaf and a pinch of thyme, cover and simmer gently until the chicken is tender. This should take about 45 minutes to an hour. Remove the chicken pieces to a hot platter and taste the sauce for seasoning. Add a little cream, about ½ to ¾ of a cup, and blend it in. If you like a thicker sauce, add pea-sized balls of butter and flour kneaded together and stir them in.

VARIATION

With mushrooms: You may add sautéed mushrooms (½ pound) and sautéed tiny white onions (8 to 12) to the pot for the last few minutes of cooking. Or cook them with the chicken, adding them during the last half hour.

CHICKEN IN CASSEROLE

Proceed as for Brown Fricassee, but transfer the pan to the oven after the broth is added and bake at 350° for 1 hour, or until the chicken is tender. Add any of the vegetables you like—mushrooms, carrots, tiny white onions, small potatoes—during the last half hour of cooking.

VARIATION

With wine: Substitute dry white wine for half of the chicken broth.

COLD CHICKEN IN ASPIC

Prepare a Plain Chicken Fricassee (page 306) and do not thicken the broth. Let the chicken cool in the stock, then remove the pieces and arrange them in a mold or large deep bowl. Strain the sauce and chill to let the fat rise to the surface and solidify. Skim off all the solid fat. If the broth has jellied, simply reheat it to melt and pour over the chicken. If it is not firm, add a little unflavored gelatin. One envelope will jelly 2 cups of liquid. If the liquid is partly firm, use half of this proportion: ½ envelope to two cups of liquid. Melt the gelatin in a few spoonfuls of cold water. Heat the broth and stir in the gelatin until it dissolves thoroughly. Pour the broth over the chicken. Place the mold or bowl in the refrigerator and chill.

Garnished: You may add any garnishes you choose to the chicken as you arrange it in the mold: olives, sliced hard-cooked egg, strips of pimiento, green pepper rings, cooked vegetables (string beans, carrot rounds, canned whole mushrooms), sliced onion or radishes.

Serve from the mold or turn out on a bed of greens and pass a bowl of well-seasoned mayonnaise.

Poached Chicken

Many people call poached chicken "boiled." If it were actually boiled it would not be very tasty. The chicken should be gently simmered, with the broth or water barely moving on the surface. The classic poached chicken is cooked whole, stuffed or unstuffed, in seasoned water or water and wine mixed. The cooked bird is arranged on a hot platter and carved in the same way as roast chicken. Use a mature fowl for this dish.

POACHED CHICKEN (Serves 4)

4- to 5-pound fowl	1 bay leaf
Boiling water, or water and wine, to cover	1 teaspoon of thyme or rosemary
1 onion	Stuffing or 2 sprigs of parsley and 1 onion
2 teaspoons of salt	
Peppercorns	

If a fowl is not available, use a roasting chicken. Wash the chicken or wipe with a damp cloth, and if you wish to stuff it, use one of the stuffings suggested for Roast Stuffed Chicken and follow the directions for stuffing (page 305). If you do not stuff the bird, put a sprig or two of parsley and a peeled onion in the cavity. Sew up securely and truss (see page 303). Place the fowl in a deep kettle and add boiling water to cover or boiling water and dry white wine mixed. Add a few peppercorns, the onion, bay leaf and thyme or rosemary. Cover tightly and simmer—do not boil—gently for 1 hour. Add the salt and continue simmering until the fowl is tender. This may take another hour. The length of time depends on the toughness of the bird. Test for doneness with a fork. A roasting chicken will take about an hour.

Arrange the cooked bird on a platter, remove the strings and carve as you would a roast chicken. Serve with creamy mashed potatoes, buttered noodles or rice.

VARIATIONS

1. Serve the broth first as a soup course.

2. Add any vegetables you like to the hot broth during the last half hour of cooking.

3. Cook the broth down and thicken it with Beurre Manié (page 348) to serve as a sauce. Taste for seasoning and add a little heavy cream if you like.

Duck

Most of the ducks sold in this country are Long Island ducks, a strain developed as an all-purpose fowl. These ducks have a heavy layer of fat under the skin and it is better to give them long, slow cooking rather than the high-heat cooking used for wild ducks or other varieties. One Long Island duck will usually serve two persons amply and four with lighter appetites. Some of the younger and smaller ducks must be served a half to a person.

When roasting duck it is wise to use a pan with a rack or a spit. The rack or spit allows the fat to cook out into the dripping pan below and keeps the duck crisp. If duck stands in a bath of its own grease it is flabby and uninteresting. Prick the skin a few times during roasting and it will be crunchier.

BROILED DUCKLING (Serves 4)

2 small ducklings	**Freshly ground black pepper**
Salt	

Split the ducklings in half with poultry shears, cutting each from the vent at the tail along the side of the breastbone to the neck opening. Then turn the duckling and cut down the center of the back until it is halved. Rub the skin of the duckling halves with salt and freshly ground black pepper. Heat the broiler until very hot and place the ducks with the bone or inside about 4 inches from the flame. Broil for 20 minutes, then turn and finish cooking until browned and crisp. Serve with wild rice or Barley Casserole.

VARIATION

Charcoal-broiled: Broil the duckling over charcoal on your outdoor grill. (See Charcoal-Broiling, page 183.) Place the duck halves about 6 inches from the coals.

ROAST DUCKLING (Serves 4)

1 large or 2 small ducklings	**Thyme or rosemary**
Salt and pepper	**1 onion stuck with 2 cloves**

Use a roasting pan with a rack to hold the duck out of the drippings. If your pan does not have a regular roasting rack, use a bread rack or any contrivance to keep the duck off the bottom of the pan. Rub the duck well with salt and pepper and a bit of thyme or rosemary if you like. Place in the cavity of the duck a peeled onion into which you have pushed two cloves. Stand it on the rack and roast in a 325° oven, allowing 1¼ hours for rare duck, 1½ for medium-rare and about 2 hours for very well-done duck. Most people prefer duck roasted medium-rare rather than well-done. After ½ hour prick the skin to release the fat, and prick several more times during roasting.

For crisp duck, increase the heat to 500° for the last 15 minutes of cooking.

Ducks are easier to carve by cutting them into halves or quarters with poultry shears; they do not slice well. Serve each person a half or quarter and with it, rice, wild rice or barley. Turnips are also an excellent accompaniment for duck.

VARIATIONS

À la Française: Roast the duck as above for about 1½ hours. It should be on the underdone side. Remove to a hot platter, cut into quarters and serve heaped with tiny French petits pois that have been cooked with tiny white onions, peeled and parboiled, and strips of ham. An orange and onion salad goes very well with this dish.

Au Poivre: Rub the duck with salt only, and roast as above. 30 minutes before the duck is done press coarsely ground black peppercorns into the breast. Return to the oven. Increase the heat to 500° for the last 15 minutes of cooking to crisp the skin.

ROAST DUCK WITH OLIVES (Serves 4)

1 large or 2 small ducklings	6 sprigs of parsley
1 green pepper	Salt and pepper
1 large onion	1 cup of white wine
3 stalks of celery	24 small green olives
1 carrot	

Cook the giblets, wing tips and neck of the duck in 2 cups of water for 45 minutes. Strain and set the broth aside. Peel the onion and carrot and seed the pepper. Chop these and the celery and parsley all rather coarsely. Arrange the chopped vegetables on the bottom of a baking dish. Rub the duck with salt and pepper and place it on top. Add the white wine to the strained broth and pour this over all. Roast in a 325° oven for 1½ to 1¾ hours, or until the duckling is brown and crisp. Baste during the roasting with the broth in the pan.

When the duck is done, remove it to a hot platter and keep it warm. Rub the vegetables and broth through a fine sieve, or put them through a food mill, or use your food processor to liquefy the vegetables thoroughly. Reheat the sauce, skim off the excess fat and taste for seasoning. Add the olives and heat them through. Serve this sauce with the duck, and accompany it with small new potatoes cooked in their jackets and tiny green peas.

ROAST DUCK WITH CURRY AND HONEY (Serves 4)

Mix 4 tablespoons of honey with 1½ tablespoons of curry powder. Roast duck according to directions for plain Roast Duckling, page 311, and after it has cooked for 55 minutes, remove it and brush well with some of the honey-curry mixture. Repeat this every 10 minutes during the next ½ hour of cooking, or until the duck skin has a fine glaze. Serve this curried glazed duck with rice and chutney and thinly sliced bananas dressed with a sharp French oil-and-vinegar dressing.

ROAST DUCK, CHINESE STYLE (Serves 4)

1 large or 2 small ducks	1 teaspoon of ground ginger
Lemon juice	4 tablespoons of honey
Soy sauce	

Rub the ducks inside and out with the lemon juice and then dry them out thoroughly by standing them in front of an electric fan for 1 hour or rubbing them well with paper towels until no dampness remains. Rub the skin and the interior with soy sauce, and rub the outside with ground ginger. Roast according to directions for Roast Duck (see page 311) in a 325° oven for 1 hour. Then brush the skin with a mixture of 1½ tablespoons of soy sauce and the ground ginger and honey. Continue cooking and brush the skin with the mixture occasionally until the duck has a nice glaze and is done.

Serve this Chinese-style duckling with steamed rice and Chinese vegetables, or with small white turnips smothered in butter and sprinkled with toasted sesame seeds.

ROAST DUCK AU GRAND MARNIER (Serves 4)

1 large or 2 small ducks	½ cup of honey
1½ cups of water	½ cup of Grand Marnier
1 large orange	½ cup of orange sections, peeled
Salt and pepper	
1½ cups of orange juice	

Cook the giblets, wing tips and neck of the duck in 1½ cups of water for 35 minutes. Strain and reserve the broth. Rub the duck skin with salt and pepper, and put an orange, cut into slices (skin and all), in the cavity of the duck. Roast on a rack in a pan according to directions for plain Roast Duckling (see page 311), basting frequently during the cooking with a mixture of 1 cup of orange juice and the honey. Roast the duck for 1 hour and 25 minutes, then remove it to a hot platter and keep warm. Skim the fat from the pan juices and place the pan over direct heat. Add the strained broth and ½ cup of orange juice. Cook over high heat for 5 minutes and then add the Grand Marnier and taste for seasoning. Heat and blend, add the orange sections and heat them through.

Pour this rich sauce over the duck and serve with a barley and mushroom casserole and an endive salad mixed with tiny whole beets.

DUCK WITH PINEAPPLE (Serves 4)

1 large or 2 small ducks	1 can of sliced pineapple
1½ cups of water	Butter
Salt and pepper	Sugar

Make a broth, salt and pepper the duck and place it on a rack in a pan, as for Roast Duck au Grand Marnier (see page 313), omitting the sliced orange in the cavity. Baste the duck during roasting with part of the juice from a can of sliced pineapple. When the duck is done, remove it to a hot platter and keep warm. Skim the fat from the pan juices and place the pan over direct heat. Add another ½ cup of pineapple juice and the broth from the giblets, and cook down a little over high heat. Sauté the slices of pineapple in butter, and as they cook sprinkle them with a little sugar to let them candy. Arrange the pineapple slices around the duck and pour the sauce over it.

If you like a thicker sauce, mix 1 teaspoon of cornstarch with a little water and stir into the sauce. Cook, stirring constantly, until thickened.

DUCK WITH LENTILS (Serves 4)

1 duckling	**1 pound of Italian sausages**
Salt and pepper	**(or frankfurters)**
2 cups of quick-cooking	**⅔ cup of chopped parsley**
lentils	**1 clove of garlic, chopped**
1 large onion, chopped	**1½ cups of red wine**
4 tablespoons of butter	**Buttered bread crumbs**
⅔ cup of water	

Roast the duck according to directions for plain Roast Duckling (see page 311). While the duck is roasting, cook the lentils until tender but not mushy (see Lentils, page 456). Drain and reserve the liquid.

Peel and chop the onion. Sauté in 4 tablespoons of butter until transparent and soft. Cook the Italian sausages (or frankfurters) in ⅔ cup of water for 12 minutes. Drain and slice.

When the duck is roasted cut it into small serving pieces. Mix the lentils with the sautéed onion, the chopped parsley and the garlic, and then mix in the sausages and duck so the meat is distributed throughout. Put this mixture into a buttered casserole and pour 1½ cups of red wine over it. Add broth from the lentils if more liquid seems necessary. Cover and bake in 350° oven for 25 minutes. Uncover and bake for another 10 minutes. Then put a good layer of buttered crumbs on top and finish cooking for 5 minutes or until browned and bubbly.

This dish can be kept in the oven for some time. Simply add more liquid (lentil broth or wine) if it tends to get dry. With this casserole serve an onion and lettuce salad dressed with olive oil and lemon juice (instead of vinegar) and a good red wine. This is a hearty spread for a skiing or skating party.

COLD ROAST DUCK (Serves 4)

Roast duck according to directions for plain Roast Duckling (see page 311). After it is cooked rub the skin well with lemon or lime juice and then chill the duck. Cut it into serving-size pieces, and serve with greens, sliced tomatoes, sliced cucumbers and a green bean salad. Pass mayonnaise flavored with orange juice and a dash of lemon juice.

VARIATION

After the duck is cooked, skin it and cut into serving pieces. Dip each piece into mayonnaise and arrange on a bed of lettuce. Garnish with sliced beets and sliced onions that have marinated in a French dressing made with orange juice instead of vinegar. Surround with orange slices, and serve with heated garlic bread.

Squab

Squab are baby pigeons, tender and delicious and considered one of the greatest delicacies. They are usually expensive but they make excellent party food because they are easy to prepare and will not be ruined by a little extra cooking if guests are late. Squab is one fowl that should be rather well done.

A squab usually weighs a pound or less. Allow one per serving.

BROILED SQUAB

Split each squab and flatten it out as you treat a chicken for broiling. Or have the butcher split and flatten it with a cleaver. (When flattened with a cleaver, squab is called *crapaudine,* because it's supposed to look like a frog.)

Broil under a medium flame, turning several times and brushing well with melted butter. Cook until very tender and done and browned on the outside. Season to taste with salt and pepper and serve with the pan juices, sautéed potatoes and tiny French peas.

Note: Squab should be eaten with the fingers. It's impossible to get all the tasty bits from the bones with knife and fork.

ROAST SQUAB

Allow one per serving. Bard the breast well with salt pork or fat bacon. Arrange in a baking pan and cook at 325° without basting for 45 minutes to 1 hour, or until well done. Remove the barding pork or bacon during the last 15 minutes of cooking to let the breast brown. Test for doneness by puncturing the thigh joint with a fork.

Note: Squab may be seared in a hot oven and then finished off with a lower heat, but if you use this method you must watch the birds carefully and baste them often. Start them in a 450° oven and baste frequently with melted butter. After 25 minutes, reduce the heat to 350° and cook for 15 to 20 minutes more, basting occasionally.

VARIATION

With tarragon: Add a bit of dried or fresh tarragon and a chunk of butter to the cavity of each bird. Baste with tarragon-flavored melted butter while cooking.

ROAST STUFFED SQUAB (Serves 4)

4 squab	¹/₄ cup of chopped parsley
1 onion, chopped fine	¹/₂ teaspoon of thyme
6 tablespoons of butter	4 pieces of fat bacon
1 cup of fine bread crumbs	Melted butter and white wine mixed (about ¹/₄ cup each)
1 cup of chopped ham	
¹/₂ cup of pine nuts	

Peel the onion and chop. Sauté in 6 tablespoons of butter until soft and transparent. Mix with the bread crumbs, ham, pine nuts, chopped parsley, and thyme, and stuff the birds with this mixture. Arrange the squab in a baking pan and cover the breast of each one with a piece of fat bacon. Roast in a 325° oven for 1 hour and 15 minutes, basting frequently with the mixture of melted butter and white wine. If more basting liquid is needed, add wine. Remove the barding bacon from the breast during the last 15 minutes of cooking.

Serve with wild rice or barley and small white onions steamed in butter.

SQUAB ON THE SPIT

Bard each squab with fat bacon and arrange them on a spit. The average-sized spit for an outdoor charcoal broiler will hold several squab. Spit them through from side to side, placing the head of the first forward and the tail of the second forward, so that the birds alternate on the spit, head to tail. In this way the squab will be evenly balanced on the spit.

Roast over charcoal until browned and tender. This will take 35 to 40 minutes.

COLD SQUAB

Serve plain roast squab or broiled squab cold for an elegant picnic. It is wise to allow 2 per person since outdoor eaters often have hearty appetites.

Turkey

The holiday choice, turkey, used to be just that: a fall and winter specialty. Today it is available all the year round and in every size from 4-pound broilers up to toms of 30 pounds or more. The smaller birds are a recent development. They are small-boned and heavily meated, with extra breadth through the middle that provides more breast meat.

When you buy turkey, look for firm, fresh-looking skin, plump legs and thighs and a thick breast. Long, scrawny turkeys are not as tender or tasty.

ROAST STUFFED TURKEY (Serves 4 to 6)

7- to 8-pound turkey	**Salt and pepper**
½ lemon	**Butter**
6 cups of stuffing	**White wine**

Rub the cavity of the turkey with the cut side of the half lemon and stuff it lightly with any of the stuffings suggested for chicken (page 305) or with half the Tarragon-Bread Crumb Stuffing (page 319). Close the vent with foil or with metal skewers, or sew it up, and then truss the bird well (page 303). Rub the turkey with butter, and season with salt and pepper. Arrange in a roaster or in a large baking pan and roast, basting frequently with butter or with butter and dry white wine mixed.

There are several theories on the proper way to roast a turkey. Some people insist on starting it in a hot oven and then reducing the heat. I feel this tends to dry out the meat. Other people like to roast turkey in a parchment wrapping, browning it at the last. This, to me, reduces the crusty brown outside that is so tasty to gnaw on. I prefer to roast it uncovered, basting frequently, in a 350° oven, allowing about 15 to 18 minutes to the pound. To be sure of doneness test by moving the thigh joint up and down. If it moves easily the turkey should be done. Puncture the thigh joint with a fork. If the juice runs red, the bird needs more roasting; if it is clear the turkey is done. Also, a meat thermometer inserted in the thickest part of the thigh (without touching the bone) should register 170° to 175°. Do not overcook turkey. The dark meat should still have a pinkish tinge. If you overcook, the meat will be dry and half the flavor gone.

Serve Roast Stuffed Turkey with sautéed tiny white onions, mashed potatoes and Giblet Sauce made with the turkey giblets and neck (see page 304).

Note: For turkeys weighing over 16 pounds, allow 12 to 14 minutes per pound. An 18-pound turkey will take about 4 hours.

VARIATIONS

Small turkey, basted: If you buy a very small turkey of about 4 pounds to roast (one of the small broiler turkeys) baste it with butter or butter and white wine every few minutes. These smaller birds do not have the heavy layer of fat and they can be very dry. Begin testing for doneness after 1 hour of roasting. They cook quickly.

Without basting: If you wish to save yourself the trouble of basting during the first half of the roasting, fold a piece of cheesecloth into several thicknesses and saturate it with melted butter mixed with olive oil. Cover the breast of the turkey with the cloth and roast until half done. Then remove the cloth and finish roasting, basting every 15 or 20 minutes.

TARRAGON-BREAD CRUMB STUFFING (for a 20-pound turkey)

12 cups fresh bread crumbs

1½ cups finely sliced scallions or shallots

½ to ¾ pound unsalted butter

2 tablespoons fresh or 1 tablespoon dried tarragon

1 cup chopped parsley

1 tablespoon salt

1½ teaspoons freshly ground black pepper

½ cup pine nuts

Use French or Italian bread, crusts trimmed, for the bread crumbs. Melt the butter in a skillet, add the scallions or shallots, and toss to coat well. Mix with the rest of the ingredients. Taste for salt. Use to stuff the breast cavity. This amount should be more than ample for a 20-pound bird.

LEFTOVER ROAST TURKEY AND STUFFING

Breaded: Dip slices of cold turkey in lightly beaten egg and then roll in fine crumbs. Brown in plenty of butter or olive oil and serve with a hot Sauce Diable (page 351) or Tomato Sauce (page 352).

Turkey Curry: Make a Rich Cream Sauce (page 349) and blend it with any leftover Giblet Sauce (page 304). Flavor to taste with curry powder and add pieces of cold turkey. Heat and serve over rice. With this serve a good chutney, toasted buttered almonds, chopped hard-cooked egg and some crisp tiny green onions.

Heated stuffing: Moisten the stuffing with Giblet Sauce and heap it in a greased casserole. Dot liberally with butter and heat in a 350° oven for 20 to 25 minutes, or until hot through. Or heat with the Giblet Sauce (page 304) in a heavy skillet.

PLAIN ROAST TURKEY

Roast turkey plain, without stuffing, in any of the ways suggested for chicken (pages 305–306) allowing 15 to 18 minutes per pound in a 350° oven for a bird up to 16 pounds. (See note for Roast Stuffed Turkey, page 317.) Baste frequently.

BROILED TURKEY

Small turkey broilers (about 4 pounds) may be split and broiled as suggested for chicken (pages 301–302). Cook for 25 minutes on each side and baste frequently. One broiler will serve 4 persons.

CREAMED TURKEY OR CHICKEN (Serves 4)

2 cups of leftover turkey or chicken

2 cups of Rich Cream Sauce (page 349)

Toast or biscuits

Sautéed mushrooms (optional)

Cut the turkey or chicken into small pieces. Make the Rich Cream Sauce and heat the meat in the sauce. Season to taste and serve on toast or hot biscuits. Garnish with sautéed mushrooms, if you like.

Salads and Salad Dressings

Salads

Salad can be anything from a bit of green with a simple oil and vinegar dressing to an elaborate concoction that contains vegetables and meat or fish with garnishes. It can be a side dish with hamburger, or it can be offered as the main course at a summer buffet dinner. No matter when it is served, or what the ingredients, a salad should always have a slightly tart taste and always be zestful.

If you use greens or raw vegetables, be sure they are fresh and crisp. If you use cooked vegetables, be sure you don't cook them until they are limp. They should still be "bitey." If you use meats, use lean, tender pieces with all fat and gristle removed. If you use seafood, be sure it is not over-cooked, mushy and tasteless.

Always taste salad before serving it. If it seems a little dull, perhaps it needs a dash of lemon juice or a bit of grated onion.

Serve salad chilled but not icy-cold. Food that is icy-cold has no flavor.

Green Salads

Not so many years ago iceberg lettuce was about the only salad green sold in the average American market. This round, hard head-lettuce was developed by growers because it ships well and keeps well. It's an ideal product from the viewpoint of shipper and grocer, but of all salad greens it is the least desirable for eating. It tends to be watery and is always tasteless.

The growing popularity of the tossed green salad led to public interest in a more varied choice of lettuces, and today most areas offer a good selection. Any of the following make a good green salad, alone or in combination. Or use them as garnishes and as beds of greens for other cold foods.

Boston lettuce: This round head has loosely packed light green leaves. Tender and delicious.

Bibb lettuce: Small, very compact head lettuce. The leaves are crisp and tender and are small enough to be left whole in a salad. A fairly expensive lettuce, generally sold by the pound.

Romaine: A long, slender, loosely headed lettuce with dark green leaves. The texture is firm and crisp and the flavor clean.

Escarole: This comes in a flat, fan-shaped bunch, shading from yellow at the center to deep green. The leaves are long and slender and curly at the edges. Firm, bitey, with a slightly bitter taste.

Curly endive (chicory): This feathery green comes in a spread-out bunch. It shades from a yellow center to pale green, crinkly ends. It is crisp, with a bitter tang that makes it an excellent accent among other greens.

Watercress: These tiny stalks with the round green leaves are bound together in bunches. The strong peppery taste is a welcome addition to a bowl of greens. Watercress is also a decorative and tasty garnish.

Spinach: Many people think of spinach only as a vegetable to cook. Try tender young spinach leaves in the salad bowl. They have a fresh flavor.

Leaf Lettuce: A loosely formed bunch of tender leaves, growing straight up from the root. It can be green, green tipped with red, or fairly reddish throughout. The red varieties give a nice change of color in salads.

Lamb's-Tongues or Field Lettuce: This is scarce but worth watching for. It comes in small clumps of tiny, tongue-shaped leaves on delicate stems. It does not ship or keep well and is found only near the areas where it is grown. Most often available in the fall in eastern markets.

Arugala: Also known as "Rocket." Flat, serrated green leaves that look like overgrown dandelion greens. The texture is coarse and the taste peppery and rather bitter. A good accent for mixed green salads.

Belgian endive: These small, pale stalks look almost like large buds. They are composed of tightly packed, narrow, pointed leaves, shading from white to pale yellow. Rinse them and split them lengthwise into halves or quarters.

BASIC GREEN SALAD

To be good, a green salad should be crisp and fresh; not watery and wilted. Choose any combination of greens you like and wash them carefully to remove all grit. Discard any wilted or discolored leaves. Using a clean, absorbent towel, dry the greens thoroughly; if you leave moisture on them it will thin down the salad dressing and give you a limp salad. Do this job gently. Some greens, such as Boston lettuce, are very tender and crush and bruise easily.

Spread the greens out on a fresh towel, roll them up very loosely and put on the bottom shelf of the refrigerator to crisp until you are ready to make the salad.

Green salad should not be made until the last minute. It wilts if it stands too long. Just before ready to serve, break the greens into bite-size pieces and put them in a salad bowl. Now mix a good French Dressing (page 343). Do not doll up delicate greens with chili sauce dressing or chopped pickle or crumbled cheese. Such additions only detract from the crisp, clean taste of the salad. Pour the freshly mixed dressing over the greens and toss lightly with a fork and spoon until each piece of green is bathed with oil. Serve quickly.

There are many ways to vary the flavor of green salad, and some additions turn it into a hearty main course for a summer luncheon. Here are some suggestions:

1. Flavor French Dressing with garlic or herbs.
2. Add onion rings or chopped raw onion.
3. Add sliced raw mushrooms.
4. Add thin strips of green pepper, chopped green onion and chopped celery.
5. Add slices or cubes of avocado and chopped chives.
6. Add cubes of peeled and seeded cucumber, sliced radishes and chopped raw onion or green onion.
7. Add cooked shrimp, chopped chives and capers.
8. Add cooked crab-leg meat, chopped chives and capers.
9. Add cooked lobster meat, chopped chives and capers.

Chef's Salad: Add strips of cold chicken, turkey, ham or tongue, and strips of Swiss cheese. Garnish with tomato quarters and sliced hard-cooked eggs.

   Note: Some people like to add tomatoes to a tossed green salad. The flavors are complementary, but the tomato seems to make the salad watery. I suggest serving sliced tomatoes or tiny peeled whole tomatoes on the side.

Avocado Salads

The most common mistake people make with avocados is serving them before they are fully ripe. A green avocado is hard, rubbery and far from delicious. A ripe avocado is rich and soft. How can you tell a ripe avocado? Frankly, it is not always easy, but here are some suggestions.

If you are buying the pear-shaped avocado with the thin green skin, test it by pressing it gently between the palms of your hands. If it has give and feels slightly soft, it should be ripe. The roundish, thick green-skinned avocados may have a little give when soft, but since the skin is thicker it is not as easy to detect. Inspect the stem end of this type. If it looks freshly picked and the stem end is bright green, it is probably still hard. If the stem end has turned dark (but not mushy), it should be ripe. There is a third variety found on the markets. It is round with a very thick, dark skin, rough and almost purple in color. Look at the stem end, if it has dried and darkened, the avocado is dead ripe. When in doubt, ask your grocer to pick one out for you.

A ripe avocado will not keep long. If you do not use it at once, store it in the refrigerator on the bottom shelf, but do not expect it to keep more than 24 hours. If you use only half of an avocado, leave the pit in the unused half, rub the flesh with a little lemon juice and wrap tightly in foil.

Firm avocados can be set aside to ripen at room temperature. This takes from one to three days, depending on how hard they are. The warmer the spot, the faster they ripen. Firm avocados can also be kept in the refrigerator for a week or so. Remove them a day or two before you plan to eat them to allow them to ripen.

Allow ½ of a medium-sized avocado per person. Do not prepare avocado until the last minute. The flesh darkens after it is cut.

AVOCADO HALVES, VINAIGRETTE

Allow ½ avocado per person. Peel them or not, as you choose, cut them in half the long way and remove the pits. Arrange the halves on beds of greens and fill the centers with Vinaigrette Sauce (page 343).

Variations

With green onions: Add a teaspoon of chopped green onions or chives to each cavity.

With garlic: Flavor the Vinaigrette Sauce with a little grated garlic.

AVOCADO AND GRAPEFRUIT SALAD (Serves 4)

1 large or 2 small avocados   **Greens**
1 large or 2 small grapefruit   **Vinaigrette Sauce**

Peel the avocado. Peel the grapefruit and cut out the sections, being careful to keep them whole. Slice the avocado the long way into crescent-shaped pieces. Alternate these with the grapefruit sections on a bed of greens. Dress with Vinaigrette Sauce (page 343).

AVOCADO AND ORANGE SALAD

For 4 persons buy 1 large or 2 small avocados and 2 oranges. Prepare as for Avocado and Grapefruit Salad (see above).

AVOCADO AND ONION SALAD

For 4 persons buy 1 large or 2 small avocados and 1 Bermuda or red Italian onion. Peel the onion and cut it in thin slices. Prepare the avocado as for Avocado and Grapefruit Salad. Alternate the avocado and onion slices on a bed of greens, and dress with Vinaigrette Sauce (page 343).

GUACAMOLE (Serves 4)

2 very ripe avocados   **1 to 1$\frac{1}{2}$ teaspoons salt**
1 or 2 chopped green chilies   **Chopped fresh coriander (optional)**
2 tablespoons lime juice or lemon juice

The avocados must be dead ripe for this Mexican salad. Peel them and mash the pulp until it is smooth. Add the chopped chilies, the lime or lemon juice, and the salt, and blend thoroughly. Heap on a bed of greens and sprinkle with chopped coriander, if you like, or serve as a dip with tortillas or corn chips.

VARIATIONS

With garlic: Add a finely chopped clove of garlic to the mixture.

With tomato: Add $\frac{1}{4}$ to $\frac{1}{3}$ cup peeled, seeded and chopped tomato.

With onion: Add $\frac{1}{4}$ cup finely chopped yellow onion or green onions.

With Jalapeño: For a spicy guacamole, omit the green chilies and use 1 very finely chopped jalapeño.

STUFFED AVOCADO

Allow ½ avocado per person. Peel it or not, as you choose. Cut in half lengthwise and remove the pit. Arrange each half on a bed of greens and stuff with any of the following mixtures:

1. Chicken or turkey salad.
2. Any seafood salad.
3. Cubes of tomato and chopped green onion mixed with Vinaigrette Sauce.
4. Chopped green pepper, chopped green onion, chopped cucumber and chopped celery marinated in Vinaigrette Sauce.

Vegetable Salads

VEGETABLES À LA GRECQUE

Some vegetables can be cooked in an à la grecque bouillon and then chilled and served on greens, as a salad or hors d'oeuvre course. For the basic à la grecque recipe, see Asparagus à la Grecque, page 384.

Other vegetables that are tasty when prepared in this manner are:

Tiny artichokes
Celery hearts or celery stalks
Cauliflowerets
Eggplant, peeled and cut into fingers
Leeks
Mushroom caps
Tiny white onions
Young green onions (cook them whole)
Zucchini, cut in slices

VEGETABLES IN VINAIGRETTE SAUCE

Cooked vegetables when cooled can be used separately or in various combinations as a salad course. Dress them with Vinaigette Sauce (page 343), arrange them on greens and garnish with mayonnaise, if you like.

The following vegetables lend themselves nicely to this treatment:

Artichokes
Asparagus
Green beans
Beets
Broccoli
Carrots

Cauliflower
Celery root (celeriac)
Celery
Leeks
Tiny green onions
Peas

SALAD À LA RUSSE

This term refers to a salad made of cubed vegetables, cooked or raw, bound together with mayonnaise. Sometimes cubes of cold cooked meat are added. Use any combination of the following vegetables:

Cooked green beans, cut in pieces
Cubed cooked beets
Diced carrots, cooked or raw
Cubed raw celery
Cubed raw cucumber
Diced raw onion or chopped green onion
Cooked green peas
Cubed cooked potatoes

Use any of the following meats:

Cubed cooked chicken or turkey
Cubed ham
Cubed tongue
Cubed veal

Mix the ingredients with mayonnaise to taste, heap on a large salad plate and garnish with any of the following:

Anchovy fillets
Capers
Sliced hard-cooked egg
Green or ripe olives
Pimientos cut into strips
Tomato quarters

Special Salads

STUFFED ARTICHOKES—See page 380.

BEET AND EGG SALAD (Serves 4)

5 cooked and peeled
   medium beets

3 hard-cooked eggs

½ cup (or more) of
   mayonnaise

Watercress or endive

Chop the beets and the eggs and blend with the mayonnaise. Arrange on a bed of watercress or on Belgian endive, cut the long way.

BEET AND ONION SALAD (Serves 4)

5 cooked and peeled
   medium beets

1 Bermuda onion or red
   Italian onion

Vinaigrette sauce or sour
   cream, lemon juice and
   salt and pepper

Greens, if desired

Slice the beets neatly. Peel and slice the onion very thin. Arrange the sliced beets and onions on greens, if you like. Dress with Vinaigrette Sauce or sour cream flavored with lemon juice and salt and pepper to taste.

BEET AND POTATO SALAD (Serves 4)

1 cup of diced cooked
   beets

1 cup of diced cooked
   potatoes

1 cup of canned tiny French
   peas

½ cup of chopped hard-
   cooked egg

¾ cup of mayonnaise

Chopped green onion

Romaine or watercress

Combine the beets, potatoes, peas and egg, and mix with mayonnaise. Arrange on romaine or watercress and garnish with chopped green onions.

BEETS IN SOUR CREAM (Serves 4)

5 cooked and peeled medium beets
Sour cream

¹/₂ cup of Vinaigrette Sauce

Slice the beets and then cut the slices into strips. Soak in the Vinaigrette Sauce for several hours, turning frequently to be sure the beet strips are evenly bathed. An hour or two before serving, drain the beets and mix with sour cream; or arrange on a plate and cover with sour cream.

CELERY SALAD (Serves 4)

1 medium-sized bunch of Pascal celery
Chopped chives or green onions

1 cup of Vinaigrette Sauce (or more)
Romaine

Clean the celery and save the outer stalks and large leaves for flavoring soups and stews. Cut the inner stalks, the heart and the small leaves into fairly small pieces. Pour the Vinaigrette Sauce over them and let stand for several hours to mellow and wilt. Turn the celery often to be sure it is evenly bathed. Serve on romaine with a garnish of chopped green onions or chives.

CELERY ROOT (CELERIAC) SALAD—See recipes in Vegetable chapter, page 405.

CUCUMBER SALAD (Serves 4)

2 medium-sized cucumbers
Greens
¹/₂ cup of Vinaigrette Sauce (or more)

Peel the cucumbers and cut them into very thin slices. Soak in the Vinaigrette Sauce, turning frequently to be sure they are evenly bathed. Let the cucumber slices stand in the sauce for several hours until they are mellow and wilted. Arrange on a bed of romaine or escarole, if you like.

CUCUMBERS IN SOUR CREAM

Season sliced cucumbers with salt and fresh or dried dill weed. Cover with sour cream and chill for 1 or 2 hours.

VARIATION

Add chopped chives and chopped parsley to the sour cream.

CAULIFLOWER SALAD—See Cold Cauliflower, page 403.

DRIED BEAN SALAD (White Pea Bean) —See page 453.

EGG AND ROMAINE SALAD

Break a small head of romaine into bite-size pieces. Slice 4 hard-cooked eggs over the top. Dress with Vinaigrette Sauce and garnish with chopped chives or little green onions. Serve with mayonnaise on the side, if you like.

ENDIVE SALAD

Split 4 of the Belgian endive into quarters the long way and arrange in a shallow salad dish. Dress with Vinaigrette Sauce.

LENTIL SALAD—See page 456.

MUSHROOM SALAD (Serves 4)

1 medium head of romaine	**Salt and pepper**
¹/₂ pound of raw mushrooms	**Vermouth**
6 tablespoons of olive oil	
2 tablespoons of red wine vinegar	

Clean the romaine and break it into pieces. Wipe the mushrooms with a damp cloth and cut them into slices. Put the romaine and mushrooms in a salad bowl. Mix the olive oil, wine vinegar, salt and pepper to taste, and add a dash of dry vermouth. Pour over the salad and toss lightly.

ORANGE AND ONION SALAD (Serves 4)

2 large red Italian onions
4 tablespoons of olive oil
2 large oranges
1 tablespoon of orange juice

1 tablespoon of lemon juice
Salt and pepper
Rosemary

Peel the oranges and onions and cut them into thin slices. Arrange the sliced oranges alternately with the sliced onions on a large platter or salad plate. Mix the olive oil, the fruit juices, salt, pepper and a touch of rosemary. Pour over the salad.

RICE SALAD (Serves 4)

1 cup of uncooked rice
6 tablespoons of olive oil
3 tablespoons of wine vinegar
1 teaspoon of salt
1 teaspoon of black pepper
$1/2$ teaspoon of tarragon
$1/4$ cup of chopped green pepper

$1/4$ cup of chopped parsley
$1/4$ cup of chopped chives
$1/2$ cup of cucumber, cut into small cubes
$1/4$ cup of chopped green onion
Vinaigrette Sauce (page 343)
Hard-cooked eggs
Pimiento

Boil the rice according to directions on page 168. Drain and mix at once with the olive oil, vinegar, salt, pepper and tarragon. Let stand to cool. Then mix with the chopped green pepper, parsley, chives, cubed cucumber and chopped green onion. Mix in Vinaigrette Sauce to taste, heap on greens and garnish with sliced hard-cooked egg and pimiento strips.

TOMATO SALAD

Allow 1 medium tomato per person. If you wish to peel the tomatoes, plunge them into boiling water for a brief minute. Rinse quickly in cold water. This should loosen the skin so that you can peel it off easily. Or, if you have a gas stove, plunge a fork into the stem end of each tomato and hold it over the gas flame, turning to heat the skin on all sides. Do this quickly, or the tomato will cook and get soft on the outside. Then rinse it quickly in cold water and peel. If you do not mind the peel left on, merely wash the tomatoes well and remove the stem end. Slice onto a bed of greens and serve with Vinaigrette Sauce or mayonnaise.

TOMATO AND ONION SALAD (Serves 4)

Allow 2 tomatoes and 2 red Italian or Bermuda onions for 4 persons. Wash the tomatoes, remove the stem ends and slice. Peel and slice the onions, cutting them very thin. Arrange the tomatoes and onions on a bed of greens and pour a vinaigrette dressing over them.

STUFFED TOMATO SALAD

Allow 1 medium tomato per person. Wash them well, cut out the stem end and hollow out the center of the tomatoes. Fill with any of the following:

1. Cottage cheese mixed with chopped chives and parsley. Serve with mayonnaise.
2. Fill with salmon or tuna salad or any seafood salad.
3. Fill with any meat or poultry salad.
4. Fill with any vegetable vinaigrette (see page 326).
5. Fill with avocado cubes soaked in Vinaigrette Sauce (page 343).
6. In each tomato place a cold poached egg and top with jellied consommé (see Aspic Salad, page 339). Garnish with mayonnaise.

WATERCRESS SALAD, CHINESE STYLE (Serves 4)

1 bunch of watercress	**Vinaigrette Sauce, made**
¼ cup of sliced water chestnuts	**with soy sauce instead of salt**
½ cup of bean sprouts	
½ cup of chopped green onions	

Wash the watercress and dry it on a soft towel. Arrange it in a bowl with the water chestnuts, bean sprouts and onions. Make Vinaigrette Sauce (page 343) but use soy sauce in place of salt. Pour this over the salad.

Coleslaw

Shredded raw cabbage salad is an old stand-by at picnics and barbecues. If well seasoned, it is tasty and refreshing. Unfortunately much of the "coleslaw" served these days is simply cabbage with oil and vinegar. This vegetable is not a delicate green. It is hearty and has a definite flavor. It needs to be dressed with a sauce that has body, a sauce that can hold its own with the vegetable.

The traditional dressing for old-fashioned, country coleslaw is boiled dressing. Another popular dressing, and one that I find very satisfactory, is sour cream dressing. There are several versions, all good.

OLD-FASHIONED COLESLAW (Serves 4 to 6)

2-pound head of cabbage	**6 tablespoons of sugar**
4 tablespoons of butter	**1 teaspoon of dry mustard**
1 tablespoon of flour	**Salt to taste**
¹/₂ cup of water	**¹/₂ cup of vinegar**
2 eggs	

Old-fashioned Coleslaw is made with a boiled dressing that has a sharp, sweet-sour taste. It takes trouble, but the results are well worth the effort.

Prepare the dressing first so it will have a chance to cool: Heat water to the boiling point in the bottom of a double boiler. In the top, put the butter and blend in the flour. Slowly add the water, stirring constantly and continue to cook and stir until it is well blended and smooth.

Beat the eggs with the sugar and mustard and add about 1 teaspoon or less of salt. Pour the hot sauce over the egg mixture, stirring as you add it. Return the sauce to the top of the double boiler and continue cooking and stirring until thickened. Do not overcook. Remove from the fire the minute it is done. Add the vinegar last, blending it in thoroughly. Set aside to cool.

Clean and shred the head of cabbage and soak in salted water for 1 hour. Drain well and pour the cooled dressing over it.

SHORTCUT COLESLAW (Serves 4 to 6)

2-pound head of cabbage
1 cup of mayonnaise
¹/₂ cup of sour cream
Juice of 1 lemon

1 tablespoon (or to taste) of sugar
1 teaspoon of dry mustard
Salt and pepper to taste

Here is a popular modern version of the Old-fashioned Coleslaw. This sauce has the same sweet-sour flavor but takes much less time and trouble.

Mix all the ingredients thoroughly and pour over shredded cabbage that has been soaked for 1 hour in salted water.

VARIATION

Add 1 tablespoon (or to taste) of horseradish to the dressing.

PUNGENT COLESLAW (Serves 4)

¹/₂ of a large head of cabbage
¹/₂ cup of mayonnaise
¹/₂ cup of sour cream

1 teaspoon of celery seeds
¹/₄ cup of capers

Shred the cabbage very fine. Mix the other ingredients and blend thoroughly with the shredded cabbage. Let stand for 1 hour to mellow.

SOUR CREAM COLESLAW (Serves 4)

¹/₂ of a large head of cabbage
1 cup of sour cream
1 tablespoon of sugar
1 teaspoon of salt (or more)

1 tablespoon of vinegar
1 teaspoon of freshly ground black pepper

Shred the cabbage very fine. Blend the other ingredients thoroughly and mix with the shredded cabbage. Let stand for 1 hour to mellow.

Potato and Macaroni Salads

Use new potatoes for potato salad. Their smooth, waxy texture is pleasing and they soak up the flavors of the seasonings and dressing without crumbling. Older potatoes tend to turn mushy after they are moistened with dressing. Prepare potato salad well in advance so there will be plenty of time to chill it and to let the flavors blend and mellow.

POTATO SALAD 1 (FRENCH POTATO SALAD) (Serves 6)

3 pounds (6 to 8) medium-sized new potatoes

1 teaspoon of salt

1 teaspoon of freshly ground black pepper

¹/₂ cup of olive oil

3 tablespoons of wine vinegar

1 cup of chopped green onions

¹/₂ cup of chopped parsley

Wash the potatoes and put them, unpeeled, in boiling water to cover. Add a pinch of salt and cook in the boiling water until they are just done. Test by piercing them with a fork. Do not overcook. Drain at once and run a little cold water over them. Do not let them stand in cold water for the potatoes should still be warm when the seasonings are added. Just get them cool enough so that you can peel them without burning your hands. Peel them quickly and cut them into slices. Put them in a deep bowl and add the salt, pepper, olive oil and vinegar, mixed. Set aside to cool and then chill in the refrigerator. About 2 hours before you are ready to serve, add the chopped onion and parsley and additional oil if necessary. Taste for seasoning and add more salt and pepper if needed. Serve in a salad bowl and garnish with sliced hard-cooked egg, strips of green pepper and sliced stuffed olives.

POTATO SALAD 2 (Serves 6)

3 pounds (6 to 8) medium-
sized new potatoes
1 cup of white wine
1 teaspoon of salt
1 teaspoon of freshly ground
black pepper
1 teaspoon of dry mustard
$^1/_2$ cup of finely cut celery

$^1/_2$ cup shaved almonds
$^1/_4$ cup grated or chopped
carrots
$^2/_3$ cup of olive oil
Juice of one lemon
$^1/_4$ cup of chopped parsley
1 cup of chopped green
onions

Wash the potatoes and put them, unpeeled, into boiling salted water to cover. Cook in the boiling water until just done when tested with a fork. Do not overcook.

While the potatoes are cooking, blanch almonds in boiling water (see page 8), slip off the skins and then cut them into thin slices. Prepare the celery and carrots.

When the potatoes are done, drain them and run them quickly under cold water until they are just barely cool enough to handle. Do not let them get cold. Peel them and slice them into a deep bowl. Pour the white wine over them and add the salt, pepper, mustard, celery, almonds and grated carrot. Set aside to cool for several hours or overnight.

Two hours before serving, add the olive oil, lemon juice, parsley and onion. Toss well and taste for seasoning. Add more salt if necessary. Serve in a salad bowl and garnish with sliced hard-cooked egg and chopped parsley and chives.

POTATO SALAD 3 (Serves 6)

3 pounds (6 to 8) medium-
sized new potatoes
$^1/_2$ cup of finely chopped
onion
$^1/_2$ cup of finely chopped
celery

$^1/_2$ cup of chopped green
pepper
$^1/_4$ cup of chopped parsley
Mayonnaise
Salt and pepper

Wash the potatoes and put them in boiling water to cover. Add a pinch of salt and cook in the boiling water until just tender when pierced with a fork. Do not overcook. While the potatoes are cooking, prepare the chopped vegetables.

Drain the cooked potatoes and run them under cold water until cool enough to handle. Peel them and cut them into small cubes. Place the potato cubes in a large bowl, add the chopped vegetables, bind with mayonnaise and season with salt and pepper, if necessary.

Serve in a salad bowl and top with more mayonnaise. Garnish with pimiento strips, sliced hard-cooked egg, sliced olives and capers.

MACARONI SALAD

Cook 1 pound of elbow macaroni according to directions on the package. Drain thoroughly and prepare as you do Potato Salad 3 (see above).

Meat Salads

CHICKEN SALAD (Serves 4)

2½ cups of cubed cold chicken	**Greens**
1 cup of chopped celery	**Garnishes**
Mayonnaise to taste	

Cut the cold cooked chicken in even cubes, being careful to remove all gristle, fat, skin and bone. You need pure, lean meat for salad. Combine 2½ cups of the cubed meat with 1 cup of chopped raw celery and blend with mayonnaise to taste. Pile on a bed of romaine or Boston lettuce and garnish with any or all of the following: tomato quarters, sliced hard-cooked egg, capers, pimiento strips, stuffed olives.

VARIATIONS

With nuts: Add ½ cup of chopped, toasted almonds, walnuts, filberts or pecans.

With green onion: Add ½ cup of chopped green onion.

TURKEY SALAD

Follow directions for Chicken Salad (see above), substituting turkey for the chicken.

VEAL SALAD

Follow directions for Chicken Salad (see page 337), substituting veal for the chicken.

LAMB SALAD (Serves 4)

2¹/₂ cups of cubed cold lamb

1 cup of Vinaigrette Sauce

¹/₂ cup of chopped celery

¹/₂ cup of chopped green onion

¹/₂ cup of toasted almonds

Curry mayonnaise to taste

Greens

Pickles

Cut the cold lamb into even-sized cubes, being careful to remove all fat and gristle. Soak in the Vinaigrette Sauce (page 343) for several hours, turning frequently to be sure the meat is evenly bathed. Drain and mix with the celery, green onion and toasted almonds, and blend in Curry Mayonnaise (page 345) to taste. Pile on a bed of romaine and garnish with a good sharp pickle.

BEEF SALAD—See page 214.

HAM SALAD

2¹/₂ cups of cubed ham

¹/₂ cup of chopped celery

¹/₂ cup of chopped green onion

¹/₄ cup of chopped gherkins

Mustard Mayonnaise

Greens

Hard-cooked egg

Cut the ham into even cubes, being careful to remove all fat and gristle. Mix with the celery, onion and gherkins, and blend with Mustard Mayonnaise (page 345) to taste. Pile on a bed of romaine or Boston lettuce and garnish with sliced hard-cooked egg.

VARIATION

Substitute cubed tongue for half of the ham.

Aspic Salads

BASIC ASPIC FOR SALADS

A good consommé (see Soup chapter) is an excellent base for an aspic salad. If you have started your broth with veal bone the consommé should jelly of its own accord when cold. If it is too runny to hold a firm shape but is partly thickened, add ½ envelope of unflavored gelatin to each 1½ cups of consommé. Dissolve the gelatin in ¼ cup of cold water. Heat the consommé, stir in the dissolved gelatin until melted, and then cool. If the consommé is completely runny, use a whole envelope of unflavored gelatin and proceed in the same manner, dissolving the gelatin in ½ cup of water.

QUICK ASPIC FOR SALADS

³/₄ cup of hot water
1 bouillon cube
Pinch of thyme
Dash of Worcestershire sauce

1 envelope of unflavored gelatin
½ cup of cold water
½ cup of tomato juice

Heat ³/₄ of a cup of water with the bouillon cube, the thyme and the Worcestershire sauce. When the bouillon cube is dissolved and the mixture blended, remove from the stove and strain. Dissolve the gelatin in the cold water, stir it into the hot bouillon mixture until melted and then add the tomato juice.

ASPIC SALADS

Use individual molds or one large mold. Brush the molds with olive oil. Then pour a thin layer of warm consommé aspic or Quick Aspic (see above) in the bottom and chill. When firm add the first layer of vegetables, cold meats or hard-cooked eggs and more aspic. Place in the refrigerator to chill until almost firm. Meanwhile, chill the rest of the consommé or bouillon aspic until thick but still runny. Do not let it get firm. When the first layer of the aspic is almost firm, fold the second layer of ingredients into the slightly thickened aspic and pour into the mold. Put back in the refrigerator to finish setting.

Unmolding aspic: Dip the bottom part of the mold into a pan of hot water. Take it out quickly to prevent the aspic from melting. Run a spatula around the edges of the mold, turn it upside down on a bed of greens and shake gently. If the aspic does not come out easily at once, lift one side of the mold slightly, and while still holding it upside down, run the spatula down the side. Turn the mold around and repeat on all sides.

Garnish with olives, pimientos, tomato quarters, stuffed eggs or any cold food you choose. Serve with mayonnaise.

SUGGESTED COMBINATIONS FOR ASPIC SALADS

Allow 1½ to 2 cups of aspic made of consommé or broth and about 2 cups of vegetables or meats for a salad for 4 persons. Here are some suggestions:

With poached eggs: Poach 4 eggs according to directions in the Egg chapter, page 89. Remove them from the hot water and drain thoroughly on absorbent paper. Trim the edges neatly and allow them to cool. Place them at the bottom of a mold, cover with aspic and chill (see above). Fold ½ cup of cooked green peas (or canned petits pois), ¼ cup of finely chopped green onion and ¼ cup of chopped pimiento into the rest of the aspic for the top layer.

With stuffed eggs: Put 4 stuffed eggs (page 35) on the bottom layer and top with ¼ cup of chopped green pepper, ¼ cup of chopped green onion and ½ cup of cut green beans (cooked and cooled).

With ham: Put 1½ cups of cubed ham on the bottom layer and top with ¼ cup of chopped chives and ¾ cup of chopped parsley.

With avocado: Cut 1 large or 2 small avocados into crescent-shaped slices (see Avocados, page 324) and arrange in the bottom of the mold. In the top layer put ¼ cup of chopped green pepper, ¼ cup of chopped green onion and ½ cup of cubed (and thoroughly drained) ripe tomato.

With cubed vegetables and meat: Use any combination of the cubed vegetables and meats suggested under Salad à la Russe (page 327).

COLD BOILED BEEF IN ASPIC

Prepare beef as for Cold Boiled Beef (see page 213). After the meat is firmly pressed and cold, cut it into thin, uniform slices and trim them neatly. Arrange in a mold with any garnishes you choose: sliced hard-cooked egg, stuffed olives, pimiento strips, onion rings. Pour consommé or aspic over the meat and let it jelly in the refrigerator.

COLD CHICKEN IN ASPIC—See page 308.

Fish and Shellfish Salads

TUNA SALAD PLATE

The finest canned tuna is solid-pack white meat and the best comes from France. This is not because European tuna is any better than our own, but because the fish is packed in olive oil, which gives it a richer flavor and a moist, yet firm, texture. There are also several good brands of Italian tuna packed in olive oil.

For each serving use 1 small (6½-ounce) can of tuna. Open the tin, drain off the oil and arrange the tuna in one piece, as it comes from the can, in the center of a bed of greens. Garnish with raw onion rings or paper thin slices of Bermuda or red Italian onions, sliced hard-cooked eggs and capers. Serve mayonnaise separately.

SALAD NIÇOISE (Serves 4)

2 6½-ounce cans of solid white meat tuna	4 hard-cooked eggs
Greens	Pimientos
3 cans of anchovy fillets	Ripe olives
4 ripe tomatoes	Vinaigrette Sauce (page 343)

Open the tins of tuna and drain off the oil. Place the tuna in the center of a large platter covered with greens. Open the anchovy tins and arrange the fillets around the edge of the tuna. Wash the tomatoes and quarter them. Quarter the hard-cooked eggs. Arrange these around the edge of the platter. Garnish with strips of pimiento and ripe olives and serve with Vinaigrette Sauce.

MIXED TUNA SALAD (Serves 4)

2 6½-ounce cans of tuna

1 cup of chopped celery

½ cup of chopped green onion

Mayonnaise

Greens

4 tomatoes

4 hard-cooked eggs

Lemon wedges

Open the canned tuna and drain off the oil. Flake the fish and combine it with the celery and onion. Blend with mayonnaise to taste and arrange on a bed of greens. Wash the tomatoes and cut them in quarters. Quarter the hard-cooked eggs. Arrange these around the tuna salad. Serve with additional mayonnaise and lemon wedges.

SALMON SALAD PLATE

Buy firmly packed, canned salmon that can be served in one piece. Remove any skin or bone and prepare as for Tuna Salad above, but substitute sliced cucumbers for the sliced eggs in the garnish.

MIXED SALMON SALAD

Follow directions for Mixed Tuna Salad, substituting salmon for the tuna.

BASIC SEAFOOD SALAD (Serves 4)

Do not try to stretch seafood. Serve good-sized hunks of crab, lobster or shrimp and allow at least ½ cup per person.

2 or more cups of crab, shrimp or lobster

Greens

Mayonnaise or other dressing

Garnishes

Arrange the seafood on a bed of greens and mask with mayonnaise, Green Mayonnaise or Sauce Rémoulade. Garnish with any of the following:

Sliced avocado

Capers

Quartered hard-cooked eggs

Sliced cucumbers
Chopped parsley and chives
Tiny green onions
Small celery stalk from the center of the bunch
Strips of green pepper
Ripe olives
Pimiento strips
Anchovy fillets
Tiny artichoke hearts, vinaigrette
Asparagus, vinaigrette or à la grecque
Tomato quarters
Small tomatoes hollowed out and stuffed with mixed cooked
vegetable salad.

Fruit as a Salad Course

The usual fruit salad—a mixture of sweet fruit dressed with mayonnaise, whipped cream or sweet dressing—hardly makes sense as a salad course. It is much more of a dessert. Some tart fruits mixed with greens make a nice contrast with rich meat dishes (see Orange and Onion Salad, page 331), but if you like to follow the meat course with sweet fruit, it seems wiser to serve it plain with a good sharp cheese and let it take the place of a sweet or dessert course.

If you insist on serving fruit as a salad, don't cut it into cubes and mix it up. Slice or halve the fruit and arrange it neatly on a platter of greens. Dress with a French Dressing and use lemon juice in place of the vinegar in the dressing. No sugar.

Salad Dressings

FRENCH DRESSING (VINAIGRETTE SAUCE)

Basic French Dressing is simply oil, vinegar, salt and pepper. The secret to a good dressing is in the quality of the oil and vinegar. Get good olive oil.

As for vinegar, look for a good wine vinegar. There are some on the market that are too sharp. Either red or white will do, but the white tends to be milder, or use a sherry vinegar. Another good vinegar for this dressing is a pear vinegar made in California. If you can't find a mild vinegar, you can substitute lemon juice.

Use freshly ground black pepper. It is always spicier and has a more definite flavor.

Now for proportions. Tastes vary, but most people prefer 3 or 4 parts of oil to 1 of vinegar. This depends, of course, on the heaviness of the oil and the sharpness of the vinegar. Taste and try. Salt and pepper to taste.

Avoid these mistakes:

Don't use sugar. If the vinegar is mild, as it should be, no sweetening is necessary.

Don't use prepared herbed vinegars. Herbs are a fine touch to a green salad, but mix them in yourself from your herb collection. Your salad will taste fresher.

Don't mix the dressing hours before you intend to use it. The fresher it is, the better.

Don't store the dressing or the oil in the refrigerator. Olive oil gets cloudy and sluggish if it is too cold. Keep it at room temperature.

VARIATIONS ON FRENCH DRESSING

With garlic: Add minced garlic to taste.

With an herb: Add dried or fresh herbs. Tarragon, chervil, chives all go excellently with greens. If you are using the dressing on sliced tomatoes, basil is a good addition.

MAYONNAISE

2 egg yolks	**1¹/₂ cups of olive oil**
1 teaspoon of salt	**Lemon juice or wine vinegar**
¹/₂ teaspoon of dry mustard	**to taste, starting with 1**
¹/₄ teaspoon of freshly	**tablespoon**
ground pepper	

Be sure all the ingredients are at room temperature. You may use a shallow dish and a fork; a bowl and an egg beater or wire whisk; or an electric beater. First beat the egg yolks, salt, mustard and pepper together. Then start adding the oil, a few drops at a time, beating it in after each addition thoroughly. If the mayonnaise starts to curdle, you are adding the oil too fast. Correct the curdling by starting over with another egg yolk and a little oil and then gradually beating the curdled mixture into this. Continue adding oil until the mixture is thick and stiff. Thin with vinegar or lemon juice.

Food processor method: Place 1 whole egg, 1 tablespoon of vinegar or lemon juice, 1 teaspoon of salt and ¼ teaspoon of pepper in the processor. Blend for a couple of seconds. Continue blending while pouring— very slowly to begin with—1½ cups of olive oil into the spout.

VARIATIONS

Mustard Mayonnaise: To 1 cup of mayonnaise, add 1 tablespoon of French mustard, or more, if you like.

Green Mayonnaise: To 1 cup of mayonnaise add ½ cup of mixed chopped green herbs; parsley, chives, tarragon, watercress, and spinach will all add green color and good flavor.

Tartar Sauce: To 1 cup of mayonnaise add 2 tablespoons of finely chopped onion, 2 tablespoons of chopped dill pickle, 2 tablespoons of chopped parsley and lemon juice to taste.

Rémoulade Sauce: To 1 cup of mayonnaise add 1 minced clove of garlic, 1 teaspoon of dry or 1 tablespoon of fresh chopped tarragon, ½ teaspoon of dry mustard, 1 finely chopped hard-cooked egg, 1 tablespoon of capers, 1 tablespoon of chopped parsley and anchovy paste to taste.

Thousand Island Dressing: To 1 cup of mayonnaise add 1 tablespoon of finely chopped onion, 3 tablespoons of chili sauce, 1 chopped hard-cooked egg, and a touch of dry mustard.

Curry Mayonnaise: To 1 cup of mayonnaise add 1½ teaspoons of curry powder (or more, to taste) that has been simmered in 1 tablespoon of butter for 2 or 3 minutes and cooled. Never add raw curry to dressings.

BOILED SALAD DRESSING

2 tablespoons of flour
1 teaspoon of dry mustard
3 tablespoons of sugar
2 egg yolks
1 cup of white wine

½ cup of wine vinegar or lemon juice
½ cup of olive oil
Salt and pepper
¼ cup of sour cream

Heat water in the lower part of a double boiler; in the upper section put the flour, mustard, sugar, wine and vinegar or lemon juice. Beat the egg yolks until light and add these to the mixture with the oil and salt and pepper to taste. Cook over the hot water, stirring constantly with a wooden spoon. *Do not let the water boil, and do not let the sauce boil,* or it will curdle. When it is thick, beat in the sour cream until thoroughly blended.

SOUR CREAM DRESSING

Mix 1 cup of sour cream with 1 tablespoon of grated fresh horseradish, or bottled horseradish thoroughly drained, 1 teaspoon of dry mustard and ½ teaspoon each of salt and freshly ground black pepper. Sprinkle with chopped parsley.

VARIATION

Omit the horseradish and add 1 tablespoon of chopped chives or grated onion.

SAUCES

In fine French restaurants, the *saucier*—the chef in charge of sauces—is a most important functionary, for on his skill depends much of the success of the cuisine. A subtle sauce turns simple fare into a party dish, and the cook who has a repertoire of the classic sauces and a deft hand at preparing them soon gains the reputation of performing "kitchen miracles."

Some advice on sauces

Don't overdo them. Too many at one meal can be overwhelming. If you are serving a rich sauce on the main dish, serve a simple vegetable as an accompaniment.

Remember, many sauces demand your undivided attention at the last minute. Take this into consideration when you plan your meal.

Some sauces should be eaten the minute they are cooked. Don't use such a sauce on the night the dinner may have to wait.

No matter how elegant the sauce, it will never disguise inferior quality or poor cooking of the basic food. Tough meat is still tough, overcooked vegetables are still uninteresting even though beautifully sauced.

Sauces are not difficult, but some do take careful attention. If you heed a few simple warnings, you will have no trouble. Thickening agents are the main source of difficulty. Flour and egg yolks are most commonly used. Flour can lump and egg yolks can curdle. Here is the way to avoid these mistakes:

Roux: In this method, the liquid is added to melted butter blended with flour. Two tablespoons of flour will thicken 1 cup of liquid. Melt the butter in a saucepan and blend in the flour. Remove the pan from the stove before you add the liquid. Or, to be even safer, do this job over hot water, using a double boiler. Add the liquid very slowly to be sure it blends without lumping. Return the pan to the stove and cook, stirring constantly, until the sauce is thickened and smooth.

If, in spite of your care, it does lump, put it through a fine strainer. After straining you may find the loss of flour in the lumps has left the sauce too thin. Start over with another Roux, reducing the amount of flour by one half.

Beurre Manié: This is flour and butter kneaded together into small balls and added to hot liquid. As in the case of Roux, 2 tablespoons of flour will thicken 1 cup of liquid. Use about twice as much flour as butter and blend them together with your fingertips. Then roll the mixture into tiny balls about the size of green peas. Turn the heat very low under the liquid and sprinkle the flour-and-butter balls over the surface, a few at a time, stirring them in to be sure they blend without lumping. The liquid must not be too hot, and by no means boiling. Continue stirring and cooking until it thickens and is smooth. If lumpy, put it through a fine strainer, and then, if too thin, add more Beurre Manié.

Egg yolks: Three egg yolks will thicken 1 cup of liquid. Egg yolks are sometimes used in addition to flour, one yolk being added to a sauce partly thickened with flour and butter. Beat the yolks lightly and stir a few spoonfuls of the hot liquid into the yolks. Be sure the heat is low under the sauce and that it is not boiling. To be safe, do this over hot water, using a double boiler. Add the egg mixture to the sauce and stir in thoroughly, using a wooden spoon. A metal spoon will sometimes turn egg sauce a dark gray. Cook and stir until heated through and thickened, but do not boil the sauce, or the egg yolk will curdle.

If you are making a sauce that must be kept hot for some time before it is used, thicken it with flour, not egg yolks. It is too difficult to keep egg sauces hot without curdling. They should be used at once.

Other thickening agents: Bread crumbs, thick tomato paste (for tomato sauces), cornstarch (for oriental dishes) and grated potato are sometimes used for thickening. Bread crumbs and tomato paste are simply stirred into the sauce. Cornstarch should be blended with a little water before being added to the sauce. One tablespoon will thicken 2 cups of liquid. When you first add the cornstarch mixture, the sauce will turn cloudy, but as the starch thickens, the sauce will become clear again. A medium-sized grated potato will thicken 3 to 4 cups of liquid. Stir it in and simmer for 5 to 10 minutes or until the starchy potato taste is gone.

A word about seasonings

A fine sauce may become a failure because the seasoning is wrong. Recipes give approximate amounts, but spices and herbs vary considerably in quality and strength. Tarragon from one firm will be highly flavorful, from another, dry and flat. Buy only the best quality dry herbs and spices, and discard them when they get too old. "Made" seasonings, such as curry, vary considerably in taste and tang. Some people enjoy the stronger curry powders; others prefer a milder blend. The seasoning or mix you buy will affect the taste of the sauce. Taste and try as you cook.

Sauces for Meat, Fish and Vegetables

BASIC WHITE SAUCE (CREAM SAUCE OR BÉCHAMEL)

2 tablespoons of butter   **1 cup of milk**
2 tablespoons of flour   **Salt and pepper**

Melt the butter and blend in the flour. Remove the pan from the heat, or place it over hot water (see instructions page 347 under Roux). Slowly add the milk, blending it in until smooth. Return to the heat and cook slowly, stirring constantly, until the sauce is thickened and smooth. Season to taste with salt and freshly ground black pepper. For a thicker sauce use 3 or 4 tablespoons of flour.

VARIATIONS

Rich Cream Sauce: This sauce can be made richer by using heavy cream for half of the milk or by reducing the amount of flour by $\frac{1}{2}$ tablespoon and adding 1 egg yolk after the sauce has been thickened. Follow directions for thickening with Egg Yolks, page 348.

With meat or fish: If you are using this sauce with meat or fish, substitute the juices or stock for the meat or fish for part of the milk.

With vegetables: Cook down the liquid from the vegetable and blend it with heavy cream for the liquid in the sauce.

Sauce Mornay: Add ¼ to ½ cup of grated Parmesan cheese and 2 tablespoons of butter.

Cheese Sauce: Add ½ cup of grated sharp cheddar, Gruyère or Emmenthaler and a dash of Tabasco or dry mustard.

Sauce Soubise: Sauté 1 sliced medium onion in the butter over low heat, covered, until tender but not brown, about 20 minutes. Stir in the flour and cook for a minute or so. Then stir in the milk. Simmer for 10 to 15 minutes. Purée in a blender or food processor. Add seasonings, and just before serving, heat through and beat in 2 tablespoons of butter, one at a time.

Mustard Sauce: Add 2 tablespoons Dijon mustard and simmer for 2 or 3 minutes.

Horseradish Sauce: Drain bottled horseradish thoroughly and add it to the sauce to taste. Or use grated fresh horseradish and a dash of wine vinegar or lemon juice.

Egg Sauce: Add 2 hard-cooked eggs, sliced.

Caper Sauce: Add 3 tablespoons of capers and a spoonful of the caper juice.

Dill Sauce: Add 1 tablespoon of fresh, chopped dill or 2 teaspoons of dried dill weed.

Creamy Curry Sauce: Cook 2 teaspoons (or more, to taste) of curry powder with the butter before adding the flour. Then proceed as for Basic White Sauce.

BASIC BROWN SAUCE (SAUCE ESPAGNOLE)

¼ pound of butter	**1 bay leaf**
½ pound of veal and ham diced	**1 quart of beef stock or broth**
1 onion, sliced	**¼ cup of tomato**
4 sliced mushrooms	**4 tablespoons of flour**
	Salt and Pepper

Melt the butter in a saucepan and add the meat, the onion, the mushrooms and bay leaf. Cook until thoroughly browned. Meanwhile, blend the stock and tomato purée, and cook together, reducing the liquid a little. Blend the flour into the meat and mushroom mixture, remove the pan from the heat, and slowly add the stock, stirring constantly to keep it from lumping. Return to the heat, cover the pan, and simmer gently for 30 or 40 minutes. Strain. Taste for seasoning and add salt and pepper. This basic sauce can be used with many additions for meats.

VARIATIONS

Bordelaise Sauce: Combine 6 chopped shallots, 1½ cups dry red wine, and 1 tablespoon chopped parsley in a saucepan. Reduce to ¾ cup over moderately high heat. Strain and stir into 1 cup Basic Brown Sauce. Bring to a boil and simmer 2 minutes. Stir in a tablespoon of butter.

With garlic: Add more tomato purée and sautéed garlic slivers, and simmer to let the flavors blend.

Madeira Sauce: Sauté 6 chopped shallots in a tablespoon of butter until just tender. Set aside. Add ⅓ cup of Madeira to 1 cup Basic Brown Sauce and bring to a boil. Add the shallots, and simmer 5 minutes. Taste for seasoning.

Wine Merchants' Sauce (Sauce Marchands de Vin): Sauté 6 small green onions in 4 tablespoons of butter until soft. Add ¾ cup of dry red wine, and cook rapidly to reduce the liquid to one half its volume. Add 1 cup of Basic Brown Sauce, heat through, and flavor with a dash of lemon juice.

Sauce Diable: Combine ¼ cup tarragon vinegar, ¾ cup of white wine, 1 chopped shallot and 1 teaspoon dried tarragon in a saucepan. Reduce by half over moderately high heat. Stir into 1¼ cups Basic Brown Sauce, with a dash of Tabasco and 2 teaspoons dry mustard. Bring to a boil and simmer 3 minutes. Give it several grinds of black pepper, and put through a strainer.

HOLLANDAISE SAUCE

¼ pound of sweet butter	**2 teaspoons of lemon juice**
3 egg yolks	**½ teaspoon of salt**

Use a double boiler for this sauce. Heat water in the lower part of the boiler and put the butter in the top section over the hot water. Beat the egg yolks lightly with the lemon juice and salt. Add them to the melted butter, beating constantly. *Do not let the water boil.* Continue beating and cooking over hot water until the sauce is thickened and hot. Serve at once.

Note: If the sauce starts to curdle while cooking, add a spoonful or so of hot water and beat it in.

VARIATIONS

With mustard: Add 1 or 2 teaspoons of Dijon mustard or ¼ teaspoon of dry mustard.

With tarragon: Add ½ teaspoon of tarragon or substitute tarragon vinegar for the lemon juice.

Quick Hollandaise: Place 3 egg yolks in a blender or food processor with 2 teaspoons of lemon juice, ½ teaspoon of salt and a few grains of cayenne pepper. Turn the blender or processor on for 2 or 3 seconds to blend the eggs and seasonings quickly. Melt ¼ pound of sweet butter in a saucepan and heat almost to the boiling point. Turn on the blender (on high) or processor and pour the hot butter steadily into the egg mixture until the butter is blended and the sauce thickened.

MOUSSELINE SAUCE

Whip heavy cream and blend in an equal amount of Hollandaise Sauce.

SAUCE BÉARNAISE

1 teaspoon of dried tarragon	**Salt and pepper**
2 teaspoons of chopped green onion	**3 tablespoons of wine vinegar**
2 teaspoons of chopped parsley	**1 tablespoon of water**
	Hollandaise Sauce

Cook the tarragon, green onion, parsley and seasonings in vinegar and water until they are cooked down almost to a glaze. Make a Hollandaise Sauce (see above), beating in this mixture after the egg yolks. Continue to beat over hot water until the sauce is thickened.

TOMATO SAUCE

1 18-ounce can of solid-pack tomatoes	**1 bay leaf**
1 teaspoon of dried basil	**½ teaspoon each of salt and pepper**
1 onion, chopped	**Lump of butter**

Simmer the tomatoes, basil, onion, bay leaf and salt and pepper over low heat for about ½ hour, or until it is reduced by ⅓. Strain, taste for seasoning, and stir in a lump of butter.

VARIATIONS

With fresh tomatoes: For the canned tomatoes substitute 6 ripe tomatoes, peeled, seeded and chopped and ½ cup of stock or broth.

With green pepper: Sauté the onion and half a green pepper (cut in strips) in butter or olive oil and add to the mixture. Substitute oregano for the basil in this version.

With garlic: Add a minced clove of garlic.

BARBECUE SAUCE

2 medium onions

¼ cup of olive oil

1 cup of tomato purée

1 teaspoon of salt

1 teaspoon of basil

½ cup of strained honey

½ cup of rich broth or stock

¼ cup of Worcestershire sauce

1 teaspoon of dry mustard

½ cup of dry red wine

Peel and chop the onions, and sauté them in the olive oil until soft. Add all the rest of the ingredients, except the wine, and simmer gently for 10 to 15 minutes. Add the wine and heat through.

VARIATIONS

With garlic: Use a minced clove of garlic for one of the onions.

With thyme or oregano: Substitute thyme or oregano for the basil.

With brown sugar: Omit the honey and use 2 tablespoons of brown sugar.

With chili sauce: Add a bit of chili sauce just before you serve.

With green pepper: Sauté half a green pepper, cut in strips, with the onion.

CURRY SAUCE

5 tablespoons of butter	Curry powder
1 large onion	1 to 1½ cups of broth, stock
1 apple	or tomato juice
2 stalks of celery	2 teaspoons of chutney
Salt	

Melt the butter. Peel and chop the onion. Core the apple and chop with the skin left on. Chop the celery. Sauté these in the butter gently until just transparent. Do not let them brown. Sprinkle with curry powder (up to 3 teaspoons for a mild curry, 1 tablespoon or more for hot curry). Season to taste with salt, and let this cook down into the vegetables and apple for 3 or 4 minutes. Add broth, stock or tomato juice to taste. About 1 to 1½ cups will serve two persons amply. You may thicken the sauce with a few tablespoons of tomato paste, or, if you prefer, add pea-sized balls of butter and flour mixed together (see instructions under Beurre Manié, page 348). Just before serving, add the chutney.

This sauce can be used with any leftover meat. Cut the meat into dice, and add it to the sauce to heat. It can also be used with canned tuna fish, with crabmeat or lobster meat, or with any leftover fish.

BUTTER SAUCES

Brown Butter (Beurre Noisette): Heat butter in a skillet until browned, but not burned.

Black Butter (Beurre Noir): Heat butter in a skillet until quite brown and add lemon juice or wine vinegar to taste.

Parsley Butter: Mix chopped parsley with softened butter. Or melt butter and add chopped parsley.

Herb Butter: Add to softened butter the herb of your choice (chervil, tarragon, rosemary, chives, parsley), to taste. Or melt the butter and add the herb. You may use several herbs mixed for this if you like. Chives, parsley and chervil are a good combination.

To ¼ pound of butter add 2 tablespoons of parsley, or two tablespoons of chives. Of other herbs, add 1 tablespoon fresh, or 1 to 1½ teaspoons dried.

Anchovy Butter: Add to butter anchovy paste, or finely chopped anchovy fillets, and a dash of lemon juice.

Buttered Crumbs: Melt ¼ cup of butter and add ¼ cup of very fine dry bread crumbs. Heat through, brown and season to taste with salt and pepper.

Whipped Butter: Let butter stand at room temperature until soft. Whip a few spoonfuls of heavy cream through it until it is light and fluffy.

Garlic Butter: Crush 1 clove of garlic and add to it ¼ pound of softened butter.

Lemon Butter: Add lemon juice to taste to butter.

Dessert Sauces

SOFT CUSTARD SAUCE

3 egg yolks	**1 cup of scalded milk**
4 tablespoons of sugar	**Flavoring**
Pinch of salt	

Heat water in the lower part of a double boiler. Beat the egg yolks lightly and put them in the top section of the boiler with a pinch of salt and the sugar. Gradually add the scalded milk, stirring it in slowly with a wooden spoon. Cook and stir until the mixture begins to form a film or coating on the spoon. *Do not let the water boil.* If this sauce is overcooked, it will curdle. As soon as the sauce coats the spoon slightly, take it from the hot water and pour into a cool bowl. Flavor with vanilla, sherry or with any favorite liquor or brandy: Grand Marnier, Cognac, rum, Benedictine.

HARD SAUCE

½ cup of butter	**Flavoring**
1 cup of confectioner's sugar	

Cream the butter until soft, and gradually add the sugar, beating it in until smooth. Flavor with vanilla or with any favorite brandy or liquor.

VARIATION

Substitute brown sugar for the confectioner's and flavor the sauce with dark rum.

BUTTERSCOTCH SAUCE

1 cup of brown sugar	**Pinch of salt**
¼ cup of butter	**Vanilla**
¼ cup of heavy cream	

Mix the sugar, butter, cream and pinch of salt together in the upper section of a double boiler, and cook gently over hot water for 30 to 45 minutes or until rich and mellow. Flavor with vanilla.

VARIATION

Flavor with rum or Cognac.

CREAMY CUSTARD SAUCE

Prepare a soft custard (page 355) and flavor with your favorite liqueur. Whip ½ pint of heavy cream until stiff but not buttery. Fold through the custard sauce.

BROWN SUGAR BRANDY SAUCE

½ cup of brown sugar	**½ teaspoon of cornstarch**
½ cup of water	**Cognac or dark rum (about**
Pinch of salt	**2 ounces)**

Put the brown sugar and water in a saucepan with the salt. Bring to a boil and cook for 3 or 4 minutes. Blend a scant half tablespoon of cornstarch in two tablespoons of water and add to the brown sugar mix, stirring it in and cooking until the mixture thickens. Remove from the stove and add Cognac or dark rum to taste.

CHOCOLATE SAUCE

12-ounce package of semi-
  sweet chocolate

2 squares of unsweetened
  chocolate

3 tablespoons of coffee

½ pint of heavy cream

2 tablespoons of Cognac

In a double boiler melt the chocolate with the coffee. Gradually stir in the heavy cream and Cognac. Stir until smooth.

This sauce may be kept in the refrigerator and reheated.

VARIATIONS

With rum: Substitute 1 ounce of dark rum for the Cognac.

With nuts: Add ⅓ cup of blanched and toasted almonds, filberts or any kind of nut you prefer.

COGNAC SAUCE (BRANDY SAUCE)

6 tablespoons of butter

⅔ cup of powdered sugar

2 egg yolks

¾ cup of heavy cream

1½ ounces of Cognac

Cream the butter with the powdered sugar. Add the egg yolks, one at a time. Place in the top of a double boiler over hot water and gradually blend in the cream, stirring constantly with a wooden spoon. As soon as the mixture coats the spoon, remove it from the heat and pour into a bowl. Flavor with the Cognac.

SOUFFLÉS

Somehow the soufflé has acquired a reputation for being a difficult, temperamental dish. This reputation is unjustified. The soufflé is simple to make and not fussy about the way it is baked. I have cooked soufflés at different temperatures and without temperature control. I have even dared to peek in the oven at a soufflé. No bad results.

The secret of a good soufflé is in the egg whites: in how they are beaten, how they are folded into the cream base. For success follow these simple rules:

1. Be sure the eggs are at room temperature when you beat them.
2. Do not use an electric mixer. If you beat them by hand, you can beat more air into them and they will be fluffier.
3. Do not beat the whites to the stiff, dry stage used for meringue. They should be stiff but still moist.
4. Always *fold* egg whites in; do not stir or beat. Fold by moving the spoon down through the mixture to the bottom, then along the bottom of the pan or bowl toward you, folding the sauce up from the bottom over the top. Repeat until fairly well mixed. This method will never blend as thoroughly as stirring will, but thorough blending is not needed.
5. Add the egg whites to the cream mixture in two portions. Fold the first portion in fairly well. Fold the second half of the whites in very lightly.
6. For added lightness, use an extra egg white.

BASIC SOUFFLÉ (Serves 4)

These are the basic ingredients and the basic steps for making soufflés. The seasonings and flavorings you choose are added after the cream base is thickened. Suggestions for specific soufflés are listed below (Cheese Soufflés, Fruit Soufflés, etc.).

3 tablespoons of butter   **4 eggs**
3 tablespoons of flour   **1 additional egg white**
1 cup of scalded milk

Melt the butter and blend in the flour. Remove the pan from the heat (or cook over hot water in a double boiler). Gradually stir in the milk, blending it in smoothly. Return to the stove and continue cooking and stirring until the mixture is thick and smooth. This step is the same as making a Basic White Sauce. Cool the sauce slightly. At this point the seasonings and flavorings are added (see below). Beat the egg yolks until light and lemon-colored and stir into the cream mixture. Let this stand while you beat the egg whites until stiff but still moist. Fold half of the egg whites into the cream sauce fairly well. Then fold the second half in just lightly. Pour the mixture into a greased soufflé dish or straight-sided casserole and bake, uncovered, in a 375° oven until the soufflé has puffed up and browned. This will take about 35 minutes.

Serve at once or it will fall.

Cheese, Vegetable, Fish Soufflés

CHEESE SOUFFLÉ (Serves 4)

Proceed as for Basic Soufflé and when the cream sauce is thick, add ½ cup of sharp, grated cheddar cheese and 1 teaspoon of salt. Then add the egg yolks, fold in the whites (see Basic Soufflé recipe) and bake as above.

Parmesan Cheese Soufflé: Use 1 cup of grated Parmesan cheese instead of the cheddar.

Swiss Cheese Soufflé: Use ½ pound of grated Switzerland Swiss cheese or Gruyère in place of the cheddar, or use half Swiss cheese and half grated Parmesan.

SPINACH SOUFFLÉ (Serves 4)

Prepare the Basic Soufflé mixture (page 359), but add an extra table-spoon of flour. When the cream sauce is thick, add 1 teaspoon of salt and stir in the beaten egg yolks. Add 1 cup of puréed or finely chopped, drained, cooked spinach and flavor with 2 teaspoons of grated onion. Fold in the egg whites and proceed as for Basic Soufflé.

BROCCOLI SOUFFLÉ (Serves 4)

Prepare the Basic Soufflé mixture (page 359), but add an extra table-spoon of flour. When the cream sauce is thickened, add 1 teaspoon of salt and stir in the egg yolks. Add 1 cup of puréed, cooked broccoli and a dash of onion juice. Fold in the egg whites and proceed as for Basic Soufflé.

TUNA SOUFFLÉ (Serves 4)

Prepare the Basic Soufflé mixture (page 359), but add 1 extra table-spoon of flour. When the mixture is thick, stir in the egg yolks. Open a can of tuna and drain and flake the meat. Add this to the cream mixture, season to taste and add a dash of lemon juice. Fold in the egg whites and proceed as for Basic Soufflé.

SALMON SOUFFLÉ (Serves 4)

Substitute salmon for the tuna in Tuna Soufflé and season with a dash of lemon juice and 1 teaspoon of grated onion.

CLAM SOUFFLÉ (Serves 4)

Open a can of minced clams. Drain off the juice and use it for part of the liquid in preparing the Basic Soufflé mixture (page 359). When the cream sauce is thickened, add the minced clams, season to taste and add the egg yolks. Proceed as for Basic Soufflé.

Dessert Soufflés

CHOCOLATE SOUFFLÉ (Serves 4)

Prepare the Basic Soufflé mixture (page 359) and when the cream sauce is thickened, stir in the egg yolks beaten with ¼ cup of sugar. Melt 2 squares of unsweetened chocolate with ¼ cup of sugar over hot water and add this chocolate mixture to the cream sauce and egg yolks. Fold in the whites according to directions for Basic Soufflé and pour the mixture into a soufflé dish that has been greased and dusted with sugar. Bake in a 375° oven for 35 to 40 minutes, or until puffed and browned.

LIQUEUR SOUFFLÉ (Serves 4)

Make the Basic Soufflé mixture (page 359), adding 1 extra tablespoon of flour. When the cream sauce is thick, stir in the egg yolks beaten with ¼ cup of sugar. Add ¼ cup of your favorite liqueur: Grand Marnier, Benedictine, Chartreuse, Crème de Cacao, Crème de Café. Continue according to recipe for Basic Soufflé.

FRUIT SOUFFLÉ (Serves 4)

Purée 1 cup of drained canned or stewed apricots or prunes. Prepare the Basic Soufflé recipe (page 359), adding an extra tablespoon of flour. Beat the egg yolks with ¼ cup of sugar and stir into the thickened cream mixture. Fold in the puréed fruit and proceed according to directions for Basic Soufflé. Pour the mixture into a soufflé dish greased and dusted with sugar and bake in a 350° oven for 35 to 45 minutes or until brown and puffed. Serve with a custard sauce.

LIGHT FRUIT SOUFFLÉ (Serves 4)

1 cup of puréed or crushed
   fruit
Sugar to taste
4 egg whites

¼ cup of liqueur (kirsch,
   Cognac or Grand
   Marnier)
Butter

Use any berries, such as raspberries, strawberries or huckleberries; or any puréed fruit, such as apricots or peaches. Crush the fruit or put it through a mill and add sugar to taste. Heat with ¼ cup of liqueur. Beat the egg whites until stiff but not too dry and fold them into the fruit purée. Pour into a soufflé dish that has been buttered and dusted with sugar. Bake in a 375° oven for 30 minutes or until puffed and brown.

Serve at once with whipped cream or a custard sauce flavored with the liqueur. This type of soufflé is far lighter and more delicate than cream base soufflés, and it falls easily. It must be served quickly.

LEMON SOUFFLÉ (Serves 4)

3 tablespoons of butter
2 tablespoons of flour
1 cup of scalded milk
Pinch of salt
3 eggs, separated

1 tablespoon of grated
   lemon rind
3 tablespoons of lemon
   juice
⅓ cup of sugar

Melt the butter in the upper part of a double boiler over hot water. With a wooden spoon blend the flour into the butter until smooth. Cook for a few minutes, then remove from the stove. Slowly add the scalded milk, stirring constantly. When the milk is thoroughly blended, return the pan to the stove and cook over hot water, stirring to keep the mixture smooth. Continue cooking and stirring until thickened. Add a pinch of salt. Remove from the stove.

Beat the egg yolks until light and lemon-colored, and beat in the lemon rind and lemon juice. Stir in a little of the milk mixture, and then add the rest of the sauce and beat thoroughly.

Beat the egg whites until stiff but not dry (they should be smooth and glossy), then beat in the sugar. Carefully fold the egg whites (see page 358) into the lemon mixture. Pour into a buttered and sugared casserole or soufflé dish and bake at 350° for 30 to 35 minutes, or until the soufflé has puffed up and is lightly browned. Serve at once.

Soups

"Can" is not a synonym for "soup." With no disrespect to this country's soup manufacturers, many of whose products are prepared with care and skill, the best soup is made at home. I admit that homemade soup is somewhat out of fashion, probably because most people won't take time to do the job. It seems to me, however, there are occasions when an old-fashioned, homemade soup is just right. Doesn't a rich, hot chicken broth sound good for a winter evening? Or a steaming bowl of chowder?

Delicate soups make excellent first courses for luncheon or dinner. Thick, hearty soups can be the main course at luncheon, supper or even a buffet dinner.

Remember that bones are important to soup. Even though you use meat for the flavor and texture, bones add the gelatinous richness. Veal bones are indispensable when you make a broth to jell naturally, without resorting to gelatin.

Soups with Beef Broth Base

The simplest way to prepare a good beef broth is to make Pot au Feu—meat, vegetables and seasonings cooked together in enough water to cover. This gives you a fine boiled dinner and also a rich meat broth delicious plain or as a base for many other soups.

CONSOMMÉ

Strain the broth from Pot au Feu through a linen napkin to be sure it is very clear. Put it in a kettle with 1½ pounds of ground beef and 1 cup of red or white wine. Bring to a boil and reduce the liquid over a high flame for 15 minutes. Lower the flame, cover the kettle and simmer gently for 1 hour. Strain through a fine linen towel. Beat an egg white until frothy and add this and the shell from the egg to the broth. Return it to the stove and cook for a few minutes, beating it with the egg beater as it cooks. Strain again through the linen towel. The egg white and eggshell gather all the impurities together, and when the soup is strained it should be perfectly clear. This is known as "clarifying." Add salt to taste.

This consommé can be served plain or with any of the following additions:

With rice: After the consommé is clarified, add 2 tablespoons of rice, return to the stove and cook gently just until the rice is done. This will take about 25 minutes.

With noodles: Cook the clarified consommé with ½ cup of broken noodles for 15 minutes.

With carrots: Cook the clarified soup with finely cut carrots for 15 to 20 minutes or until the carrots are done.

With peas: Cook the clarified consommé with a few green peas and a little grated carrot for 15 minutes.

With mushrooms: Cook the clarified consommé with 3 or 4 thinly sliced mushrooms for 5 minutes.

With avocado: Add paper-thin slices of avocado to the soup cups just before dishing out the consommé.

POT AU FEU

4 pounds of shin beef

1 beef bone or veal bone

1 piece of salt pork

1 onion, peeled and stuck
with 2 cloves

4 leeks if available (or 2
extra onions), split
lengthwise

4 carrots, peeled

2 small white turnips,
peeled

1 clove of garlic, peeled

1 bay leaf

1 teaspoon of thyme

1 sprig of parsley

1 tablespoon of salt

6 quarts of water

Boiled potatoes, cooked
separately

Place the beef, the bone and the salt pork in the bottom of a very large kettle, add the vegetables and all the seasonings. Cover with water and bring to a boil. Boil for 5 to 10 minutes and then skim off any scum that has come to the surface. Cover the kettle, reduce the heat and simmer gently for 3 or 4 hours. If the liquid cooks down too much, add more water during the simmering.

When the Pot au Feu is done, skim the fat from the surface with a large spoon. If the broth still seems fatty to you, pour it through a strainer lined with a linen napkin or towel.

Traditionally Pot au Feu is served as follows: first a bowl of broth; then slices of the beef and salt pork with the vegetables and boiled potatoes, sour pickles and hot mustard. The rest of the broth can be used as a base for any of the following soups.

OLD-FASHIONED VEGETABLE SOUP

6 cups of beef broth (from
Pot au Feu)

2 onions, thinly sliced

2 carrots, thinly sliced

4 celery stalks, cut in fine
bits

1 turnip, cut in small dice

3 leeks, thinly sliced

12 string beans, cut in small
pieces

1/4 head of cabbage,
shredded

2 potatoes, cut in small dice

1 cup of green peas

1 cup of broken macaroni
bits

Wash the vegetables carefully and peel the onions, carrots, turnip and potatoes. Cut all into slices or bits as suggested at left. Put the beef broth in a large kettle, taste for seasoning and add salt if necessary. Bring to a boil and add the vegetables. Cover the pan, lower the flame and simmer gently until the vegetables are done and well blended with the broth. This will take about ½ to ¾ hour. Serve with grated Parmesan cheese and crisp buttered toast.

FRENCH ONION SOUP

6 cups of beef broth (from Pot au Feu)

4 large onions, thinly sliced

6 tablespoons of butter

¼ cup of sherry

½ cup of grated Switzerland Swiss cheese

6 pieces of toasted French bread

Grated Parmesan cheese

Peel the onions and cut them in thin slices. Heat the butter and sauté the onion slices in the melted butter until they are brown and soft. If you like your onion soup to have a deeper color, add a sprinkling of sugar to the sautéed onions and allow it to caramelize. Bring the broth to a boil and add it to the onions. Add the sherry, taste for seasoning and add salt if necessary. Add the grated Switzerland Swiss cheese and pour the soup into a large casserole, or into individual casseroles, and bake in a 350° oven for 15 minutes. Top with the toasted bread slices, sprinkle with grated Parmesan cheese and serve.

BORSCHT (Serves 6 to 8)

Borscht (or Borsht or Borsch) comes in many versions, and this is one I have known since I was young. It makes an excellent one-dish meal, served with good black bread and sweet butter.

3 quarts beef broth, well seasoned

4 raw beets, peeled and shredded

4 potatoes, peeled and diced

2 onions, peeled and chopped

2 cups finely shredded cabbage

¼ to ½ cup lemon juice

2 or 3 tablespoons sugar

2 cups boiled beef, diced

The vegetables for this dish should be of medium size. In a large pot bring the broth to a boil, add the beets, and simmer 15 minutes. Add the other vegetables and cook till soft. Add the lemon juice and sugar to taste. The dish should have a sweet-sour balance. Finally stir in the beef and cook just long enough to heat through.

VARIATION

Chilled Borscht: Omit the meat. When the vegetables are done, drain off the broth and reserve. Purée the vegetables, and combine again with the broth. Chill thoroughly. Serve in bowls with a dollop of sour cream.

Soups with Chicken Broth Base

If your local market sells lesser chicken parts, you will find that the necks, backs and gizzards make excellent broth at very small cost. Otherwise, buy a whole fowl and use the cooked chicken meat for salad or hash.

CHICKEN BROTH

1 fowl or 4 pounds of
   chicken necks and backs
1 onion, peeled and stuck
   with 2 cloves
1 stalk of celery

1 sprig of parsley
Salt and pepper
Water

Put the fowl (or backs and necks) in a kettle, add the onion, celery, parsley and salt and pepper to taste. Pour over enough water to cover and a little extra. Put a lid on the kettle and bring to a boil. Reduce the heat and simmer gently for 2 hours. If you are using a whole fowl and wish to use the meat in a salad or hash, remove the chicken from the broth and cut the meat from the breast, thighs and drumsticks. Then return the bones to the broth and simmer for another ¾ hour. Strain the bones from the broth and then strain the broth through a linen napkin to remove the excess fat.

Serve the broth plain or with any of the additions suggested above for Consommé (see page 364).

DOUBLE CHICKEN BROTH

This rich broth is an elegant choice for a dinner party. It is also just the thing for the convalescent's tray.

Prepare the chicken broth above and strain it. Return it to the stove and add another chicken. Bring to a boil, cover, lower the flame and simmer gently for 3 hours. Remove the chicken, taste the broth for seasoning and add salt if necessary. Then strain the broth through a linen towel or napkin. If you wish, you may clarify the broth with egg white and eggshell (see recipe for Consommé, page 364).

LEEK AND POTATO SOUP (Serves 6)

5 or 6 leeks	**Salt to taste**
5 tablespoons butter	**Cayenne**
3 cups diced potatoes	**Nutmeg**
1 quart chicken broth	**2 tablespoons flour**

Trim and wash the leeks thoroughly to remove all sand. Split lengthwise, then cut in thin slices. Sauté in a large saucepan over moderate heat in 3 tablespoons of butter for 4 minutes. Add the potatoes and broth, bring to a boil, and reduce to heat. Cover and simmer till the potatoes are soft. Season to taste with salt (the broth may provide enough), cayenne and nutmeg. Drain off the broth and reserve. Purée the vegetables in a food mill, ricer or food processor. Combine again with the broth. Melt the remaining 2 tablespoons of butter in a saucepan over low heat, stir in the flour, and cook for a few seconds. Add 1½ cups of the soup and stir until the mixture is thickened. Stir back into the rest of the soup, and bring to a boil. Serve with a dash of cayenne or nutmeg.

VARIATIONS

Do not purée the vegetables, but leave them in coarse pieces in the thickened soup.

Vichyssoise: Prepare the soup in the main recipe and allow it to cool. Blend in 1½ cups heavy cream. Chill thoroughly. Serve with a sprinkling of chopped chives.

Soups Made with Legumes

It is wise to plan a legume soup after you have had a ham dinner. Save the bone from the ham to cook with the legumes. Otherwise buy a shank end of ham, cook it with the legumes and use the meat from the shank for a separate course or another meal.

SPLIT PEA SOUP

1½ cups of split peas

Ham bone

1 onion, stuck with 2 cloves

1 stalk of celery

1 bay leaf

2 to 3 quarts of water

½ cup of tomato purée

½ cup of heavy cream

In a large kettle, put the peas, ham bone, onion, celery, bay leaf, and 2 to 3 quarts of water. Bring to a boil, then lower the heat and simmer gently until the split peas are soft and mushy enough to be sieved, about 2 hours. Remove the ham bone and purée the soup by putting it in a food processor or through a food mill. Taste for seasoning and add salt if necessary. Add the tomato purée and cream and return to the stove. Bring to a boil. Serve with croutons fried in butter until crisp.

Note: If you prefer, you may substitute bacon rind, a slice of ham or a small pork butt for the ham bone.

VARIATIONS

With kidney beans: Substitute red kidney beans for the split peas and flavor with a few dashes of Madeira or sherry wine at the last minute.

With black beans: Substitute black beans for the split peas and flavor with Madeira or sherry wine. Serve with lemon slices.

With white pea beans: Substitute white pea beans for the split peas and serve topped with crumbled bacon bits.

LENTIL SOUP

1½ cups of lentils	2 to 3 quarts of water
Ham bone	¼ cup of chopped parsley
1 onion, peeled and stuck with 2 cloves	¼ cup of finely chopped onion
1 bay leaf	Frankfurters or garlic sausage
Sprig of parsley	

Place the lentils in a deep kettle with the ham bone, onion, bay leaf and parsley. Add 2 to 3 quarts of water and bring to a boil. Reduce the heat and simmer gently for 1 hour. Remove the ham bone and the onion. Taste for seasoning and add salt if necessary. Stir in the chopped parsley and chopped onion. Serve with slices of frankfurters in each bowl (simmer the frankfurters for 15 minutes and then slice), or with slices of garlic sausage (simmered for 30 minutes and then sliced).

This hearty soup, with crisp Italian or French bread, a good tossed salad and some cheese and fruit, makes a very satisfying dinner.

Cream Soups

An excellent cream soup is rich and flavorful and worthy of the featured place on a luncheon or supper menu. Too often what passes for cream soup is a dreary milk mixture thickened with flour. Properly made, this type of soup has a broth base, enriched with pure cream and thickened with egg yolks. Here is the basic recipe:

BASIC CREAM SOUP

2 cups of broth (chicken or beef)	¼ cup of chopped parsley
	Salt and pepper
1 cup of finely cut vegetable	1 cup of cream
	2 egg yolks
1 small onion, minced or grated	

Use beef or chicken broth made according to the recipes on pages 363 and 367 or buy a fine canned broth. Simmer 1 cup of finely cut raw vegetable in the broth. While it is cooking add the onion and chopped parsley. Or sauté the onion gently in butter and then add it to the broth and vegetable. When the vegetable is tender, drain it, purée it and then return it to the broth. Or put the broth and vegetables in a food processor and blend thoroughly. Taste for seasoning and add salt and pepper if needed. Put the mixture in the top of a double boiler over hot, but not boiling, water. Beat 2 egg yolks until light and then beat the cream into the yolks. Slowly add this egg-cream mixture to the soup in the top of the boiler and stir it in with a wooden spoon until thick. It is done when the mixture coats the spoon with a slight film. Do not let the mixture boil and do not overcook.

Suggested vegetables for cream soups:

1 cup of finely cut fresh asparagus
1 cup of finely cut carrots
1 cup of finely cut celery
1 cup of fresh green peas
1 cup of finely cut fresh broccoli
1 cup of finely chopped onion
1 cup of chopped fresh spinach

CREAM OF CORN SOUP

Use 1 cup of cooked corn kernels and heat in the broth. Follow instructions for Basic Cream Soup (page 370) but omit the puréeing. Simply transfer the kernels and broth, when heated through, to the top of the double boiler and thicken with the egg yolks and cream.

CREAM OF MUSHROOM SOUP

Sauté ½ pound of sliced mushrooms in 3 tablespoons of butter until soft. Then proceed as for Cream of Corn Soup.

CREAM OF TOMATO SOUP (Serves 4)

6 medium very ripe
   tomatoes, peeled, seeded
   and chopped

1 small onion, finely
   chopped

3 tablespoons butter

Salt

Freshly ground black
   pepper

¼ teaspoon baking soda

1 cup heavy cream or
   evaporated milk

¼ teaspoon dried sage,
   crumbled

Chopped parsley

In a saucepan sauté the onion in the butter until translucent. Add the tomatoes, salt and pepper to taste, baking soda, and sage. Cook over moderate heat for 10 to 12 minutes or until thickened. Remove from the heat, and stir in the cream or evaporated milk. Taste for salt. Heat to just under the boiling point. Serve in bowls with a sprinkling of parsley.

VARIATION

Cold Tomato Soup: Purée the soup, and chill thoroughly. Serve with sour cream and chopped parsley.

Chowders

Old-fashioned fish chowder is not made with tomatoes. It is made with a base of onion, salt pork, potatoes and milk or cream. This may be flavored with any fish, but clam is most popular. Corn chowder is also tasty and can be cooked quickly for unexpected supper guests.

CLAM CHOWDER

1½ cups of minced clams
(or about 2 cups of
shucked clams)

3 or 4 slices of salt pork (or
bacon), cut into small
cubes

2 medium potatoes, peeled
and diced

1 medium onion, peeled and
chopped

Salt and pepper

2 cups of light cream

Pinch of thyme

Paprika

You may use fresh hard-shell or soft-shell (razor) clams or canned minced clams. If you use fresh clams and do not know how to shuck them (remove the shells), ask the fish dealer to do this for you, or buy them already shucked. You will need about 1½ cups of clams after they have been minced or chopped. One quart of unshucked or 1 pint of shucked clams should be ample. If you use canned clams, buy 2 cans of the minced variety.

If you are using fresh clams, wash them well and then chop them or put them through a coarse grinder, being sure to save all the liquor. Fry the salt pork or bacon and cook the potato in salted boiling water until soft. When the salt pork or bacon is brown, remove it from the pan and sauté the chopped onion in the fat. Drain the cooked potato, saving the liquid, and return the potato water to the stove to cook down a bit. Combine the salt pork (or bacon), the sautéed onion, the cooked potatoes, the potato water, the liquor from the clams, and the chopped raw clams. (If you are using canned clams, add just the liquor from the cans.) Bring this to a boil, lower the heat and simmer gently for 5 to 10 minutes. Season to taste with salt and pepper and add the cream slowly. (If you are using canned minced clams, add them with the cream.) Heat the soup gently just to the boiling point, but do not let it boil. Stir in a tiny pinch of thyme just before you dish it up and dust the top of each bowl with a little paprika.

FISH CHOWDER

Follow the directions for Clam Chowder (see page 373) but use ½ to 2 cups of any cooked, flaked fish in place of the clams. Add the fish at the last minute with the cream.

CORN CHOWDER

Follow directions for Clam Chowder but substitute 1½ cups of cooked corn kernels, canned corn kernels, or canned cream-style corn for the clams and add them with the corn juice when you add the cream.

Cold Soups

COLD CUCUMBER SOUP (Serves 6)

2 cucumbers, peeled, seeded and chopped

2 cups chicken broth

1 tablespoon finely chopped onion

Salt

Freshly ground black pepper

1 teaspoon fresh dill

2 cups yoghurt

Finely chopped cucumber or dill for a garnish

Put the cucumbers, broth and onion in a saucepan, cover, and cook over low heat until the cucumbers are tender, about 20 minutes. Put through a food mill or purée in a food processor. Add salt and pepper to taste and the fresh dill. Allow to cool. Blend in the yoghurt, and taste for salt. Chill. Serve in chilled bowls with a garnish of chopped cucumber or dill.

GAZPACHO (Serves 6)

This is one of the most popular of all cold soups, and there are many versions of it. Here is one that hails from California.

3 pounds fresh tomatoes, peeled, seeded and chopped

1 clove of garlic, finely chopped

2 cucumbers, peeled, seeded, and coarsely chopped

½ cup minced green pepper

½ cup minced onion

2 cups iced tomato juice

⅓ cup olive oil

3 tablespoons vinegar

Salt

Freshly ground black pepper

¼ teaspoon Tabasco

For garnishing:

6 ice cubes of tomato juice   Croutons (see below)

In a large bowl combine the tomatoes with the rest of the ingredients, cover and chill thoroughly. Taste for salt and garlic content, adding more to taste.

For the croutons: Sauté 1 cup of small (¼ inch) cubes of white bread in 2 tablespoons of olive oil with 1 small clove of garlic, finely chopped, until lightly browned. Drain on paper towels and cool.

Serve the Gazpacho with a cube of frozen tomato juice in each bowl and a garnish of croutons.

CHILLED BORSCHT—See variation under Borscht, page 367.

COLD TOMATO SOUP—See variation under Cream of Tomato Soup, page 372.

VICHYSSOISE—See variation under Leek and Potato Soup, page 368.

Vegetables
and Legumes

Vegetables

There are few sights in the market so handsome as a display of fresh vegetables piled in colorful pyramids or laid out in neat rows. But how sad to think of the future many of them face. What once was a snowy head of cauliflower will appear on a dining room table as a soggy, yellow lump. Crisp green beans will be cooked until they are grayish and limp.

It's hard to say whether vegetables are often poorly prepared because people dislike them or disliked because poorly prepared. Some food experts claim vegetables are eaten mainly because they are supposed to be good for us, and that our hearty ancestors ignored them and concentrated on vast meals of game, meat, poultry and sweets. Many fabulous old menus list no vegetables of any sort; but the omission can be explained by the fact that the most impressive menus of the past are derived from Christmas and New Year's celebrations. In former times, people had no knowledge of canning, no refrigerated transportation to bring foods from far away. Winter was a time without fresh produce, but in warmer months our ancestors eagerly ate vegetables from their kitchen gardens. Plans of these gardens show they grew a vast array of vegetables, herbs and fruits, a much larger selection than most modern families eat.

A very old cookbook from the fourteenth century, one giving recipes of the chief cooks for King Richard II, describes how to prepare spinach, cabbage and a truly royal "salat" composed of leeks, fennel, cresses (watercress), porette (greens), onions and many herbs—these to be flavored with oil, vinegar and salt. Very tasty.

The Chinese and French, two peoples famed for their cookery, both respect vegetables and give them fine treatment. In the Orient, tender asparagus, snow peas or young green beans are cooked gently, just to the done stage, and served up still a little on the bitey side. The French excel in using various seasonings with vegetables, giving them an added richness and flavor. We can learn from both French and Chinese.

General rules for buying vegetables

The first step toward having tasty vegetable dishes is to select a good product. Of course, the fresher and crisper the vegetable is, the better. Wilted, tired vegetables can be freshened to some degree by soaking in icy water, but there hardly seems much point in buying them in the first place for they will never recapture the true fresh flavor. If you can buy direct from the grower, so much the better. You can have a steady supply of fresh products. Otherwise, select a market that takes care of its produce well, keeping it damped down and cool.

It is usually wise to buy the foods that are in season. They have a shorter distance to travel and are generally cheaper. The food page of most urban newspapers will give information on seasonal produce. Out-of-season vegetables, though sometimes excellent, are apt to be expensive. These days we have such a fine choice of frozen vegetables, picked at the height of the season, that winter menus offer no problems. Sometimes, too, canned vegetables are a good choice. Compare price and quality before deciding.

Try to buy your fresh vegetables often, rather than buying larger amounts at a time and storing them in your refrigerator. They stay crisp, it is true, but they do lose some flavor.

Don't stick to the old, familiar favorites. We have a large variety of vegetables available in our markets, and if you experiment a little, you may have some pleasant surprises.

General rules for cooking vegetables

Most vegetables—particularly the nontuberous ones, those that grow above ground—are delicate pieces of plant life. They should be cooked quickly in as little liquid as possible and served up at once while they still have their fresh taste. Five minutes too long in an oven will not absolutely ruin a beef roast, but five minutes too long in boiling water will turn the finest green vegetable to mush.

Plunge vegetables into boiling water slightly salted (about ½ teaspoon of salt to 2 cups of water) and use as little water as possible. If the vegetables are green, do not cover the pan, this helps them retain the green color.

White vegetables (cauliflower, onions, celeriac, white turnips, etc.) will stay whiter if the pan is covered. A dash of lemon juice or vinegar helps too.

Cook gently in boiling water, testing with a fork at frequent intervals. As soon as the vegetable is done (and do not let it get too done; it will be best if still a little firm), remove it from the fire and drain immediately. If you let cooked vegetables stand in the hot water, they lose their color and go limp.

Frozen vegetables have adequate instructions for cooking on the package. Be sure to follow them accurately.

The following recipes give specific instructions for cooking the best-known vegetables in a variety of ways, and include suggestions for seasoning or sauces. At the end of the chapter are recipes for dishes combining several vegetables.

Artichoke (Globe or French)

This winter vegetable, known as the globe or French artichoke, looks like a large green thistle. Many people have never tried it because it presents such a formidable appearance; they don't know how to eat it. This is sad indeed, for they miss one of the tastiest and richest of vegetables. How-to-eat instructions follow, but first, how to buy: Look for artichokes that are bright green and have tightly packed leaves. Force a few of the leaves apart slightly and look inside for worm damage. Worms can nibble away at the base of the leaves and not show on the outer part of the thistle. Brownish streaks and spots mean age or frost damage. Such artichokes are sometimes still good eating, but look inside to see if the inner part of the leaves is still fresh and crisp, and do not pay a high price for them. The size of the artichoke does not affect quality. Buy one per person.

Eating the artichoke is fairly complicated. Because it demands the eater's undivided attention, it is usually served as a separate course—either as a first course or immediately following the meat. If served *with* the meat, it should be served on a separate plate, large enough to hold all the discarded leaves. With each artichoke goes an individual bowl of sauce—melted butter, mayonnaise or Hollandaise.

To eat, pull the leaves off one at a time, dip the base of each leaf in the sauce and nibble off the fleshy end. Discard the rest of the leaf. Use your fingers for this operation, of course. When all the outer leaves are removed, you come to the tiny undeveloped leaves growing out of the heart. Pull these off and discard them, and with a knife cut out the feathery "choke" underneath. This exposes the most delectable part of the artichoke—the base. Cut this in bite-size pieces with your fork, spear each one, and dip it in the sauce.

And now for the cooking:

BOILED ARTICHOKES

1 artichoke per person
Water to cover
Salt

4 tablespoons of sauce per person (melted butter, Hollandaise or mayonnaise)

Be sure you have a deep kettle, large enough to hold all the artichokes standing upright. Fill the kettle with enough water to cover the artichokes and add 1 teaspoon of salt for each quart of water. Bring this to a boil. Meanwhile, cut the stem ends off so that the artichokes will stand upright. Some people like to trim off the tops and the ends of the large leaves because of the prickles, but this is a troublesome job and hardly necessary. Wash the artichokes thoroughly under running water, or soak in cold water for a half hour before cooking. This will remove any bugs lurking inside.

Plunge the artichokes into the boiling water and cook uncovered until they are tender when tested at the base with a fork. This will take anywhere from 30 minutes to 1 hour, depending on the size of the artichokes. When done, drain thoroughly upside down. Arrange on individual plates, with bowls of sauce for each person. Use melted butter, Hollandaise Sauce or mayonnaise.

STUFFED ARTICHOKES

4 artichokes
Water to cover
Salt
Butter
1 clove of garlic, chopped
6 to 8 mushrooms, chopped
$^1/_2$ cup of chopped ham
1 cup of dry bread crumbs

4 tablespoons of grated Parmesan cheese (optional)
$^1/_2$ teaspoon of salt
$^1/_2$ teaspoon of pepper
$^1/_4$ cup of chopped parsley
Melted butter
1 cup of broth or dry white wine

For 4 people, buy 4 large artichokes. Prepare as for boiled artichokes and cook until half done, or tender enough so that the leaves can be separated.

Meanwhile, prepare the following stuffing: Melt 4 tablespoons of butter in a skillet, add the chopped garlic, mushrooms and ham. When the mushrooms are tender, blend in the dry bread crumbs, salt, pepper and chopped parsley. Blend and remove from the fire.

When the artichokes are tender enough, drain them well and let them cool until you can handle them. Spread the leaves apart at the center, reach in and remove the underdeveloped leaves at the heart and then with a spoon cut out the feathery choke. Fill this space with stuffing and push a little between the outer leaves. You may sprinkle 1 tablespoon of grated Parmesan cheese in each artichoke, if you like. Press the leaves back in shape and tie each artichoke around the middle with string to hold it in shape. Stand the artichokes upright in a deep casserole, brush with melted butter, add 1 cup of broth (this can be made with hot water and a bouillon cube) or dry white wine. Bake in a 375° oven for $^1/_2$ hour, basting frequently with the broth or wine in the pan.

COLD ARTICHOKE

1 artichoke per person
Water to cover
Salt

3 to 4 tablespoons of mayonnaise per person or 3 tablespoons of Vinaigrette Sauce per person

This can be served as a first course, as a salad course or as a side dish on a cold buffet. Prepare and cook as for Boiled Artichokes. When they are done, cool them and then chill in the refrigerator. Serve with mayonnaise or Vinaigrette Sauce (see Salad Dressings).

COLD STUFFED ARTICHOKE

1 artichoke per person	**¹/₃ to ¹/₂ cup of seafood salad per person**
Water to cover	
Salt	**2 tablespoons of mayonnaise per person**

This is a refreshing salad for a luncheon or supper party. Prepare and cook as for Boiled Artichokes. Cook and then chill in the refrigerator. When ready to serve, gently push aside the center leaves and remove the undeveloped leaves at the heart. Then remove the feathery choke with a spoon. Be careful not to break the artichoke apart. Fill the center with any seafood salad (page 342), using ¹/₃ to ¹/₂ cup per artichoke. Press back into shape and serve with additional mayonnaise.

ARTICHOKE AS AN HORS D'OEUVRE

1 artichoke for 2 to 3 persons	**Salt**
Water to cover	**Dip sauce or mayonnaise**

Allow about 1 artichoke to every 2 or 3 persons. Prepare and cook them as for Boiled Artichoke. Cool and chill. Remove all the outer leaves and arrange them in a circle around the edge of a large chop plate or platter. Discard the undeveloped leaves at the heart and the feathery choke. Cut the heart of the artichoke into bite-size pieces and spear each one with a toothpick. Heap these in the center of the platter. Place on the cocktail table with a bowl of dip sauce (see pages 26–27) or mayonnaise.

Asparagus

Asparagus lovers, like sweet-corn addicts, devote hours and days to gorging on this delightful green stalk during the height of the season. They even make whole meals of it. And indeed there are few food treats to equal fresh asparagus, cooked just to the bitey stage, bathed in plenty of melted butter. The French even give it the dignity of a separate course on the menu, following the meat course.

Some people will tell you that ½ pound of asparagus is ample for 1 person. Actually most people can easily consume ¾ pound. If the asparagus has a great amount of white, tough stalk, which must be discarded, then even a pound per serving may be needed. Look for young green stalks, tightly budded at the top and as nearly uniform in size as possible. Stalks of various sizes cook at various rates, and you will have some done before others begin to cook through. Asparagus with too much white stalk is a waste of money, unless it is being sold at a bargain price.

If you prefer to serve only the tips of the asparagus, save the green stalks for soup or a soufflé. Hot, fresh asparagus is delicious enough served with plain melted butter. If you want a more elaborate sauce, serve Hollandaise (page 357), crumbs browned in butter or browned butter. Cold asparagus should be served with Vinaigrette Sauce or mayonnaise (pages 343–344).

BOILED ASPARAGUS

¾ to 1 pound of asparagus per person	**1 tablespoon of melted butter or 1½ tablespoons of Hollandaise Sauce per person**
Water to cover	
Salt	

Wash asparagus thoroughly. There may be sandy grit lurking in the tips. Cut off the tough ends of the stalks and peel the stalk up for 2 or 3 inches. There are two ways to boil asparagus. You may place the stalks flat in a shallow skillet with just enough boiling salted water to cover them. (Use ½ teaspoon of salt to 2 cups of water.) In this case, cook them without a lid, and be sure to remove them as soon as the tips are tender. The stalks will still be bitey, but this crunchy texture is very good. Overcooked tips go mushy.

If you prefer an even doneness for your asparagus, use an asparagus cooker or a tall container and stand the stalks upright with the tips out of the water. You can use the bottom part of a double boiler, inverting the top as a cover, or you can use a coffee percolator with the percolating part removed. Fill the container with enough boiling, salted water to cover the stalks but not the tips. Tie the asparagus together with string, or wrap a collar of aluminum foil around it to hold it in place, and stand it in the boiling water. Cover and cook until the stalks are just tender. By this time the tips should be steamed to doneness. Asparagus cooked in this manner, because covered, will not be as green as that cooked in an open skillet, but it will be more evenly done.

Cooking time for asparagus varies with the thickness of the stalks. Allow about 10 to 12 minutes in an open skillet and 15 or so if cooked upright. Do not let the asparagus stand in the water after it is done. Drain at once and serve with melted butter or Hollandaise Sauce (page 351).

VARIATIONS

With crumbs: For each serving, toss 1 tablespoon of dry bread crumbs in a saucepan with 1 tablespoon of butter. Pour the brown buttered crumbs over the tips of the asparagus just before serving.

With cheese: For 2 persons, arrange 1 pound of cooked asparagus stalks in an oven-proof dish that has been well buttered. Pour over them 2 tablespoons of melted butter, sprinkle with 2 tablespoons of grated Parmesan cheese and 2 tablespoons of buttered crumbs (page 53). Place in a moderate oven or under the broiler flame until the cheese melts and the top is brown and bubbly.

ASPARAGUS, HELEN EVANS BROWN

½ pound of asparagus per person	Salt
Water to barely cover	1½ tablespoons of melted butter per person

Allow ½ pound of asparagus per person. Wash and clean as for Boiled Asparagus, and cut into diagonal slices about ¼ inch thick. This will enable the asparagus to cook in the briefest time. Cook it in the smallest possible amount of boiling, salted water until just barely tender, but still bitey. It should only take 2 to 3 minutes at the most. Drain at once and serve with plenty of butter.

ASPARAGUS, FRENCH STYLE

1 pound of asparagus for 2 persons	3 or 4 large outside lettuce leaves
3 or more tablespoons of butter	Salt

For 2 persons, buy 1 pound of asparagus and wash and slice it diagonally as for the preceding Chinese-style recipe. Melt 3 tablespoons of butter in a skillet and add the asparagus. Cover with the washed lettuce leaves, with water still clinging to them, and put a lid on the skillet. Steam the asparagus over very low heat until tender, adding more butter if necessary. This method will take longer—about 10 minutes. When the asparagus is done, discard the lettuce, sprinkle the asparagus with salt to taste and serve.

VARIATION

Cook whole asparagus stalks by this method.

ASPARAGUS, ITALIAN STYLE

Cook whole asparagus stalks as for the French Style above, but substitute olive oil for the butter in the recipe.

COLD ASPARAGUS, PLAIN

Prepare boiled asparagus and let it cool. Chill in the refrigerator and serve with mayonnaise.

COLD ASPARAGUS VINAIGRETTE

Prepare boiled asparagus and let it cool. Serve with a Vinaigrette Sauce (page 343), using about ½ cup of sauce per pound of asparagus.

ASPARAGUS Á LA GRECQUE

Boil 2 pounds of asparagus until barely tender in water to which you have added ¼ cup of olive oil, 1 crushed clove of garlic, the juice of 1 lemon, a sprig of parsley, a pinch of thyme, a pinch of tarragon, a bay leaf and 3 or 4 peppercorns. Drain and cool. Serve with Vinaigrette Sauce (page 343) or mayonnaise.

Green Beans (Snap Beans)

Probably not more than one person in a hundred has tasted that delicate tidbit—a properly cooked, tender green bean. Maybe green beans are so common that few people feel they deserve any special care. They are always with us, they are plentiful and they are cheap. Yet anyone who has enjoyed the results of a summer vegetable garden knows how delectable tiny new green beans can be when cooked just right, drained, buttered well and served piping hot. They crunch just a bit when you bite into them and have all the fresh garden flavor.

You can duplicate this without a garden if you select your green beans with care and treat them with respect. One pound of beans will serve four persons. Look for those that are young, fresh and bright green; the tinier they are, the better, for then they can be cooked whole. Break one in two; it should have a firm snap. Inside, the beans should be immature—barely formed—and embedded in moist, firm flesh. The larger ones, paler in color and with fully matured beans inside, will be tough and tasteless no matter what you do to them. Pass them by, and if no young beans are available, buy frozen green beans.

BOILED GREEN BEANS (Serves 4)

1 pound of green beans	**Salt**
Water to barely cover	**4 to 6 tablespoons of butter**

Wash 1 pound of green beans. If they are tiny, leave them whole, but snip off the tip ends. If they seem too large to cook whole, cut them diagonally into 1-inch pieces. Or you can slice them French fashion—the long way. (There are special slicers available to do this job.) However, young tender beans will be just as tasty cut diagonally, and they even seem to retain more of their fresh flavor if they are not so thoroughly shredded.

Plunge the beans into boiling salted water (½ teaspoon salt to 2 cups of water)—just enough to cover them—and cook without a lid until they are barely tender. They should still have some crispness left. This should take no more than 10 to 12 minutes—at the most, 15. Drain at once and dress with 4 to 6 tablespoons of melted butter.

VARIATIONS

With bacon: Prepare the beans as above, and while they are cooking, cut 4 or 5 bacon slices into small pieces. Fry the bacon until it is brown and crisp. When the beans are done, drain them, add the melted butter and sprinkle the bacon over the top.

With almonds: Prepare the beans as above and while they are cooking, blanch ¼ cup of almonds and then cut them in slivers. Melt 4 to 6 tablespoons of butter in a skillet and toss the almonds about in the hot butter until they are slightly browned. (Or you can use canned toasted almonds.) Drain the beans and toss them in the skillet with the buttered almonds.

With mushrooms: Prepare the beans as above and while they are cooking, wash and slice ¼ pound of fresh mushrooms. Melt 5 tablespoons of butter in a skillet and sauté the mushrooms until brown and tender. Drain the beans and toss them with the mushrooms.

With onions: Prepare the beans as above and while they are cooking, wash 6 scallions and cut them into 1-inch pieces. Melt 5 tablespoons of butter in a saucepan and add the onions. Cover tightly and steam until tender. (You may substitute tiny white onions—use about 1 dozen—and they should be no bigger around than a five-cent piece.) Drain the beans and toss them with the onions.

With cheese: Prepare the beans as above and when they are done, drain them well. Add 4 tablespoons of butter and 6 tablespoons of grated Italian-style or imported Swiss cheese. Toss and mix well.

GREEN BEANS, ITALIAN STYLE (Serves 4)

1 pound green beans	1½ teaspoons lemon rind, finely chopped
3 tablespoons olive oil	
2 finely chopped cloves of garlic	½ teaspoon freshly ground black pepper
1½ tablespoons lemon juice	¼ cup grated Parmesan cheese

Cook the beans according the the recipe for Boiled Green Beans (page 385). Drain. Heat the olive oil in a skillet or the pan in which the beans were cooked, and sauté the garlic until just lightly browned, about a minute. Add the beans and toss with the garlic and oil. Add the lemon juice and rind and the pepper. Toss again. Transfer to a serving dish, and sprinkle with the Parmesan. Serve with roast chicken or a veal dish.

HOT BEAN SALAD (Serves 4)

1 pound of green beans	2 tablespoons of mild vinegar
Water to cover	
Salt	Lemon vinegar
4 strips of bacon	1 teaspoon of sugar
3 medium onions, thinly sliced	Pepper

Prepare the beans as for boiling, and while they are cooking cut up the strips of bacon and fry until crisp. Remove the bacon from the skillet and add the sliced onions to the bacon fat. Sauté these until just done. Add vinegar (a mild white wine vinegar is best), a dash of lemon juice and a sprinkling of sugar (about 1 teaspoon or less). Season with ½ teaspoon of freshly ground black pepper and taste for salt. When the beans are done, drain them and pour the sauce over them. Add the bacon bits and mix well.

GREEN BEANS VINAIGRETTE

1 pound of green beans   **Salt**
Water to cover   **½ cup of Vinaigrette Sauce**

Cook beans as for boiling. When done, drain and cool. Pour the Vinaigrette Sauce (page 343) over them and turn to be sure they are thoroughly bathed in the sauce.

Lima Beans

Fresh lima beans have a bland flavor, but there are many times when a bland vegetable is just what you want: with a highly seasoned pork sausage, for example. Their blandness also enables them to combine well with other flavorings, such as mushrooms, bacon bits, sour cream and chives. Then of course, there is that American Indian specialty, the lima bean and corn dish called succotash. This is delicious, especially with plenty of butter, freshly ground black pepper and a good spoonful or two of thick cream.

When you buy fresh lima beans, always buy them in the pod. Shelled beans soon turn tough. One pound of unshelled baby limas will serve two persons. Look for pods that are young and fresh. Feel them. Remember you want tiny beans. If the pods have big bumps, you can be sure the beans are too mature and will be starchy. If you can't get baby limas, buy dried lima beans. They are starchy, it's true, but you will get more for your money. Or buy frozen lima beans.

BOILED LIMA BEANS (Serves 2)

1 pound of unshelled lima beans for 2 persons	**¹/₂ teaspoon of freshly ground black pepper**
Water to cover	**2 tablespoons of melted butter**
Salt	

Shell the limas the last minute before cooking so the beans will stay fresh. Open the shells at the rounded end and the beans will slip out easily. Cook in just enough boiling salted water (¹/₂ teaspoon of salt to 2 cups of water) to cover. Cook without a lid for 15 to 20 minutes, or until one of the larger beans is tender. Drain and add the freshly ground black pepper and melted butter.

VARIATIONS

With mushrooms: Prepare the beans as above and while they are cooking, wash and slice ¹/₃ pound of fresh mushrooms. Melt 3 tablespoons of butter in a skillet and sauté the mushrooms until tender and brown. Drain the beans and toss them in the skillet with the mushrooms, adding ¹/₂ teaspoon of freshly ground black pepper.

With bacon: Prepare lima beans as above, and while they are cooking cut 3 slices of bacon into pieces and fry. Chop one onion and add it to the hot bacon fat. Sauté the onion until tender. When the beans are done, drain them and add them to the onion and bacon bits. Season with ¹/₂ teaspoon of freshly ground black pepper.

With sour cream: Cook lima beans as above. Drain them and add ¹/₂ teaspoon of freshly ground black pepper, ¹/₂ cup of sour cream, 1 tablespoon of melted butter and 2 tablespoons of chopped chives. Heat through, but do not boil or the sour cream will curdle.

SUCCOTASH (Serves 4)

1 pound of unshelled lima beans	**4 tablespoons of melted butter**
2 to 3 ears of sweet corn	**³/₄ teaspoon of freshly ground black pepper**
Water to cover	
Salt	**4 tablespoons of heavy cream**

For this dish you need equal amounts of sweet corn and lima beans. To 1 pound of limas use about 2 to 3 ears of corn, depending on their size. This amount will make about 4 servings. Cook the beans as for boiled limas. Cook the corn in boiling salted water for 3 or 4 minutes. Remove the ears from the water and cut off the kernels, slicing lengthwise with a sharp knife. Drain the beans and add them to the corn. Add the melted butter, freshly ground black pepper and cream. Stir and heat well.

VARIATION

Use fresh green beans in place of the lima beans.

Beets

Why beets? And why not beets? Without beets there would be no red flannel hash, no New England boiled dinner, no borscht. And even the most stubborn beet boycotter has been known to succumb to beets in sour cream with chives and parsley. The reaction all depends on the quality of the beet.

As with most vegetables, beets are best when small and young. The large older beets tend to be woody and strong in flavor. Look for beets that are smooth and firm—not withered—and about 2 inches or less in diameter. The condition of the beet tops, or greens, is no indication of the quality of the vegetable, for the tops wither easily in transport. Small beets run about 6 or 7 to a bunch, and a bunch will serve 2 to 3 persons.

BOILED BEETS (Serves 2 to 3)

1 bunch of beets	**Salt**
Water to cover	**3 tablespoons of butter**

Cut the stems off about 2 inches from the beet—no closer. Do not peel or chop the beets before cooking or cut the stems too close, or the beets will bleed. That is, the red color will run out and you will be left with a whitish-pink, tasteless root vegetable. Wash the beets well and plunge into boiling, salted water ($\frac{1}{2}$ teaspoon of salt to 2 cups of water) to cover. Put a tight lid on the pan and cook for 20 to 30 minutes or until tender. Do not test with a fork until nearly done, as this will tend to make the beets bleed. When they are done, rinse them in cold water until cool enough to handle. Slip off the skins and stems, and slice, or leave whole, if very small. Melt 3 tablespoons of butter in a pan, add the beets and reheat.

VARIATIONS

Beets with sour cream: Prepare the beets as above. When the butter is melted add 1 tablespoon of chopped chives and 1 tablespoon of chopped parsley. Then add the beets, heat and add 4 tablespoons of sour cream. Heat through but do not boil or the cream will curdle.

Beets with onion: Cook beets as above. Melt the butter in a skillet and add 1 medium onion, peeled and sliced. Sauté until tender. Add the beets and 2 tablespoons of chopped parsley. Heat.

Hot pickled beets: Cook beets as above. Melt the butter in a skillet, add 1½ tablespoons of wine vinegar, a dash of lemon juice and ½ teaspoon of sugar. Add the beets and heat.

COLD BEETS VINAIGRETTE (Serves 2 to 3)

1 bunch of beets	**Salt**
Water to cover	**½ cup of Vinaigrette Sauce**

Cook beets as for Boiled Beets. Peel, cool and slice. Soak in Vinaigrette Sauce (page 343) for 1 or 2 hours. Serve in a salad.

VARIATION

Add 2 medium-sized sweet onions, peeled and sliced, to the beets while they soak in the sauce. Serve as a pickle relish or as garnish on a salad or meat platter.

COLD BEETS WITH SOUR CREAM (Serves 2 to 3)

1 bunch of beets	**½ cup of sour cream**
Water to cover	**½ teaspoon of salt**
Salt	**½ teaspoon of pepper**
1 medium onion, chopped	**1 teaspoon of horseradish**

Cook beets as for Boiled Beets. Cool, peel and slice. Arrange the slices in a bowl and top with the chopped onion. Season sour cream with salt, freshly ground black pepper and grated horseradish. Spread this mixture over the beets and chopped onion.

Broccoli

We tend to think of broccoli as being a relatively new vegetable, since it has become popular in this country only during the last seventy or so years. Actually, Americans knew about it in colonial days and even grew it in their own gardens. Old cookbooks of the eighteenth century give recipes for preparing "brockala," and old order lists for garden seeds include it.

Why it was slow in catching on with the general public is a mystery. Today it is grown in California in large quantities and shipped all over the country. It ships well and is available through winter months when other green vegetables are hard to come by.

Broccoli is usually sold in 2-pound bunches, enough to serve four persons. Look for firm, bright green heads, tightly budded. Avoid broccoli that is beginning to open into tiny yellow flowers. It is too mature and will be tough and strong flavored.

BOILED BROCCOLI (Serves 4)

2 pounds of broccoli	**Salt and pepper**
Water	**4 to 6 tablespoons of butter**

Cut off the lower tough portion of the broccoli stalks and then peel the remaining stalks up an inch or so. Trim off any wilted leaves. If the bunches are not of uniform size, split the larger ones lengthwise so that all stalks will be the same thickness. Soak in cold water and a teaspoon of salt for 15 to 20 minutes to coax out any tiny insects.

In a kettle, put enough water to cover the broccoli and bring it to a boil. Add the vegetable and cook gently, uncovered. After 5 minutes add a teaspoon of salt and continue cooking until the stalks are tender when pierced with a fork. Total cooking time should be about 10 to 15 minutes. Be careful not to overcook. The tender buds will turn mushy, the broccoli will lose its color and the flavor will be too strong.

As with asparagus, the buds cook more quickly than the stalks. If you wish to be sure that they will not be overdone, prop the broccoli up in the kettle with the heads out of the water (or tie the stalks in bunches as you do asparagus) and cover the pan. Cook gently until just tender—about 10 to 12 minutes. Or separate the stems from the buds. Cook the stems until nearly tender, and then add the buds.

Drain the broccoli, season to taste with salt and pepper and serve with melted butter.

You may also serve the broccoli with lemon butter (add 1 tablespoon of lemon juice to each 4 tablespoons of melted butter), Hollandaise Sauce, Buttered Bread Crumbs or sprinkled with grated Parmesan cheese and then glazed under the broiler flame.

ITALIAN-STYLE BROCCOLI

Prepare the broccoli as above. Meanwhile heat ¼ cup of olive oil in a skillet with 1 minced clove of garlic. Add the drained broccoli and sauté very quickly in the hot oil. Sprinkle with grated Parmesan cheese or buttered crumbs.

VARIATION

If you wish to use only the heads of broccoli for vegetable at a company dinner, reserve the stalks and cook them the next day Italian style.

PURÉED BROCCOLI

Prepare 2 pounds of broccoli and boil until just tender. (See Boiled Broccoli, page 391). Put the cooked and drained stalks through a food mill or purée in a food processor. Melt 4 tablespoons of butter in a skillet and reheat the puréed broccoli in the hot butter, stirring to blend thoroughly. Season to taste with salt and freshly ground black pepper.

VARIATIONS

With onion: Add 1 tablespoon of grated onion.

With cream: Add 2 tablespoons of heavy cream.

COLD BROCCOLI, PLAIN—Follow directions for Cold Asparagus, Plain page 384).

COLD BROCCOLI VINAIGRETTE

An English cookbook, almost 200 years ago, stated of "brockala": "the French eat oil and vinegar with it." To prepare broccoli in this fashion, follow directions for Cold Asparagus Vinaigrette (page 384).

Brussels Sprouts

These miniature members of the cabbage family are excellent winter standbys. They go well with all pork dishes. Brussels sprouts have been maligned by people who have only encountered them cooked to a gray mush. Cook them until just tender and serve them up still bright green. Brussels sprouts are sold by the pound or in pint and quart baskets. One pound or 1 quart basket will serve 4 persons. As with all green vegetables, Brussels sprouts should be firm and fresh-looking.

BOILED BRUSSELS SPROUTS

1 quart or 1 pound of Brussels sprouts	Salt and pepper
Water	4 tablespoons of melted butter

Trim the stems off close to the sprouts and remove any discolored leaves. Put the sprouts to soak for 15 to 20 minutes in water to which you have added 1 teaspoon of salt.

In a kettle put enough water to cover the Brussels sprouts and add 1 teaspoon of salt. Bring this to a boil and add the vegetable. Do not cover. Cook gently until just tender when pierced with a fork. This should take about 15 minutes.

Drain well and serve with melted butter and salt and pepper to taste. Some people like a dash of vinegar or some lemon juice added.

SAUTÉED BRUSSELS SPROUTS

Clean and soak the sprouts as above. In a large skillet melt 4 tablespoons of butter. Add the well-drained Brussels sprouts and cover tightly. Lower the flame and cook very slowly until the sprouts are barely tender. Season to taste with salt and freshly ground black pepper and add a tablespoon of grated onion.

VARIATION

At the very last minute, add 2 tablespoons of grated Parmesan cheese.

BRUSSELS SPROUTS WITH MUSHROOMS

Prepare sprouts as for Boiled Brussels Sprouts (page 393). While they are cooking, melt 4 tablespoons of butter in a skillet. Clean ½ pound of fresh mushrooms and sauté them gently in the melted butter.

When the sprouts are done, add them to the mushrooms in the skillet and toss them about to blend with the juices. Add a dash or so of lemon juice and season to taste with salt and freshly ground black pepper.

BRUSSELS SPROUTS WITH GREEN ONIONS

Prepare as for Brussels Sprouts with Mushrooms (see above), substituting 6 chopped green onions (scallions) for the fresh mushrooms.

BRUSSELS SPROUTS WITH BACON

Prepare as for Boiled Brussels Sprouts (page 393), and while the sprouts are cooking, fry 6 slices of bacon. When crisp, remove and chop fine. Drain off all but 4 tablespoons of the bacon fat. Return the chopped bacon to the pan and add the cooked and drained sprouts. Season with 1 tablespoon of grated onion.

BRAISED BRUSSELS SPROUTS

Clean and soak as for Boiled Brussels Sprouts (page 393). Melt 4 tablespoons of butter in a skillet and add the drained sprouts. Cook quickly for a few minutes to sear the sprouts lightly in the butter. Add ½ cup of broth or stock (you may use ½ cup of hot water and 1 bouillon cube), cover the pan and cook the vegetable over a very low heat until tender.

Cabbage

The importance of cabbage has never been thoroughly assessed. Indeed, without its existence the history of the Western world might have been radically different. For centuries it has been a mainstay in the diet of much of Europe, Britain and many regions of North America. Lowly though it may seem, it has no rival in versatility except the potato. It is available the year round; it can be eaten raw or cooked in almost any manner—boiled, steamed, braised, sautéed, baked; and a list of recipes calling for cabbage would fill a book.

There are several varieties of cabbage found in our markets. The common or green cabbage is sold everywhere. In summer the fresh young heads are bright green and rather small (2 to 3 pounds); the late or winter crop is lighter in color, sometimes almost white, firmer and larger (up to 6 pounds). In some areas of the country Savoy cabbage is sold. This is bright green with a curly leaf and more delicate in flavor. Red cabbage is popular in certain German and Pennsylvania Dutch dishes. It is attractive, but must be cooked with some acid added—vinegar, lemon juice or tart apple. Without acid it turns a grayish purple. The long-leafed, curly Chinese cabbage is available in some parts of the country.

A small head of cabbage, 2 to 3 pounds, will serve 4 persons. Some grocers will cut a larger cabbage in half if you cannot use the whole head.

Whatever you do, don't cook cabbage for hours. This old-fashioned method accounts for too much cabbage smell, and results in a mushy, gray vegetable, unappetizing and completely lacking in any food value. Like most green vegetables cabbage benefits by being cooked quickly in a small amount of water just to the bitey stage.

SHREDDED BOILED CABBAGE (Serves 4)

If you cook cabbage by this method you will be more certain to have a crisp, refreshing dish. It takes less cooking time but more preparation and more attention.

2- to 3-pound head of cabbage	**Salt**
Water	**6 tablespoons of melted butter**

Remove any outer wilted leaves and trim off the stalk end of the cabbage. With a sharp knife, cut through the head in thin slices, shredding it as you would for coleslaw. Soak for 20 to 30 minutes in cold water to which you have added 1 teaspoon of salt.

In a wide skillet place a small amount of water—about 2 inches or so. Add a teaspoon of salt and bring to a boil. Add the drained cabbage and cover. Cook quickly, turning once or twice during the cooking to be sure all the cabbage is evenly cooked. Test for doneness with a fork and remove from the fire and drain as soon as the cabbage is barely tender. Young green cabbage will cook in this manner in about 4 minutes; older winter cabbage may take twice as long. Savoy cabbage, which is the most delicate, will take about 3 minutes.

Drain well, season to taste with salt and freshly ground black pepper and pour melted butter over the cabbage.

Note: Red cabbage needs the addition of acid. If you shred it and boil it, be sure to add 1 tablespoon of vinegar or lemon juice to the water in which it cooks. Actually red cabbage seems to taste better when sautéed (page 398).

QUARTERED BOILED CABBAGE (Serves 4)

This method takes less preparation but a little longer cooking time.

2- to 3-pound head of cabbage	**Salt**
Water	**6 tablespoons of melted butter**

Clean as for Shredded Boiled Cabbage (see page 395) and cut the head in quarters. Soak in salted water for 20 to 30 minutes. In a large kettle put enough water to cover the cabbage quarters and add 1 teaspoon of salt. Bring it to a boil and add the cabbage. Cook until just barely tender. If the cabbage is young and green, leave the cover off the pan to help retain the green color. Young cabbage will cook in about 6 to 8 minutes; older winter cabbage in about 15 minutes; Savoy takes only about 6 minutes.

When it is done, drain it, season to taste with salt and freshly ground black pepper and pour the melted butter over it.

If you like a tart or sour taste with cabbage, pass the vinegar cruet.

Note: If you are buying a larger head for more servings, cut it in eighths before cooking.

CREAMED CABBAGE (Serves 4)

2- to 3-pound head of cabbage	**Salt and pepper**
1½ cups of Béchamel Sauce (page 349)	**½ cup of buttered crumbs (page 53)**
Butter	

Prepare and cook the cabbage as for Shredded Boiled Cabbage (page 395). Butter a large casserole, place a layer of the cooked cabbage in the bottom, season to taste with salt and pepper and add a layer of Béchamel Sauce. Repeat these layers until all the ingredients are used up, being sure the top layer is Béchamel Sauce. Sprinkle with buttered crumbs and bake in a 375° oven for 10 to 15 minutes, or until the top is browned and the mixture is hot through and bubbly.

VARIATION

With cheese: Sprinkle each layer of sauce with grated Parmesan, Swiss or Gruyère cheese and top with grated cheese.

BRAISED CABBAGE (Serves 4)

2- to 3-pound head of cabbage

3 to 4 tablespoons of butter or bacon fat

³/₄ cup of meat stock (or 1 bouillon cube and ³/₄ cup of boiling water)

Clean and shred the cabbage as for Shredded Boiled Cabbage (page 395). Soak in salted water for 20 to 30 minutes. In a large skillet melt the butter or bacon fat, add the drained cabbage and gently sauté it in the hot fat. Turn it frequently with a spatula to be sure it is evenly browned. When slightly colored (in about 2 to 3 minutes) pour the hot bouillon or stock over the cabbage, cover it tightly and simmer gently until just done. This should take about 5 minutes.

COUNTRY-FRIED CABBAGE (Serves 4)

2- to 3-pound head of cabbage

1 tablespoon of vinegar

3 to 4 tablespoons of bacon fat

4 tablespoons of heavy cream

Clean and shred the cabbage as for Shredded Boiled Cabbage and soak in salted water (see page 395). In a large skillet melt the bacon fat. Add the well-drained cabbage and brown it in the hot fat, turning with a spatula to be sure it cooks evenly. When browned, cover with a tight lid and continue cooking until tender. Taste for seasoning. If the bacon fat is not salty enough, add salt to taste. Sprinkle with the vinegar and heavy cream, and continue cooking just until the cream is hot through.

SAUTÉED RED CABBAGE (Serves 4)

2- to 3-pound head of red
   cabbage
3 to 4 tablespoons of bacon
   fat
Salt and pepper
1 cup of red wine

2 tart apples
2 tablespoons of brown
   sugar
1 tablespoon of vinegar

Clean and shred the cabbage as for Shredded Boiled Cabbage and soak in salted water (see page 395). In a large skillet melt the bacon fat. Add the well-drained cabbage and sauté, turning to cook on all sides. Season to taste with salt and pepper and add the red wine. Simmer for 5 to 6 minutes and add the 2 apples, cored and diced but not peeled. Sprinkle with the brown sugar and vinegar, cover and simmer until the apples and cabbage are tender.

This dish is particularly good with pork, duck or goose.

BAKED CABBAGE WITH SAUSAGE (Serves 4)

2- to 3-pound head of
   cabbage
$^1/_4$ pound of bacon
Salt and pepper
1 small onion, finely
   chopped

$^1/_2$ cup of white wine
$^1/_2$ cup of meat stock (or 1
   bouillon cube and $^1/_2$ cup
   of boiling water)
1 pound of pork sausage
   links

Clean and quarter the cabbage as for Quartered Boiled Cabbage (page 396) and soak in salted water. Line a large casserole with the bacon strips. Add the quartered cabbage, season to taste with salt and pepper and sprinkle with the chopped onion. Pour over this the white wine and meat stock and top with the sausage links. Bake in a 350° oven until the cabbage is tender and the sausage done and well browned. This will take $^3/_4$ of an hour to 1 hour.

COLESLAW—See pages 333–334.

Carrots

The carrot has long been a favorite of rabbits and donkeys, and also of mine, provided it is the tender young vegetable. Old woody carrots are never tasty, though they do add flavor to soups and stews. Look for the tiniest you can find, young, firm and fresh-looking.

Carrots are sold by the bunch and one bunch usually weighs 1 pound. This amount serves 3 to 4 persons, depending on appetites, but if you are serving 4, it is safer to cook 1½ bunches. (You can use the other half bunch in a meat stew or a casserole or as raw carrot strips.)

Cook tiny young carrots whole without peeling. Larger carrots should be peeled or scraped and cut in long strips. They can, of course, be cut in rounds, but for some reason these are not as tasty.

The frequent combination of carrots and peas is an insult to both vegetables. They do not complement each other. It would make just as much sense to combine turnips and asparagus. Serve them separately.

BOILED CARROTS (Serves 4)

1½ bunches of carrots	Pepper
Water to cover	4 tablespoons of melted
Pinch of salt	butter
Salt	

If the carrots are tiny, simply wash them well and cut off the tops. In a skillet or saucepan, put just enough water to cover the carrots, add a pinch of salt and bring to a boil. Add the carrots whole, placing them flat in the pan. Cover tightly and simmer gently until just tender when tested with a fork. Tiny whole carrots take about 15 minutes.

If the carrots seem too large to cook whole (that is, if they are over ¾ inch thick), split them in half lengthwise. Bigger carrots should be scraped or peeled and cut into strips.

When the carrots are cooked, drain them well, season to taste with salt and freshly ground black pepper and pour melted butter over them.

VARIATIONS

With chives and parsley: Add 1 teaspoon of chopped chives and 1 teaspoon of chopped parsley to the melted butter.

With lemon juice: Add 1 tablespoon of lemon juice to the melted butter.

With green onions: Add 4 green onions, chopped and sautéed in butter, to the seasoned carrots.

STEAMED CARROTS

For this dish, tiny young carrots are by far the best. Melt 4 tablespoons of butter in a heavy skillet with a tight lid. Add tiny whole carrots and a bit of salt and pepper. Cover tightly and steam over very low heat until tender when pierced with a fork.

GLAZED CARROTS (Serves 4)

1½ bunches of carrots, cooked and drained	1 tablespoon of chopped parsley
2 tablespoons of butter	Salt to taste
2 tablespoons of strained honey	Dash of lemon juice

Melt the butter in the skillet and add the honey, parsley and cooked carrots. Season to taste with salt. Simmer very gently for a few minutes until all the ingredients are well blended. Add a dash of lemon juice and serve.

BRAISED CARROTS (Serves 4)

1 bunch of carrots	Pepper
3 tablespoons of butter	½ cup of broth or stock
Salt	

Leave the carrots whole if they are tiny and young. Peel larger carrots and cut in half lengthwise. Melt butter in a heavy skillet and arrange the carrots flat in the pan. Cook them over fairly high heat for a few minutes, seasoning to taste with a little salt and pepper. (Use the salt lightly if the broth or stock you plan to use is heavily seasoned.) Add the broth (you can make this with hot water and a bouillon cube), cover the pan and simmer gently over a low flame until the carrots are just tender when pierced with a fork.

Cauliflower

As most people know, Mark Twain said cauliflower was nothing but cabbage with a college education. It is most certainly a refined vegetable and very delicate when treated with respect. It delights us by coming on the market in abundant supply at the time when summer vegetables are tapering off. You will find it in all sizes, from small heads of ½ to ¾ pound, on up to giants weighing as much as 5 or 6 pounds. Allow about ½ pound per person. Choose heads that are snowy white with firm, tightly packed buds. Avoid those that have brown spots or any discoloring.

There is nothing handsomer in the vegetable line than a whole cooked head of cauliflower, white, glistening with melted butter and surrounded with tiny whole carrots and small whole green beans. It is equally elegant cooked and chilled and served with other cooked vegetables and a well-seasoned mayonnaise. This makes a fine salad luncheon.

To clean cauliflower, cut off the stem end and remove the green leaves. Soak the head in 2 quarts of cold water to which you have added 1 teaspoon of salt. Let the cauliflower stand in the water for about ½ hour to draw out any tiny insects. If you do not intend to cook the head whole, break or cut off the small bunches of flowerets. These are the tightly packed bunches, each with a separate stem attached to the main stalk or center of the head. Cut off these stems as close to the head as possible, starting with those around the outside. Soak in cold water with salt added.

BOILED CAULIFLOWER (Serves 4)

2-pound head of cauliflower
Boiling salted water to cover

6 tablespoons of melted butter
Salt and pepper

Cut off the stem end and remove the green leaves. Soak the cauliflower, according to directions above, in cold, salted water for ½ hour. In a deep kettle put enough water to cover the cauliflower and add 1 teaspoon of salt. Bring this to a boil, put the cauliflower in the boiling water and place a lid on the kettle. Cook gently until the vegetable is just tender when pierced at the stem end with a fork. Do not overcook cauliflower or the head will be mushy and fall apart. Overcooking also tends to turn the white head a dull gray or yellow color. A 2-pound head of cauliflower will take 20 to 25 minutes to cook.

Drain well, arrange on a platter or in a vegetable bowl and pour melted butter over. Season to taste with salt and freshly ground black pepper.

Or arrange on a large platter and surround with other cooked vegetables.

Cauliflower and buttered almonds: Chop blanched almonds and brown them lightly in hot butter. Pour over the cooked cauliflower head and season with salt and pepper.

Cheesed cauliflower: Place a cooked, drained head of cauliflower in a casserole, dot it liberally with butter, season to taste with salt and freshly ground black pepper, and sprinkle with grated Parmesan cheese, Switzerland Swiss cheese or sharp cheddar. Heat in a hot oven (450°) until the cheese melts.

Crumbed cauliflower: Brown fine toasted crumbs in melted butter. Spread these over the cooked, drained cauliflower head and season with salt and pepper.

Cauliflower with bacon bits: Fry 3 or 4 slices of bacon until brown and crisp. Crumble and sprinkle over the cooked, drained cauliflower. Add melted butter.

Herbed cauliflower: Melt butter and add chopped parsley and chives (1 tablespoon of each to 6 tablespoons of butter). Pour this over the cooked, drained cauliflower and season to taste with salt and freshly ground black pepper.

Cauliflower Hollandaise: Serve hot cauliflower with Hollandaise Sauce (page 351).

BOILED CAULIFLOWERETS

Follow directions for Boiled Cauliflower (page 401) but first break the cauliflower head into flowerets, cutting each individual bunch off as near the center of the head as possible. Cook in boiling salted water to cover until tender but *not mushy*. This will take about 10 to 15 minutes. Drain thoroughly and serve with melted butter, salt and pepper. Or use any of the variations listed above under Boiled Cauliflower.

CAULIFLOWER AND CHEESE CASSEROLE

Break a cauliflower head into flowerets and cook as for Boiled Cauli-flowerets (page 402). Drain and arrange in a buttered casserole. Cover with 1 cup of Rich Cream Sauce (page 349), sprinkle with ½ cup of grated Switzerland Swiss cheese and ⅓ cup of fine toasted bread crumbs browned in butter. Heat in a 450° oven until the cheese is melted and the top browned and bubbly.

COLD CAULIFLOWER

Cook a whole head of cauliflower according to directions under Boiled Cauliflower (page 401). Drain and arrange the head in the center of a large platter. Surround it with any combination of cold cooked or raw vegetables you choose. Or arrange the cauliflower alone on a bed of greens. Serve with Vinaigrette Sauce, mayonnaise, mayonnaise flavored with mustard or chili sauce, or with a sour cream dressing.

Celeriac or Celery Root

This round, brownish root with a rough skin and green tops is sometimes called "knob celery." Though it is of the same family, it is not the root of the regular stalk celery, as some people think.

Celeriac is usually sold in individual knobs, which vary in size from about 2½ inches to 4 to 5 inches in diameter. One pound will serve 4 persons.

BOILED CELERIAC (Serves 4)

1 pound of celeriac
Boiling water to cover
Salt and pepper

4 tablespoons of melted butter

Wash the roots and cut off the tops. Peel them and place in cold water to which you have added 1 teaspoon of salt. This keeps the vegetables from turning dark. Let it stand in the water until you are ready to cook. In a kettle put enough water to cover the vegetable, add 1 teaspoon of salt and bring to a boil. Cut the roots into slices or cubes and drop them into the boiling water. Cover the pan and cook until the celeriac is just tender. This will take about 10 minutes. Drain thoroughly and dress with melted butter and salt and freshly ground pepper.

VARIATIONS

Crumbed celeriac: Brown fine toasted crumbs in melted butter and sprinkle over cooked celeriac. Season with salt and pepper.

Cheesed celeriac: Drain cooked celeriac and arrange in a buttered casserole. Dot with butter and sprinkle liberally with grated Parmesan cheese and Switzerland Swiss cheese. Run under the broiler flame to melt the cheese and brown lightly.

Puréed: Combine equal amounts of puréed celeriac and potato. Add butter and salt and pepper to taste.

Celeriac Hollandaise: Serve cooked celeriac with Hollandaise Sauce (page 351).

SCALLOPED CELERIAC AND POTATOES

Alternate layers of thinly sliced raw celeriac and raw potato in a buttered casserole. Add beef broth to nearly cover, dot with butter, and bake, covered, at 350° for about 45 minutes, or until tender. Add grated cheese, preferably Swiss, and bake, uncovered, for another 15 minutes.

CELERIAC STEAMED IN BUTTER (Serves 4)

1 pound of celeriac	**Salt**
4 tablespoons of butter	**Pepper**

Wash the roots, cut off the tops and peel them. Soak in cold salted water until ready to cook. Melt the butter in a large skillet. Slice the roots very thin and arrange the slices over the bottom of the skillet in the melted butter. Season to taste with salt and freshly ground black pepper. If you must put several layers of the slices in the skillet, shift them once or twice during the cooking, moving those on top to the bottom of the pan so they will all cook evenly. Cover the skillet with a tight-fitting lid and steam gently over low heat until the celeriac is tender. This will take 15 to 20 minutes.

VARIATION

Sprinkle the slices with grated Parmesan cheese just before they finish cooking.

COLD CELERIAC

Soak cold celeriac in Vinaigrette Sauce (page 343) and serve on a bed of greens with or without mayonnaise. Combine it with other cold cooked vegetables and serve in the same way.

RAW CELERIAC SALAD (Serves 4)

2 medium-sized celery roots

3 tablespoons of mayonnaise

1 teaspoon of dry mustard

1 tablespoon of chopped parsley

1 teaspoon of finely chopped onion

1 tablespoon of chopped onion

Salt and pepper

Wash the roots, trim off the tops and peel them. Put them in cold salted water until you are ready to use. Then grate them or cut in thin strips (julienne) and mix with all other ingredients. Heap on a bed of greens and garnish with hard-cooked egg, raw onion rings and green pepper rings. Serve with additional mayonnaise if you wish.

Rémoulade: Cut the celeriac into fine julienne and toss with mayonnaise flavored with Dijon mustard to taste. Serve as an appetizer.

Celery

There are two kinds of celery available in most markets: the large, hearty green bunches topped with green leaves (this variety is sometimes called Pascal); and the pale, almost white celery with yellowish leaves. This pale color is achieved by bleaching. Some people think it is more attractive, but green celery is far tastier and has more food value. Pascal celery comes in very large, sometimes gigantic, bunches, but extra celery is no problem. It can be eaten plain with salt, added to sandwich fillings, or used in salads, soups, stews, stuffings or sauces. A bunch weighing 1½ pounds will serve 4 persons amply. Look for those bunches that are fresh and crisp.

Celery often has soil clinging to the base of the stalks and must be washed thoroughly. Cut off about 1 inch of the root end, separate the stalks, trim off the green leaves and wash the celery in cold water, rubbing off any dirt. Trim the bottom of the root end, wash the dirt from the crevices and save the root, along with the leaves, for flavoring in soups and stews. The tiny, tender leaves at the heart of the bunch can be left on the stalks as if you are going to eat them raw, or can be added to green salads.

BOILED CELERY (Serves 4)

1 to 1½ pounds of celery	**Pepper**
Water	**4 tablespoons of melted**
Salt	**butter**

Cut off the root end of the celery and separate the stalks. Trim off the leaves. Save the heart for salads, the root and leaves for flavoring soups and stews. Wash the stalks well and remove any tough strings. Cut them into 1- to 2-inch pieces and soak in salted water (1 teaspoon of salt to 2 quarts of water) until ready to cook. In a kettle put just enough water to cover the celery, add 1 teaspoon of salt and bring to a boil. Add the celery and cook gently, uncovered, until just tender when pierced with a fork. This will take about 10 minutes. Drain well, season to taste with salt and freshly ground black pepper and pour melted butter over.

VARIATIONS

Creamed: Serve the cooked celery covered with a Rich Cream Sauce (page 349).

Hollandaise: Serve cooked celery with a Hollandaise Sauce (page 351).

With almonds: Sliver blanched almonds and brown them lightly in melted butter. Pour this over cooked celery and season to taste with salt and freshly ground black pepper.

BRAISED CELERY (Serves 4)

1- to 1¹/₂-pound bunch of celery

4 tablespoons of butter

³/₄ cup of broth or stock

Salt

Pepper

Clean the celery as for Boiled Celery (page 406) but leave the stalks whole. Cut the stalks into fairly uniform lengths—about 6 to 8 inches long. If any are exceptionally thick through, cut them in half once lengthwise. Melt the butter in a large skillet and place the celery stalks flat in the pan. Brown them lightly in the butter over fairly high heat, turning once. When lightly colored, add the broth (this can be made with hot water and a bouillon cube) lower the heat and cover the skillet. Cook gently until the celery is just tender. Season to taste with salt and pepper.

VARIATION

Add ¹/₂ cup of slivered blanched almonds to the celery to brown in the butter and cook in the broth.

COLD CELERY

Soak cold cooked celery in Vinaigrette Sauce (page 343) and serve on a bed of greens or in combination with other cold vegetables as a salad.

RAW CELERY

1. Cut into uniform strips and serve with a good dip sauce (pages 26–28).
2. Add chopped raw celery to green salads.
3. Cut the stalks into uniform lengths and fill the hollows with mashed blue cheese thinned with heavy cream. Use as an hors d'oeuvre or as a garnish on salad plates.

Corn

The sooner corn is cooked after picking, the better it is. If you can't buy directly from the grower, go to a good greengrocer—one who is supplied daily with fresh corn in season. The ears should be displayed on beds of ice and be kept cold and damp. Open the husks a bit to be sure the kernels are firm and fresh. Look for tiny young kernels. Pierce one with your fingernail; it should be milky inside, not mealy. Corn that is too mature or too old will be tough. Never buy corn already husked.

Keep the corn cold and damp in the refrigerator until just before cooking. Then peel off the outside husk and remove the silken threads. Don't cut off the stem end unless you own some of those metal corn holders. The ears will be easier to hold if you have a stem attached.

Since the season is all too short, make a feast of corn when you can get it. Buy at least 2 ears per person. Personally, I can eat 3 or 4 easily.

BOILED CORN

2 to 3 ears of corn per person

Water to cover

Salt and pepper

Butter

In a large skillet, put enough water to cover the corn. Do not add salt. This tends to toughen the corn. While the water is coming to a boil, husk the ears and remove the silk. Plunge them into the boiling water, let it return to a boil and cook 3 to 5 minutes. Tender young corn needs no more than 3 minutes of boiling. Too much cooking makes it tough and mealy.

Remove the ears quickly and arrange them in a deep bowl lined with a napkin. Fold the napkin over the corn to hold in the heat. Serve with individual dishes of salt, pepper grinders and plenty of sweet butter.

VARIATION

You can put the corn in a kettle of cold water and bring it just to a boil. The corn should then be done.

SAUTÉED CORN

2 ears of corn per person

2 to 3 tablespoons of butter

Salt

Pepper

Husk the corn and remove the silk. With a sharp knife, cut the kernels off, slicing down from the stem to the tip of each ear. Melt the butter in a skillet, add the kernels and cook gently for 5 minutes, stirring frequently to be sure the corn does not stick. Season to taste with salt and freshly ground black pepper.

With cream: Just before the corn is cooked, add ½ cup of heavy cream and heat it through.

With green pepper: Use an extra tablespoon of butter and cook 1 green pepper cut in thin strips before you add the corn. Let the pepper cook gently for 3 to 4 minutes and then add the kernels. Proceed as above.

With green onion: Use an extra tablespoon of butter and cook 4 chopped green onions before you add the corn. After the onions have cooked gently for 3 minutes, add the corn kernels and proceed as above.

Eggplant

This is the beautiful pear-shaped purple vegetable, often used as a decorative piece in a harvest display. I'm afraid many people buy it only for this purpose and never cook and eat it. Actually, it is a most versatile member of the vegetable family, for its flavor takes well to a variety of sauces and seasonings and it combines nicely with other foods.

Select the smaller eggplants; larger ones are apt to be less tasty. They should be firm, unblemished and shiny. About 1½ pounds will serve 4 persons.

This vegetable is usually peeled and sliced or cubed before cooking. It is fried, broiled or baked. For some reason, it is never boiled, maybe because it would look unappetizing.

SAUTÉED EGGPLANT (Serves 4)

1½ pounds of eggplant	**4 to 6 tablespoons of butter**
Flour	**2 tablespoons of olive oil**
Salt and pepper	

Peel the eggplant and cut it into slices ½ inch thick. Salt the slices and allow them to stand in a collander for at least a half hour to draw out the bitter juices. Drain and pat dry with paper towels. Dip each slice in flour seasoned with salt and freshly ground black pepper. Put enough butter and olive oil in a skillet to make a ¼-inch depth of hot fat. Sauté the eggplant slices until they are cooked through and browned on both sides. If you have a large number of slices, cook a few at a time and as they finish cooking put them in a casserole in a very low oven to keep warm.

VARIATIONS

Cheesed: Sprinkle each slice of eggplant lightly with grated Parmesan cheese a minute or two before it is done. Or arrange sautéed eggplant slices in a shallow, flame-proof dish, sprinkle with grated Parmesan cheese and run under the broiler to brown.

With barbecue sauce: Serve sautéed eggplant slices with a spicy barbecue sauce (page 353).

With tomato and onion: Serve sautéed eggplant slices topped with grilled tomato and sautéed onion slices.

BROILED EGGPLANT

Prepare eggplant as for sautéing (page 409). After dipping the slices in seasoned flour, arrange them on an oiled or buttered baking sheet, dot liberally with butter and run them under the broiler flame to brown. When they are brown, turn, butter the other side of each slice and return to the broiler to finish cooking. Serve as you would sautéed eggplant.

PIQUANT BROILED EGGPLANT (Serves 4)

1½ pounds of eggplant   **1 cup of Vinaigrette Sauce**

Peel the eggplant and cut it into ½-inch slices. Salt and drain, as for Sautéed Eggplant. Place the Vinaigrette Sauce (page 343) in a deep bowl and put the slices in the sauce. Let them stand for 2 or 3 hours, turning frequently to be sure they are evenly bathed. Arrange the slices on an oiled baking sheet and broil until brown on top. Then turn and finish cooking on the other side. Serve plain or with a sharp barbecue sauce.

BAKED EGGPLANT (Serves 4)

1½ pounds of eggplant
2 large onions
Flour
Salt and pepper
½ cup of olive oil or oil and
 butter mixed

½ cup of fine, toasted
 crumbs
½ cup of grated Parmesan
 cheese

Peel the eggplant and cut into ½-inch slices. Salt and drain, as for Sautéed Eggplant (page 409). Peel and slice the onions. Dip the sliced eggplant in flour seasoned with salt and freshly ground black pepper. Heat oil (or oil and butter mixed) in a large skillet, brown the eggplant on both sides and sauté the onion slices.

Oil or grease a casserole and place a layer of the browned eggplant in the bottom; add a layer of onion; season with salt and pepper; and continue alternating layers of the two vegetables until they are used up. Top with crumbs and grated Parmesan cheese, mixed. Pour the oil or butter left in the skillet over the casserole and add more if it seems to dry. Bake in a 350° oven for 20 to 25 minutes, or until brown and bubbly.

EGGPLANT AND TOMATO CASSEROLE (Serves 4)

1½ pounds of eggplant
1 large onion (or 2
 medium)
2 medium fresh tomatoes
Flour
Salt and pepper
Olive oil, or oil and butter
 mixed

1 teaspoon of basil
½ cup of fine, toasted
 crumbs
½ cup of grated Parmesan
 cheese

Peel the eggplant and cut into ½-inch slices. Salt and drain, as for Sautéed Eggplant (page 409). Peel and slice the onion and tomatoes. Dip the eggplant slices in flour seasoned with salt and pepper and sauté quickly in hot oil, or oil and butter mixed, until browned on both sides. Sauté the onion slices quickly.

Oil or grease a casserole and put a layer of the browned eggplant slices in the bottom. Top with a layer of onion and then a layer of sliced tomatoes. Season with salt, pepper and a pinch of basil. Repeat the layers until all the vegetables are used. Top with crumbs and grated Parmesan cheese mixed, and pour the oil and butter from the skillet over the casserole. Add more oil or butter if it seems too dry. Bake in a 350° oven for 20 to 30 minutes, or until browned on top and done through.

FRENCH-FRIED EGGPLANT (Serves 4)

1½ pounds of eggplant	Fine bread crumbs
Flour	Oil for deep frying
2 or more eggs, beaten	Salt and pepper

Peel the eggplant and cut it into slices ¾ inch thick. Then cut each slice into strips about ¾ inch wide. Salt and drain, as for Sautéed Eggplant. Beat the eggs lightly. Heat oil in a deep fryer to 380°. Dip each eggplant strip into flour, then into the beaten egg and finally into fine crumbs. Fry, a few at a time, in the hot fat until golden brown. Recheck the heat of the fat after frying each batch of eggplant strips. Drain the cooked eggplant on absorbent paper and season with salt and freshly ground black pepper.

EGGPLANT À LA GRECQUE (Serves 4)

1½ pounds of eggplant	½ teaspoon of pepper
⅓ cup of olive oil	2 sprigs of parsley
2 tablespoons of wine vinegar	Pinch of thyme or oregano
1 clove of garlic, chopped	Water
½ teaspoon of salt	

Peel the eggplant and cut it into 1-inch cubes. Salt and drain, as for Sautéed Eggplant. Mix the oil, vinegar, chopped garlic and seasonings with enough water to cover the eggplant cubes. Before adding the cubes, bring this mixture to a boil, lower the flame and simmer for 5 minutes to blend the flavors. Then add the cubed eggplant and cook gently until tender. This will take about 10 minutes. Remove from the stove and let the eggplant cool in the liquid. Drain thoroughly and chill.

This may be served as an appetizer or salad. Add Vinaigrette Sauce if you like.

RATATOUILLE (Serves 4)

⅓ cup of olive oil

1 medium onion, chopped very fine

1 clove of garlic, chopped very fine

1½-pound eggplant, peeled and cubed

2 medium-sized zucchini, sliced with peel on

3 large peppers, cut in strips

Salt and pepper

Basil

6 ripe tomatoes, peeled and seeded, or 1 16-oz. of solid-pack tomatoes

Sauté the onion and garlic until soft. Add the eggplant (which has been salted and drained, as for Sautéed Eggplant) and zucchini; toss well. Then add the pepper strips, salt and pepper to taste and the basil. Simmer, covered, until the vegetables are soft. Add tomatoes and allow them to cook down with the vegetables until the mixture is thick and well blended.

Serve hot or chilled, with additional oil and lemon juice.

MOUSSAKA—See page 262.

Leeks

This vegetable is not well known in America and is hard to find in the markets in some areas. Its scarcity is regrettable for leeks are the most elegant of the onion family and essential in many a fine dish—the popular cold soup Vichyssoise, for example. You will recognize them by their resemblance to the green onion, or scallion, though leeks are much larger. They vary in size from ½ inch in diameter to about 1½ inches. Size does not affect the taste, but it's wise to buy those that are uniform in thickness so that they will all cook in the same amount of time.

Besides being delicious in Vichyssoise and other soups and stews, leeks are a delicate and tasty vegetable, served hot or cold. Allow 3 to 4 leeks (depending on size) per person.

BOILED LEEKS (Serves 4)

12 to 16 leeks	**4 tablespoons of melted**
Water to cover	**butter**
Salt and pepper	

Cut off the root ends and all but 1 inch of the green tops. Peel the thin filmy skin from the white and then soak the leeks thoroughly in cold water for 20 minutes or more. Run water into the tops and down through the stalks to be sure they are well washed. Leeks can be very gritty, and if any soil lurks inside, they will not be tasty.

In a large kettle, put enough water to cover the leeks and add 1 teaspoon of salt. Bring to a boil and add the vegetable. Cook uncovered until the green tops are tender when pierced with a fork. This will take 15 to 20 minutes, depending on the thickness of the leeks. Drain thoroughly, season to taste with salt and freshly ground black pepper and dress with melted butter.

VARIATIONS

With Hollandaise: Serve with Hollandaise Sauce (page 351).

Creamed: Serve with Rich Cream Sauce (page 349).

Cheesed: Drain the leeks, arrange them in a flat flame-proof dish, top with buttered crumbs and grated Parmesan cheese and run under the broiler flame to brown.

LEEKS À LA GRECQUE

Cook leeks in an à la grecque sauce (see Eggplant à la Grecque, page 412) and let them cool in the sauce. Drain and chill. Serve as an appetizer or salad course.

COLD LEEKS VINAIGRETTE

Boil leeks (above), drain and cool. Soak in a Vinaigrette Sauce (page 343) for an hour or so and serve on a bed of greens as a salad course.

Lettuce

Most people think lettuce and similar greens are used only for salads or garnishes. Yet certain varieties, when properly cooked, become delicately flavored hot vegetables. Shop for the following greens:

Boston lettuce: This comes in rather soft heads of smooth, tender leaves. It is more delicate than most greens and is easily bruised, but generally this affects only the outside.

Cos or romaine: This is a hardy lettuce with firm, oblong leaves loosely headed into long bunches. It ships well and is crisp.

Leaf lettuce: This tender delicacy, as its name implies, does not "head." It comes in separate leaves.

Escarole: This green comes in flared bunches. The leaves are long, firm and smooth with rippling edges.

Belgian endive: The small, elongated budlike bunches of this elegant vegetable are as beautiful as they are tasty. The leaves are flat and firmly folded together. They are white, shading to pale green at the tips.

Here are ways to use these greens as hot vegetables.

BRAISED LETTUCE (OR ESCAROLE)

Any of the above greens, except leaf lettuce, may be used successfully in this recipe. Cook Boston lettuce and Belgian endive whole. If you are using cos or romaine, remove the coarse outer leaves and save for salad. Cook the center of the head whole or halved, depending on size. To cook escarole, trim off the coarse outer leaves and cut the head into serving-size sections.

Greens for 4 servings	**Salt**
4 tablespoons of butter	**Pepper**
3/4 cup of stock or broth	

Wash the greens thoroughly, making sure all of the grit is removed. Separate the leaves slightly, pushing them apart to let the water run between them. Remove outer coarse or crushed leaves. Drain thoroughly and dry on paper towels. Melt the butter in a large skillet and sauté the greens in it quickly over fairly high heat. Add the stock or broth (this can be made with hot water and a bouillon cube), cover the pan and simmer gently just until the greens are wilted and tender. Season to taste with salt and freshly ground black pepper.

BRAISED BELGIAN ENDIVE

Allow 1 or 2 endives per serving. Split the endives lengthwise. Lay them flat in a shallow pan, add broth to just cover, and simmer until tender, turning once. Remove the endives, and reduce the liquid over high heat until it is almost a glaze. Stir in a little butter and return the endives to the pan for another minute to heat through. Salt and pepper to taste.

WILTED LETTUCE (Serves 4)

For this recipe, use any of the above greens except Belgian endive. Break the greens into bite-size pieces, as for tossed green salad.

2 medium-sized heads of Boston lettuce or substitute 1 medium head of romaine, 1 medium head of escarole or the equivalent of leaf lettuce	**6 slices of bacon** **$^1/_3$ cup of mild wine vinegar** **Salt** **Pepper**

Wash the greens thoroughly and break them into bite-size pieces. Cut the bacon in small squares and fry it until brown and crisp. Remove the bacon bits; add to the remaining fat the vinegar and salt and freshly ground black pepper to taste. When the mixture boils, add the greens, tossing them in the hot liquid just until wilted and hot through. For Boston or leaf lettuce this will only take a minute or two. Escarole and romaine, having firmer leaves, will take a little longer. Serve with the crumbled bacon bits sprinkled on top.

VARIATION

You may add chopped green onions, a grated onion or 2 tablespoons of chopped chives to the hot liquid before you toss the greens in it.

Mushrooms

Like the onion, the mushroom is not only delectable by itself but also valuable for flavoring soups, stews, stuffings and sauces. It is one of the most elegant garnishes for meat, fish or vegetable dishes, and raw, sliced mushrooms turn a plain tossed salad into something very special.

Not too many years ago it was difficult to buy fresh mushrooms in some parts of the country, but "mushroom farms" have sprung up all over and mushrooms are now widely distributed. They come in sizes ranging from about 1 inch across up to huge ones 4 to 5 inches across. The size has no effect on the flavor. Freshness does. Buy mushrooms that are firm and show no signs of deterioration. Whereas markets used to sell only the white button-type, still widely available, nowadays shoppers are offered a choice of shiitake, oyster, Black Forest, cremoni, and other types. These can be used in any of the recipes given here. A pound will serve 4 persons as a vegetable; half that amount will do for garnishing.

Do not peel mushrooms or soak them in water. Simply wipe them off with a damp cloth. Much of the flavor is in the skin and if you wash them vigorously, you will lose part of the goodness. If, by chance, you have old mushrooms with dark wrinkled skins, then peel them. They will be tough if you don't. Do not discard the stems; though not as tender as the caps, they have excellent flavor. If you are serving guests and wish to use only the caps, for elegance's sake, break off the stems and save them for the next day; or chop them and add to sauces, stuffings or soups. In most cases, it is preferable to cook the mushrooms, stem and all. If you are slicing them, slice the long way right through the cap and stem.

SAUTÉED MUSHROOMS (Serves 4)

This is a rich and tasty dish and makes a fine main course for a luncheon or supper. It is also an excellent accompaniment to steak, or any other beef cut, and to roast or broiled fowl.

1 pound of mushrooms	**Salt and pepper**
5 tablespoons of butter	

Wipe the mushrooms with a damp cloth and cut them through lengthwise, stems and all, in thin slices. Or cook them whole. Melt the butter in a skillet, add the mushrooms and cook over a medium flame until brown and tender. Stir occasionally to be sure they are cooking evenly. The mushrooms should be done in 6 to 10 minutes. Season to taste with salt and freshly ground black pepper and serve on buttered toast.

VARIATIONS

With bacon: Garnish with crisp bacon curls.

With herbs and cream: Just before the mushrooms are done, add 1 tablespoon of chopped parsley, 1 tablespoon of chopped chives (or tops of green onion) and ¼ cup of heavy cream. Heat through, season to taste and serve on buttered toast.

With sour cream: Before you remove the mushrooms from the skillet, add 1 cup of sour cream. Heat through, but do not boil or the cream will curdle. Season to taste and serve on toast.

BROILED MUSHROOMS (Serves 4)

For this recipe, use the caps only, saving the stems for later use. Allow 4 mushrooms caps per person for a first course.

16 medium-sized   **Salt and pepper**
   mushrooms
Melted butter

Wipe the caps with a damp cloth and arrange them, cap side up, on a buttered baking sheet. Brush them well with melted butter, season to taste with salt and freshly ground black pepper and broil for 8 to 10 minutes, or until tender when pierced with a fork. Serve on hot buttered toast as a first course.

VARIATION

With cheese: Sprinkle the caps with grated Parmesan cheese during the last minute of broiling.

STUFFED MUSHROOMS (Serves 4)

For this recipe, buy good-sized mushrooms, 2 to 3 inches across, so the caps will be large enough for stuffing. Allow 2 per person for a first course at dinner, or 4 per person for a main course at luncheon.

16 mushrooms	1 tablespoon of chopped
Butter (about ¼ pound)	chives (or minced onion)
½ cup of fine dry bread crumbs	Salt and pepper
	Parmesan cheese
2 eggs, lightly beaten	Broth
1 tablespoons of chopped parsley	

Remove the stems of the mushrooms, scrape them and chop them fairly fine. Wipe the mushroom caps with a damp cloth. Heat 2 or 3 tablespoons of butter in a skillet and sauté the chopped mushroom stems lightly. Mix these with the bread crumbs, eggs, parsley, chives or onions and ½ teaspoon each of salt and freshly ground black pepper. Brush the mushroom caps with melted butter and arrange them, cup side up, on a buttered baking dish. Fill each cup with some of the stuffing, sprinkle with grated Parmesan cheese (or use Switzerland Swiss), dot well with butter and add a little broth to the pan to keep them from sticking and burning. Bake in a 375° oven for 15 to 20 minutes, or until tender when pierced with a fork. Baste during the cooking with additional butter to keep the mushrooms moist.

VARIATIONS

With seafood: Substitute crabmeat, chopped shrimp or lobster meat for the mushroom stems in the stuffing.

With meat: Substitute any leftover meat, chopped, for the mushroom stems.

With wine: Put a little white wine in the baking dish and baste the mushrooms with white wine during the cooking.

MUSHROOMS STUFFED WITH SNAILS (Serves 4 to 6)

4 dozen mushroom caps, 1
inch in diameter

4 dozen canned snails,
rinsed under cold water

4 to 6 tablespoons butter

Snail butter

Chopped parsley

For the Snail butter:

¼ pound slightly softened
butter

3 tablespoons shallots, finely
chopped

1 to 2 tablespoons puréed
garlic, to taste

Salt

Freshly ground black pepper

First make the Snail Butter: Cream the softened butter with the shallots, garlic, ¼ cup of chopped parsley, and salt and pepper to taste. Sauté the mushroom caps in butter until just cooked through. Arrange on a baking sheet hollow side up. Coat the snails with the snail butter, and place one in each cap. Sprinkle with additional chopped parsley. Heat in a 450° for 10 minutes and serve immediately.

MUSHROOMS À LA GRECQUE

Buy small mushrooms and remove the stems. Wipe the caps with a damp cloth and cook gently in a sauce à la grecque (see Eggplant à la Grecque, page 412). Cool in the sauce and then drain and chill. Serve as an hors d'oeuvre.

Onions

The lowly onion is our best friend in the kitchen. Try cooking without it for one week and see how tasteless your food becomes. It is used in some form for every course except dessert. Besides being versatile, it comes in many varieties and has important near relatives: the leek, the shallot and garlic.

The common, medium-sized cooking onion with the dry, yellow skin is most often used for flavoring boiled dinners, broths, soups, stews and pot roasts. The larger, round, yellow onion, known as the Bermuda or Spanish onion, is milder, with a rather sweet flavor. This is popular, sliced and broiled, with steak and hamburger, or served raw with sliced tomatoes. The red-skinned onion, called Italian onion, has colorful red streaks through the meat. It is mild and a good choice for salad or garnish on cold platters. Then there is the tiny white onion with a dry skin. This is the choice for boiling and serving as a vegetable. Fresh green onions, or scallions, as they are sometimes called, are excellent as a hot vegetable, alone or in combination with other fresh garden vegetables, as well as raw in salads or plain with salt.

The recipes to follow include all these onion varieties. The type of onion recommended for each dish is specified.

BOILED WHITE ONIONS (Serves 4)

Buy the tiny white onions and allow 4 or 5 per person, and even more if your family loves onions.

16 to 20 white onions	**Pepper**
Water	**4 tablespoons of butter**
Salt	

Cut off the two ends of the onions and peel off the dry outer skin. Plunge into cold water until ready to cook. (If your eyes water while you peel onions, try doing this job while holding the onion under running water.)

In a kettle put enough water to cover the onions and add 1 teaspoon of salt. Bring it to a boil, add the onions, cover the pan and cook until the onions are just tender when pierced with a fork. Do not overcook or they will turn mushy and fall apart. Cooking time will be about 15 to 20 minutes. Drain them well, season to taste with salt and freshly ground black pepper and pour melted butter over them.

VARIATIONS

Creamed: Serve with a Rich Cream Sauce (page 349).

With cheese: Arrange the boiled onions in a baking dish, dot liberally with butter and sprinkle with grated Parmesan, Switzerland Swiss or cheddar cheese. Run under the broiler flame to melt the cheese.

ONIONS STEAMED IN BUTTER (Serves 4)

16 to 20 small white onions   **Salt**
4 to 6 tablespoons of butter   **Pepper**

Prepare the onions for cooking according to the directions for Boiled White Onions (page 421). In a heavy skillet, with a tight-fitting lid, melt the butter. Arrange the onions in the butter, season them to taste with salt and freshly ground black pepper, cover and steam gently over a low heat until they are just tender. This will take a little longer than boiling.

VARIATION

A few minutes before the onions are done, sprinkle them with grated Parmesan cheese.

GREEN ONIONS STEAMED IN BUTTER (Serves 4)

20 to 25 tiny green onions   **Salt**
4 to 6 tablespoons of   **Pepper**
    butter

Buy bunches of tiny green onions, allowing about 5 or 6 onions per person.

Cut the bunches apart, trim off the root ends of the onions and trim the green tops, leaving about 4 to 5 inches of green on each onion. Remove any outer layer of skin that seems tough. Wash thoroughly. Melt the butter in a heavy skillet with a tight lid, arrange the onions in the butter and season to taste with salt and freshly ground black pepper. Cover and steam gently until the onions are just tender. This will take about 10 minutes.

GLAZED ONIONS (Serves 4)

16 to 20 small white onions   **Pepper**
4 to 5 tablespoons of   **Sugar**
    butter
Salt

Clean the onions as for Boiled White Onions (page 421). Melt the butter in a heavy skillet and sauté the onions quickly, letting them color a bit. Cover and finish cooking over a low heat. Just before the onions are done, sprinkle them lightly with a little sugar (about $1\frac{1}{2}$ to 2 teaspoons is ample) and cook them uncovered, shaking the pan to let the sugar glaze the onions and brown them evenly. Season to taste with salt and pepper.

SAUTÉED ONIONS (Serves 4)

The large Bermuda or Spanish onions are best for this cooking method, although any of the other varieties of dry onions may be used. Allow about 3 large onions for 4 persons. If you use the regular yellow-skinned cooking onions, allow 1 per person.

3 Bermuda onions	**Salt**
5 tablespoons of butter	**Pepper**

Cut off the ends of the onions and remove the dry outer skin. Cut them in thin slices and soak in water with 1 teaspoon of salt added. Let them stand for $\frac{1}{2}$ hour. Melt the butter in a skillet. Drain the onion slices and dry them on paper towels. Then sauté them in the hot butter gently until tender and delicately colored. This will take 10 to 15 minutes. Stir them frequently to be sure they are not sticking to the pan and to cook them evenly. Season to taste with salt and freshly ground black pepper.

GRILLED ONIONS

These are very good with steak or hamburger. Use Bermuda onions and allow $\frac{1}{2}$ onion per person. Cut off the ends of the onions, peel off the dry outer skin and cut them in slices $\frac{1}{4}$ inch thick. Grease a broiling rack and arrange the slices on it. Season to taste with salt and freshly ground black pepper and brush well with the melted butter. Cook under the broiler flame or over charcoal until lightly browned. Do not turn. These grilled onion slices will be slightly crunchy and not quite cooked through. But with a hearty meat course they are better at this stage.

FRENCH-FRIED ONIONS (Serves 4 to 6)

4 Bermuda onions	**Oil for deep frying**
Milk	**Salt and pepper**
Flour	

Use the large Bermuda onions for French-frying.

Cut off the ends of the onions, peel off the outer skin and cut them into slices ½ inch thick. Gently push the slices in the middle to separate them into rings. Heat fat or oil in a deep fryer to 380°. Dip each onion ring in milk and then in flour. Drop a few at a time into the fryer and cook until lightly browned and crisp. This will take about 5 minutes. Recheck the temperature of the fat between each batch of onion rings to be sure it stays near 380°. Drain the cooked onions on absorbent paper and season to taste with salt and freshly ground black pepper.

BAKED ONIONS (Serves 4)

4 onions	**Butter**
½ cup of beef broth or bouillon	**Grated Switzerland Swiss or Parmesan cheese**
Salt and pepper	

Allow 1 medium-sized Bermuda onion or red Italian onion per person.

Cut off the ends of the onions and peel off the dry outer skin. Arrange them in a buttered casserole and add the broth or bouillon. (This can be made with hot water and a bouillon cube.) Sprinkle lightly with salt and freshly ground black pepper and dot liberally with butter. Cover the casserole and bake in a 350° oven for about 1 hour, or until the onions are tender when pierced with a fork. Add more broth to the pan if the liquid evaporates too fast. When the onions are done, remove the casserole from the oven, take off the cover and sprinkle the onions with cheese (grated Parmesan, Switzerland Swiss or sharp cheddar) and run them under the broiler or return to the oven to melt the cheese.

Parsnips

This is one of the most neglected and most maligned of vegetables, though why, I don't understand. Properly cooked they are a very satisfying vegetable, and puréed they are my favorite Thanksgiving vegetable. Despite their poor reputation they are available in the market the year round.

BOILED PARSNIPS

You will need 2½ to 3 pounds of parsnips for 4 persons. Trim and brush them. Boil in their skins in salted water 20 to 40 minutes, depending on their size, or until just tender. Drain and cool, then peel. Cut into serving pieces. Melt 4 tablespoons of butter in a pan, add the parsnips, and cook over low heat until hot through. Sprinkle with salt and pepper to taste.

PURÉED PARSNIPS (Serves 4)

3 pounds parsnips	**¼ pound melted butter**
1 teaspoon salt	**¼ cup Madeira**
1 teaspoon sugar	**Buttered breadcrumbs**

Boil the parsnips as directed above. When cool enough to handle, peel them and put through a food mill or purée in a food processor. You should have 2½ to 3 cups of purée. Add the rest of the ingredients, except for the breadcrumbs, and whip thoroughly. Put into a 1-quart baking dish, sprinkle with the buttered breadcrumbs and bake at 350° 25 to 35 minutes. Serve with roast turkey, chicken or beef.

Peas

According to a cookbook published in the early nineteenth century, green peas must be quite young, picked early in the day while the morning dew is still on them, kept in a cool place and shelled just before cooking. This is still the best advice on the subject. Of course, those of us who do not have green peas growing at our back doors must forgo the pleasure of picking them while the morning dew is still on them, but we can select the freshest and youngest when we buy.

Look for small, shiny pods (never buy peas already shelled) and break open a pod to see if the peas inside are tiny and young. Nibble one. It should be tender and sweet. Don't buy peas with faded or discolored pods, or pods with such large peas inside that they are almost bursting. Such peas are too old or mature and will be tough and mealy.

Keep peas unshelled in your refrigerator until you are ready to cook them and don't soak them in water after they are shelled. They lose flavor. Cook in as small amount of water as possible and for as short a time as possible.

Two pounds of peas in the shell will serve 4 persons. Don't try to stretch them with carrots. This is a poor combination.

BOILED GREEN PEAS (Serves 4)

2 pounds of unshelled peas
1¹/₂ to 2 cups of water
Salt

Pepper
4 tablespoons of melted butter

Shell the peas just before cooking and do not soak them in water. Bring a small amount of unsalted water (1¹/₂ cups should be enough, but certainly not more than 2 cups) to a boil. Peas should not be drowned in water; in fact, they need not be completely covered. Add the peas to the boiling water and cook uncovered until just barely tender when pierced with a fork. This will take no more than 10 minutes for very young peas and about 5 minutes longer for larger peas. If the peas are overly mature, no amount of cooking will make them tender. Drain as soon as they are done, season to taste with salt and freshly ground black pepper and pour melted butter over them.

VARIATIONS

With onions: Combine cooked peas with tiny white onions boiled until just tender. Season with salt and pepper and pour melted butter over them.

With mushrooms: Combine cooked peas with mushrooms sautéed in butter and season to taste with salt and pepper.

With herbs: Mix chopped chives and parsley with the melted butter before you pour it over the cooked peas.

FRENCH STEAMED PEAS (Serves 4)

This French method for cooking young green peas preserves their fresh flavor and bright color. It takes longer than boiling, but the results are worth the extra time and trouble.

2 pounds of unshelled peas	Salt
Several large outside lettuce leaves	Pepper
4 tablespoons of butter	

Shell the peas just before cooking. In a large skillet with a tight-fitting lid put 1 tablespoon of butter. Over this spread 2 or 3 large outside lettuce leaves, well washed with a bit of the water still clinging to them. Heap the peas on top, add the other three tablespoons of butter in small pieces and cover with more lettuce leaves. Put a tight lid on the pan and cook over high heat until the butter is bubbly hot. Then lower the heat and steam very gently just until the peas are tender. This should take about 15 minutes. Discard the lettuce, season the peas with salt and pepper and serve piping hot.

VARIATIONS

With green onions: Add four finely chopped little green onions to the pan with the peas.

With herbs: Stir 1 tablespoon of chopped parsley and 1 tablespoon of chopped chives into the peas after they have finished cooking.

PETITS POIS

These tiny canned peas, imported from France, make an elegant vegetable dish. An American firm also markets canned petits pois, put up in Le Sueur, Minnesota, and the product is just as good as the imported variety.

Prepare petits pois by simply heating them, or flavor with any of the additions suggested for fresh peas (see above). Petit pois are also available frozen.

SNOW PEAS (CHINESE PEAS) (Serves 4)

These pod peas are cooked and eaten pod and all. Allow 1 pound for 4 persons.

| 1 pound of snow peas | Butter |
| Salted water or broth to cover | |

Wash the peas well and remove any stems. Heat salted water, chicken or meat broth (enough to cover the peas) until boiling. Add the peas and simmer gently for 5 to 7 minutes, or until tender. Drain. If you cook the peas in seasoned broth, they will need no additional seasoning. Simply dress them with a little melted butter, if you like. If you cook them in water, add salt to taste to the cooked peas and dress with butter.

VARIATIONS

With almonds: Toss blanched, slivered almonds in a little hot butter until they are heated through but not too brown and crisp. Mix these with the snow peas.

With chicken: Cook snow peas in chicken broth and mix with bits of cooked chicken.

SUGAR SNAP PEAS

Sugar snap peas, a recent arrival in American markets, have both edible pods and fully developed peas. They should be cooked for only a few minutes in rapidly boiling salted water.

Peppers

The beautiful bright green, red or yellow peppers, called bell peppers, are more often appreciated for their appearance than for their flavor. We encounter them too often only in decorative vegetable arrangements, as a garnish on salads or cold meat platters or as containers for hash made from leftover meats. Try using them as a flavoring in soups and stews. You will find their delicate, sweet tang is a great addition. As a hot vegetable they are a welcome change and go exceptionally well with steak, hamburger, and various lamb dishes, such as shish kebab.

Buy fresh-looking, plump peppers with shiny skins. As a vegetable, allow 1 large pepper per person. If you plan to stuff them, buy peppers of uniform size.

SAUTÉED PEPPERS (Serves 4)

4 large peppers	**Salt**
4 tablespoons of butter or butter and olive oil mixed	**Pepper**

Wash the peppers, cut them open and remove the seeds, the white membrane and the core. Cut them into strips about ½ inch wide. Heat the butter, or oil and butter, in a skillet and add the pepper strips. Cook gently, stirring occasionally, to be sure the pepper strips cook evenly and do not stick. Cook until tender. This will take about 10 to 15 minutes. Season to taste with salt and freshly ground black pepper.

Serve these sautéed peppers with steak or other broiled meats.

VARIATIONS

With green onion: Add 4 tiny green onions, finely cut, to the pan and sauté them with the pepper strips.

With garlic: Add a finely chopped clove of garlic to the pan to sauté with the pepper strips.

With tomato: Cook a chopped clove of garlic with the peppers, and 3 or 4 minutes before they are done add 2 peeled, seeded and chopped fresh tomatoes and a tiny pinch of basil. Cover the pan and finish cooking until the peppers are tender and the tomatoes cooked down. Season to taste with salt and pepper.

With oil and vinegar: Cook any of the above combinations in olive oil instead of oil and butter. Just before done add a dash or two of wine vinegar. Season to taste with salt and freshly ground black pepper and serve hot or cold as a relish with broiled meats.

BROILED PEPPER SLICES

Cut peppers through into ½-inch slices. Remove the seeds and core. Brush with oil or butter and grill over charcoal or in the broiler for several minutes. Season to taste with salt and freshly ground black pepper and serve with steak or hamburger.

GRILLED (ROASTED) PEPPERS

I find the skin of most bell peppers, either raw or cooked, rather disagreeable, so I prefer to grill my peppers before using them, which can be done on a charcoal grill, under the broiler or over a gas flame. Lay the whole peppers on the grill or on a broiling pan close to to the heat (or hold over a gas flame on a long fork), and cook until the skin blackens on each side. Then carefully scrape off the skin with a knife. It should come away easily. The flesh of the pepper will have cooked during the grilling. Remove the stem and seeds, and cut into strips or quarters. Use in any dish calling for cooked bell peppers, or serve as an appetizer, dressed with Vinaigrette Sauce and garnished with anchovy fillets and chopped parsley.

STUFFED PEPPERS

1 large pepper per person
Stuffing
Butter

Fine bread crumbs
Grated Parmesan cheese
Broth or stock

Use the stuffing suggested for Stuffed Artichokes or for Stuffed Mushrooms (page 380 or page 419), and allow $\frac{1}{2}$ to $\frac{3}{4}$ cup per pepper, depending on the size of the peppers. Cut the tops from the peppers and scoop out the seeds and core. Fill a kettle with enough water to cover the peppers and bring to a boil. Add the peppers and cook for 2 or 3 minutes to soften them slightly. Remove from the water and drain thoroughly. Arrange them in a buttered baking dish or casserole and fill each with the stuffing. Top with fine crumbs, plenty of butter and a liberal sprinkle of grated Parmesan cheese. Add a little broth or stock (this can be made with hot water and a bouillon cube) to the pan. Put in enough liquid to keep the peppers from sticking. Bake in a 350° oven for about 30 minutes, basting with the pan juices from time to time. When the peppers are brown on top and cooked through, remove them to a hot platter. Serve plain or with a tomato sauce or barbecue sauce.

Potatoes

It might be said that the potato is the "basic black dress" of the vegetable family. It can be served plain or dressed up for elegance. Like good bread, it has an unobtrusive flavor and hearty quality that make it welcome at all meals. It goes with a wide variety of seasonings and flavorings and can be cooked by any method.

When you buy, select the potato best suited to your purpose. Baking potatoes are larger than average and elongated in shape. They have a fine, mealy texture when roasted or baked in the oven. Those from Idaho are considered outstanding mainly because of their gigantic size, but baking potatoes from other states cook just as well. The regular, or Irish, potato, smaller and rounder, is less expensive. It is used for general cooking purposes: boiling, mashing, frying, sautéing, and in soups and stews. Actually, it bakes well too, and is fine roasted with meat in the oven. New potatoes come in two colors: some have reddish skins; others are pale brown. They taste the same. Red-skinned potatoes are popular because they add a spot of color to the table. New potatoes range in size from tiny ones, no bigger than walnuts, on up to those the size of regular Irish potatoes. The smallest are elegant cooked whole with their skins left on and bathed liberally with butter. Larger new potatoes are good sliced and sautéed and are the best choice for potato salad. New potatoes do not bake well.

Allow 1 baking potato per person, or if they are extra large, ½ potato will be ample. The usual portion of the regular potato for boiling is 1 or 2, depending upon size. New potatoes vary so in size that you must judge for yourself the amount you need. Certainly you will need at least 4 and sometimes 8 of the tiny ones for a serving.

Whenever possible, cook potatoes with their skins on. Much of the food value lies just under the skin and is lost if peeled away. After cooking, the skins will slip off easily, if you prefer serving them without their jackets. Wash potatoes thoroughly and scrub them with a stiff brush to remove any dirt or soil. If you do peel them, plunge them into cold water until you cook them, to keep them from turning brown.

BOILED POTATOES (Serves 4)

Good boiled potatoes are dry and mealy, not soggy. Sogginess comes from overcooking, not drying out the potatoes after they are drained, or letting them stand in a tightly covered dish where steam can accumulate. Be sure to use potatoes of uniform size or cut them into uniform pieces. Do not peel until after boiling unless the skin has many blemishes. Allow 1 large or 2 medium-sized potatoes per serving.

4 to 8 potatoes	**Salt and pepper**
Water to cover	**Butter**

Wash the potatoes well and scrub them with a stiff brush. If they are large, or if they are not of uniform size, cut them into uniform pieces. Do not cut them too small. The potatoes should be halved or quartered. If the skins have blemishes, peel the potatoes and plunge them into cold water until ready to cook.

In a large kettle, put enough water to cover the potatoes and add 1 teaspoon of salt. Bring this to a boil, add the potatoes, cover the pan and cook in boiling water just until tender when pierced with a fork. This will take about 20 to 25 minutes. Do not let them overcook and get watery. Drain the potatoes at once, sprinkle with salt and freshly ground black pepper and put back on the stove over very low heat for a few minutes to dry out and get mealy. Serve in their skins with plenty of melted butter.

VARIATIONS

Peeled: If you like the skins removed, peel the potatoes after they are drained, season with salt and pepper and put back on the stove to dry and fluff. Pour melted butter over them and serve.

With parsley: Add 4 tablespoons of chopped parsley to the pan while the potatoes are drying; or add the parsley to the butter.

With chives and parsley: Add 2 tablespoons of chopped chives and 2 tablespoons of chopped parsley to the butter.

BOILED TINY NEW POTATOES

4 to 8 potatoes per person   **Salt and pepper**
    (depending on size)   **Butter**
Water

Wash the potatoes well and cook them whole with their skins on in boiling, salted water to cover. Place a lid on the pan and cook until the potatoes are just tender. This will take 10 to 15 minutes. Do not overcook. Drain well and serve with plenty of salt, freshly ground black pepper and butter.

VARIATION

You may add chopped parsley, or chopped parsley and chives mixed, to the butter; or sprinkle over the potatoes after they are cooked and drained.

MASHED POTATOES (Serves 4)

4 to 8 potatoes   **4 tablespoons of butter**
Water to cover   **4 tablespoons of heated**
Salt   **cream or whole milk**
Pepper

Peel the potatoes, cut into uniform pieces and cook as for Boiled Potatoes (see page 431). When done, drain them thoroughly and put them through a ricer or mash with a potato masher. Return the potatoes to the pan, season to taste with salt and freshly ground black pepper and add the butter. Beat thoroughly with a wooden spoon or wire whisk. (Do not attempt to purée potatoes in a food processor; they become pasty.) Add the heated cream or milk a bit at a time and beat it in well. If the potatoes seem too stiff, add a little extra cream. Reheat over hot water and serve with an extra lump of butter on top.

VARIATIONS

With parsley: Add 4 tablespoons of chopped parsley to the potatoes after they have been mashed.

With chives: Add 2 tablespoons of chopped chives to the mashed potatoes and sprinkle chopped parsley on top when you serve them.

With bacon: Sprinkle the top of the mashed potatoes with crumbled crisp bacon.

With cheese: Sprinkle the top of the mashed potatoes with grated Parmesan or Switzerland Swiss cheese, dot liberally with butter and run under the broiler flame for a minute to brown.

MASHED POTATO PATTIES

Shape cold mashed potatoes into small patties. Dust these with flour and cook in butter until brown on both sides. Serve plain or with a sprinkling of chopped parsley.

BAKED POTATOES

1 baking potato per person   **Salt and pepper**
Butter or olive oil

Wash and scrub the potatoes. If they are extra large, they can be cut in half. Dry them and rub them well in oil or butter, and slit the top skin with a sharp knife for about ½ inch—just enough to let the steam escape as the potato cooks. Bake in a 375° oven until soft when pierced with a sharp fork. This will take from 30 minutes to an hour, depending on the size of the potatoes.

When they are done, remove them from the oven, split open the tops and add a good-sized lump of butter to each one. Season to taste with salt and freshly ground black pepper and serve with additional butter, salt and pepper.

VARIATIONS

With parsley: When the potatoes are done, slit them down the top and press the ends to spread the slit open. Scoop out the insides of the potatoes and put through a ricer or mash with a potato masher. Add 1 tablespoon of butter for each potato, salt and freshly ground black pepper to taste and 1 tablespoon of parsley for each potato. Blend well, heap back in the shells, dot with additional butter and return to the oven to heat through.

With chives: Follow directions for the first variation, but add 1 tablespoon of chives as well as the parsley for each potato.

Au gratin: Make either the parsley or the chive variation and sprinkle the top with grated Parmesan cheese and buttered crumbs. Reheat.

With grated cheese: Scoop out the insides of the potatoes, add butter, salt, pepper and 1 tablespoon of sharp, grated cheese for each potato. Return to the shells and top with a sprinkling of paprika. Reheat.

With sour cream: Serve plain baked potatoes with sour cream, salt, freshly ground black pepper and chopped chives; or scoop out the insides and blend with these ingredients. Return to the shells and reheat.

With bacon: Substitute crumbled crisp bacon for the chopped chives in any of the above variations.

SCALLOPED POTATOES (Serves 4)

4 medium potatoes	**Whole milk, milk and cream**
Butter	**mixed or broth**
Salt and pepper	

Butter a casserole well. Wash and peel the potatoes and cut them into thin slices. Put a layer of potato slices in the bottom of the casserole, season to taste with salt and freshly ground black pepper and dot liberally with butter. Continue the layers until all the potato is used up. Dot the top liberally with the butter and add just enough milk, milk and cream or broth to fill the casserole even with the top layer of potatoes. Cover and bake in a 375° oven for 30 minutes. Remove the cover and continue cooking until the potatoes are tender when pierced with a fork and the top is lightly browned.

With cheese: Sprinkle each layer with grated Parmesan or Switzerland Swiss cheese.

With chives and parsley: Sprinkle each layer with chopped herbs.

With onion: Top each layer of potato slices with a thin layer of sliced onions.

With ham: Top each layer of potatoes with a layer of chopped or ground ham; or top with layers or thinly sliced Canadian bacon.

SCALLOPED POTATOES AND CELERIAC—See page 404.

POTATOES ANNA (Serves 4)

4 medium potatoes	**Salt**
Butter	**Pepper**

Select a large, shallow baking dish or pie tin and butter it thoroughly. Wash the potatoes, peel them and slice them very thin. Arrange a layer of the potato slices on the bottom of the baking dish in an even pattern. If the dish is round, arrange the slices in a spiral. If it is square or oblong, arrange the slices in rows. Let them overlap just slightly. Season to taste with salt and freshly ground black pepper and spread with butter. Repeat the layers until all the potato slices are used. Top liberally with butter spread evenly. Bake in a 400° oven for 30 to 40 minutes, or until the potatoes are tender when tested with a fork or toothpick. Turn the baking dish upside down on a platter or large flat plate so the potatoes will come out crusty side up.

VARIATION

Potato Galette: This is a version of Potatoes Anna done on top of the stove. Use a heavy skillet and prepare the potatoes as in the recipe above. Cover and cook over low heat until the potatoes are tender.

OVEN-FRIED POTATOES (Serves 4)

4 medium potatoes	**Salt**
Bacon fat, beef drippings or butter	**Pepper**

Use a large, flat baking dish and grease it well with fat. Wash, peel and slice the potatoes. Put them in the baking dish, season to taste with salt and freshly ground black pepper and pour a little melted fat over them. Bake in a hot oven (400°) stirring occasionally to see that they cook evenly. Add extra fat, if needed. Test with a fork. They are done when they are brown and tender.

VARIATION

Cut the potatoes in long fingers, as for French-fried Potatoes.

FRIED POTATOES (Serves 4)

4 large potatoes	**Salt**
Butter, bacon fat or beef drippings	**Pepper**

Wash the potatoes, peel them and cut them in thin slices. Melt about 6 tablespoons of fat in a heavy skillet, add the potato slices and cook them over a medium flame. Turn the slices often with a spatula or pancake turner to be sure they cook and brown evenly, and season them to taste with salt and freshly ground black pepper as they cook. When all the potatoes are tender and browned around the edges, they are done.

VARIATIONS

Soft fried: Some people prefer a softer, less crisp fried potato. For this result, use only 4 tablespoons of fat, add the potato slices, salt and pepper and cover the pan. Cook over low heat for about 20 minutes. Then remove the cover, turn the heat up and brown the potatoes. These will be less bitey.

With green onions: Add 4 to 6 chopped small green onions to the pan to cook with the potatoes.

With sliced onions: Add 2 or 3 sliced onions to the pan to cook with the potatoes.

With parsley: Add 2 tablespoons of chopped parsley to the potatoes just before they finish cooking.

With parsley and chives: Add chopped parsley and chopped chives mixed during the last minute of cooking.

With cheese: Sprinkle with grated Parmesan cheese, grated Switzerland Swiss or grated sharp cheddar during the last 2 or 3 minutes of cooking.

FRIED OR SAUTÉED NEW POTATOES (Serves 4)

6 medium-sized new potatoes or 16 tiny ones	**Salt**
4 tablespoons of butter	**Pepper**

Wash the potatoes well but do not peel them. Slice medium-sized potatoes, or cut tiny ones in half. Melt the butter in a heavy skillet. Add the potatoes, season to taste with salt and freshly ground black pepper and cook over medium heat, stirring frequently to be sure they do not stick. When they are browned, crisp on the outside and tender, they are done.

VARIATION

Use any of the variations listed for Fried Potatoes (page 436).

NEW POTATOES STEAMED IN BUTTER (Serves 4)

16 small new potatoes	**Salt and pepper**
4 tablespoons of butter	

Wash the potatoes and trim a thin strip of the skin off around the middle of each potato. Melt the butter in a heavy skillet, add the whole potatoes, season to taste with salt and freshly ground black pepper and cover tightly. Steam the potatoes over very low heat until tender. Shake the pan occasionally to be sure the potatoes are not sticking and are cooking evenly. Serve with a sprinkling of chopped parsley or chopped chives and parsley mixed.

FRIED COOKED POTATOES (HOME-FRIED POTATOES)

1 or 2 cooked potatoes per person	**Pepper**
	Salt
1 tablespoon of bacon fat or butter	

Peel the potatoes (if they have been boiled with their skins on) and cut them in medium slices. Melt the fat in a skillet, add the potatoes, season to taste with salt and freshly ground black pepper and cook quickly. Turn the slices to brown them on both sides. These fried potatoes will only take a few minutes since the potatoes have already been cooked.

When they are hot through and thoroughly browned, they are done. Serve plain or garnished with bacon bits and chopped parsley.

VARIATION

Lyonnaise Potatoes: Sauté 2 sliced onions in butter or bacon fat and add them to the fried potatoes a few minutes before the potatoes are done. Blend the onions in with the potato slices.

HASHED BROWN POTATOES (Serves 4)

6 to 8 boiled potatoes   **4 tablespoons of bacon fat**
Salt and pepper   **or butter**

Peel the boiled potatoes and cut them into very small cubes or chop them. Season to taste with salt and freshly ground black pepper. Melt the fat in a skillet, add the potatoes and press them down firmly with a spatula. Cover the pan lightly and let the potatoes cook over fairly low heat until a golden brown crust forms on the bottom. This will take 20 to 30 minutes. Check to see if they are brown by lifting the edges gently with the spatula. Turn upside down on a plate, or fold over like an omelet.

VARIATION

Mix chopped parsley or chopped chives and parsley with the potatoes before you cook them.

POTATOES HASHED IN CREAM

Follow the directions for Hashed Brown Potatoes (above) and just before the potatoes are done, add ½ to ¾ cup of hot cream. Let this cook into the potatoes for a minute or so before serving.

FRENCH-FRIED POTATOES (Serves 4)

Use baking potatoes for this dish, and if you like French-fried foods allow at least 1½ large potatoes per person. For the deep fat, use vegetable oil or shortening; or buy beef suet and render it. You will find that suet gives a fine flavor to the potatoes.

6 baking potatoes   **Salt**
1½ quarts of oil or fat, at   **Pepper**
**   least**

Peel the potatoes and cut them in slices about ½ inch thick lengthwise. Then cut the slices into strips ½ inch wide. Soak these potato strips in cold water for ½ hour. Bring the fat or oil to 375° in a deep-fat fryer. If you have no thermometer, test it with a small bread cube. It is hot enough for frying when it cooks the bread brown and crisp in 30 seconds. Dry the potato strips on paper towels and fry them in the frying basket a few at a time until they are brown and crisp. This should take about 4 minutes. Recheck the temperature of the oil between each batch of potatoes. Drain the cooked potatoes on absorbent paper.

If you can cook these in advance and then recrisp the potatoes for a minute in hot oil just before serving, you will have a crisper, firmer vegetable. The double cooking process keeps them from getting soggy. Season to taste, after draining, with salt and freshly ground black pepper.

VARIATIONS

Shoestring Potatoes (Potatoes Julienne) are made the same way. Cut them into very thin strips and cook as for French-fried, allowing about 1 minute instead of 4 in the hot oil.

Potato Chips: Cut the potatoes into extremely thin slices and proceed as for French fries, allowing 1 minute cooking time in the hot oil.

POTATO PANCAKES (Serves 4)

4 medium potatoes	**1 teaspoon of salt**
1 medium onion	**½ teaspoon of pepper**
1 egg, lightly beaten	**Butter or bacon fat**
2 tablespoons of fine, dry bread crumbs	

Wash the potatoes and peel them. Grate with a fine grater and drain off all the liquid that collects in the bowl. Wash and peel the onion. Grate the onion into the potato and mix in the egg, the bread crumbs and the salt and pepper. Heat the butter or bacon fat (you will need about 1 tablespoon at a time) in a large skillet or on a griddle. Put 4 large spoonfuls of the mixture on the griddle to make 4 pancakes. Cook gently until brown on the bottom, turn with a pancake turner and brown the other side. Add more fat to the griddle and continue cooking until all the mixture is used.

Spinach

Buy spinach young, fresh and crisp. Two pounds will serve 4 persons. Wash spinach thoroughly to be sure it is free of grit and soil. Hold it under running water, separating the leaves to let the water wash each one. Pile it in a pan with cold water and swirl it around a bit. Then lift it out, discard the water and rinse the pan of grit. Repeat. Then break off any wilted or discolored leaves and any coarse stems or roots. If you buy the already cleaned spinach sold in plastic packages, you will save yourself a lot of trouble. But be sure it is fresh and crisp.

Don't drown spinach in water and don't cook it to death.

BOILED SPINACH (Serves 4)

2 pounds of spinach   **Butter**
Salt and pepper

Wash the spinach thoroughly. (If you use the packaged variety, you need only rinse it lightly.) Put the spinach in a saucepan or kettle without water. The water clinging to the leaves is enough moisture for cooking. Sprinkle with a bit of salt and cook gently, uncovered, until the greens are thoroughly wilted and tender. Drain well, season to taste with salt, freshly ground black pepper and plenty of butter.

Serve with lemon sections or a cruet of vinegar. Some people like a tart touch to their spinach.

VARIATIONS

Italian style: Dress with grated garlic, olive oil, salt and pepper.

With onion: Add a grated onion to the butter before you put it on the spinach. Serve garnished with sliced hard-cooked egg.

With herbs: To the butter add 2 tablespoons of chopped chives and 1 teaspoon of dried tarragon, or 1 tablespoon of fresh tarragon. Dress the spinach with this herbed butter, salt and freshly ground black pepper, and serve it with lemon quarters.

Chopped: Chop the spinach coarsely before seasoning and serving.

Creamed 1: Chop the spinach coarsely. Melt 2 tablespoons of butter in a skillet and add 4 tablespoons of heavy cream. Blend the chopped spinach into this mixture, season to taste with salt and pepper and serve.

Creamed 2: Chop the spinach coarsely and fold into 1 cup of Rich Cream Sauce (page 349).

With mushrooms: Chop the spinach coarsely and mix with ½ pound of mushrooms, sliced and sautéed in butter. Season to taste.

Puréed: Put the cooked spinach through a food mill and season with any of the flavorings suggested above.

Wilted: Cook according to directions for Wilted Lettuce (page 416).

Note: Any of the following greens can be cooked according to the directions for spinach:

Swiss chard	Dandelion greens
Beet tops	Mustard greens
Turnip tops	Chicory
Collards	Kale

Squash

There are two general sorts of squash: summer and winter. The best known varieties of summer squash are the round white scalloped, the yellow crook-necked and the long green zucchini. They cook quickly and have a delicate flavor. When you buy them, look for ones that are young, with tender skins; select the smallest and freshest. Large summer squash has tough skin, too many seeds, and is not tasty.

Allow about 2 pounds for 4 persons, but you can usually judge the amount you need by the size of the squash: 3 or 4 very small scalloped squash will serve 1 person; one 8-inch crook-necked will serve 2; 2 or 3 small 6-inch zucchini will serve one. Summer squash are cooked and eaten with their skins on.

The most popular varieties of winter squash are the Hubbard and the acorn. The acorn is a small round vegetable with a tough green and orange skin. It is generally cut in half and baked, one half an acorn squash a serving. The flesh of the squash is scooped out of the shell (the tough skin) and eaten. The Hubbard resembles the acorn but is very large. It averages 3 to 6 pounds and one will serve at least 6 persons. It is cut in serving-size pieces and baked with the skin on. As with the acorn, it is served in the shell, but only the flesh is eaten.

BOILED SUMMER SQUASH (Serves 4)

The best choice for this dish is the yellow crook-necked variety, though the scalloped white squash may be used too. The latter has less flavor and really needs the addition of a little onion.

2 pounds of crook-necked or scalloped summer squash	**Pepper**
	Butter
Water	**Onion (optional)**
Salt	

Wash the squash. Leave tiny scalloped squash whole. Cut yellow crook-necked squash into very thick slices—about 1½ to 2 inches thick. In a kettle put enough water to cover the vegetable and add 1 teaspoon of salt. Bring to a boil and add the squash. (Add 1 minced onion for additional flavor, if you wish.) Cook, uncovered, until the squash is tender. This will take 10 to 15 minutes. Do not overcook or the vegetable will be watery. Drain thoroughly, season to taste with salt and freshly ground black pepper and add a liberal amount of butter.

BOILED ZUCCHINI (Serves 4)

2 pounds of zucchini	**Pepper**
Water	**Butter**
Salt	

Wash the zucchini and be sure to remove any grit or rough spots on the skin, but do not peel. Cut into slices about ½ inch thick. Bring a very small amount of water to a boil and add 1 teaspoon of salt. The zucchini does not need to be covered with the water; it will steam done. Add the vegetable, cover the pan and simmer gently just until the zucchini is tender. Do not overcook. The slices should still be a little firm. Drain thoroughly and season with salt, freshly ground black pepper and plenty of butter.

SUMMER SQUASH CASSEROLE (Serves 4)

2 pounds of summer squash, crook-necked or zucchini

2 onions

1 green pepper

Salt

Pepper

Butter

Wash the squash and cut it in slices about ½ inch thick. Peel and slice the onions and cut the green pepper into strips. Melt 3 tablespoons of butter in a skillet and sauté the onion and green pepper lightly until about half tender. Butter a casserole and put a layer of squash in the bottom. Season with salt and freshly ground black pepper and dot with butter. Add a layer of onion and pepper slices. Repeat these layers until all the vegetables are used up. Pour the butter from the skillet over the casserole and bake in a 350° oven for about 30 minutes, or until the squash is tender and bubbly.

VARIATIONS

With cheese: A few minutes before the vegetables are done, sprinkle the top of the casserole with grated Parmesan cheese. Finish cooking.

With garlic: Add a minced clove of garlic to the onion and green pepper when you sauté them.

With green onion: Substitute 8 tiny green onions, chopped, for the onion slices.

SAUTÉED ZUCCHINI (Serves 4)

2 pounds of zucchini

Butter or olive oil (or both)

Salt

Pepper

Wash the zucchini and cut it into ½-inch slices. If very tiny, cut it in slices the long way or on the diagonal. In a large skillet heat enough butter, olive oil, or butter and oil mixed, to cover the bottom of the pan well. You will need about ¼ cup. When it is hot, add the zucchini slices and sauté them gently, turning to cook on both sides. Do not let them get mushy. Cook just until slightly browned and tender. Add more butter or oil, if needed. Season to taste with salt and freshly ground black pepper.

With garlic: Add 1 minced clove of garlic to the skillet.

With onion: Add 1 large onion, cut in slices, to the skillet.

With tomato: When the zucchini is half cooked, add 2 tomatoes, peeled, seeded and chopped.

With cheese: Just before the zucchini is done, sprinkle it with grated Parmesan cheese, cover the pan and finish cooking.

FRENCH-FRIED ZUCCHINI

Wash and slice zucchini as for Sautéed Zucchini (see above). Dip each slice in flour and fry in deep fat (see French-fried Potatoes, page 438) until brown and crisp. This will take only about 2 minutes. Drain on absorbent paper and season with salt and freshly ground black pepper.

BAKED ACORN SQUASH (Serves 4)

2 acorn squash	**Salt**
4 tablespoons of butter	**Pepper**

Cut the squash in halves and scoop out the seeds. Arrange the halves on a baking sheet, cut side up. Spread each liberally with soft butter leaving a good-sized piece in the hollow of each half. Season to taste with salt and freshly ground black pepper. Bake in a 350° oven for 45 minutes, or until tender when tested with a fork. Serve the squash in the shell with additional butter, salt and pepper.

VARIATIONS

With bacon: Substitute 1 slice of bacon cut in small squares for the butter in each half acorn. Do not salt.

With brown sugar: Brush each half with butter and season with salt. Add a rounded teaspoon of brown sugar to the hollow and a good lump of butter. Bake as above.

With bacon and sugar: Put 1 cut-up slice of bacon and 1 teaspoon of brown sugar in the hollow of each squash half. Bake as above.

BAKED HUBBARD SQUASH

Cut Hubbard squash into serving-size sections. Arrange on a baking sheet and season in any of the ways suggested for acorn squash. Bake according to directions for Baked Acorn Squash (see above).

MASHED HUBBARD SQUASH

Bake Hubbard squash sections according to directions for Baked Acorn Squash (see page 444). When done, scoop out the flesh, add 4 to 6 tablespoons of melted butter, salt and freshly ground black pepper to taste and beat until smooth. Serve topped with crumbled bacon bits.

Sweet Potatoes

There are two sorts of sweet potatoes: the yam with the orange-colored flesh: and the plain, or Jersey, sweet potato with the yellowish flesh. The yam has a more decided flavor and is very oily. The plain sweet is dry and firm and needs to be served with an extra amount of butter. Both are cooked in the same manner. Allow 1 medium-sized sweet potato per person.

BOILED SWEET POTATOES (Serves 4)

4 medium-sized sweet potatoes	Pepper
Water to cover	4 to 6 tablespoons of butter
Salt	

Wash the potatoes, cut off the tips and cut them in quarters. Do not peel. In a saucepan put enough water to cover the potatoes and 1 teaspoon of salt. Bring this to a boil, add the potatoes and cook, covered, until just tender when pierced with a fork. This will take 8 to 10 minutes. Drain the potatoes and remove the skins. Season to taste with salt and pepper and serve with butter, allowing plenty for Jersey sweets.

MASHED SWEET POTATOES

Boil sweet potatoes as above, drain, skin and mash with a potato masher. Season to taste with salt and freshly ground black pepper and add 4 tablespoons of butter for yams, 6 for Jersey sweets.

VARIATION

Top the mashed sweets with crumbled bacon bits.

FRIED SWEET POTATOES

Boil sweet potatoes as above, drain and skin. Cut into slices about ½ inch thick and fry in hot bacon fat or butter until brown on both sides. Season to taste with salt and pepper.

VARIATIONS

Crisped: Dust the potato slices with a little flour for a crisper finish. Serve these with Fried Apple Rings (page 145) and crisp bacon slices.

Sugared: Fry the potatoes in butter and after you have turned them to brown on the second side, sprinkle with a little brown sugar and dot with extra butter.

CANDIED SWEET POTATOES (Serves 4)

4 quartered boiled sweet potatoes

Salt and pepper

6 tablespoons of butter

4 tablespoons of brown sugar

Peel the boiled sweet potatoes. Butter a casserole and put a layer of the quartered potatoes in the bottom. Season to taste with salt and pepper, sprinkle with brown sugar and dot liberally with butter. Repeat these layers until all the potatoes are used. Bake in a 375° oven until hot through, brown and bubbly.

Some people like this dish with baked ham.

BAKED SWEET POTATOES

Wash sweet potatoes and rub the skins with oil or butter. Bake in a 375° oven for 30 to 45 minutes, or until done when tested with a fork. Serve with plenty of butter, salt and pepper.

Tomatoes

This beautiful member of the vegetable family is one reason we should all be thankful we weren't born before Columbus sailed across the Atlantic. Along with some other interesting foods (notably the potato, the green pepper, corn and beans) the tomato is the gift of the Americas to the world.

Strangely enough, many of our forefathers thought tomatoes were poisonous and refused to eat them, though they grew them for decorative purposes. They called them "love apples," and perhaps the puritanical background of some of the colonials led them to suspect the innocent vegetable of having sinful effects.

Europeans, on the other hand, accepted tomatoes at once. They were sent to Spain from the Spanish colonies and spread from there to southern France and Italy. At least one variety of tomato has traveled back across the Atlantic since then to become popular in this country—the Italian plum tomato. This small plum-shaped tomato has a strong, rich, sweet flavor. It is delicious plain and is by far the best choice for making sauces.

Other well-known varieties are the beefsteak, a large meaty tomato that is excellent sliced raw or broiled and served with steak; the tiny marble-sized cherry tomatoes that are so tasty with hors d'oeuvre; and the regular, or garden, tomato used for all purposes.

Hothouse tomatoes are widely distributed in the winter months. I find them a disappointment. They never seem to ripen into the firm red vegetable that a good tomato should be. They tend to get mushy and always seem a little bitter. Another bad choice is the tomato picked too green and shipped too far. Green-picked tomatoes never become meaty and sweet.

To peel tomatoes: For most cooking methods, tomatoes should be peeled. There is a simple way to do this job. Spear the tomato at the blossom end with a fork and hold it in a gas flame turning it quickly around. Do not cook it. Heat it for only a minute to loosen the skin. You will find the skin then slips off easily. Or plunge the tomatoes into boiling water for 1 minute. Then drain and plunge at once into cold water. Slip off the skins.

STEWED TOMATOES (Serves 4)

6 to 8 medium-sized tomatoes	**Sugar**
Salt and pepper	**4 tablespoons of butter**

Peel the tomatoes (see above) and cut out the cores. Then cut them in quarters. Put the tomato quarters in a saucepan, season to taste with salt, freshly ground black pepper and a tiny pinch of sugar to cut the acid. Cook very gently until tender. Add the butter and let it melt into the tomatoes.

VARIATIONS

With onion: Grate 1 onion and add it to the tomatoes as they cook.

With basil: Add a few leaves of fresh basil or 1 teaspoon of dried basil to the tomatoes as they cook.

With croutons: If you like your stewed tomatoes thicker, add small cubes of bread that have been fried in butter. Stir them in at the last minute.

BAKED STUFFED TOMATOES (Serves 4)

4 large beefsteak tomatoes	**Butter**
2 cups of stuffing (page 419)	**Grated cheese**
Salt	**Broth or water**
Pepper	

Wash the tomatoes, but do not peel them. Remove the core at the stem end of each tomato and cut out the seeds and some of the pulp, making a hollow large enough to hold ½ cup of stuffing in each tomato. Season the inside of the tomatoes with salt and pepper and arrange them in a greased baking dish.

Select any of the stuffings suggested for Stuffed Mushrooms (page 419) and prepare 2 cups. Fill the tomatoes with this mixture, dot them with butter and sprinkle liberally with grated Parmesan, Switzerland Swiss or sharp cheddar cheese. Add a little broth or water to the baking dish to keep the tomatoes from sticking. Bake in a 375° oven for 30 minutes, or until hot and cooked through.

SCALLOPED TOMATOES (Serves 4)

6 to 8 medium-sized tomatoes	**Salt and pepper**
	Sugar
2 onions, sliced	**Buttered crumbs**
Butter	

Prepare the tomatoes as for Stewed Tomatoes (page 447). Peel and slice the onions and sauté them in 2 tablespoons of butter until about half done. Butter a casserole and put a layer of tomato quarters on the bottom. Top with part of the onions, dot liberally with butter and sprinkle with salt, freshly ground black pepper and a tiny pinch of sugar. Repeat the layers until all the vegetables are used up. Top with a layer of crumbs that have been browned in plenty of butter. Bake in a 375° oven for 30 minutes, or until the tomatoes and onions are thoroughly tender.

VARIATIONS

With cheese: A few minutes before the tomatoes are done, sprinkle the top of the casserole with grated Parmesan cheese. Finish cooking.
With additional crumbs: Add a layer of buttered crumbs in between each layer of vegetables. This will be a thicker casserole, as the crumbs absorb some of the liquid from the tomatoes.

FRIED TOMATOES (Serves 4)

These fried tomato slices go excellently with sausage or bacon and are a nice change from the usual fried apple ring.

4 tomatoes	**Salt and pepper**
Flour	**Butter or bacon fat**

Wash the tomatoes and core them but do not peel. Cut them in slices about ½ to ¾ inch thick and dip each slice in flour. Melt butter or bacon fat, allowing about 1 tablespoon of fat for each tomato. Fry the slices in the hot fat until brown on the bottom, then turn, season with salt and freshly ground black pepper and brown on the other side. Add more fat as needed.

PENNSYLVANIA DUTCH FRIED TOMATOES (Serves 4)

4 tomatoes	**Butter**
Flour	**Brown sugar**
Salt and pepper	**½ cup of heavy cream**

Prepare the tomatoes as for Fried Tomatoes (above). Dredge the slices in flour seasoned with salt and freshly ground black pepper and fry them in hot butter. When they are brown on the bottom, sprinkle with a little brown sugar and turn to brown on the other side. Sprinkle the top of the slices with a little more brown sugar. Keep the heat very low so the sugar and butter will not burn. Just before the tomatoes are done add about ½ cup of cream to the pan and let it heat through. Remove the tomato slices to a hot dish, blend the juices in the pan and pour them over the tomatoes.

BROILED TOMATOES (Serves 4)

4 large tomatoes	**Butter**
Salt and pepper	**Buttered crumbs**

Wash the tomatoes and core them but do not peel. Cut them in half and arrange them cut side up on a baking sheet or rack. Season to taste with salt and freshly ground black pepper, sprinkle lightly with fine buttered crumbs and top with a liberal dab of butter for each tomato half. Broil under the broiler flame until browned and bubbly. This will take about 5 minutes.

VARIATIONS

With onion: Mix grated onion with buttered crumbs.

With cheese: Mix grated Parmesan cheese with the buttered crumbs.

With chives and parsley: Mix chopped chives and chopped parsley with the buttered crumbs.

With basil: Mix chopped fresh basil or a bit of dried basil with the buttered crumbs.

Turnips

Both the small white turnips and the large yellow turnips, known as rutabagas, have a definite flavor and are considered excellent additions to stews and boiled dinners. They go exceptionally well with game, and the mashed yellow turnip is traditional in some regions with stuffed roast turkey.

Buy 1½ pounds of either variety to serve 4 persons.

BOILED WHITE TURNIPS (Serves 4)

1½ pounds of young white turnips

Water

Salt and pepper

Butter

Wash and peel the turnips. In a kettle put enough water to cover the vegetables and add 1 teaspoon of salt. Bring it to a boil, add the turnips whole, cover the pan and cook until the turnips are tender when tested with a fork. This will take 15 to 20 minutes. Drain thoroughly, season to taste with salt and freshly ground black pepper, and dress with plenty of butter.

MASHED RUTABAGA (Serves 4)

1½-pound yellow turnip

Water

Salt

Pepper

Butter

Wash and peel the rutabaga and cut it into slices or cubes. Put enough water in a kettle to cover the vegetable, add a teaspoon of salt and bring to a boil. Add the rutabaga, cover the pan and cook until the vegetable is tender. This will take about 15 minutes. Drain the cooked rutabaga and mash thoroughly with a potato masher or put through the ricer. Season to taste with salt and freshly ground black pepper and add a generous amount of butter—at least 6 tablespoons. Blend well. Return to the pan and reheat over hot water.

VARIATIONS

With cream: Add ½ cup of heavy cream or sour cream and beat it through the mashed rutabaga.

With bacon: Serve mashed rutabaga sprinkled with bacon bits.

With potatoes: Combine with an equal amount of mashed potatoes and add butter, cream and seasoning to taste.

Legumes

Dried Beans, Lentils and Peas

The word "legume" means any vegetable that grows in a pod. In cooking, however, "legumes" generally means the dried peas or beans that go into soups and casseroles. These hearty foods are among mankind's oldest standbys. Even the most primitive people knew that dried vegetables would keep through the long winter months and could be eaten as substitutes for fresh vegetables or in place of meat.

As with pastas and grains, legumes have such a bland flavor that successful cookery depends on your skill in seasoning and flavoring them. Onion, garlic and cured, smoked or salt meat are the most popular additions to legumes. Various national or regional groups have special ways of flavoring them. Mexicans like to add garlic and chili; Mediterranean peoples like garlic and oregano; the British like mustard and bay leaf; New Englanders like brown sugar and molasses. Whatever seasonings you use, be sure to cook legumes slowly until they are thoroughly done. Long, slow cooking blends the seasonings and intensifies the flavors.

You can buy packaged dried beans and peas in the markets today labeled "quick-cooking." These have been cleaned and processed and need only be cooked. If you do not buy the "quick-cooking" variety, be sure to pick over the legumes to remove any bits of pod or any damaged beans, and then soak them in plenty of water for 5 or 6 hours before cooking.

PLAIN WHITE BEANS (Serves 4)

White pea beans cooked in the basic fashion may be dressed or flavored in a variety of ways before serving.

2 cups of white pea beans	**1$^1/_2$ teaspoons of salt**
1 bay leaf	**$^1/_2$ teaspoon of pepper**
1 onion, peeled and stuck with 2 cloves	**1 clove of garlic, peeled**

Pick over the beans and discard any that are damaged and any bits of pod or stone. Put them to soak in 8 cups of cold water for six hours. (Or use the "quick-cooking" beans.) Drain off the water, put the beans in a deep kettle and cover with fresh water. Add the rest of the ingredients. Bring to a boil, lower the heat, cover and simmer gently until the beans are tender. Unprocessed beans will take about 1 to 3 hours; "quick-cooking" ones will be done in about ½ hour.

Drain the beans and discard the onion, garlic and bay leaf. Dress in any of the following ways:

With herbs: Add 3 tablespoons of butter, 4 tablespoons of finely chopped parsley and 3 tablespoons of chopped chives.

With bacon and onion: Fry 6 slices of bacon until crisp. Remove the bacon from the pan and sauté 2 large onions cut into thin slices in the hot bacon fat. Crumble the bacon and mix these bits and the sautéed onion with the beans. Top with chopped parsley.

With onion, green pepper and tomato: Sauté 2 thinly sliced onions and 1 chopped green pepper in 6 tablespoons of butter. When soft, add 3 ripe tomatoes, peeled, seeded and chopped, and cook down. Mix this with the cooked beans and top with chopped parsley.

Casserole, with pork or ham: When you drain the beans, save the liquid. Arrange ½ of the drained beans in a buttered casserole, add a layer of leftover cooked pork or ham, and then the rest of the beans. Mix the bean liquid with ½ cup of tomato purée and enough stock from the meat (or stock made with boiling water and bouillon cubes) to cover the beans. Pour this into the casserole and top with buttered crumbs or crumbs mixed with grated Parmesan cheese. Bake in a 350° oven for 30 to 40 minutes or until the liquid is cooked down and the beans are browned on top.

With ham: Cook as for Plain White Beans, but omit the garlic clove and add a ham bone, ham shank, or two or three slices of ham. Drain the beans, dress with chopped parsley, sautéed onion and the meat from the ham, cut into bite-size pieces.

With Roast Leg of Lamb: Cook the beans as for Plain White Beans, but add ¼ cup of tomato purée halfway through the cooking. Drain the beans and mix them with the pan juices from the roast. Add ½ cup of chopped parsley and serve with the meat.

WHITE BEAN SALAD

Cook the beans as for Plain White Beans, drain and chill. Mix with 3 tablespoons of chopped green pepper, 4 tablespoons of chopped parsley,

3 tablespoons of chopped chives and Vinaigrette Sauce (page 343). Serve in a large bowl lined with romaine.

BOSTON BAKED BEANS (Serves 4)

2 cups of white pea beans

1 scant teaspoon of salt

1 medium onion, peeled

³/₄ pound of salt pork

¹/₃ cup of brown sugar or molasses

2 teaspoons of dry mustard

1 teaspoon of black pepper

Boiling water

If you use "quick-cooking" beans they need no sorting or soaking. If you use unprocessed beans, look them over and discard any bits of stone or pod. Put them to soak in 2 quarts of water for 6 hours. Soak the salt pork for 2 or 3 hours in cold water. When the beans have soaked, drain them and put them in a large kettle. Add a bit of salt and enough water to reach 2 inches above the beans. Bring to a boil, lower the heat and simmer gently until the beans are just barely tender. This will take about 30 to 40 minutes for unprocessed beans and about 20 minutes for the "quick-cooking" variety. Drain well.

Place the onion in the bottom of a large earthenware casserole or bean pot with a tight lid. Top with a layer of the drained beans and add half of the salt pork cut into pieces about 1 inch square and ½ inch thick. Add the rest of the beans and top with the rest of the salt pork. Mix the brown sugar (or molasses), mustard and black pepper and add this to the beans and pork. Add boiling water to cover, put on the lid and bake in a 250° oven. Add boiling water frequently to be sure the beans are always covered. Bake 4 to 5 hours. Then remove the lid and let the beans finish cooking, uncovered and without additional water, for about ³/₄ hour.

VARIATION

With spareribs: Some New Englanders like to use pork spareribs in place of the salt pork. Place 4 to 6 spareribs in the bottom of the casserole with the onion. Add the beans and proceed as above.

PUNGENT BEAN CASSEROLE (Serves 4)

2 cups of kidney beans or
pinto beans

Scant teaspoon of salt

1/2 pound of hot sausage
(Italian or Spanish)

1/2 pound of smoked ham

1 teaspoon of oregano

1 clove of garlic, minced

1 large green pepper,
chopped

1/2 cup of chopped parsley

1/2 cup of red wine

Grated Parmesan cheese

Use the "quick-cooking" beans that need no sorting or soaking. If you use the unprocessed beans, be sure to look them over carefully and discard any bits of pod or shriveled or discolored beans. Then soak them in 8 cups of water for 6 hours. Drain the beans, put them in a kettle and pour over enough fresh water to cover them well. Add the salt, bring to a boil, lower the flame and cook gently until the beans are thoroughly tender, but not mushy. "Quick-cooking" beans will be done in about 30 minutes. Unprocessed beans take from 1½ to 2 hours. Drain and save the liquid.

Sauté the sausage until browned and done, turning to cook on all sides. Cut the ham into bite-size pieces. In a casserole place a layer of the beans, then a layer of the meat and a bit of the oregano, minced garlic, chopped green pepper and chopped parsley. Repeat these layers until all the ingredients are used. Mix the bean liquid with the red wine and pour this over the beans and meat. Bake in a 350° oven for 45 minutes. Sprinkle the surface of the casserole with a liberal amount of grated Parmesan cheese and continue baking for another 15 to 20 minutes.

VARIATIONS

With chili: Add 2 tablespoons of chili powder to the bean broth and red wine before you pour it over the casserole.

With onion and tomato: Add layers of sautéed onion slices to the casserole, and substitute tomato juice thickened with a little tomato paste for the bean liquid.

LENTIL CASSEROLE (Serves 4)

2 cups of lentils	**4 to 6 knockwurst**
Pinch of salt	**Butter or bacon fat**
1 onion, peeled and stuck with 2 cloves	**Bacon strips**
	Chopped parsley
1 bay leaf	

Use the "quick-cooking" lentils that need no soaking. Or, if you use the unprocessed lentils, pick them over carefully to remove any bits of rock or grass. Soak for several hours in 6 to 7 cups of water. Drain and put in a kettle with water to cover and the pinch of salt. Add the onion and a bay leaf to the lentils. Bring to a boil, lower the flame and simmer gently until the lentils are tender. Do not let them get mushy. The "quick-cooking" variety will be done in about 25 to 30 minutes. Unprocessed lentils take about twice as long. Drain and save the liquid. Discard the onion and bay leaf.

Split the knockwurst in half the long way and sauté it in butter or bacon fat until nicely browned on both sides. In a large casserole put a layer of the cooked lentils, a layer of the knockwurst, more lentils and the rest of the knockwurst. Top with the rest of the lentils. Pour the lentil liquid over the casserole and bake in a 350° oven for 40 minutes. Cover the top of the casserole with strips of bacon and continue baking until the bacon is crisp and brown.

VARIATIONS

With pork chops: Substitute browned pork chops for the knockwurst.

With cheese: Omit the bacon and sprinkle the top of the casserole with grated Parmesan cheese during the last few minutes of cooking.

With lamb: Substitute cooked, leftover lamb for the knockwurst and sprinkle each layer with minced garlic, chopped parsley and a tiny pinch of oregano. Add 2 peeled, seeded and chopped tomatoes to the top of the casserole. Bake for 40 minutes and then sprinkle with grated Parmesan cheese and buttered crumbs, mixed. Finish baking until browned on top.

With ham: Substitute pieces of ham for the knockwurst.

LENTIL SALAD

Prepare lentils as for the Lentil Casserole (above) and cook in water to cover with an onion stuck with 2 cloves, a bay leaf and a little salt. Drain, discard the onion and bay leaf and set the lentils aside to cool. When chilled mix them with 1 bunch of little green onions or scallions chopped, 1 cup of chopped parsley and oil and vinegar dressing.

BEAN SOUP—See Variations, page 369.

LENTIL SOUP—See page 370.

SPLIT PEA SOUP—See page 369.

Index